The Senecan
Amble

The Senecan Amble

A STUDY IN PROSE FORM
FROM BACON TO COLLIER

BY

GEORGE WILLIAMSON

*'It is a world to see how Englishmen
desire to hear finer speech than
the language will allow. . . .
But I let pass their fineness, which
can no way excuse my folly.'*
JOHN LYLY

THE UNIVERSITY OF CHICAGO PRESS
CHICAGO, ILLINOIS

THE UNIVERSITY OF CHICAGO PRESS
CHICAGO 37
W. J. Gage & Co., Limited, Toronto 2B, Canada
Faber and Faber, Ltd., London, W.C. 1, England

Contents

FOREWORD

This is not a history of prose style in the seventeenth century, but an account of its most incisive pattern. Yet, as it deals with one of the extremes that serve to define contemporary styles, it becomes more than the story of a fashion. It is at bottom, however, an expanded revision of 'Senecan Style in the Seventeenth Century', for the use of which thanks are due to the editors of *Philological Quarterly*. Shaftesbury, who found in the Senecan mode a 'uniform Pace', complained that 'the common Amble or Canterbury is not . . . more tiresome to a good Rider, than this see-saw of Essay-Writers is to an able Reader'. Though but one of several metaphors that were used to describe the mannered structure and movement of Senecan style, the 'Amble' may extend to the easy gait of that prose. With exceptional address Morris W. Croll has treated the same subject in various essays on the broad European scene, giving considerable attention to England. But most of the writers involved in this study are illustrated in *English Prose*, the selections edited by Sir Henry Craik.

For an earlier period there are two works of importance. G. P. Krapp, in *The Rise of English Literary Prose* (1915), traces the development of artistic prose from Wyclif to Bacon. R. W. Chambers, in *The Continuity of English Prose* (1932), attempts that which Krapp thought impossible, to trace its continuity back to Alfred and Ælfric. But Krapp is not concerned, like Croll, with the Ciceronian and Attic traditions as such, nor with any general Senecan or Patristic imitation. And Chambers is content with native tradition; for him English style is like the long bow, even if Ascham required something more to write *Toxophilus*. For the later period there is W. Fraser Mitchell's *English Pulpit Oratory from Andrewes to Tillotson* (1932), which crosses this study at various points, but is centred on the development of prose style as related to 'metaphysical' preaching. Another point of view is found in the articles by

R. F. Jones (1930–2), which challenge the position of Croll by advancing the claims of science in the alteration of prose.

Since Croll is both pioneer and master in the present subject, further exploration becomes at once easier and more difficult; but the English aspect of the subject invited, and still invites, curiosity. One incentive to this study, and perhaps its final refuge, is the fact that English critics, though not unaware, were much less articulate on style than continental critics. It is to be hoped that the effort to draw them out has not made them say more than they would, or talk beside the point. The rest is a construction which assumes that it is more definitive and less distorting to describe the stylistic complex of a time by its chief mode than to reduce it either to general qualities or particular facts; not only that fashions are the best definitions, but that they are more clearly seen in the original designs than in the various copies.

The debts of this study are beyond its powers to repay, but the more conscious ones are acknowledged by the references. To those who, without mention, have said things that I say, or contrary things, and said them better, I extend apologies for my negligence. I am aware, however, that some of my additions to the original essay have been anticipated, but their repetition was required in this context. 'Neither affected I', remarked Selden, 'to muster up many petie and late names for proofe of what is had wholly by all from ancient Fountains.' The intent without the slur I applaud, but I have fallen short of the achievement. Where I have not been able to borrow 'what best cleered them', I have no doubt added sediment of my own.

G. W.

The University of Chicago
March 1948

1. *Preface to Anti-Ciceronianism*

'Then', says *The Advancement of Learning*, 'did Erasmus take occasion to make the scoffing Echo: *Decem annos consumpsi in legendo Cicerone*; and the Echo answered in Greek, *"Ove, Asine*'. 'I have spent ten years compiling Cicero'; and Echo answered, 'Thou burro.' If *legendo* means no more than reading Cicero, then Bacon does not point Erasmus at the collection of 'Nizolian Paper-books', as Sidney called them; but to make the scoff plain he adds a Latin gloss to the echo which rhymes Cicero with ass. In 1634 the Echo is no longer a Grecian, but also 'no Ciceronian, nor apt for fluent styles, but a Lipsian right, and fitter for a brief manner of speech dialogue wise'. Thus spoke *A Strange Metamorphosis of Man*, and this antithesis defined the Anti-Ciceronian movement. In its broad sense this movement began as an opposition to the exclusive imitation of Cicero—an imitation which Gabriel Harvey, following Erasmus and Ramus, re-defined in his *Ciceronianus* of 1577.

I

A study of Anti-Ciceronianism in England must begin, as Bacon suggests, with Erasmus, and particularly with the *Ciceronianus* which he published in 1528.[1] To the elements of such a study there is no better introduction, but for a proper understanding of the movement in general the various studies of 'Attic Prose' by Morris W. Croll are indispensable.[2] Essentially the *Ciceronianus* renews the contro-

---

[1] The scoffing echo derives from the *Colloquies*: '*Juvenis* and *Echo*'. For another attack on Ciceronianism see Foster Watson, *Vives on Education*. The first native attack is found in John Jewell's *Oratio contra Rhetoricam* (*c.* 1548); translated by H. H. Hudson, *Quarterly Journal of Speech*, xiv. 374–92.

[2] 'Juste Lipse et le mouvement anti-cicéronien', *Revue du seizième siècle*, ii (1914).

'Attic Prose in the Seventeenth Century', *Studies in Philology*, xviii (1921).

'Attic Prose: Lipsius, Montaigne, Bacon', *Schelling Anniversary Papers*, New York, 1923.

'Muret and the History of "Attic" Prose', *PMLA*, xxxix (1924).

'The Baroque Style in Prose', *Studies in English Philology*, ed. Malone and Ruud, Minneapolis, 1929.

versy between Cicero and the Atticists which is recorded in the rhetorical works of Cicero, Tacitus, and Quintilian. If it did not introduce a new school of Attic writers, it did administer a vigorous rebuff to Ciceronian imitation; and it raised once more the old quarrel between philosophy and rhetoric, which in terms of style meant the essay or plain style as opposed to the oratorical or grand style. Hence, so far as schools of style are concerned, Erasmus sets the plain Attic in opposition to the ornate Ciceronian; but he also distinguishes Ciceronian style from Isocratic structure.

It will be useful to isolate, so far as possible, the character of the styles thus opposed. It would not be desirable, even if it were possible, to separate these styles from their imitators, for then we should fail to perceive their contemporary form and pressure. We must be prepared to find them associated, often by contrast, with different writers; and only those writers who are significant for our study will be selected. It is hardly necessary to remark, except as a reminder, that style in the Renaissance, not only in Latin but also in the vernacular, found its great models in the classical languages. It is perhaps necessary to add that Renaissance style was none the less the product of a long rhetorical tradition, which is exhibited, for instance, in the section on figures that is found in all grammars after Donatus.

In his famous dialogue Erasmus ridicules the extremes to which Ciceronian imitation went. His Ciceronian has collected three volumes from the works of Cicero: the first is a lexicon of words; the second a lexicon of phrases or formulas of speech; the third a compilation of 'all the metrical feet with which Cicero ever begins or ends his periods and their subdivisions, the rhythms which he uses in between, and the cadences which he chooses for each kind of sentence'.[1] Of his actual preparation for writing, the Ciceronian gives a most solemn account; even a letter costs him no less than days of painful labour:

I read as many letters of Cicero as possible; I consult all my lists; I select some words strikingly Ciceronian, some tropes, and phrases, and rhythms. Finally, when furnished sufficiently with this kind of material, I examine what figures of speech I can use and where I can use them.

[1] Translation by Izora Scott, *Controversies over the Imitation of Cicero* (New York, 1910), part ii, p. 24. The opposition in this dialogue will be indicated by using the names 'Ciceronian' and 'Anti-Ciceronian' for the opposing speakers.

Then I return to the question of sentences. For it is now a work of art to find meanings for these verbal embellishments.[1]

He concludes his labour by inventing his matter. It was against similar, if less exaggerated, practices that Erasmus directed his satire.

When the Anti-Ciceronian objects that Cicero is deficient in some virtues, he begins with wit and proceeds to *sententiae*. Being granted that 'sentences' are gems or shining lights, he opposes Seneca to Cicero: 'Truly, from Seneca's reflections you can find something to imitate more easily than from others where maxims are neither frequent nor striking.'[2] But imitation raises another problem when the Anti-Ciceronian argues that slavish imitation leads to the defects of virtues.[3] Here he draws upon Horace for support, thereby introducing three schools of style:

> I prove obscure in trying to be terse;
> Attempts at ease emasculate my verse;
> Who aims at grandeur into bombast falls.

Thus those who aim at the Attic style become dry instead of clever and charming; at the Rhodian, diffuse; at the Asiatic, bombastic.[4]

'Brevity is praised in the work of Sallust. Would there not be danger of becoming unduly concise and abrupt, if one should try to imitate this with painful precision?' Demosthenes exemplifies both adequacy and concision, but too anxious imitation might result in saying too little. 'Isocrates is praised for structure and rhythm. He who strives greatly for this may weary his reader by too much precision of periods and may forfeit confidence by the ostentation of his art.'[5] On the other hand, 'Seneca is praised for fluency. The heedless and

---

[1] Ibid., p. 31. Contrast the Anti-Ciceronian method in Montaigne's *Essayes* (I. xxxix): 'A Consideration upon Cicero.'

[2] Ibid., p. 37.

[3] On the hazards of imitation compare Quintilian, x. ii. 15–18.

[4] Scott, *Controversies*, ii. 55. See Horace's *Ars Poetica*, 25–7.

[5] R. C. Jebb (*The Attic Orators*, London, 1893, ii. 61) describes the Gorgian figures in Isocrates: 'The specially Isocratic figures of language are those which depend on a parallelism. These are chiefly three. (1) A parallelism in sense—Antithesis. . . . (2) A parallelism in form and size merely between two or more clauses or sentences—Parisosis. (3) A parallelism of sound—Paromoiosis: when the latter of two clauses gives to the ear an echo of the former, either in its opening or at its close or throughout.' Hermogenes, says Jebb, observes that Demosthenes, on the contrary, 'has rarely a direct and absolute symmetry or consonance of clauses'; he interrupts his balance, or avoids symmetrical structure in clauses of equal length, or shifts one of the two words that would have jingled.

enthusiastic imitator runs a risk of becoming redundant and extravagant instead of fluent.'[1]

Moreover, some characteristics are so prominent in writers 'that they might be considered faults if they were not offset by allied virtues: for example, in Seneca an abruptness and a profusion of aphorisms are offset by the moral purity of his precepts, the splendour of his themes, the charm of his language; in Isocrates the faults of composition are offset by clearness and weight of thought'.[2] For Cicero the moral of this argument is cumulative, since 'his diction is so fluent that he might be criticized at times as loose and free; so exuberant that he could be called redundant; so rhetorical that he seems a declaimer'.[3] These comments serve to discriminate the styles of Seneca, Cicero, and Isocrates as they could be described in the time of Erasmus. Both the fluent and the aphoristic aspects of Seneca are remarked. It should be observed that structure apart from rhythm in Isocrates must involve either euphony or symmetry, or both; and that Isocrates is regarded as much more precise than Cicero in composition or the arrangement of words.

While satirizing those who would rather be Ciceronians than Christians, Erasmus puts into the mouth of his startled Ciceronian this question, 'Do you advise us to use the phrases of Thomas Aquinas and Duns Scotus?' To which the Anti-Ciceronian replies: 'If propriety is an essential, it is better in speaking of sacred things than to copy Cicero. And yet there is a certain happy mean between the Scotists and the extreme Ciceronians.'[4] This aspect of the conflict between philosophy and rhetoric, and consequently between

---

[1] Scott, *Controversies*, ii. 56. For a similar method of characterizing styles by a salient quality, often the same quality, see Quintilian, bks. X and XII.

[2] Croll (*Euphues*, ed. Croll and Clemons, p. xxv) finds that the Gorgian figures in Isocrates, though infrequent, 'are always used with a careful study of variety in form and rhythm which is in sharp contrast with Lyly's study of uniformity and exactness'. Octave Navarre (*Essai sur la rhétorique grecque avant Aristote*, Paris, 1900, p. 199) observes that besides euphony and rhythm, Isocrates uses the Gorgian figures to render his sentence musical.

[3] Scott, *Controversies*, ii. 57. The defects of Cicero reflect the charges against him made by the 'Atticists' and reported by Quintilian (XII. x. 12 ff.) and Tacitus (*Dialogue*, 18). L. Laurand (*Études sur le style des discours de Cicéron*, Paris, 1907, liv. III, chap. viii) describes Cicero, after Molon's teaching, as Rhodian, mingling the virtues of Attic and Asiatic.

[4] Scott, *Controversies*, ii. 68. See p. 78 for another propriety: 'If you wish to express Cicero exactly, you cannot express yourself. If you do not express yourself, your speech will be a false mirror. . . .'

styles, had its counterpart in another aspect which more nearly concerned Bacon. It is suggested in this comment on Glareanus, who held Erasmian views: 'He preferred to spend his time on philosophy and mathematics rather than to imitate Ciceronian phrase, which hardly fits the subtleties of mathematicians.'[1] Both aspects, it may be noted, are relevant to Bacon's review of the Ciceronian movement in his *Advancement of Learning*.[2] Moreover, the Anti-Ciceronian argues that not only is the Ciceronian constantly in danger of violating propriety, but his imitation cannot be intelligent without a knowledge of rhetoric; and no one has taught rhetoric so wisely or so well as Quintilian.[3]

Propriety, furthermore, makes its demands upon those who are committed to a definite view of life. Cicero's language, observes the Anti-Ciceronian, would not have pleased the age of Cato the Censor; it did not please the Stoics of his own time: 'Aye, even when Cicero lived, there were men who breathed forth that early severity—Cato of Utica, for example, and Brutus, and Asinius Pollio—who vainly sought in Cicero's eloquence something more severe, less theatrical, more masculine.'[4] In the Renaissance as in the Golden Age of Rome —and Bacon was aware of the parallel—such aversion was followed by the Anti-Ciceronian movement.

The latter part of the dialogue employs the satiric device of a long roll-call by which to prove that there is no true Ciceronian but Cicero himself. It will be useful to notice, among the candidates examined, some of the Church Fathers and a group of English writers. Although the Ciceronian will not allow Lactantius to be a Ciceronian, the Anti-Ciceronian points out marks of Ciceronian imitation: 'it is characteristic of Cicero to emphasize a thing by two

[1] Ibid., p. 108.

[2] See Everyman ed., pp. 23-5.

[3] Erasmus derives a great deal from Quintilian, not least being his criticism of Isocrates. In 1531 Sir Thomas Elyot (*Gouernour*, bk. 1, chap. xi) found the art of the orator in 'that parte of logike that is called *Topica*' and 'in that parte of rhethorike, principally, which concerneth persuasion'. For the former he named Cicero and Agricola; for the latter, Hermogenes and Quintilian; or, in shorter form, Cicero's *Partitiones* and Erasmus's *De Copia*.

[4] Scott, *Controversies*, ii. 84. Again the charges of the Atticists. They objected to exuberance and verbosity, rhythmical cadences, and frigidity of wit. See introduction to Cicero's *Orator* in the Loeb Classical Library. To the scholars represented in this library let me express my indebtedness, for the references to classical authors are commonly to their volumes.

words meaning the same, or almost the same'; and Lactantius has copied the metrical endings or periodical cadences of Cicero. But to St. Augustine the Ciceronian gives this character: 'He is like Cicero in that he makes his periods very long and involved. But he is not so clever in breaking up the extended structure of his oration into divisions, nor has he Cicero's ready speech and felicity in handling subjects.'[1] When St. Ambrose is suggested, the Ciceronian responds:

You cite a Roman orator, not a Ciceronian. He delights in clever allusions and general reflections, expresses himself only in aphorisms, abounds in rhythmical divisions and clauses and nicely balanced periods, has his own inimitable style but it is very different from Cicero's.[2]

If this character portrays a Roman orator rather than a Ciceronian, it describes a style at once Senecan in its *sententiae* and Gorgian in its symmetry.

Pope Gregory I fares little better: 'He is more like Cicero than St. Ambrose, but his speech flows sluggishly and shows the influence of Isocrates, which is foreign to Cicero, for in his boyhood he had been so trained in the schools.[3] Subservience to Isocratic structure— 'et Isocraticae structurae quasi servit'—was foreign to Cicero chiefly in point of euphony, but symmetry would have more effect on rhythm; and Gorgian symmetry, though not less obtrusive in the early Cicero than in Isocrates, helps to distinguish St. Ambrose from Cicero. To a Ciceronian, at any rate, Isocrates would present a niceness of composition, both in sound and symmetry, that could well be considered foreign to Cicero. Since Isocrates himself declares in his last works that he has given up 'antitheses and parisoses and those other figures which compel applause', it may be recalled that

[1] Scott, *Controversies*, ii. 92–3.

[2] Ibid., p. 93. Croll (*Euphues*, p. xlii, n. 2) quotes the *Ciceronianus* on St. Ambrose: 'membris incisis comparibus numerosus ac modulatus suum quoddam dicendi genus habet aliis inimitabile, sed a Tulliano genere diversissimum. *Opera*, Leyden, 1703–6, vol. i. 1008. ("Made rhythmic and measured by short members of equal length, his style has something peculiar to himself, inimitable by others, but most unlike the Ciceronian style.") This is a typical humanist way of apologizing for the barbarism of the Latinity of the fathers of the church.' Yet Croll (p. xl) makes Wilson on 'equal members' perceive 'what is really characteristic of Isocrates' and no barbarism.

[3] Cf. Eduard Norden (*Die Antike Kunstprosa*, ii. 654), who cites this remark of 1705: 'Gregorius fere semper graditur periodis bimembribus et quasi bipedibus similiter cadentibus.' On like-endings Croll (*Euphues*, p. xli, n. 1) refers to Bede's *De schematis et tropis*: 'He gives examples from Gregory, and says that this is the figure called by Jerome *concinnas rhetorum declamationes*.'

the criticism of Isocrates in ancient times was inclined to blame his
Gorgian symmetries; nothing, said Dionysius, more 'paralyses his
force'.[1] At least, to be Isocratic is for Gregory to be less Ciceronian,
and he owes this misfortune to his training in the schools.[2]

In venturing upon English writers, the Anti-Ciceronian indulges
in an oblique attack on Ciceronianism:

If I cite William Grocyn, you will say that there is nothing extant of his
except a single letter, very carefully elaborated, clever, and in good Latin.
Fitted for epistolary cleverness, he loved brevity and propriety; you would
call him a representative of the Attic school in this surely, for he aimed
at nothing else and could not endure Cicero's fulness of expression. He
was laconic not only in writing but also in speaking.[3]

Diffidence is only proper, for these are the ideals of the Anti-
Ciceronian movement, both ancient and modern. No such hesitation,
however, is required in proposing Thomas Linacre. But the Ciceronian, asserting that Linacre would have preferred to be like Quintilian, objects vigorously:

Thus, you see, he was not much more kindly disposed toward Cicero
than the common run of Greeks are. Urbanity he never strives for; he
surpasses an Attic in the repression of his feelings; brevity and elegance
he loves, and he is extremely didactic. He studiously copies Aristotle and
Quintilian. You may bestow upon him as much praise as you wish but he
cannot be called a Ciceronian, for he has studied to be unlike Cicero.[4]

[1] Cf. R. C. Jebb, *Attic Orators*, ii. 62, notes 1 and 2. Cf. Philostratus (*Lives of the Sophists*, Loeb ed., 17. 503): 'The Siren which stands on the tomb of Isocrates the sophist—its pose is that of one singing—testifies to the man's persuasive charm, which he combined with the conventions and customs of rhetoric. For though he was not the inventor of clauses that exactly balance, antitheses, and similar endings, since they had already been invented, nevertheless he employed those devices with great skill. He also paid great attention to rhetorical amplification, rhythm, structure, and a striking effect. . . .'

[2] See Croll's account (*Euphues*, p. xxxiv) of the passage of Gorgian rhetoric 'to its great medieval destinies' by way of Isocrates, the Sophists' schools, Imperial Rome, and the Church Fathers, 'especially perhaps through the mediation of Gregory the Great'.

[3] Scott, *Controversies*, ii. 103.

[4] Ibid. It may be recalled that Linacre was a teacher of Erasmus and More. Here Linacre is close to the defects or 'frigidities' of Attic virtues which are so often assigned to the Stoics by Cicero. In the *Orator* (20-1), where he is replying to the Atticists and particularly the Attic-Stoic Brutus, he distinguishes two varieties of plain style: 'Within this class some were adroit but unpolished and intentionally resembled untrained and unskilful speakers; others had the same dryness of style, but were neater, elegant, even brilliant, and to a slight degree ornate.' The former resemble the older Stoics, the latter the newer Atticists. To the plain style Cicero assigns an intellectual appeal, to the grand an emotional appeal.

B

Mark again the characteristics—here more Stoic than Attic—and also the models that oppose one to Cicero.

For the sake of comparison here in brief is Cicero's own description of the orator whom his opponents, as he suggests, thought the only true Attic:

He is restrained and plain, he follows the ordinary usage . . . and is loose but not rambling. . . . His very freedom from periodic structure obliges him to see that his short and concise clauses are not handled carelessly, for there is such a thing even as a careful negligence. . . . All noticeable ornament will be excluded . . . only elegance and neatness will remain. The language will be pure Latin, plain and clear; propriety will always be the chief aim. . . . He will employ an abundance of apposite maxims (*acutae sententiae*) . . . this will be the dominant feature in this orator. . . . Metaphor may be employed because it is of the commonest occurrence in the language of townsman and rustic alike. . . . Gorgian symmetry must be avoided. . . . But wit is certainly an outstanding mark of Attic style.[1]

Although this is a pattern of the plain orator and style, it is not unrealistic; the Attic requirements are tempered rather than altered.[2] Brevity and wit are the qualities which Erasmus most constantly associates with the Attic style.

Thomas More, admits the Ciceronian, is a most fortunate genius, but his education was most unfortunate. In his boyhood 'scarcely a trace of the better literature had crossed into England', and he was obliged 'to learn English Law, the farthest possible from literature'. Only at odd hours could he turn his attention to the study of oratory; and when called to the affairs of state, 'he could love study but could

---

[1] *Orator*, 75–90. Cicero suggests that wit may be connected with Gorgian figures when he describes (ibid. 38) the Sophistic style: 'Datur etiam venia concinnitati sententiarum et argutiis. . . .' Cicero held (ibid. 28–32) that the better kind of Atticist imitated Lysias; the more perverse imitated Thucydides, modelling 'choppy, disconnected phrases' on his 'dark and obscure sentences'. But neither model can be described as free from Gorgian figures. R. C. Jebb (*Attic Orators*, i. 167) observes: 'There is one kind of ornament, however, which Lysias uses largely, and in respect to which he deserts the character of the plain style. He delights in the artistic parallelism (or opposition) of clauses.' Likewise W. R. M. Lamb (*Lysias*, Loeb ed., p. xvii) remarks on the pleadings of Lysias: 'Their only artifice is the steady poise imparted by antithesis, which gives way, as in Thucydides, to a more rapid and looser system for the vivid presentment of scenes and characters.' N. R. Tempest (*The Rhythm of English Prose*, p. 113) concludes that 'balance is the only attempt at rhythmical effect to be found in the plain style'—the simple style of short groups.

[2] Cicero is, of course, sensitive to the criticism of the Atticists, to whom he is replying, and hence gives their demands a slight bias in his favour. They wanted a plain style with little ornament, no rhythm, and almost no emotional appeal.

not cultivate it'. The consequence, we are apparently to infer, was a strange harmony of genius and education: 'Though the style he gained tended rather to Isocratic rhythm (*structuram*) and logical subtlety than to the outpouring river of Ciceronian eloquence, yet he is not inferior at all in culture to Cicero.'[1] But his genius could not rescue his style, and to be Isocratic is still not to be Ciceronian. It is hardly probable that Isocratic structure here means rhythm apart from Isocratic antithesis, an appropriate mode for dialectic subtlety, and a real contrast to the diffuse flow (*fusum flumen*) of Cicero.

With an allusion to William Latimer as a pious man who prefers theology, another to Reginald Pole as not a bad imitator of Cicero, and a compliment to the king, the Anti-Ciceronian concludes the review of English writers. This summary, however, omits an earlier mention of Richard Pace, who could have been a Ciceronian if business had not interfered. Among these writers of Latin, Thomas More stands alone as an Isocratic.

There can be little doubt that Erasmus's own preference was the Attic style. In a letter written in 1527, the year before his *Ciceronianus*, he declares:

Even if I could attain perfection in portraying the figure of Ciceronian phrase, I should prefer a style of speaking more genuine, more concise, more forceful, less ornate, and more masculine. And yet, though ornamentation has been lightly considered by me, I should not spurn elegance when it comes of its own free will. However, I have not time to polish what I write. Let them be Cicero's brothers who have leisure to spend three months on one short epistle.[2]

Here, as before, Attic and Stoic virtues are mingled rather than distinguished. It was from this point of view that Erasmus wrote his *Ciceronianus*, in which he reminded his contemporaries that Cicero had been challenged by worthy men in his own time, and that there was, after all, a rational basis for imitation.

In Bacon's time William Bedell described Erasmus's style in these words:

Some, not able themselves to judge betwixt imitating and aping, are bold to censure his style, (though, by their own confession, pure, copious,

---

[1] Scott, *Controversies*, ii. 103-4. On the study of law see Sir Thomas Elyot, *The Gouernour*, bk. I, chap. xiv.
[2] Ibid. i. 27; *Ep.* 899.

flexible, and extemporary,) as not every where elevated to the true light of the Ciceronian pole. He can run but goingly, who ties himself to another man's footsteps. Erasmus had his own genius as well as Cicero; held a bull as complete a creature as a baboon, and that most comely which was most genuine and masculine; not so much taken with the cadency and chiming of words, as the sententious density of the matter; and therefore rather chose with St. Augustine to retain some few words in common use, though less Ciceronian, than, by changing them into more eloquent, but less intelligible, torture his simple readers upon the continual rack of their dictionaries.[1]

If this adds little to Erasmus's own remarks, it reminds us of his preference for 'the sententious density of matter' rather than 'the cadency and chiming of words', in which Cicero and Isocrates excelled; and in this preference he is joined by Bacon.

II

Erasmus's persistent opposition of Isocratic and Ciceronian style raises a question of importance to students of the Anti-Ciceronian movement, and that is the relation of Isocratic structure to various prose styles. If the importance is not obvious, it may be recalled that Anti-Ciceronianism for Croll is partially defined by asymmetry versus symmetry. If asymmetry is allowed to be a valid distinction, the reader is still faced with the problem of distinguishing between wilful asymmetry and imperfect execution. Symmetry, of course, involves the figures of parallelism, and they raise some controversial issues. The basic question for our study is whether they serve not only to create oratorical pattern but also to display ideas, or whether both functions are ultimately Gorgian. If they produce harmony in the period, can they also point thought in the epigram? Or since they provide important elements of oral design, are they excluded from making the form of ideas salient? And if they may serve both functions, do they all contribute to these diverse effects, or how does their elaboration differ in the two modes? It is to such questions that Isocratic structure directs our attention.

Feuillerat would make the imitation of Isocrates almost decisive

---

[1] 'Life of Erasmus', Thomas Fuller's *Abel Redivivus*, ed. William Nichols (London, 1867), i. 88–9. In short, Erasmus was not a Ciceronian ape, and in diction he kept to the standard of the plain style. Apparently the 'chiming of words' could be Ciceronian.

in the formation of Euphuistic style;[1] but Whipple denies that Isocrates either was or could be associated with Euphuism.[2] Neither would dissociate Isocrates and Cicero. Whipple argues that good classicists like Elyot and Ascham, in imitation of Cicero and Isocrates, subordinated the Gorgian schemes to rhythm or 'the full sentence and flowing style', and minimized the similarities of sound. Both points are important to Ciceronian imitation, for it is the schemes which contribute primarily to rhythmic design that are important to oratory. But Erasmus—also a good classicist—offers the relevant objection in one of Whipple's own citations: the speech of Pope Gregory I 'flows sluggishly, [and] as if it were subservient to the Isocratic structure—a thing which is foreign to Cicero'.[3] In disciples, at least, rhythm could become subordinate to the Isocratic schemes. From other remarks we know that Erasmus did not exempt Isocrates from this charge; bad classicists may have been even less perceptive. In fact, to charge Isocrates with an artificial rhythm was by no means a novelty.

In the rhythm of Isocrates antithetic structure is fundamental, but also both obtrusive and monotonous; it is created by the figures of parallelism—in sense, form, and sound—all of which depend upon the idea of symmetry or balance; it even governs his discourse as a whole.[4] 'There is a leading idea', says Jebb, 'which is worked out on the principle of antithesis. Every contrast which it can yield is developed.' Thus the figure of antithesis provided not only rhetorical opportunities for its complementary figures but also a governing principle for the periodic rhythm. It is orthodox to hold with Croll that Isocrates, a disciple of Gorgias, elaborated the form of the rhythmic period in conjunction with the Gorgian schemes;[5] but this does not mean that the innovator, whatever his merits, has always

[1] Albert Feuillerat, *John Lyly* (Cambridge, 1910), pp. 461 ff.
[2] T. K. Whipple, 'Isocrates and Euphuism', *Modern Language Review*, xi (1916), 15–27, 129–35.
[3] Ibid., p. 22.   [4] Cf. R. C. Jebb, *Attic Orators*, ii. 59, 61, 62, 65.
[5] O. Navarre (*Essai sur la rhétorique grecque*, p. 197) derives a hint of Isocrates' notion of the period from a fragment of his 'que toute pensée doit former un cercle complet et circonscrit en lui-même'. And for the period, says Navarre, Isocrates' counsel is important: 'Que de deux conjonctions la conséquente réponde immédiatement à son antécédente.' 'It is in effect', he concludes, 'to the symmetrical balancing of two correlative particles that a great number of the periods of Isocrates, and of those the longest and most complex, owe their precise equilibrium as well as the harmony and lucid distribution of all their parts.' Of the Gorgian rhythm Navarre remarks

overshadowed the disciple. Nor does it mean that Isocrates could not add life and reputation to the Gorgian figures. Aulus Gellius quotes a passage from Lucilius in which the satirist ridicules those who wish to seem Isocratic and therefore indulge in these figures.[1] Actually neither ancient nor modern criticism has found it easy to minimize the Gorgian element in Isocrates.

It is relevant to ask how his disciple Cicero regarded him. Cicero's mature opinion is to be found in his *Orator*. There he concludes that the Sophists 'show many clever phrases, but these are like a new and immature product, choppy, resembling verselets, and some-times over-ornamented'.[2] Then he considers the progress made by Isocrates:

In the next generation came Isocrates, who is always praised by me more than the others of this group, not without an occasional quiet and scholarly objection from you, Brutus; but you may, perhaps, grant my point if I tell you what I praise in him. For inasmuch as Thrasymachus and Gorgias—the first according to tradition to attempt an artificial arrangement of words—seemed to him to be cut up into short rhythmical phrases, and Theodorus on the other hand seemed too rugged and not 'round' enough, as one may say, Isocrates was the first to undertake to expand his phrases, and round out the sentences with softer rhythms.[3]

This statement, which also stresses the rhythmic period, has been preceded by the observation that the Gorgian figures—which Iso-crates, remarks Cicero, by his own confession cultivated eagerly—must be used 'less frequently and certainly less obviously' in foren-

(p. 93): 'Au plus important des éléments poétiques qui ne pouvaient être transportés dans la prose, le *vers*, Gorgias s'est efforcé du moins de trouver un équivalent. Cet équivalent est la *parisose*, définie plus haut [defined as equality of length in members, sometimes rigorous correspondence of words]. Très fréquente dans la prose de Gorgias, la parisose y joue un rôle comparable à celui du vers dans la poésie: elle en est en quelque sorte l'unité de rythme.'

[1] See Jebb, *Attic Orators*, ii. 62, n. 1; Aulus Gellius, *NA*, xviii. 8.

[2] *Orator*, 39. 'The result', says Quintilian (VIII. v. 13–14) of the cult of *sententiae*, 'is a number of tiny epigrams, affected, irrelevant, and disjointed.' This cult was found in the schools of declamation.

[3] *Orator*, 40. Note the short cola of the early Sophists. H. J. Rose (*Handbook of Greek Literature*, London, 1934, p. 279) describes their achievements as follows: Gorgias' 'chief contribution was the so-called Gorgian figures (*schemata*), in other words an elaborate arrangement of thought and language alike in a series of effective antitheses, elaborately worked out to give a rhythmical effect by the pairing of clauses (often riming) of the same length (*parisosis*)'. Thrasymachus introduced 'the use of the period, or complex, rounded sentence which is characteristic of the best oratory, both Greek and Latin, and with it a sort of natural punctuation, by the employment of a definite rhythm, the paean (one long and three short syllables) to mark the beginning and end.'

sic oratory. Some idea of the Gorgian manner may be had from this fragment 'imitated from his funeral oration delivered, or professing to be delivered, over the Athenian dead':

Servants of the undeservedly unfortunate, punishers of the undeservedly fortunate; advantageously of bold intent, in fit season ready to relent; by the minds' prudence overcoming valour's rudeness; froward against the froward, gentle to the gentle, fearless against the fearless, dread in the hour of dread.[1]

To understand Cicero's statement, however, it is necessary to have before us his distinction between the periodic rhythm and the Gorgian rhythm:

Sentences are rounded off either by the arrangement of words—spontaneously, as it were—or by using a certain class of words in which there is an inherent symmetry. If they have similar case-endings, or if clauses are equally balanced, or if contrary ideas are opposed, the sentence becomes rhythmical by its very nature, even if no rhythm is intended. It is said that Gorgias was the first to strive for this sort of symmetry. An example of it is found in the following passage from my oration *In Defence of Milo*: 'For this law, gentlemen of the jury, is not written, but born; we did not learn, receive and read it, but we seized, plucked and wrested it from Nature herself; for this we were not taught, but made; we know it not by training, but by instinct.'[2]

Here Cicero begins to distinguish between the inherent rhythm of the Gorgian figures, which produce their own rounded form, and the intentional rhythm which gives each sentence an appropriate movement and cadence, so that form and thought keep pace. It may be observed that an answering rhythm of the parts is not the same as a larger rhythm of the whole; indeed, the one may destroy the other. Since the example in translation does not reveal all of its symmetries, especially the equal members and similar endings, here is the Latin:

Est enim, iudices, haec non scripta sed nata lex, quam non didicimus,

---

[1] See H. J. Rose, *Handbook of Greek Literature*, p. 279. O. Navarre (*Essai sur la rhétorique grecque*, pp. 86–92) explains the innovations of Gorgias by an analysis of the fragment of his *Epitaphios*: above all, antithesis, 'which matches ideas or opposes them by couples'. The servants of antithesis are *parisosis* (or *isocolon*), equality of length, sometimes rigorous correspondence of words, between clauses; final assonance (*homoioteleuton*); initial assonance (*homoiokatarckton*); *paronomasia*, which gathers up the antithesis in two words of a common root; and *parechesis* or alliteration.

[2] *Orator*, 164–5. The subject is introduced in *Orator*, 149.

accepimus, legimus, verum ex natura ipsa arripuimus, hausimus, expressimus, ad quam non docti sed facti, non instituti sed imbuti sumus.[1]

One further comment will relate this distinction and its example to the passage on Isocrates: 'The ancients even before the time of Isocrates were fond of this style—Gorgias particularly so; in his prose symmetry of itself frequently produces rhythm.' Cicero concludes that when Isocrates had finally relaxed the 'extreme strictness' of his rhythm, 'he had corrected not only his predecessors, but also himself'.[2] This strictness resulted from his devotion to isocolon or equal members.

The apparently spontaneous and less formal rounding of sentences is another matter; in the early writers it was accidental.[3] Here the proportioning of phrases or members, or the combination of long and short syllables, in which the ear can feel both deficiency and excess, produces the rhythm which gives movement to the period and becomes most definite as final cadences.[4] Cicero distinguishes three ways in which prose becomes rhythmical: by the use of definite rhythms, which is purposeful rhythm; by the natural arrangement of words, in which rhythm is accidental; and by the symmetrical figures of speech, in which rhythm is inherent. But rhythm may be concealed by variety even when it comes by design.[5] In the functional use of rhythm the members of a period are brought to a close now with one, now with another cadence; but an earlier cadence may anticipate a later cadence.[6] It is rhythm in this sense, as Erasmus

---

[1] L. Laurand (*Études*, p. 125) remarks that of the Gorgian figures Cicero was perhaps too prodigal in his youth. This period is a common example in Renaissance rhetorics.

[2] *Orator*, 167, 176.

[3] See Laurand, *Études*, liv. II, esp. chap. i, where he points out that *numerus* for Cicero has a large sense, including all the elements which contribute to rhythm, and a narrow sense, referring to combinations of long and short syllables. The rhythm here distinguished as Gorgian is, of course, only an element in the larger sense of rhythm. Its assonances, as Laurand remarks, brought out the contours of the period.

[4] Cf. *Orator*, 178, 187. Laurand (*Études*, p. 121, n. 1) observes that making the last members of the sentence longer than the first produces a sort of progression in the rhythm, which contributes to the majesty of the period.

[5] Cf. *Orator*, 197, 219–20.

[6] Ibid. 199–200. Laurand points out that Cicero's favourite cadence or clausula, the dichoree, came from Asia and Hegesias. For Cicero, as for Aristotle, prose should be bound or restricted by rhythm, but it should not contain actual verses (187). Its proper rhythm is defined between the extremes of verse and common speech; the one is too strict and confined, the other too loose and rambling (195–6). Prose should be neither loose nor wholly rhythmical; though its rhythm approaches the metrical, it does not cease to be speech (198).

recognized, to which Cicero devoted himself both in theory and in practice.[1] Cicero's period is not only logically articulated but distributed in proportioned members, measured by a sensible cadence.

To the friends of Brutus, who 'deliver broken and choppy sentences and upbraid those who produce rounded and finished periods', Cicero replies that 'as a matter of fact this invidious rhythm does nothing except to form the words into a well-knit sentence'.[2] To the admirers of Isocrates, moreover, he objects that Isocrates derived rhythm from Thrasymachus and structure from Gorgias, though he was more restrained in his use of them.[3] Cicero, in fact, regarded the Gorgian or Sophistic style as more appropriate to show-pieces than to practical oratory; and after his early excesses, he moderated his use of it accordingly. Quite obviously, to Brutus the Stoic and Atticist, both Isocrates and periodic rhythm were offensive subjects; but Cicero does not retreat beyond his conviction when he extends a qualified approval to Isocrates. In short, although Isocrates is Gorgian and for much of his career too strictly rhythmical, he deserves praise for his development of periodic rhythm as opposed to Gorgian rhythm.

Plutarch, on the other hand, is less sympathetic. It is appropriate that Plutarch should discuss oratory in his essay 'Of Hearing'; appropriate, too, that he should take the side of philosophy against rhetoric. He condemns both those who demand 'merely that the style shall be plain and pure Attic' and those who 'mind nothing but words and jingle', for both prefer expression to philosophy—a preference responsible for 'that abundance of subtilty and sophistry which is crept into the schools'.[4] It is not surprising, therefore, that his essay 'Whether the Athenians were more Warlike or Learned' should call upon Isocrates for the unheroic side of an antithesis in which his life is spent

knitting and joining together antithetical and equally balanced clauses, and words of similar endings, all but smoothing and adapting his periods and sentences with files, planes, or chisels . . . afraid of suffering one vowel

---

[1] His doctrine of rhythm was more often derived from the *De Oratore* (III. xliv ff.). There although the good orator 'restricts his style to periods and to measures, yet he relieves and unbends it by varying the stops and cadence' (xliv). 'But there is no time where there are no stops' (xlviii). Therefore the members of a period ought to be under some regulation—the later equal to or longer than the foregoing; they should have measure, but no regular returns. [2] *Orator*, 170.

[3] Ibid. 175–6. [4] Seneca expresses a similar view in *Ep.* 52.

to clash with another, or to pronounce a sentence where but one syllable was wanting.[1]

This exaggerates what Erasmus calls the too great precision of his periods.

In neo-classical days, when Blair lectured on rhetoric, such a description still had its moral for the use of parallel structure. Too much correspondent structure, warns Blair,

leads to a disagreeable uniformity; produces a regularly returning clink in the period, which tires the ear; and plainly discovers affectation. Among the ancients, the style of Isocrates is faulty in this respect; and on that account, by some of their best critics, particularly by Dionysius of Hali-carnassus, he is severely censured.[2]

If Isocrates eventually could share the disability of the heroic couplet, it is useless to quarrel with those for whom his Gorgian structure remained obtrusive. Although this structure was not alien to Cicero, as Erasmus's Ciceronian contended, no one can believe Erasmus a fool for thinking it native to Isocrates.

Erasmus also gives notice of the relation of Isocratic structure to an English writer, if not to English style. For the purposes of our study it is instructive to compare the most recent view of More's English style with the Erasmian remark that his Latin style 'tends rather to Isocratic structure and dialectic subtlety than to the copious river of Ciceronian diction'. But first it would be useful to have some conception of the native tradition in prose, such as that which emerges from Krapp's *Rise of English Literary Prose*. There the native tradition in prose, going back to medieval times, is based on the simple colloquial or aggregative sentence, with sprawling members, loosely connected by temporal and co-ordinating conjunctions, unemphatic in effect. It uses the simplest kind of amplification—cataloguing, the heaping of synonyms, words of similar meaning, or phrases of similar construction; for oral ornament it employs alliteration and synonymous word-pairs.[3] It was essentially a polysyndetic

---

[1] *Morals*, ed. W. W. Goodwin (Boston, 1870), v. 409. Laurand (*Études*, p. 121, n. 2) observes that logically antithesis is a species of parison, but its importance has made it a genre apart. In ancient theory it is co-ordinate, not subordinate, to parison.

[2] Hugh Blair, *Lectures on Rhetoric*, lect. XII.

[3] See G. P. Krapp's *English Literary Prose* on Wyclif's style (p. 50) and on Latimer's style (pp. 180-4). To pass from this to schematic prose is to pass from shapelessness to formal pattern; between the two come various degrees of shape, various kinds of form. Latimer, for example, improves upon the native tradition in the direction of simple

and highly co-ordinated style. In a more disciplined form the English Bible transmits, through Tyndale, the native tradition of prose as shaped in the fifteenth century. 'The style which lay at the base of Tindale's translation', says Krapp, 'was the easy, polysyndetic, and naive style of simple narrative.'[1]

In *The Continuity of English Prose from Alfred to More and his School*, R. W. Chambers, after tracing that continuity through the homiletic tradition, arrives at this appraisal of More:

More brings English eloquence from the cloister where it had taken refuge, and applies it to the needs of Sixteenth-Century England. Thereby he deserves the title which Mackintosh gave him long ago, of restorer of political eloquence. He knows all the tricks. He couples synonyms together when it suits his purpose; but he does not do it with the maddening persistency which Berners, or Elyot, or Hall, or even Fisher displays: a persistency which had become a real danger to English style. In the same way More uses balanced sentences, and sometimes emphasizes the balance with alliteration, sometimes even with cross-alliteration; the most characteristic cadences of Lyly's *Euphues* are anticipated. But when More has once achieved them, he goes on and tries something else, instead of repeating the trick with the reiterated folly of Lyly.[2]

Now the practice of coupling synonyms, as we have seen, is Ciceronian to Erasmus; and the Euphuistic tricks he doubtless would regard as Isocratic structure, which is patterned by the Gorgian figures.[3] In any event the schemes, Thomas Wilson remarked, are 'contrary to the vulgar custom of our speech'.[4]

order in structure and sound. His alliteration or like-sounds are used in simple patterns; but though not devoid of pattern, they are relatively deficient in schematic form. The colloquial tradition is also strong in Richard Taverner.

[1] Cf. *English Literary Prose*, pp. 102–7, 233–42, 252–6. This polysyndetic background served to make more striking even feeble imitations of the asyndetic Senecan style. Tyndale thought that 'the Greek tongue agreeth more with the English than with Latin, and the properties of the Hebrew tongue agreeth a thousand times more with English than with the Latin'.

[2] Introduction, *Harpsfield's Life of More* (E.E.T.S., 1932), pp. clv–clvi. 'It is from this homiletic tradition', Chambers has said, 'that More sometimes borrows the trick of balanced sentences, many of which can be scanned as rough alliterative lines. It is a tradition which we can trace from Ælfric, through the group of Saints' Lives contemporary with the *Ancren Riwle*, and through Rolle.' But Bede's *De schematis et tropis* would have led Chambers to a tradition that shaped the tradition which he connects only with alliterative verse. Cf. G. H. Gerould, 'Abbot Ælfric's Rhythmic Prose', *Modern Philology*, xxii. 353–66.

[3] On the Euphuistic tricks in More, Elyot, and Fisher see A. Feuillerat, *John Lyly*, pp. 452–9. In these examples More's *Richard III* figures prominently.

[4] *Arte of Rhetorique*, ed. Mair, p. 176. On the elevation of English style see Krapp, *English Literary Prose*, pp. 306–12.

Of the Euphuistic element in More, let us place an example chosen by Chambers beside another chosen by Feuillerat:

. . . lest those that have not letted to put them in duresse without colour, wil let as lytle to procure their distruccion without cause.

Neither to thatchieu*yng* of temper*ance* in prosper*itie*/, nor to the purchas*ing* of paci*ence* in aduers*itie*/, nor to the dispis*ing* of world*ly* van*itie*/, nor to the desir*ing* of heauen*ly* felic*itie*.[1]

The first example illustrates what Chambers calls emphasizing the balance with alliteration—so often observed in Euphuism—but the second example illustrates something much more significant—rhymed prose, which is connected with Gorgias, homiletic tradition, and Euphuism. In Chambers's account of the continuity of English prose, we miss the perception which students of style like Norden and Croll might have lent the historian peering into the cloister. More knows all the tricks and he had them from the cloister. But of this Chambers has little to say, except that More's use of the schemes avoids the 'reiterated folly of Lyly'; thus the reiteration becomes a difference in wisdom rather than in rhetoric.[2] If More 'borrows the trick of balanced sentences' from the homiletic tradition, and this same trick associates him with Lyly, we may wonder whether this trick is supposed to be at once a part of the 'eccentricity' of Lyly and a portion of the inheritance of More.[3] It is not, I presume, to be regarded as a legacy of the 'prose style—straightforward, vivid, simple in the best sense'—which More passed on to his school.[4]

The connexion of this Euphuistic element with the prose of the fourteenth century does not engage the attention of Chambers; he ignores Croll on that subject and even his own hint.[5] If he had not blinked this problem, he might have had to weigh the probability that forces which helped to shape the prose of Rolle and Hilton

[1] For the first see Chambers, *Harpsfield's Life of More*, p. clvi; for the second, Feuillerat, *John Lyly*, p. 455.

[2] Croll holds that More is not Euphuistic, but concludes (*Euphues*, p. xlvi) that his *Dialogue of Comfort* and *Richard III* are more schematic (and therefore more medieval) than his *Pico* and *Utopia*.

[3] Cf. Chambers, *Harpsfield's Life of More*, p. clxxii. For schematic effects in earlier translated prose see S. K. Workman, *Fifteenth Century Translation as an Influence on English Prose* (Princeton, 1940), esp. chaps. i and vii.

[4] In this connexion see Krapp (*English Literary Prose*, pp. 100 ff.) on the styles of More and Tyndale.

[5] See Croll, *Euphues*, pp. lv ff., 'The Uses of the Schemata in Middle-English Prose'.

also helped to shape the prose of Lyly.[1] Such a consideration would not have committed him to an equation of the simpler fourteenth-century use of the schemes with the more sophisticated use of Lyly, but it might have saved him from a rather simple conception of the homiletic tradition. Some attention to rhymed sermons as treated by G. R. Owst might have been admonitory; but one must add that Owst, writing after Norden and Croll, could have written to greater purpose on this subject.[2] Although Erasmus was writing about Latin style, it is ironical that in his account the style which descended from More according to Chambers had a better chance of deriving from Grocyn and Linacre.

Yet another English writer, often thought important to the development of English prose, has been associated, both in his own time and in ours, with Isocrates. Of course I refer to Roger Ascham.[3] Bacon found reason to include Ascham in his sketch of the Ciceronian movement; but Harvey, though once a Ciceronian, believed 'M. Ascham's Period the Siren of Isocrates'.[4] In our time Ascham has been explained as a forerunner of Euphuism. Yet when Harvey, commenting on Quintilian, declared 'Ascham in his fine discourse of Imitation, somewhat too precise and scrupulous for Tully only in all points', he also thought paromoion—'similar cadences, terminations, and inflexions'—'somewhat overmuch affected by M. Ascham in our vulgar Tongue'.[5] Was the latter fault a consequence of Ciceronian imitation or of the 'Siren of Isocrates'?

Whipple is ready to admit that Ascham 'had a special liking for the parallel or antithetic sentence-structure which he found in Isocrates', but not that he indulged in paromoion.[6] Whipple cites this sentence from Ascham to illustrate 'something of the Isocratic ring':

No, I will never so return thither again, to spend my age there in need

[1] Cf. J. P. Schneider, *The Prose Style of Richard Rolle of Hampole with Special Reference to its Euphuistic Tendencies* (Baltimore, 1906).

[2] *Preaching in Medieval England* (Cambridge, 1926), pp. 312, 328–9. On the metrical homily see pp. 273 ff.

[3] On his style see Krapp, *English Literary Prose*, pp. 295 ff.

[4] See Philostratus, *Lives of the Sophists* (Loeb ed., p. 51), for 'the Siren which stands on the tomb of Isocrates the sophist'.

[5] *Marginalia*, ed. Moore Smith, pp. 117, 115. Cf. Quintilian (IX. iv. 42) on the latter fault: 'si cadentia similiter & similiter desinentia, & eodem modo declinata, multa iungantur'.

[6] See *Modern Language Review*, xi. 16.

and care, where I led my youth in plenty and hope, but will follow rather Isocrates' counsel, to get me thither where I am less known, there to live, though not with less care, at least with less shame.

'Here', he continues, 'we have the utmost of precise and involved balance, but none of the exact euphuistic similarities of sound.'[1] In this balance, it may be noted, the use of isocolon (syllabic equality between members) is both striking and Isocratic. Yet Croll, who allows Ascham a partly Euphuistic character, finds an Ascham letter to be peculiarly Ciceronian:

> I do not know of any other attempt to reproduce Cicero which is so successful. A single sentence will illustrate the difference between balance as carried out on the Ciceronian model and the same thing in the Euphuistic form: 'Which sentences I heard very gladly then, and felt them soon after myself to be true.'[2]

Compared with the preceding example, this sentence exhibits the difference which Hermogenes found between Isocrates and Demosthenes: the avoidance of 'direct and absolute symmetry or consonance of clauses'. Here Ascham has avoided symmetrical structure in clauses of equal length, but not Cicero's objection to too strict a rhythm. This is a good example of disguised symmetry.

It would appear that the use of precise balance distinguishes both Isocrates and Euphuism from Cicero; it might be inferred that the use of similarities of sound distinguishes Euphuism from Isocrates as well as from Cicero. Both elements, however, have served to characterize Isocrates, and even the early Cicero, for classical scholars; and this makes it difficult to distinguish the Euphuist from the Ciceronian. But Erasmus, borrowing Quintilian's apology for the early Cicero, suggests that the faults of composition in Isocrates were extenuated by clearness and weight of thought. Thus the great representative of Sophistic rhetoric could be saved.

Certainly for Erasmus the kinds of style that appeared most distinct were the Ciceronian, the Isocratic, and the Attic. And this is not irrelevant to English style, for prose in the Renaissance, except in pedestrian use, tended to approximate the classical tradition of stylistic forms. By Erasmus the Ciceronian was opposed to the Attic and likewise to the Isocratic, which was too Gorgian: in the first

---

[1] See *Modern Language Review*, xi. 135. But Ascham is not devoid of repetitions of sound.

[2] *Euphues*, p. xlvi, n. 1.

instance as fullness to brevity; in the second as flowing period to mannered structure. In the later Renaissance the truth is not quite so simple, and the difficulty lies not merely in the relation of the Isocratic to the other two styles but in its relation to a new style—Euphuism. It would be easy to say that Euphuism was a new name for the Isocratic, but less easy to accept the consequences for Ascham and Lyly. Perhaps if we divide the Gorgian figures into schemes of rhythm and schemes of point, we can argue that in contradistinction the Ciceronian and Isocratean, the Isocratean and Euphuistic, over-lap in their use of isocolon and parison; the Euphuistic and Senecan overlap in their use of antithesis and paromoion. For the accurate definition of a prose style it is necessary to determine not only what figures are used but how they are used. Ascham the Ciceronian, Isocratean, and Euphuist in turn—and all by virtue of his figures of language or *schemata verborum*—is a case in point. How would the *Ciceronianus* have classified him? At least we may assume that Echo would not have answered 'Attic'.

2. *The Rhetorical Forms of Style*

Gorgias, the inventor of Sophistic style and one of the great innovators in prose, has survived as the apostle of symmetry. His significance for Anti-Ciceronian style, therefore, would seem to be negligible, if that style is characterized by asymmetry. For Croll the style of Sir Thomas Browne is just such a style; but is it untouched by the innovations of Gorgias? In a discussion of prose rhythm by Kenneth Burke the following sentence from Browne is cited: 'Even Sylla, that thought himself safe in his urn, / could not prevent revenging tongues, / and stones thrown at his monument.' In this example Burke analyses 'many complexities of asymmetric balance' on the basis of syntax, observing their conflict with rhythmic intervals;[1] but he misses the real balance because he neglects, though not by intention, the rhetorical aspect. After the first comma, the phrases or members, which Burke marks, display isocolon or syllabic equality; and not only is the member which modifies Sylla antithetic to the actions he could not prevent, but his disabilities are evenly divided. Thus Sir Thomas Browne has employed disguised symmetry, here and elsewhere, as unobtrusively as Ascham in the example already cited.

In prose as in verse, form may be more or less obtrusive, as exemplified in the contrast between the earlier sample from Gorgias and this from Browne. In the rise of prose form, as both Aristotle and Cicero indicate, Gorgias was the most significant pioneer. Hence any consideration of the rhetorical forms of style is bound to involve his innovations, although by way of improvements upon them, modifications of them, or departures from them. And some treatment of the forms of style is essential to the orientation of our subject, not to mention nicer internal discriminations.

[1] See *Counter-Statement* (New York, 1931), p. 168. Burke's divisions ought to include one after 'Sylla' (i.e. Sulla).

I

Sophistic style, to which Isocratic structure is related, may be
further defined by Euphuism; and for our study this style requires
more attention. The analysis of Euphuism made by Feuillerat draws
upon Sophistic style, and differs from that of Croll chiefly in emphasis and total significance; moreover, it provides an instructive
experiment in the definition of style.

Feuillerat begins with the abuse of antithesis and the abuse of
comparison, but so does the schoolbook definition.[1] They are, none
the less, characteristic Gorgian abuses. He realizes, however, that
the form of the style is not less characteristic. He observes that the
development of ideas is not logical, but is conducted by the simple
juxtaposition of different facets or confirmations of the thought to
be expressed; and that this juxtaposition is accomplished by the
mode of parallelism: antithesis follows antithesis, and comparison,
comparison.[2] In sentence structure this parallelism becomes balance,
and a Lylian sentence can nearly always be broken down into pairs
of co-ordinate propositions limited by conjunctions.[3] Feuillerat
stresses the connexion between thought and form; but the connexion
between form and figure is no less apparent, since the figures employed are those which produce the antithetic period.[4]

The impulse to this form, as described by Blair, arises when two
things are compared or contrasted to each other:

Where either a resemblance or an opposition is intended to be expressed,
some resemblance in the language and construction should be preserved.
For when the things themselves correspond to each other, we naturally
expect to find the words corresponding too. We are disappointed when
it is otherwise; and the comparison, or contrast, appears more imperfect.[5]

Thus Lyly's form is connected with the figures which he abused;
but for Blair the abuse of the form is represented by Isocrates. No

---

[1] See A. Feuillerat, *John Lyly* (Cambridge, 1910), pp. 411 ff. On the abuse of
similitudes Feuillerat makes a remark the importance of which will appear later: 'Elles
n'ont pas pour but de faire appel à l'imagination du lecteur; leur rôle est d'expliquer et
de prouver les idées avancées par l'auteur.'

[2] Ibid., p. 431. Cf. Cicero's illustration, already cited, of the Gorgian sentence, which
is one way of making Isocrates' 'circle'.

[3] Ibid., p. 434.

[4] As Demetrius remarks (*On Style*, 59), 'the figures of speech are themselves a form
of composition'.

[5] Hugh Blair, *Lectures on Rhetoric*, lect. XII.

one, however, is obliged to think in continual similes and antitheses; nor is there any necessity for expressing them in parallel or
balanced form; but if one desires such a style, antitheses and comparisons are the logical material for exploiting the form.

The mode of parallelism has a further extension. The structure
of Lyly's sentence, observes Feuillerat, is rendered more striking
by devices of a purely euphonic character. These he divides into
alliteration and rhyming effects: the rhyme nearly always accents
the structure; the alliteration may be employed for its jingle alone.[1]
Such an extension might lead one to ask whether Lyly's style merely
subserves his thought—whether his thought has not been moulded
so as to exploit a style. When Feuillerat concludes that Lyly's style
is characterized by an approach to poetic form, he supports such a
conclusion; and he is led to it by Lyly's use of balance with rhyming
effects and a tendency to isocolon.[2]

In this exaggeration of rhythmical form he finds the great defect
of Euphuism, and thus relates it in another way to the Gorgian
ancestry from which it descends. On the basis of rhythm he distinguishes Lyly from Guevara: the antithetic balance in Guevara is
submerged in the waves of a Ciceronian period; the 'tic-tac métro-
nomique et mécanique' of Lyly is only too audible, for he preferred
co-ordinate structure.[3] Here we may invoke Cicero's distinction
between periodic and Gorgian rhythm, and recall Erasmus's distinction between the rhythms of Cicero and Isocrates. Lyly's
euphonic devices are a natural extension of the correspondent character of his sentence, as in Gorgias; and his rhythm is inherent in
the figures which constitute that sentence.

But Feuillerat leads us in another direction when he concludes
with respect to the periodic movement:

North, comme Guevara, est un cicéronien; et il ressemble à Sidney
qui, lui aussi, a dans sa phrase beaucoup de l'emphase et de l'enchevêtre-
ment espagnols, et non à Lyly qui, par sa vivacité alerte, coupée et
épigrammatique, fait plutôt songer à la manière française.[4]

This is less an opposition of a Ciceronian and a Gorgian style than
of a Ciceronian and a Senecan, or even an Attic as described by

---

[1] *John Lyly*, pp. 435 ff.   [2] Ibid., p. 439.
[3] Ibid., pp. 449–50. Cf. G. P. Krapp (*English Literary Prose*, p. 315) on the style
of Guevara.
[4] *John Lyly*, p. 450.

Erasmus. Blair, who calls these styles the *style périodique* and the *style coupé*, also regards the *style coupé* as the French manner;[1] but Feuillerat presumably ought not to be reminded of that manner by an approach to poetic form. Thus Lyly's style is made to look two ways, toward both schematic and pointed prose, and we encounter a problem that will reappear in our study. Various questions are provoked. Can a style employing certain figures be at once Senecan and Gorgian? If Euphuism were to drop most of its euphonic devices, would we have left anything like the curt Senecan style? Croll, of course, differs from Feuillerat chiefly in maintaining unequivocally that the euphonic aspect of Lyly's style is the paramount concern, and that everything else is made to serve it; he treats Euphuism as schematic or rhymed prose, not as both rhymed and pointed prose.

Finally, we may notice a statement in which Feuillerat, while discussing the origins of Euphuism, brings the problem of figures to a head:

> Depuis le jour où Gorgias et Isocrate eurent révélé les effets du balancement (isocôlon ou parison), de l'antithèse, de la rime (homoioteleuton), des jeux de mots ou assonances et consonances (paronomasia), ces figures ne cessèrent pas d'être la presque unique ressource des stylistes.[2]

In confirmation, following Norden, he lists many writers who have made use of them—from the Greeks to the African school of Church Fathers; and among these writers we find not only Cicero but the chief Anti-Ciceronians. Medieval practice seems to lend support to this apparently exaggerated claim for some of the *schemata verborum*.

But this, it might be objected, is to state a half-truth at best, for it obscures another resource with which Isocrates was connected. The other great contribution to the formal support of prose W. R. M. Lamb has put into these words:

> But the aim of making *metre* the chief formal support of prose was started by Thrasymachus of Chalcedon; who seems to have largely determined the rhythmic method of Isocrates, and thus to have opened up a field of experiment hardly less important than the work of Gorgias to European literature.[3]

[1] *Lectures on Rhetoric*, lect. XI. Cf. Bouhours, *Entretien d'Ariste et d'Eugène*, ed. Radouant, p. 59.
[2] *John Lyly*, p. 461.
[3] *Clio Enthroned: A Study of Prose-Form in Thucydides* (Cambridge, 1914), p. 246.

Cadences are not the same as balance or the rhythm inherent in the Gorgian figures; but balance and sentence cadences are the two modes of rhythm in prose. Cadence will be considered in relation to the period.

The figures of parallelism provided Gorgias with the rhetoric for his 'jingling Epigrams', which in turn emphasize the twofold powers of these figures. Hence he bequeathed to posterity the means not only to schematic jingle but also to epigram, enabling Lamb to discuss him as a witty or pointed writer.[1] His rhetoric contributed to prose one of its great formal supports, serving point as well as pattern and rhythm; indeed, that rhetoric and schematic prose are synonymous. The Gorgian figures, it has been said, 'reduce the idea and its expression to a regular design'.[2] And 'the chief benefit resulting to us now', as Lamb remarks, 'is the establishment of balance in the constitution of a sentence'.[3] The pointed style, which is also indebted to Gorgias, has been described by Alexander Bain:

The profuse employment of the Balanced Sentence, in conjunction with antithesis, epigram, and climax, determines the Pointed Style. This combination is seen in Pope, Junius, and in a less degree in many others. It is also termed the 'Epigrammatic' style. The French excel in epigram and point. The excess of this quality in Tacitus, Lucan, and Seneca, is usually identified with the decline of the Latin language.[4]

Here we are reminded of the gamut between virtue and excess in the pointed style. Having reviewed the dual aspect of the Gorgian achievement, it is now time to recall that Cicero recognized, in words which I have quoted, both aspects of this contribution to the formal support of prose—both the ingenuity and the rhythm of its symmetry.

Clearly, as the almost unique resource of stylists, these figures must be differentiated in writers by their use; but Feuillerat is not enough concerned with that requirement. Croll, on the other hand, would differentiate styles too much by the kind of figures employed. Thus he finds that Euphuism is related to Ciceronian style, but not to Senecan style; for if Euphuism is a school of antithesis, it is anti-

---

[1] *Clio Enthroned*, pp. 152–8. 'He had', says Lamb, 'the happy gift of seizing and turning to account the material from which proverbs, epigrams and other self-supporting, self-recording sentences are made.'

[2] J. M. Campbell, *The Influence of the Second Sophistic on the Style of St. Basil the Great* (Washington, 1922), chap. x.

[3] *Clio Enthroned*, p. 157.

[4] *English Composition and Rhetoric* (New York, 1890), p. 148.

thesis as a structural figure, a figure of language, not a figure of thought or wit. This instance is all the more pat because the difference might appear to lie in use. But when Feuillerat makes Lyly approach the French manner, he describes a style that is Senecan rather than Gorgian, witty rather than oratorical; that contrives a different effect out of the same figures. Altogether, he leaves Lyly with something of the dual character that has been discovered in Gorgias but usually has not been ascribed to Isocrates.

II

Both Erasmus and Feuillerat advance the problem of formal distinctions in prose analysis. Erasmus deals in salient qualities, but he usually points to their rhetorical causes: if Isocrates produces an effect of undue precision, the causes are to be found in his structure. In fact, as Croll suggests, the basic forms of the period or sentence, which were distinguished by the ancient rhetoricians, are indispensable for any attempt to discriminate between fashions or movements in prose style.[1] With these forms in mind, it will be easier to determine whether certain figures of language are essential or accidental to a particular style, and then how they are used in that style. These forms will enable us to grasp the structure of the styles that Erasmus found indispensable to his analysis—Attic, Isocratic or Sophistic, and Ciceronian—styles no less necessary to the analysis of later prose.

When Aristotle accused Gorgias of bringing poetry into prose, he put us in the way of understanding not only the development of artistic prose but his own analysis. It all centres in the question of providing prose with formal support or, as for Aristotle, with formal limitation. Thus Aristotle divided prose into the kind which had formal support and the kind which did not. Where he called these modes of structure the periodic and the continuous, Demetrius

---

[1] Croll (*Studies in English Philology*, ed. Malone and Ruud, p. 429) specifies the 'several elements of prose technique: diction, or the choice of words; the choice of figures; the principle of balance or rhythm; the form of the period, or sentence'; and then concludes that 'the last-mentioned of them—the form of the period—is, however, the most important and the determinant of the others'. The extent to which the form of the sentence tells the story of the development of English prose may be seen in G. P. Krapp's *Rise of English Literary Prose*; e.g. pp. 146, 279, 334, 357, 359–60, 374. In this study I am concerned necessarily with the species of style rather than with individual styles.

called them the compacted and disjointed; for Quintilian they were the compacted and resolved, and for us they are the periodic and loose.[1] Structurally, of course, style is concerned primarily with the relation of members, although the character of the members, such as form and length, is also important.[2] Hence style must begin with the distinct types of membered sentences: the co-ordinate and the complex, which provide different ways of ordering thought, but are not synonymous with the rhetorical forms mentioned above.

Either type of sentence may be written in the well-knit form or the loose form, but as ways of ordering thought they have distinct characters. The co-ordinate sentence, which is most fully exploited in balance, equates thought, emphasizes alike, and disperses unity and coherence. Structurally the relation between members of a co-ordinate sentence devoid of balance is the same as that between sentences.[3] The complex sentence, which is most fully exploited in the cumulative period, subordinates thought to thought, distributes emphasis, and promotes or focuses unity and coherence. It provides its thought with an articulate logic, and in periodic form is well-knit both grammatically and rhetorically; for when so compacted it is shaped so as to accumulate force and sonority.[4] Of course sub-dependence is the great complicator of sentence structure. Using such sentences, the rhetorically well-knit form exploits the formal arrangements or supports of prose, the loose form neglects or avoids them; thus variations of these two types of sentence and style are

[1] William Mure in his *Critical History* (1850–7) calls these two styles the Periodic and the Sententious. The mode of structure for the Sententious is the 'jointed' of Aristotle and the 'disjointed' of Demetrius. The mode of structure for the Periodic is 'involution of language' or subordinate clauses grouped into a unified body. Macaulay's style, he remarks, is jointed or sententious; it has the characteristic virtue of that style—perspicuity at the expense of incoherence of structure. Mure's division of styles is like Blair's French division: the *style coupé* and the *style périodique*.
[2] Cf. Demetrius (*On Style*, 1): 'As verse is articulated by measures so prose style is articulated by members.' In medieval terms a member or *distinctio* could be of three kinds: *dependens*, *constans* (a statement complete but continuing), and *finitiva*, that member in which the whole sentence is finished. Cf. C. S. Baldwin, *Medieval Rhetoric and Poetic* (New York, 1928), p. 218.
[3] Members when united in paratactic structure and unified in thought do not advance logically; they repeat or vary the main idea, or present different aspects of it. When thrown into parallel form they acquire a formal unity.
[4] Hypotaxis is the structural principle of climax in a sentence or period; it permits the energy and meaning of a sentence to be centred in a comprehensive rounding. On the relation of emphasis to various styles see H. J. C. Grierson, *Rhetoric and English Composition* (1945), pp. 102–14.

38

created. Still greater variety is attained through hybrids; but nothing really new is introduced by the single-membered sentence, even if it becomes the basis of a style. In such a sentence, antithesis, being intra-clausal, is necessarily less formal. This type of sentence with antithesis may, however, be exploited in epigram, usually by prominently opposed words, in which two ideas of the same order are given symmetrical form. It is found in Euphuism. Its general use produces the most discrete form of style—the formal extreme to the periodic style. Fundamentally, these syntactic forms, when subjected to rhetorical exploitation, yield the basic patterns of the most distinctive characters of style; and these characters are defined by extremes. It must be observed, however, that the relation of co-ordinate structure to the representation of thought limits its appearance in discourse; therefore even a highly paratactic style will reveal a preponderance of subordinate structure, so that the effect of parataxis is out of proportion to its incidence.

The study of sentence structure itself has yielded some interesting suggestions for the history of English prose style.[1] These are found in a tabulation of the connective usage of a list of writers—chiefly as essayists—including Caxton, Lyly, Sidney, Bacon, Dryden, Addison, Johnson, and Macaulay, studied with respect to their initial, internal (co-ordinate), subordinate, and correlative connectives.[2] Since the effect of any prose derives in considerable part from its use of connectives, it makes some difference that Bacon is represented in this tabulation by the more connected *Essays* of 1625. But some of the findings that concern the relation of members deserve particular attention.

Except for Macaulay, Lyly and Bacon have the smallest, and almost the same, amount of subordinate structure; Johnson of the *Lives* is next, and then Dryden of the *Preface to the Fables*. Lyly has the most correlative structure, more than twice that of Bacon; but Lyly is low and Bacon high in the initial connexion of sentences.[3]

[1] See R. R. Aurner, 'The History of Certain Aspects of the Structure of the English Sentence', *Philological Quarterly*, ii (1923), 187–208. These aspects relate to the simplifying of the sentence both in number of clauses and complexity of their relations.

[2] Cf. R. R. Aurner, 'Caxton and the English Sentence', *Wisconsin Studies in Language and Literature*, no. 18 (1923), p. 50. The older, largely co-ordinate prose is still represented in the King James Version of the Bible.

[3] In correlative structure Lyly is Isocratic or Sophistic; in initial connexion Bacon is highest in the 1625 edition, and such connexion is in the native tradition.

Not counting initial connexion, the ratio of co-ordinate to subordinate structure is highest in Lyly, with Bacon second, and Macaulay third. Sidney's *Arcadia* and Dryden's *Essay of Dramatic Poesy* are nearly parallel on all counts, but Dryden's *Preface to the Fables* shows a marked advance over Sidney's *Defense of Poesy* in the ratio of co-ordinate to subordinate structure. Johnson's *Lives* shows a similar advance over *The Rambler*. Macaulay's *Essay on Milton* shows the least multiplication of members in its sentences. Of course this table does not show the precision with which these sentences are organized by their connectives; but it does show the relative weight of co-ordinate and subordinate structure, and the relative simplicity of sentence with respect to the number of clauses and the intricacy of their relations. Moreover, the development of the sentence in these aspects of structure is related to the development of patterns of style. Though such samplings are indicative rather than definitive, they are more positive than our impressions, and help to confirm the patterns of style to which they are related. Of this relation we shall be more aware in due course.

The distinctive characters of style—'lofty, mean, or lowly' as Milton called them—have long had implicit in them, whatever their origin, the definition of styles by extremes. Although these characters are not present in Aristotle, the use of extremes to define style is, and even the basic difference between the plain and the elevated style.[1] In his *Rhetoric* (III. ii) the chief merits of style, at least on the level of diction, are perspicuity and propriety. Proper words give perspicuity; all the others mentioned in *Poetics*, 21 give elevation or dignity.[2] For style language must be given an uncommon air or distinction. But this effort should be governed by propriety, for propriety will conceal the art, and only the natural persuades. Extremes are present here, for complete clarity would make language completely common, whereas too much of the unusual would make it unintelligible. *Poetics*, 22, where similar doctrine is set forth, shows more clearly the conflict between clarity and distinction which

---

[1] On Aristotle's conception of style see G. L. Hendrickson, 'The Origin and Meaning of the Ancient Characters of Style', *American Journal of Philology*, xxvi. 253 ff. See also his 'Peripatetic Mean of Style and the Three Stylistic Characters' (ibid., vol. xxv), on the relation of the 'lofty' and 'mean' styles to oratory, the 'lowly' to philosophy.

[2] And thus Blair (*Rhetoric*, x): 'All the qualities of good style may be ranged under two heads, perspicuity and ornament.'

must be resolved for a good style. Again in the *Rhetoric* (III. xii) he remarks:

> For why, if not to please, need it be clear, not mean, but appropriate? If it be too diffuse, or too concise, it will not be clear; but it is plain that the mean is most suitable. What we have said will make the style pleasant, if it contains a happy mixture of proper and 'foreign' words, of rhythm, and of persuasiveness resulting from propriety.

Thus it may be said that the uncommon gives distinction as rhythm gives form, while propriety secures the naturalness that persuades and perspicuity achieves the end of communication.[1] The use of extremes to define the best qualities of style can be observed in such pairs as the proper and the foreign, the diffuse and the concise, the metrical and the unrhythmical.[2] Prose style itself is defined for Aristotle by the extremes which poetry and geometry offer in relation to language and the ends of pleasure or instruction. The end of style is to please in language, and everything beyond the requirements of perspicuity may fall into the category of ornament, subject to the propriety which lends persuasion.

Dionysius of Halicarnassus defines three styles of composition by means of extremes: the austere or severe; the smooth, polished, or florid; and the harmoniously blended.[3] The last is a mean of varying character between the two extremes. Of this Dionysius remarks:

> I cannot see whether it is formed by eliminating the two extremes or by fusing them—it is not easy to hit on any clear answer. Perhaps, then, it is better to say that it is by relaxation and tension of the extremes that the means, which are very numerous, arise.

At least, the middle style in writing does not 'stand at an equal distance from each of the extremes'; it has too many forms for that. The austere style seeks strength, impressive rhythm, but not clauses 'parallel in structure or sound, nor slaves to a rigid sequence'. It

---

[1] On communication see *Rhetoric*, III. i. 6; on rhythm, III. viii. 2: 'Now all things are limited by number, and the number belonging to the form of diction is rhythm, of which the metres are divisions.' Of course there are other aspects of the form of diction.

[2] Metaphor or tropes and strange words give a foreign air. In the arrangement of words figures introduce strangeness or distinction in order, and so does rhythm; the familiar produces or maintains clarity. Both in words and in the arrangement of words style is found between the extremes of the familiar and the strange, or in their judicious mixture. Frigidity of style springs from improprieties of words with respect to the medium or subject.

[3] See *Greek Literary Criticism*, ed. J. D. Denniston (London, 1924), pp. 145–50.

does not seek formal periods, but rather an 'unstudied and simple character', marked by flexible arrangement and few connectives. In prose Thucydides is the prime example. The florid style is exactly opposite in its aims. It combines and interweaves its parts into formal periods. 'It could not endure to construct a passage without periods, nor a period without clauses, nor a clause without symmetry.' Moreover, 'it requires its periods to march as with steps regulated by line and rule, and to close with a rhythmical fall'. In prose Isocrates is the prime example. The harmoniously blended style is a varying 'union of the severe and polished forms of arrangement'. Herodotus in history and Demosthenes in oratory are prime examples.

When Demetrius distinguishes styles by a dominant quality or effect, he also makes use of extremes or contraries. The contraries—plain and elevated—may be combined with the extremes—elegant and forcible—but not with each other. The extremes may be harmonized with one another, but less easily than with the others, since the area of conflict is greater.[1] These opposites give four simple types of style and various composite types. Although the elevated and the plain cannot be combined, they can be varied toward either or both of the other opposites, force and elegance. Among the composite types, for example, a combination of the plain and the elegant gives the epistolary style. In composition the four simple styles may be characterized as follows: the elevated cultivates stately rhythm in suspended periods; the elegant cultivates disguised metre, symmetry, and effective pointing; the plain seeks no formal rhythm, no prolonged endings, but detached clauses; the forcible cultivates brevity and abruptness in pointed periods. For the elegant, composition is less distinctive than its cultivation of all the ornaments of charm and wit. As for the length of members, the plain is short; the elevated, long; and the forcible, very short. Where Aristotle defined distinction of style as opposed to the language of poetry and the language of geometry, both Dionysius and Demetrius

[1] See Demetrius, *On Style*, part ii. The elegant resembles the Sophistic style, including its turn and point. The forceful is a periodic style devoid of elegance, compacted by brevity, and directed toward power rather than dignity. In composition the plain is neither periodic nor rounded, the elevated is both; the elegant is rounded but not periodic, the forcible is periodic but not rounded. The plain, elegant, and elevated may be regarded as the three characters of style, with the forcible a special variety of the elevated; or the plain and the elevated may be regarded as extremes with two means, the elegant and the forcible.

seek to define kinds of distinction appropriate to different subject-matters.

Cicero, in his turn, defined the three styles as extremes with a mean;[1] and remarked that the ornament of the Sophists, scorned by the simple and rejected by the grand, found a resting-place in the middle style. For contrast to the grand style he speaks of 'one who has studied the plain and pointed style so as to be able to speak adroitly and neatly', and thereby gives a significant, indeed an 'Atticist', turn to the plain style.[2]

Quintilian defines not only characters but schools of style by means of extremes. For him the Attics are compressed and energetic as opposed to the Asiatics, who are inflated and deficient in force. The Rhodian style is a middle character between the other two, partaking of each, but neither concise nor exuberant.[3] Distinguishing 'the different forms of eloquence', he finds between the extremes of the plain and the grand a mean style, sometimes called the florid. There is not only a mean between the *simple* and the *energetic*, but also degrees in each and means between any two degrees.[4] If the Attic and Asiatic styles are opposed as the concise and energetic to the copious and weak, the plain and the grand styles are opposed as the simple and concise to the vehement and copious.[5] In these oppositions of fundamentally concise and copious styles, a difference in energy is remarked; in the first it derives from closeness of expression, but in the second from the full use of rhetoric, the plain denoting a frugal use.[6]

Thus the relation of different styles to the length and character of members, sentences, and periods becomes more evident. For composition or the arrangement of words, the forms of style are in fact basic, not merely to structure but also to rhythm. And no less manifest is the importance of extremes in any attempt to discrimi-

---

[1] See *Orator*, 20-1, 75-90, 91-6, 97-9.

[2] Cf. ibid. 98: 'qui in illo subtili et acuto elaboravit, ut callide arguteque diceret.'

[3] Cf. *Institutes of Oratory*, XII. x. 16-18.

[4] Ibid. 58-67. 'There is something fuller, and something more simple, than the *simple* kind; there is something more gentle, and more energetic, than the *energetic* kind; and the *middle* kind both rises to what is stronger, and stoops to what is weaker.'

[5] Ibid. 20-4, 64-5.

[6] For Quintilian the difference between the grand and the Asiatic style is one between true and false eloquence; the Attic style becomes a comprehensive term, meaning the best style.

nate styles, for without extremes both the art and the analysis of prose would be fuzzy and ill defined, indeed amorphous. In particular we have learned something about the kinds of extremes that may serve to define the diction and composition of styles. We have now to examine the basic forms themselves.

The loose mode of structure is the early and natural way of writing; the periodic is later and the result of art. The former is a free structure, loosely knit by connectives, and, lacking formal support, has no rhetorical form; the latter is a limited structure, closely knit not only by syntactic means but also by the formal supports of rhythm, parallelism, and rhetorical or rhythmical climax.[1] Basically, as Demetrius insists, the period is not a form of thought like the enthymeme, but a form of composition or expression, an arrangement of words. You may invert the order of the members without altering the thought, but you will destroy the course by which the members round to a climax or comprehension; you will alter the relation of beginning and end or the order of thought, not thought itself. But an arrangement of words inevitably relates to syntax, which is an instrument of order as well as thought. In brief, if a period is not a form of thought, it is an order of thoughts incident to a compacted form, which involves rhythm.

In the two extremes of style, the grand and the plain, Demetrius sharply distinguishes the appropriate order of words or composition. In the elevated style the order is one of increasing vividness, secured by an artificial, inverted disposition of words; in the plain style the order is one of clearness, dependent on a natural disposition of words.[2] The grand style employs the rounded periodic form; the plain, the loose structure. Throughout he describes the literary effect of the former as forcible, elaborate, artificial, and the literary effect of the latter as naïve, simple, natural. St. Augustine described the suspension found in the rounded form when he said of the period, 'the clauses of which are suspended on the voice of the speaker till the whole is completed by the last clause'.[3] Related to

[1] In rhythmical gradation, as in the rhopalic period, the members or parts lengthen proportionately throughout. 'The congruent and harmonious fitting of parts in a sentence', as Jonson remarks in his *Discoveries* (cxx), 'hath almost the fastening and force of knitting and connection; as in stones well squared, which will rise strong a great way without mortar.'

[2] Cf. *On Style*, 50-3, 199-201.

[3] *De Doctrina Christiana*, IV. 7. 11. Here the period cannot have less than two clauses.

thought, the period is an arrangement of members; related to words, it is an arrangement of similar patterns or rhythms. These patterns and rhythms give formal support to the arrangement of thought. Together they are related much as the rhetoric and metre are related to thought in the classical couplet.[1]

Both Aristotle and Demetrius recognized two varieties of periodic structure, for though all periods are circular, not all are antithetic.[2] The antithetic or balanced period of Gorgias is the first effort in the direction of compacted prose. Where the circular period exploits subordinate structure, the antithetic exploits co-ordinate structure, and derives its periodology from extended antithesis or parallelism, in which its members acquire their mutual support and rhythm, by which they are rounded.[3] This rhythm is an answering or antiphonal rhythm—not the symphonic rhythm of the circular period; it may obstruct the latter just as the returning clink of heroic couplets works against a paragraph rhythm.[4] In the period with clausal antithesis, the complementary parts of the opposition are related as beginning to end. These parts may be multiplied into

[1] Failure to make the sense coincide with the rhythmic divisions is illustrated by verse in Aristotle's *Rhetoric*, III. ix. 4. Suggestions on the philosophical relation of form to order, especially in pattern and rhythm, may be found in Herbert Read's 'Implications of Behaviorism', *Criterion*, vii (1928), 64–75.

[2] The Isocratic period appears to be Aristotle's norm when he classifies (and illustrates) periods as 'divided' and 'antithetical', and makes the hearer's expectation the measure for the length of members. That this expectation is established by rhythmic balances not only seems obvious but is suggested by the remark that 'language when in periodic form can be numbered'; or by the earlier remark that 'it is the numerical limitation of the form of a composition that constitutes rhythm, of which metres are definite sections'. As paeans the latter are proper only to mark the beginning and end of periods. The divided period, then, consists of balanced members; the antithetic has an opposition of parts as well. To these features may be added strict equality in length of members and oral likeness between their terminal words. In general the members of a period are expected to complete the thought within the compass of a certain rhythm, which can be measured by the ear.

[3] Of the effort to arrange this 'bead-stringing' style of prose into periodic groups, W. R. M. Lamb (*Clio Enthroned*, p. 106) remarks: 'As in the case of verse, the primary object is to erect a framework that will create a feeling of *suspense*, and defer the satisfaction of the ear while the mind is intent on the meaning. Then, as the writer came to be less dependent on skilful recitation to help out the emphasis and connection, the completeness of the period was made to coincide with a completeness of grammar.'

[4] Cf. Norman R. Tempest, *The Rhythm of English Prose* (Cambridge, 1930), p. 116. Of antiphonic prose Tempest remarks: 'In it, the elements of balance and antithesis, which are almost the only rhythmical devices of the simple style, are brought to the front and developed into complicated systems.' Symphonic prose, on the contrary, is continuously arranged, avoids repetition of movement (even in parallelisms), the appearance of artifice, or arrangements that interrupt the flow.

repetitive forms of parallel oppositions; but if the periodic character is to be sustained, unity of thought must be preserved. In other words, if this unity is preserved, the pattern may be described more than once, as in the Cicero example, without ceasing to be a limited circle of meaning.[1] The antithetic period acquires its artistic coherence from a repetitive design, though it may suggest rhythmical progress if its members lengthen. In cultivating symmetry it lends itself to the exploitation of rhyming effects. Thus the balanced pattern gives us the responsive or Sophistic period.

The circular or cumulative period attains the height of artistic coherence by employing all of the formal supports of prose—rounded form, balance, cadence.[2] It creates a cumulative effect by means of rhetorical gradation, implemented by subordination and by more continuous arrangement, which parallelism is not allowed to interrupt. Clausal antithesis, for instance, may be submerged in the circular period by subordinating one or both members. Thus Blair observes that Cicero, in arranging the members of a period, 'makes both the sense and the sound rise together, with a very magnificent swell'.[3] Each wave or member rises a little higher or runs a little longer, until both sense and sound fall away in a rhythmical cadence.[4] Thus the circular pattern, accumulating both rhythm and sense, gives us the cumulative Ciceronian period.

---

[1] The antiphonic has a more obvious periodicity or movement in balanced parts. The symphonic develops continuity in the parts rather than simple recurrence; the rhythmic parts, instead of falling into structural oppositions, fall into longer movements.

[2] Cf. Croll, *Studies in English Philology*, ed. Malone and Ruud, p. 447: 'In the oratorical period the arrangement of the members is "round" or "circular", in the sense that they are all so placed with reference to a central or climactic member that they point forward or back to it and give it its appropriate emphasis.'

[3] *Lectures on Rhetoric*, lect. XII. In lect. XVII Blair speaks of amplification—the art of magnifying or extenuating: 'But the principal instrument by which it works, is by a climax. . . . I spoke formerly of a climax in sound; a climax in sense, when well carried on, is a figure which never fails to amplify strongly.' Blair's theory of rhythm (lect. XIII) also derives from Cicero; e.g. *De Oratore*, III. xliv–xlviii; but is supplemented from Quintilian (IX. iv).

[4] The so-called 'rhopalic' period, by analogy with 'ropalic verses', grew by incremental rhythm or the equal lengthening of its successive phrases or members; see G. Guillaumie, *Balzac et la prose française*, p. 488. On the rhythm and sonority of periods Blair again remarks (lect. XIII) that 'the members of the period swell one above another . . . till the ear, prepared by this gradual rise, is conducted to that full close on which it rests with pleasure'. On the principle of harmony he observes (lect. XIII): 'it is this sort of flowing measure, this regular and proportional division of the members of his sentences, which renders Sir William Temple's style always agreeable.' Harmony also requires the 'musical close' or cadence.

The importance of rhythm to the period is made evident by Aristotle, for he discusses in connexion with it both cadence and balance, including Gorgian balance. It should be remembered that isocolon is one way of measuring language. For cadences or metrical runs Aristotle favoured the paean; and cadences, another mode of rhythm, constitute one of the formal supports of prose. Periodic rhythm is a kind of punctuation which controls and directs the force of the sentence; it can be explained, Aristotle suggests, by analogy with antistrophic rhythm, for it includes a beginning movement and a returning or concluding movement, and it commonly involves a definite sense of a turn. But the too regular pauses of isocolon, to which Isocrates was devoted, produce a mechanical return in the period which discovers an artificial rhythm.[1] Cicero, as Blair indicates, avoided these strict divisions in his prose antistrophes. While the rhetorical form of the period is ordered by the principle of emphasis, which governs the arrangement of members, the period may be rounded either by symmetry of structure or by rhythmical arrangement, or both. The period finds its limits in a rhythmical pattern to which the thought must conform, so that a stage of thought finishes with a stage of rhythm, a thought member with a rhythmic member.

It may be useful at this point to summarize the means, apart from numerical balance, by which classical and native elements combine in English rhythm.[2] The comments of a classical scholar, A. C.

[1] Gibert (see Baillet, *Jugemens des Savans* (Amsterdam, 1725), viii. 69) contrasts the style of Demetrius with the periodic style of Isocrates, 'tout renfermé dans certains nombres & dans certains cadences, à peu près comme un Poëme'. That which produces this style, he says, is the equality of the members which compose the periods, or the turn which is given them, or their oppositions, or their similar cadences, or all these things together.

[2] Cf. M. W. Croll, 'The Cadence of English Oratorical Prose', *Studies in Philology*, xvi (1919); N. R. Tempest, *The Rhythm of English Prose* (Cambridge, 1930). The classical doctrine of prose rhythm as found in Cicero's *Orator* was interpreted for French by Gibert upon the occasion of criticizing Abbé Cassagnes' application of that doctrine to the famous Guez de Balzac (cf. Baillet, *Jugemens des Savans* (Amsterdam, 1725), viii. 95–6). Although the measures which resemble the feet of verse, he observes, are not applicable to French, yet the Greeks and Latins had other things which contribute equally to harmony. 'There is the *turn of the sentence*, which we call the *circonduction*, to take this term in a very general sense; there are members which in themselves strongly resemble verses, although they are not. There is sometimes a *rapport* between certain members, either because of their *opposition*, or because of their *equality*, or even because of their *inequality*, and sometimes a *mélange* of the longer with the shorter. These are the only things that can make rhythm (number) and harmony in French.' And these sources of harmony have a place in all languages; they are the elements that fall into Cicero's larger meaning of rhythm.

Clark, on Saintsbury's *History of English Prose Rhythm* set in relief the important facts.[1] Clark builds upon two statements made by Saintsbury. 'The first is that in Old English or Anglo-Saxon the rhythm is mainly trochaic.'[2] The second is 'that in Middle English the "trochaic tyranny" was mitigated by the disuse of inflection and the introduction of a more polysyllabic vocabulary taken from the Romance languages and from Latin'. Hence the rhythm of Middle English is composite, that is, partly native and partly Latin. Against this background, Clark criticizes Saintsbury for neglecting cadence and attributing too much importance to variety in the rhythm of prose; for without some system, however loose, the result is chaos. Two principles are involved—'that of recurrence and that of variety'; for metre is involved in prose, 'but the metre is not complete'.[3] We have noticed other aspects of the principle of recurrence.

'The rhythm natural to a language depends upon its vocabulary.' Latin is essentially polysyllabic, while English is monosyllabic or disyllabic.[4] This difference is fundamental. Yet the trochaic cadence is characteristic of both languages. In Latin the trochaic rhythm is found chiefly in the *clausula*, and the three forms of the *cursus* or 'run' came into English from Latin.

When Latin words were naturalized, they brought with them the cadences in which the genius of the Latin tongue found best expression. The introduction of such words was largely due to their occurrence in the liturgy of the Church, and to their consequent adoption by the authors

---

[1] *Prose Rhythm in English* (Oxford, 1913).

[2] Ibid., p. 8. This 'trochaic hum' is 'due to the character of the language, which, being "largely monosyllabic and at the same time inflected, necessarily begets trochees ready made in still larger quantities" '. But in 'English Prose Numbers' Oliver Elton (*A Sheaf of Papers*) finds that 'rising or waved rhythm is far commoner than falling rhythm'.

[3] *Prose Rhythm in English*, p. 18. P. Fijn van Draat in *Rhythm in English Prose* (Heidelberg, 1910) insists on the principle of recurrence and will not admit the clashing of stresses; but he accepts an ancient guide when he turns to poetry for rhythmic principles: 'here we shall find a systematic application of every rhythmical device to which prose-language occasionally has recourse.' This guide would have revealed clashing stresses in Milton's *Paradise Lost*.

[4] Cf. Richard Carew, *The Excellency of the English Tongue*: 'Againe, the longe wordes that wee borrowe, being intermingled with the shorte of our owne store, make vp a perfitt harmonye, by culling from out which mixture (with Iudgment) yow maye frame your speech according to the matter you must worke on, maiesticall, pleasaunte, delicate, or manly, more or lesse, in what sorte you please' (G. G. Smith, *Elizabethan Critical Essays*, ii. 293).

of the Prayer Book and the translators of the Bible. These cadences, however, were modified when they became Anglicized, owing to the lack of
polysyllables. The English *cursus* presses monosyllables into its service
with the result that, although the scheme of accentuation is the same, the
caesuras are more numerous and more varied.[1]

Consequently, 'the native elements, viz. the trochaic roll and the
stressed monosyllable, were combined with the exotic'. One native
result of the stressed monosyllable is 'the collision of stressed monosyllables', producing a 'hammer stroke' rhythm, as in Sir Thomas
Browne's 'Now since these dead bones'.[2] Of course Browne also
produces the harmony which derived from the Latin rhythms introduced by his vocabulary, and in which English ears had been trained
by the Book of Common Prayer.

The sublimest effects in English prose, adds Clark, are produced
by the native rhythm, and the two chief means employed are 'the
collision of accents which is alien to the binary movement of medieval
prose and the prolongation of the trochaic roll with its tendency
towards blank verse'. On the other hand, 'the object of the *cursus*
was to procure a smooth ending, or, as its name implies, a "run".
It produces harmony, not grandeur, and imparts to prose an element
of tune.'[3] For this reason, it may be added, Cicero's 'esse videatur'
became almost a byword among the Anti-Ciceronians, and Mon-

[1] A. C. Clark, *Prose Rhythm in English*, p. 19. For its unity the English *cursus* therefore is more dependent upon a final 'comma' or phrase. The Bible thus combines native
and classical elements in its rhythm. On the *cursus* see R. L. Poole, *Lectures on the History of the Papal Chancery* (Cambridge, 1915), chap. iv.

[2] Stressed monosyllables do not nullify movement; they slow it down and give it
weight by clustering accents that carry a rhetorical burden. In the juxtaposition of these
monosyllables the tendency to assert their individual force is countered by the rhetorical
groupings imposed on them, and hence they are not equally strong or equally separated.
As Obadiah Walker (*Instructions for Oratory*, 1659, pp. 120–1) observes: 'Now those
words which the voice is chiefly to stay upon, and give an extraordinary *Emphasis* to,
are such, in which there lies some figure, as all *Antitheta's* and *correspondents*, and words
relating to another. . . .' Apply this rule to Browne's words in context: 'Now since these
dead bones have already out-lasted the living ones of Methuselah,' &c. But a succession
of monosyllables, if not governed by a rhetorical pattern, tends to become inert.

[3] This rhythmic run or fall at clause ends was classified in medieval times into three
types: the *planus* or even run, the *tardus* or slow run, the *velox* or quick run. For some
idea of the *cursus* it may be said that these sections of falling rhythm all had a common
base plus a different ending to mark a different rate of movement. Thus the *cursus
planus* is composed of a dactyl and a trochee; the *cursus tardus* of two dactyls; and the
cursus velox of a dactyl and two trochees, the first trochee carrying a lighter stress. If
the first type is the normal rate of the run or fall, the second is slower because it does
not change, and the third is quicker because of the double trochee. Croll and Tempest
have explored their significance for English prose rhythm.

D

taigne preferred a 'cadence that falleth shorter, cut like Iambikes'.[1]
By which Montaigne, the good Anti-Ciceronian, indicated his preference for more abrupt, less ceremonious, endings. Only the more
formal prose cultivated such means to rhythm. Besides these metrical sections, other means to rhythm were the numerical balance of
clauses, or a structural balance which developed temporal or stress
correspondences. Perhaps this caveat against prose scansion should
be entered. Rhythm in prose, quite beyond verse, moves by phrases
rather than by feet. Since accentual patterns in prose do not cut
across words, except in the *cursus*, they are bound by phrases; and
these are measured by principles of rhythmic equivalence or regular
gradation. In rhythmic form recurrence in prose, apart from numerical balance, does not operate metrically, but either in loosely
measured stresses—such types of rhythm as rising, falling, waved—
or in measured change of movement. In the *cursus* or native
cadence, however, this rhythm falls into metre, appropriately, falling
metre.

The loose mode of structure, to return to our main subject, may
also be exploited in different ways. Its members, as Croll has observed, stand farther apart than do those of the periodic mode. In
Weil's schematism the loose structure falls into the analytic order
of words or the descending construction secured by backward dependence; the periodic falls into the synthetic order or ascending
construction secured by forward dependence.[2] Although the loose
mode, having no compacted character, has no necessary order—the
end, or inclusive predication, may even come before the beginning,
or included predications—it may imitate a natural order by following
the order of thought.[3] This was the ideal of the fluent, or loose and

---

[1] *Essayes*, 'Of Bookes'. Cf. Quintilian (IX. iv. 76) on the admission of verse into the
beginnings and endings of periods: 'Iambic verses are less observable, because that
kind of verse is nearer akin to prose. Such verses, accordingly, often escape us unawares;
Brutus, through his very anxiety for elegance in composition, makes them very frequently; Asinius Pollio not seldom; and even Cicero himself at times. . . .' Blair considers English cadence: 'In general it seems to hold, that a musical close, in our language,
requires either the last syllable, or the last but one, to be a long syllable. Words which
consist only of short syllables, as, *contrary*, *particular*, *retrospect*, seldom conclude a
sentence harmoniously, unless a run of long syllables, before, has rendered them agreeable to the ear' (lect. XIII).

[2] Cf. Henri Weil, *Essay on the Order of Words in the Ancient Languages.*

[3] Quintilian (IX. iv. 23 ff.) discusses natural versus artificial order. Medieval rhetoric
(cf. C. S. Baldwin, *Medieval Rhetoric*, chap. viii) distinguished three orders of composition: natural (dictated by nature), casual (fortuitous), and apt (artistic). Thus

free, mode of Seneca. In fact, the loose mode achieves its character by avoiding periodology or premeditated effects; it may accentuate its character by relaxing even the tight construction which subordinating connectives usually impose. At bottom it is joined only by conjunctions, not by rhythm and structure.

One variation of this mode is the loose period, which is really a hybrid; it combines the loose order with periodic characteristics of rhythm and parallelism.[1] Without being committed to a coincidence of grammatical and rhetorical progression, it achieves an effect of culminative force by creating mental or oral suspense, commonly supported by some formal elements. In English it is often the difference between the typical elevated sentence of Browne and that of Milton.

Another variation of this mode is the curt style. In it the members are sharply separated, and acquire their strongest emphasis. This is truly a disjointed mode; for by omitting conjunctions, or employing only weak co-ordinating ones (*and, or, nor*), its paratactic members stand still farther apart, being deprived of logical articulation. The effect of the staccato rhetoric is increased by shortening the members. Of course other ends of this style are served by brevity; for, as Demetrius says, 'there is greater force and intensity when much meaning is conveyed in a few words . . . and it is a mark of superior skill to compress much thought in a little space'.[2] This mode may, however, bind itself together by parallelism, and then it approaches the Sophistic in character. This is the Senecan variety of the 'cut' style mentioned by Cicero as an alternative to the periodic. It is the one variety of loose style that has a positive rhetoric of its own. Parallelism both supports and secures its elliptical development.

Geoffroi de Vinsauf: 'A noble gravity comes from order itself when what is joined by syntax is separated by order' (or hyperbaton).

[1] Cf. Lamb, *Clio Enthroned*, p. 107: 'Periodic structures may be found where the grammar is, strictly speaking, complete before the period ends or is even half accomplished. In such cases, the sense of expectation which leads us to call the system a period is raised in us either by clearly hinting to our *minds* that something is about to be explained or justified or controverted, or by so arranging the phrases that they suggest to our *ears*, already accustomed to the cadence of a grammatical climax, that the regular sort and amount of sound is to follow. But in whatever degree of distinctness the mental or oral suspense is contrived, it will be convenient to speak of the grammatical as the true or original period, and of the looser systems, derivative therefrom, as *periodic* structures or forms.'

[2] *On Style*, 7-9.

The Attic as a variety of resolved style approaches the curt in its cultivation of brevity.[1] If compared with the Senecan variety, it appears brief and plain rather than brief and pointed, avoiding artful devices, but is not therefore a different character of style. Cicero's account of the Atticists is instructive, even for the Second Sophistic. In the *Orator* (28–32) he tells us that the better kind of Atticist imitated Lysias; the poorer kind imitated Thucydides, writing in 'choppy, disconnected phrases'. We may add that this inferior Atticism, which was modified by Sophistic style, passed from Thucydides to Sallust and thence to Seneca and Tacitus. But even the better Attic style sought at times, as in Lysias, some relief from its plainness, some element of rhythm, in the use of parallelism.[2] Lamb has noted two styles in Lysias, as in Thucydides, an antithetic style and 'a more rapid and looser' style.[3] There is a similar combination in Seneca and the Anti-Ciceronians. It is clear that Cicero connected the staccato style with one kind of Roman Atticist. An extreme variety of this style is found in the condensed, asymmetrical, even dislocated, style of Tacitus, the disciple of Sallust.

On the relation of form to thought, we may conclude that structurally the circular is built upon suspension, the antithetic upon correspondence, and the loose upon linear addition. Rhythm of course varies in its relation to these different kinds of form. In this classification, which is exhaustive enough from the structural point of view, the Ciceronian style belongs to the circular type; the Euphuistic to the antithetic; and the Senecan to the loose. The Senecan in its curt form tends to parataxis without conjunctions; in its fluent form it uses more hypotaxis, but loosens the tighter construction which that implies. Both the Senecan and the Attic belong to the disjointed or loose mode, but are differentiated by the extent to which they employ elements of the antithetic mode. In movement the Ciceronian style capitalizes on continuity, the Senecan on discontinuity. It should be understood, following Demetrius, that as the periodic framework, in which the members are compacted and

[1] 'Resolved' here indicates a loosening beyond that of *oratio soluta* or prose as language released from the stricter bonds of verse rhythm.

[2] Quintilian (XII. x. 21) describes the better Attic style when he objects to those who limit Attic style to 'such as are simple, clear, expressive, restricting themselves, as it were, to a certain frugality in the use of their eloquence, and always keeping their hand within their cloak'.

[3] See *Lysias*, Loeb ed., p. xvii.

brought to a focus, is braced or relaxed, periods with a tension appropriate to different uses are produced. Parallelism or symmetry is of three kinds—rhythmic, assonant, structural; and when employed in the circular period, structural symmetry becomes an element in the pattern rather than the pattern itself. This is the crux of the Isocratic quarrel.

III

These styles provide necessary rhetorical forms for the course of this study. For present illustration, though only of well-knit structures, let us begin with an example from the moderated Euphuism of Lyly's plays:

Beleeue mee Eumenides, Desire dyes in the same moment that Beautie sickens, and Beauty fadeth in the same instant that it flourisheth. When aduersities flowe, then loue ebbes: but friendship standeth stifflie in stormes. Time draweth wrinckles in a fayre face, but addeth fresh colours to a fast friende, which neither heate, nor cold, nor miserie, nor place, nor destiny, can alter or diminish.[1]

The general character of this style is established by correspondent co-ordination; but in the second sentence one side of the antithesis develops its inner antithesis by simple subordination, and in the last sentence the symmetry is broken by attaching an extra limb at the end, which softens and rounds out the rhythm.[2] Up to this point the rhythmic balance has been rather insistent; now it is broken by a member that collects the trials to which one side of the antithesis is superior.

But let us observe Euphuistic symmetry as it is employed in a circular period by William Warner:

But hope ouercomming dispaire, for that in the one is possibilitie, in the other no remedie, knowing that as the Gods haue power by iustice to punish, so they haue will by mercie to pardon, and considering that Fortune is painted with two faces, frowning with the one, and smiling with the other, that winter doth bite but sommer burnish, we haue made necessitie a vertue, continuance a custome, and patience our protector.[3]

---

[1] *Endimion*, III. iv. 130; Feuillerat, *John Lyly*, pp. 443-4. This illustrates what Feuillerat calls alliteration employed for its jingle alone, but the schematic variety is not absent.

[2] Of course no style is confined to one form of sentence or period, or everywhere reveals its distinctive manner; but every style fashions its salient character out of some fundamental form, by which or in terms of which it may be described.

[3] *Pan his Syrinx* (1584), chap. ii; Feuillerat, *John Lyly*, p. 482, n. 2. As Bain (*Rhetoric*,

Here the larger suspension of the period, using the resources of subordination, sets up an expectation that is finally gratified; but meanwhile the parallel structure has set up and gratified minor expectations.[1] It is significant that the progressive movement subsumes the repetitive movements. 'Le rythme de la phrase', as Feuillerat remarks, 'est cependant moins net que chez Lyly, arrondi qu'il est par la recherche d'un certain moelleux dans l'harmonie de la période.'[2] In fact, Warner does to Lyly what Cicero describes Isocrates as doing to Gorgias.

It must be said, however, that both rhythm and parallelism of phrase in Warner, though subordinated to the period, are more obvious than in a sober Ciceronian period. How different, for example, is Hooker!

Though for no other cause, yet for this; that posterity may know we have not loosely through silence permitted things to pass away as in a dream, there shall be for men's information extant thus much concerning the present state of the Church of God established amongst us, and their careful endeavour which would have upheld the same.[3]

Warner's symmetry has little place in the undulate suspension which accumulates the minor suspensions of this period, hanging them upon such particles as *though*, *yet*, *that*, *there*, and most nearly matching the parts connected by *and*. Seldom has more touching dignity been given to the theme 'though only to let posterity know that we tried' than is achieved by this periodic structure.

To account for this sentence in modern theory we can turn to the doctrine of prose style set forth by Stevenson:

... the true business of the literary artist is to plait or weave his meaning, involving it around itself; so that each sentence, by successive phrases, shall first come into a kind of knot, and then, after a moment of suspended

1890, p. 134) remarks, 'the participial construction is one of the hinges of the period'. Note the various kinds of like-sounds in this period.

[1] Note the particles or words in this structure that are points of suspension: besides the participles and relatives, the turns on *as—so, one—other*.

[2] *John Lyly*, p. 482, n. 2.

[3] Opening sentence of preface to *Laws of Ecclesiastical Polity*. Hooker's 'this : that' construction is an interesting means of obtaining suspension in English; and above rhythmic reasons the period illustrates the statement that 'a noble gravity comes from order itself when what is joined by syntax is separated by order'. In the 'strung-together' style, as Lamb observes, the clauses are merely tacked on; there is no working up to a turning point, no 'intention of building for continuous effect', no attempt to create a single but complicated impression during one stretch of attention.

meaning, solve and clear itself. In every properly constructed sentence there should be observed this knot or hitch; so that (however delicately) we are led to foresee, to expect, and then to welcome the successive phrases. The pleasure may be heightened by an element of surprise, as, very grossly, in the common figure of the antithesis, or, with much greater subtlety, where an antithesis is first suggested and then deftly evaded. Each phrase, besides, is to be comely in itself; and between the implication and the evolution of the sentence there should be a satisfying equipoise of sound; for nothing more often disappoints the ear than a sentence solemnly and sonorously prepared, and hastily and weakly finished. Nor should the balance be too striking and exact, for the one rule is to be infinitely various . . . and yet still to give the effect of an ingenious neatness.[1]

Presently, as we should expect, Cicero is brought forward as an expert in weaving this web or pattern.[2] The immediate interest of the Stevenson passage, however, lies in its attention to the psychology of the period, which is a psychology of expectation. By arousing expectations of balance, structural or rhythmical, of contrast or parallel, of resolution, contradiction, or simple completion, the period keeps the mind in suspense until those expectations have been satisfied, and concludes when they are.[3] In the loose style this structure is spasmodic, and the sentence is always beginning anew, however connected syntactically; the expectations, in Stevenson's terms, are not plaited or woven together, but raised and requited intermittently.

But Croll, among others, has pointed out the difficulty of imitating the Ciceronian period in English. The Ciceronian manner of writing in comprehensive periods requires an implicated style, as Stevenson suggests; but such a style is dependent upon a complex suspended syntax which imposes the greatest difficulties upon an uninflected language. The eighteenth-century rhetoricians never forgot the earlier attempts to rear such structures by means of unnatural inversions and transpositions. The Senecan manner of writing, however,

[1] Robert Louis Stevenson, *On Some Technical Elements in Style*. The significance of Aristotle's beginning and end in the period is elucidated by Stevenson's implication and evolution.

[2] Cicero had himself remarked (*Orator*, 222): 'The full period, then consists of four members each about equal to a hexameter verse. In each of these members appear the binding knots (*nodi continuationis*) which we unite in a period.' The *nodi continuationis* are the suspending particles.

[3] Of course the sense of rhythm is involved. The cumulative period depends, psychologically, upon suspense of mind; structurally, upon suspension of syntax: rythmically upon equipoise of members.

avoids the cumulative period and employs a resolved style that is more natural to modern analytical languages. Such periods as may be produced in this manner are of a very different character; loosely connected, chiefly by means of mental or oral hints, they neither seek nor achieve the involution exemplified by Cicero.

The struggle between the Ciceronian and the Senecan manner in the seventeenth century seems to have issued in the structural classification employed by Blair in the eighteenth century; the object of imitation for each is there preserved in sharp outline. Here is the new division of style—and yet hardly new, for it had been anticipated by Cicero, and was basic to his quarrel with Brutus about Attic style:

With regard to the length and construction of sentences, the French critics make a very just distinction of style, into *style périodique* and *style coupé*. The *style périodique* is where the sentences are composed of several members linked together, and hanging upon one another; so that the sense of the whole is not brought out till the close. This is the most pompous, musical, and oratorical manner of composing. . . . Cicero abounds with sentences constructed after this manner.

The *style coupé* is where the sense is formed into short independent propositions, each complete within itself. . . . This is very much the French method of writing; and always suits gay and easy subjects. The *style périodique* gives an air of gravity and dignity to composition. The *style coupé* is more lively and striking. According to the nature of the composition, therefore, and the general character it ought to bear, the one or other may be predominant.[1]

The *style périodique* is illustrated from Temple, and the *style coupé* from Pope. Advice to intermix the two styles is supported by a quotation from Cicero declaring that style should not always be periodic, but often cut up into members. Elsewhere Seneca joins Pope in his devotion to antithesis and epigram;[2] he derived this corrupt manner of expression from the cult of point and antithesis in the schools of declamation.[3]

[1] Blair, *Lectures on Rhetoric*, lect. XI. Cf. Abbé Batteux, 'Of Oratorical Elocution', *A Course of the Belles Lettres* (London, 1761), iv. 168 ff.

[2] Lect. XVII. Uniformity is the charge against Seneca as well as Isocrates, for 'the frequent use of antithesis, especially where the opposition in the words is nice and quaint, is apt to render style disagreeable. . . . A maxim or moral saying, properly enough receives this form. . . . But where a string of such sentences succeed each other; where this becomes an author's favourite and prevailing manner of expressing himself, his style is faulty; and it is upon this account Seneca has been often, and justly, censured.' Cf. lectures XVIII and XXXVII.

[3] Lect. XXVI.

Thus we may discern the background for this division of styles, and it is no longer the division of Aristotle and Demetrius, but a division established by the divergence of Cicero and Seneca—not a division between a formal and a formless style, but between a close-knit and a sharply separated style. Important doctrine for these two styles had been provided by Quintilian: for the curt style in his chapter on *sententiae*, where he criticizes the discontinuous style which their cultivation produces;[1] for the periodic in his chapter on composition, where he distinguishes the periodic from the loose, but does not deprive the latter of all rhythm and cohesion.[2] This division sets the periodic and non-periodic forms in their sharpest opposition, emphasizing the distinctive rhetoric of the curt style; it summarizes the subject of this study. In our period the Ciceronian and the Senecan again define the extremes of style, between which other styles must in turn be defined. For this time they are the elevated and plain styles in relation to which other styles find their character.

The more indefinite middle style, which is sometimes made the achievement of the seventeenth century, could move toward either extreme without producing an obvious impropriety, and hence embraced more various occasions. Ben Jonson, in his description of the three styles out of Vives, suggests an inclination toward the middle style:

Some men are tall, and bigge, so some Language is high and great. Then the words are chosen, their sound ample, the composition full, the

---

[1] *Institutes*, VIII. v. 27: 'This pursuit of fine thoughts, also, makes style too curt; for every thought makes as it were a stand, as being complete in itself; and after it there must necessarily be the commencement of another sentence. Hence language is rendered too unconnected, and being composed, not of members, but of bits (*frustis*), has no proper construction; for these round and polished portions refuse to unite with each other.'

[2] Ibid. IX. iv. While order, junction, and rhythm must be considered in all composition, they apply especially to oratorical style. The proper order, both of words and phrases or members, is secured by the principle of gradation or climax; it is best to close the sense with the verb, 'for the force of language lies in verbs'. For connexion certain collocations of words must be avoided; but more important still is rhythm (45), 'for all *structure*, and *measure*, and *connexion of words*, is concerned either with numbers, (by numbers I wish *rhythm* to be understood,) or with *metres*, that is, certain dimensions of syllables'. Though both rhythm and metre are composed of feet, they are not the same; 'for *rhythm*, that is *numbers*, consists of lengths of times; *metre*, besides length, requires the times to be in a certain order; and thus the one seems to refer to quantity, the other to quality'. Rhythm requires certain proportions in the feet, but metre refuses to admit substitutions, which violate order.

absolution plenteous, and powr'd out, all grave, sinnewye and strong. Some are little, and Dwarfes; so of speech it is humble, and low, the words poore and flat: the members and *Periods*, thinne and weake, without knitting, or number. The middle are of a just stature. There the language is plaine, and pleasing: even without stopping, round without swelling; all well-torn'd, compos'd, elegant, and accurate.[1]

In Vives the middle style is described out of Seneca on Fabianus; and this is reflected in Jonson, especially in the opposition of the low and middle styles, which gives the low style the defects of the plain that were often attributed to the Stoics. In Jonson's description the middle style—like that of Fabianus—lacks the potential excess of the high style and the actual defect of the low; it is both plain and pleasing, neither flat nor tumid.

Of these extremes in style, to differentiate a little more sharply, there are several varieties of immediate concern to this study. Fundamentally, for style in prose, arrangement as well as diction must have both clearness and distinction. Custom is the standard for both elements. The customary gives clearness; the unusual, distinction. Artificial arrangement, as opposed to the natural, introduces rhetoric or considerations beyond those of clearness. While clarity, so far as arrangement is concerned, depends on customary order, the effect of naturalness in conversational prose is often produced by violations of customary order that seem still more natural because even less formal than the customary.

The artificial order employs principles of rhythm or amplification and figures of repetition or symmetry; its purpose is to make the language of prose both pleasing and effective. Here the art of prose is to render it periodic or figurative, to develop its chief formal aspects or possibilities. The figures of repetition, which provide sound patterns, may develop the sounds into forms more like rhyme than rhythm, but disposed with some proportion. Prose is made periodic or becomes *prose mesurée* by the principles of periodic

---

[1] *Discoveries*, ed. Castelain (Paris, 1906), p. 104. Jonson then turns to what Aristotle calls frigidity in the medium: 'The vitious Language is vast, and gaping, swelling and irregular; when it contends to be high, full of Rocke, Mountaine, and pointednesse: As it affects to be low, it is abject, and creeps, full of bogs and holes. And according to their Subject, these stiles vary, and lose their names.' By propriety to subject Jonson points the excesses and defects that result from improprieties in the medium. Again the emphasis on extremes favours the mean. The association of 'pointedness' with the tumid may be noted.

rhythm.[1] The natural or customary order and the artificial order are exploited in the extreme characters of style, the plain and the grand.

If discourse begins with the psychological order, in which thought is allowed to run on just as it passes through the mind, its first form is colloquial discourse, which has an emergent order, the loosest of construction, the least committed syntax. Hence a conversational style may be said to sacrifice the psychological order as little as possible to logical and grammatical requirements, not at all to rhetorical order. At the other extreme is the periodic style, which satisfies all of these demands and cultivates the most ordered movement or rhythm. Schematic prose also satisfies these demands, but cultivates phrasal pattern rather than rhythm.

Pointed prose, on the other hand, cultivates verbal ingenuity for the sake of point rather than pattern. Here we may distinguish two varieties: antithetic point and schematic point. Antithetic point, of course, cultivates antithesis with the balance required to make it sharp. Schematic point adds to antithesis the devices of word-play to show it off. However, since this prose may be pointed by brevity alone, we may also divide it on that basis, distinguishing a plain and a pointed brevity. Thus plain brevity may use antithesis, but not all the means to show it off, for the plain variety cultivates brevity without verbal wit. Pointed brevity cultivates verbal wit in excess of antithesis, and thus makes use of all the means to point. The former may be called plain because antithesis in itself is not a departure from the plain style; but the latter, with its added rhetoric, introduces such a departure. Here pointed is opposed to plain, but allied to schematic point as the plain is allied to antithetic point. It is merely a question of whether brevity or antithesis be taken as basic.

The varieties of pointed style are related to the curt style and ultimately to the loose, from which they rise toward various degrees and kinds of form. If colloquial prose may be called free or formless, then pointed prose is an advance toward form, schematic prose a

[1] Periods comprehend, like a circle, all the thoughts that are members of the body of a sentence, expressed in equal intervals, and supported by connecting particles. The art is to equal or proportion the expressions of each member of a sentence so that the ear can perceive with ease the distinction or union of its members. The period gives the sense of a whole composed of equal or balanced parts; the ear is gratified by the proportioned members, but is not satisfied so long as the voice (or sense) remains suspended.

greater advance, and periodic prose the ultimate achievement. It is, of course, less the degree than the kind of form that counts. In logical form pointed prose is closer to the colloquial, and schematic prose to the periodic. For our study, to apply these distinctions, plain brevity or plain antithesis may be called the Stoic (or Attic) style, and pointed brevity or schematic antithesis may be called the Senecan style; the second simply adds word-play to word-contrast, though the plain may be written without formal antithesis. This is to separate for analysis what was not distinguished in fact, for Seneca was a Stoic and Lipsius a Neo-Stoic, and in general to write with brevity was to write with point. But these varieties of curt style will enable us to discriminate types of concise style that may be opposed to the Ciceronian.

3. *Schematic Prose and Pointed Prose*

When Bacon described the first vanity in learning as Ciceronian imitation, 'for men began to hunt more after words than matter', he reversed the judgement of the Ciceronian Ascham: 'Ye know not what hurt ye do to learning, that care not for words but for matter.'[1] Bacon's objection to 'that delicate and polished kind of learning' includes no real allusion to Euphuists:

Then grew the flowing and watery vein of Osorius the Portugal bishop, to be in price. Then did Sturmius spend such infinite and curious pains upon Cicero the Orator, and Hermogenes the Rhetorician, besides his own books of Periods and Imitation, and the like. Then did Car of Cambridge, and Ascham with their lectures and writings almost deify Cicero and Demosthenes, and allure all young men that were studious, unto that delicate and polished kind of learning.[2]

But Croll has described the Anti-Ciceronian movement as one 'which arose at the end of the sixteenth century in reaction from the various forms of ornate, formal style in the preceding age, such as Euphuism itself, Ciceronian imitation, and so on'.[3] Thus we are

[1] If this opposition is not fair to Ascham, it serves to point an issue—which is Ciceronian, though Bacon makes it broadly oratorical. Ascham's concern for purity of style appears in a letter to Sturm in 1550: 'I do not know what all the Oxford men are about, but some months ago, at Court, I fell in with a man from that University who, by his preference of Lucian, Plutarch, Herodian, Seneca, Aulus Gellius, and Apuleius, seemed to bring both of those tongues down to their latest and most debased age' (*Works*, ed. Giles, I. i, pp. lxii and 190). Ascham would have been horrified at Ben Jonson's taste in Latin.

[2] *Advancement of Learning*, Everyman ed., p. 24. I omit the 'scoffing Echo', now quoted at the head of Chap. I. It was also omitted in the *De Augmentis Scientiarum*, which was addressed to a European audience. Finally, Bacon adds the hurt to learning—and it must have cost him a pang: 'Then grew the learning of the schoolmen to be utterly dispised as barbarous.' On Ciceronian imitation see Ascham's letter to Sturm in Morhof's *Polyhistor* (I, 2, 13, 17). Morhof (I, 2, 10, 19) observes that Sturm condemned the pointed style.

[3] See 'The Sources of Euphuistic Rhetoric', *Euphues*, ed. Croll and Clemons (London, 1916), p. xvii. He has also observed (p. xxv) that in contrast to the normal periodicity of Cicero 'in Lyly there is no periodicity, and the members are usually short and sharp'. When he admits (p. xlvii) that classical imitation could become Euphuistic, as in Ascham or Sturm, he makes Bacon's inclusion of their names a possible confusion of Euphuism and Ciceronianism, though he would otherwise discriminate them.

confronted by the problem, as yet undetermined, of the exact relation of Senecan style to Euphuism; its opposition to Ciceronianism, especially in periodicity, is clear enough.

If Ciceronianism and Euphuism could meet in Ascham, could Euphuism and Senecanism meet in Andrewes? or have anything in common with Bacon? In short, was the older use of *Euphuism* to cover early seventeenth-century style without any foundation?[1] The failure of Bacon to include Euphuism specifically—and it was not easily overlooked—either in his attack on Ciceronianism or in his attack on Senecanism poses the problem of relationship in its most concrete form. If we are to reach any solution, we shall have to observe Euphuism, as schematic prose, in some historical perspective.

I

Croll's definition of Euphuism has received further confirmation by the printing of John Hoskins's *Directions for Speech and Style.* 'The essential feature of the style', remarks Croll, 'is a vocal, or oral, pattern, and all its other characteristics, such as the use of antithesis, and the constant use of simile, are only means by which the Euphuist effects his various devices of sound-design.'[2] The schemes or figures commonly involved in the schematic structure of Euphuism as defined by Croll are isocolon, parison, and paromoion—like-length, like-form, and like-sounds in successive members.[3] The 'euphuing of similes' and the play of antitheses provide materials for the construction of this oral pattern, the former also supplying a kind of learned ornament. The figures 'which are most characteristic of Euphuism' for Croll are '*parison* with the various kinds of *paromoion*'.[4] But there is reason to say that the essential feature of the style, in its own time, was paromoion, which vocalized the pattern supplied by parison. While we know that the 'euphuing

[1] Speaking of antithesis Croll (ibid.) concludes that 'it is a pity to use as the test of style a figure which may lead to the identification—and, alas, still does lead to it—of styles so different in kind as that of Browne and that of Lyly'.

[2] Ibid., p. xvi.

[3] Croll (p. xvi) defines 'parison, or equality of sound' in terms of formal likeness, 'so that word corresponds to word'. Hobbes called such correspondence *antitheta*; the *Ad Herennium* called it *compar*. Parison as equality of sound is hard to distinguish from isocolon; as correspondence of structure, from clausal antithesis, which has been called a species of parison.

[4] Ibid., p. xxxiii.

of similes' provoked a good deal of contemporary criticism, can we say as much for the schematic structure? Historically, it is easier to trace the course of Euphuism by the latter than by the former, for it was the wider phenomenon.[1] Of course the style is only Euphuistic in the strict sense when the two are found together.

Wilson's *Arte of Rhetorique*—which, with his logic, Harvey called 'the daily bread of our common pleaders and discoursers'—supplies instruction for both ingredients some time before Lyly put them together in the vernacular.[2] Wilson also teaches another lesson which Lyly knew thoroughly: that is amplification by 'heaps' of 'sentences' and proverbs.[3] In fact Wilson has not a little to say about the sentences, similitudes, and examples which Quintilian (V. xi) had treated as kinds of proof, and which Erasmus had gathered in his various collections. For Wilson also they were materials for amplification and means to persuasion.[4] What is important, however, is that Wilson not only offers the first English criticism of the schematic prose that was to become Euphuistic, but also indicates its provenance.

This interesting matter is found in his treatment of 'like ending, and like falling', or *similiter desinens, similiter cadens*:

Then the sentences are said to end like, when those wordes doe ende in like sillables which do lacke cases. Thou liues wickedly, thou speakest naughtly. . . . Sentences also are said to fall like when diuers wordes in one sentence ende in like cases, and that in rime. By greate trauaile is gotten much auaile, by earnest affection men learne discretion.

These two kindes of Exornation are then most delitefull, when contrary things are repeated to gether: when that once againe is vttered which before was spoken: when sentences are turned and letters are altered. Of the first this may be an example: where learning is loued, there labour is esteemed: but when slothe is thought solace, there rudenesse taketh place.

---

[1] On the diffusion of Euphuistic elements, more or less formally organized, see Ludwig Wendelstein, *Beitrag zur Vorgeschichte des Euphuismus* (Halle A.S., 1902).

[2] Cf. *Rhetorique*, ed. G. H. Mair (Oxford, 1909), pp. 188 ff. and 202 ff. See Harvey, *Marginalia*, ed. Moore Smith, p. 122. The first and shorter edition of Wilson's *Rhetorique* appeared in 1553; the longer in 1560.

[3] Ibid., pp. 116 ff.

[4] Cf. M. P. Tilley, *Elizabethan Proverb Lore* (New York, 1926), chap. III. As Quintilian prepares to consider amplification (VIII. iv) he remarks that it is the chief power of the orator and its sources are found both in matter and in words. This idea provided the basis for Erasmus's *De Copia Verborum ac Rerum* (cf. T. W. Baldwin, *Small Latine and Lesse Greeke*, ii. 182); and the *Copia* as well as his *Ecclesiastae* in turn influenced Wilson (cf. R. H. Wagner, *Quarterly Journal of Speech*, xv. 531 ff.).

A king is honoured that is a King in deede: will you drinke or you go, or will you go or you drinke. There is a difference betwixt an Hors-milne, and a Milne horse. He is a meeter man to driue the cart, then to serue the court: through labor cometh honor, through idle liuing foloweth hanging.[1]

Of paromoion, similarity of sound between words or syllables, Wilson illustrates not only like-endings (homoioteleuton), but like-beginnings (alliteration); not only the repetition of sounds, but also the repetition of words with inversion (antimetabole), and the likeness of words, though 'letters are altered', with difference of meaning (paronomasia).[2] The last example combines transverse alliteration and like-endings. Another complex variety of repetition is polyptoton or the repetition of the same stem with a different inflexion—often associated with paronomasia. When Wilson states that 'like-endings' are most delightful when accompanied by antithesis, repetition, antimetabole, or paronomasia, and includes parison in his examples, he suggests the auxiliary character of other figures in the schematic use of paromoion.[3]

From description Wilson passes to the criticism of schematic prose:

Diuers in this our time delite much in this kinde of writing, which beeing measurably vsed, deliteth much the hearers, otherwise it offendeth, and wearieth mens eares with sacietie. S. *Augustine* had a goodly gift in this behalfe, and yet some thinkes he forgot measure, and vsed ouermuch this kind of figure. Notwithstanding, the people were such where he liued, that they tooke much delite in rimed sentences, and in Orations made ballade wise. Yea, thei were so nice and so waiward to please, that except

---

[1] *Rhetorique*, pp. 202–3. Under 'Faultes in composition' Wilson objects (pp. 167–8) to 'ouermuch repetition' of one letter or word and to ending 'sentences all alike': 'I heard a preacher deliting much in this kind of composition, who vsed so often to ende his sentences with wordes like vnto that which went before, that in my iudgement there was not a dosen sentences in his whole sermon, but they ended all in Rime for the most parte.' His contemporary, Thomas Becon, could illustrate this text in a style which combined native and learned elements. See G. P. Krapp, *English Literary Prose*, pp. 337–9.

[2] Croll remarks (p. xxxviii) that the phrase 'letters are altered' refers to syllabic antithesis and that Child discusses the figure under *annomination* (or paronomasia). Wilson has dealt with 'Altering part of a worde' (*Paulum immutatum verbum*) on p. 201, but that is an orthographical scheme not illustrated here. This probably refers to the difference which makes a chime more striking—the sound-play most exploited in paronomasia or agnomination.

[3] He defines parison (p. 204) as 'Like among themselues' (*Similia inter se*). These figures are based, as Wilson says, on Cicero's treatment, *De Oratore*, III.

the Preacher from time to time could rime out his sermon, they would not long abide the hearing. *Tacitus* also sheweth that in his time, the Iudges and Seriantes at the lawe, were driuen to vse this kinde of phrase, both in their writing, and also in their speaking. Yea, great Lordes would thinke themselues contemned, if learned men (when they speake before them) sought not to speake in this sort. So that for the flowing stile and full sentence, crept in Minstrels elocution, talking matters altogether in rime, and for waightinesse and grauitie of wordes, succeding nothing els but wantonnesse of inuention. *Tullie* was forsaken, with *Liuie*, *Caesar*, and other: *Apuleius*, *Ausonius*, with such Minstrell makers were altogether followed.... I speake thus much of these ii. figures, not that I thinke folie to vse them (for they are pleasant and praise worthy) but my talke is to this ende, that they should neither onely nor chiefly be vsed, as I know some in this our time, do ouermuch vse them in their writings.[1]

If this minstrel's elocution is to be avoided, paromoion should 'neither only nor chiefly be used'; the sound effects are emphasized rather than created by the other figures of symmetry. Schematic prose is thus criticized for excessive use of the most vocal of the oral devices that were to form the patterned prose of Euphuism; and two possible models are suggested, patristic in St. Augustine, and Silver Age in writers who forsook Cicero.

While the patristic is the more immediate source for this rhetoric the connexion with the Silver Age must not be ignored—as Croll ignores it by not quoting the reference to Tacitus. But Croll argues that medieval rhetorical tradition was the immediate and efficient cause of schematic prose in the vernacular.[2] And the schematic style is properly described as a descent to the Renaissance, whereas the purely classical or Ciceronian style was a recovery, and a revolt against the medieval tradition. Wilson indicates that paromoion was its most characteristic feature in the vernacular, and later criticism seems to bear him out. Isocolon or 'equal members' he associates with Isocrates: 'Isocrates passeth in this behalf, who is thought to write altogether in number, keeping just proportion in framing of his sentence.'[3] Croll tends to ignore isocolon as a 'scheme' to which

---

[1] Ibid., p. 203. The reference to Tacitus is no doubt to *Dialogus* 26 (*Dialogue on Oratory*). Though moved to speak, Wilson does not condemn, but urges discretion.

[2] Croll (*Euphues*, pp. xli–xliii) declares that this passage argues the medieval associations of such rhetoric for Wilson. The medieval background is amplified by M. B. Ogle, 'Some Aspects of Medieval Latin Style', *Speculum*, i (1926), 170–89.

[3] *Rhetorique*, p. 204. In defining 'egall members' Wilson modifies a strictness for which Isocrates was sometimes blamed, 'not that the Sillables of necessitie should bee

objection was made by critics of schematic prose, especially in Isocrates.[1] Essentially Wilson's account of schematic prose remains unchanged by explanations given almost a half-century later.

Thomas Fuller bears witness to the use of a lower order of 'like sounds' in the preaching of 1558.[2] His example is interesting because it illustrates the random use of like-sounds without regard to supporting parallelism. In schematic prose parison and isocolon provide the metre for the rhyme, and so pattern the identities; but the metre without the rhyme is less obvious than the rhyme without the metre, though more essential to oratorical prose. Fuller's citation from the preface to Sir John Cheke's book, *The Hurt of Sedition, or The true Subject to the Rebel*, as reprinted at Oxford in 1641, provides a useful contrast to the examples given by Wilson:

Surely, preaching now ran very low, if it be true what I read, that Mr. Tavernour, of Water Eaton in Oxfordshire, high sheriff of the county, came, in pure charity, not ostentation, and gave the scholars a sermon in St. Mary's, with his gold chain about his neck and his sword by his side, beginning with these words: 'Arriving at the mount of St. Mary's in the stony stage where I now stand, I have brought you some fine biscuits, baked in the oven of charity, and carefully conserved for the chickens of the church, the sparrows of the Spirit, and the sweet swallows of salvation.'[3]

It is impossible to distinguish such unschematized jingles from what Sir Philip Sidney later criticizes as the 'coursing of a Letter' or the 'method of a Dictionary'. But such like-sounds are discussed in the

of iust number, but that the eare might iudge them to be so egall, that there may appeare small difference'. For English style this definition should be borne in mind.

[1] See his *Euphues*, p. xl, where he quotes a passage from Salutati condemning 'that artificial rhythm' (isocolon), and then cites this passage from Wilson as evidence of humanistic approval of the 'rhythmical' character of Isocrates. The former passage, which is derived from Norden, is quoted especially for similar endings: 'it does not trifle with that artificial rhythm; there is none of that equality of syllables which is not wont to happen without exact counting; there are none of those clausules which end or fall alike. For this is reprehended by our Cicero as nothing else than a puerile thing which is far from decent in serious matters or when used by men of gravity. Blessed be God that we now see one sermon in which this ferment has not been at work, which can be read without a tune or an effeminate prattle of consonance (*sine concentu et effeminata consonantiae cantilena*).' This illuminates Wilson's concern for schematic prose.

[2] Cf. Croll's discussion of Latimer, *Euphues*, p. xlix.

[3] *Church History of Britain*, ed. J. Nichols (London, 1868), ii. 522–3. Dr. Gerard Langbaine wrote the preface to this edition of Cheke's work. Richard Taverner was made High Sheriff of Oxford County in 1569; cf. Wood's account, *Athenae Oxonienses* (London, 1721), col. 183. Wood says, 'Which way of preaching was then mostly in fashion, and commended by the Generality of Scholars'.

rhetorics under paronomasia and agnomination, which include both the alliteration and the echo of words and syllables found in Euphuism.[1]

Another contrast may be had from Cheke's book itself (1549)—an example of marked parallelism emphasized by verbal echoes:

Ye rise for religion: what religion taught you that? If ye were offered persecution for religion, ye ought to flee; so Christ teacheth you, and yet you intend to fight. If ye would stand in the truth, ye ought to suffer like martyrs; and ye would slay like tyrants. Thus for religion ye keep no religion; and neither will follow the counsel of Christ, nor the constancy of martyrs.[2]

Although Cheke was capable of phrasing such as 'to disobey your betters, and to obey your tanners; to change your obedience from a King to a Ket', this passage affords a more normal sample of the skill attested by Wilson, better 'in our English speech to judge of the Phrases and properties of words and to divide sentences than any else that I have known'.[3] If the principle of balance is sufficiently obvious in his division of sentences, the use of sound to emphasize that balance is more adroit than in Taverner. Yet it might be concluded that Cheke tends to narrow Croll's distinction between the humanistic and the medieval use of the schemes. If Croll could not deny that 'Ascham liked the frailer beauties of oratory too',[4] it can scarcely be said that Cheke was averse to them. Neither Cheke nor Ascham is free from sound-play of the classical variety, and Ascham sometimes approaches Taverner in the native variety.

---

[1] Cf. Hoskins, *Directions*, ed. Hudson, pp. 15–16. But note '*Parimion*, or the Figure of like letter' in Puttenham's *Arte of English Poesie*, ed. Willcock and Walker, p. 174. Wilson, as already observed, includes alliteration among the 'faultes in composition': 'Some vse ouermuch repetition of some one letter.' And likewise 'some end their sentences all alike, making their talke rather to appeare rimed Meeter, then to seeme plaine speeche'.

[2] Cf. John Strype, *Life of Sir John Cheke* (Oxford, 1821), p. 41.

[3] 'Epistle', *Three Orations of Demosthenes*, 1570. In his preface Wilson condemns the Ciceronian, who only follows Cicero and 'his large veyne and vehement manner', but exalts Demosthenes for his 'playne familiar maner of writing and speakyng'. This was the attitude of the 'Grecian'. Richard Carew, in *The Excellency of the English Tongue*, remarks: 'Adde hereunto, that what soeuer grace any other Languadge carryeth, in Verse or Prose, in Tropes or Metaphors, in Ecchoes or Agnominations, they maye all be liuely and exactly represented in ours. Will you have *Platos* vayne? reede Sir *Thomas Smith*: The *Ionick*? Sir *Tho. Moor*: *Ciceros*? *Aschame*: *Varro*? *Chaucer*: *Demosthenes*? Sir *Iohn Cheeke* (who in his treatise to the Rebells hath comprised all the figures of Rhetorick).' See G. G. Smith, *Elizabethan Critical Essays*, ii. 293.

[4] *Euphues*, p. xlvii.

If this style was Ciceronian, it did not lack criticism. It is no doubt appropriate, as Bacon could witness, that an Aristotelian in logic should be an Anti-Ciceronian in style, even to the extent of anticipating Bacon's chief apprehension. In 1573 Ralph Lever published *The Arte of Reason, rightly termed Witcraft*, in which he put Aristotle above all profane writers, not only in matter but also in words:

for that his manner and trade of writing, is more perfect and playner, then any others is that I haue red. As for Ciceronians & sugertongued fellowes, which labour more for finenes of speach, then for knowledge of good matter, they oft speake much to small purpose and shaking foorth a number of choise words, and picked sentences, they hinder good learning, wyth their fond chatte.[1]

Thus Ascham already had his answer before Bacon made the same indictment of Ciceronianism in his own terms. The antagonism between Ciceronian and schoolman is represented by the works of Nizolius, for he not only espoused Cicero but attacked the schoolmen for their barbarous language and logical terminology.

Sidney's *Apology for Poetry* sets forth the ways in which eloquence was disguised in his time: now by 'far-fetched words', now by 'coursing of a Letter', and now by 'figures and flowers, extremely winter-starved'.[2] Sidney adds this illustrative comment with regard to alliteration: 'But I would this fault were only peculiar to Versifiers, and had not as large possession among Prose-printers, and (which is to be meruailed) among many Schollers, and (which is to be pitied) among some Preachers.' In such schematic effects the scholars are worse than the preachers; and, alluding to the famous *Thesaurus Ciceronianus*, he objects that the imitators of Cicero and Demosthenes keep 'Nizolian Paper-books of their figures and phrases'.[3] Besides the play on sounds, the similitudes of the Euphuists come in for castigation as 'a surfeit to the ears': 'for the force of a similitude not being to prove anything to a contrary Disputer but only

---

[1] Cf. T. W. Baldwin, *Small Latine and Lesse Greeke*, ii. 52–3.

[2] *Elizabethan Critical Essays*, ed. G. G. Smith (Oxford, 1904), i. 202. Alliteration, a simpler kind of paromoion and more practicable for English, was rooted in the English tradition of verse and largely replaced like-endings—especially as inflections were lost—in the schematic prose of the vernacular.

[3] See Nashe's account of the university of Wittenberg in *The Unfortunate Traveller* (1594), where he comments on Ciceronianism in the universities; *Works*, ed. McKerrow, ii. 246, 251.

to explain to a willing hearer, when that is done, the rest is a most tedious prattling'.[1] Persuasive value, however, was not always denied to the similitude, even for the Euphuist, and so Quintilian could have reminded him.

But the criticism which carries us back to Wilson comes just before the passage on similitudes in Ponsonby's text:

How well store of *Similiter Cadenses* doth sounde with the grauitie of the Pulpit, I woulde but inuoke Demosthenes soule to tell: who with a rare daintinesse vseth them. . . . So these men bringing in such a kinde of eloquence, well may they obtaine an opinion of a seeming finenesse, but perswade few, which should be the ende of their finenesse.[2]

Discretion—unfortunately, not absence—marked the use of such figures in the classics, but excess in the Euphuists, such as Gosson.[3] Yet Sidney was not very sympathetic to Ciceronianism.[4] In 1574 Languet had warned him: 'But beware of falling into the heresy of those who think that the height of excellence consists in the imitation of Cicero, and pass their lives in labouring at it.'[5] Sidney himself writes to his brother Robert in 1580: 'So you can speak and

[1] In oratory the similitude has for Sidney the function of making something understood or evident; it does not convince. As Bacon would say, in difficult or remote subjects one 'must pray in aid of similitudes' before one can argue.

[2] *Elizabethan Critical Essays*, ed. Smith, i. 401; *Works*, ed. Feuillerat, iii. 42. Lyly disclaimed 'fineness' in his preface to *Euphues*. Cf. Thomas Campion, *Observations in the Art of English Poesie* (1602): 'By Rime is vnderstoode that which ends in the like sound, so that verses in such maner composed yeeld but a continual repetition of that Rhetoricall figure which we tearme *similiter desinentia*, and that, being but *figura verbi*, ought (as *Tully* and all other Rhetoritians have iudicially obseru'd) sparingly to be vs'd, least it should offend the eare with tedious affectation. Such was that absurd following of the letter amongst our English so much of late affected, but now hist out of Paules Churchyard: which foolish figuratiue repetition crept also into the Latine toong' (Smith, ii. 330).

[3] Gosson is less precise than Lyly in his balance and less adroit in euphonic devices, seldom rising above alliterative effects. His epigraph for *The Schoole of Abuse*, which derives from Seneca (*Ep.* 116. 8), betrays the 'minstrels elocution' described by Wilson, and is therefore appropriate in style as well as thought: 'Vitia nostra, quia amamus, defendimus; et malumus excusare, quam excutere.' Pettie, likewise, in his *Petite Pallace* falls short of Lyly in relating euphonic devices to balance; his verbal echoes are less functional, or less ordered by symmetrical patterns. Consequently, Pettie is less neat, but perhaps also less monotonous; his schematic effects have more of Taverner and less of Cheke.

[4] It should be observed that after his 'digression' to oratory in the *Apology*, Sidney apologizes: 'me thinkes I deserve to be pounded for straying from Poetrie to Oratorie.' His excuse (Smith, i. 203) is that both have 'an affinity in this wordish consideration', that is, *elocutio*; and in this Aristotle would have agreed with him, and likewise Puttenham.

[5] *Correspondence of Sir Philip Sidney and Hubert Languet*, ed. Steuart A. Pears (London, 1845), p. 20.

write Latin, not barbarously, I never require great study in Ciceronianism, the chief abuse of Oxford, "qui dum verba sectantur, res
ipsas negligunt".[1] On matter as opposed to words Sidney agrees
with Bacon rather than with Ascham; on imitation he would have
had little sympathy with Ascham's complaint that 'Quintilian writeth
of it, shortly and coldly for the matter, yet hotly and spitefully
enough against the Imitation of Tully'.[2] But Sidney would no doubt
approve of the way in which parallelism is employed in Ascham's
sentence, certainly as opposed to Wilson's examples. For classical
use of the figures of parallelism was not 'barbarous'; it differed from
patristic use in nothing so much as in the requirement that they
were 'neither only nor chiefly to be used'.

William Webbe, on the other hand, is not displeased with English
prose, which seems to him more advanced than English verse in
1586. Nor is he moved to this view solely by his concern for classical
imitation in verse—that counterpart to Ciceronianism. It is rather
because English prose has a better tradition than English verse, and
not because it is more classical; 'our ancient Chroniclers' hardly
come into that category, yet for Webbe they belong among those
who have 'polished and bettered' our speech.

Among whom I thinke there is none that will gainsay but Master Iohn
Lilly hath deserued moste high commendations, as he which hath stept
one steppe further therein then any either before or since he first began the
wyttie discourse of his *Euphues*. Whose workes, surely in respecte of his
singuler eloquence and braue composition of apt words and sentences,
let the learned examine and make tryall thereof thorough all the partes of
Rethoricke, in fitte phrases, in pithy sentences, in gallant tropes, in flowing
speeche, in plain sense, and surely, in my iudgment, I thinke he wyll
yeelde him that verdict which Quintilian giueth of bothe the best Orators
Demosthenes and *Tully*, that from the one nothing may be taken away, to
the other nothing may be added.[3]

The pithy and flowing Lyly has outdone rather than imitated both
the idols of that time. Yet for all of Webbe's extravagance he recognized what Sidney failed to recognize, but Shakespeare put to ad-

---

[1] *Correspondence of Sir Philip Sidney and Hubert Languet*, ed. Steuart A. Pears
(London, 1845), p. 201; *Works*, ed. Feuillerat, iii. 132. On Sidney's own style see G. P.
Krapp, *English Literary Prose*, pp. 374–82.

[2] Smith, i. 13. This view of Quintilian is worth remarking because of the way in
which he is often alined in the criticism of Ciceronian style.

[3] Ibid. 255–6. Notice that Webbe itemizes 'pithy sentences' but not the schemes.

vantage, that in the rhetorical virtue of 'plain sense' Lyly had advanced one step farther. To conventional opinion this is still the most anomalous of all the formal virtues that may be found in Lyly.

But the other side of Euphuism was becoming apparent to William Warner in 1589 when he remarked in his preface to *Albion's England*: 'Only this error may be thought hatching in our English, that to run on the letter we often run from the matter: and being over prodigal in similes we become less profitable in sentences and more prolixious to sense.' And this is to warn against coursing the letter in its own language,[1] but it is also, and more properly, to write schematic prose.

Puttenham, whose *Arte* (1589) reveals a long period of composition, makes no allusion to Lyly, unless it is concealed in this comment on antithesis:

Isocrates the Greek Oratour was a litle too full of this figure, & so was the Spaniard that wrote the life of *Marcus Aurelius*, & many of our moderne writers in vulgar, vse it in excesse & incurre the vice of fond affectation: otherwise the figure is very cōmendable.[2]

For Puttenham the cult of antithesis not only marks Isocrates and Guevara but stamps the modern writers of the vernacular. Though 'modern' for Puttenham might extend back to Ascham, it probably falls closer to the date of publication or at least to the new courtly poets, Dyer, Sidney, and Greville. But this possible range of time makes Puttenham's remarks on prose even more interesting.

Like Wilson, he observes rhyme to be characteristic of late Latin and medieval prose:

Yea their Oratours proses nor the Doctors Sermons were acceptable to Princes nor yet to the common people vnlesse it went in manner of tunable rime or metricall sentences, as appeares by many of the auncient writers, about that time and since.[3]

In dealing with homoioteleuton, which approaches 'our vulgar

---

[1] Hoskins (*Directions*, p. 16) criticized Warner for his indulgence in paronomasia.

[2] *The Arte of English Poesie*, ed. Willcock and Walker (Cambridge, 1936), p. 211. Puttenham does allude to Sidney's *Arcadia*. J. E. Hollingsworth (*Antithesis in the Attic Orators*, pp. 54–5) concludes that 'formal antithesis reached the climax of its development in Isocrates' and that in him 'not only the modified verse rhythm, but also parison, paronomasia, and homoeoteleuton are the almost constant accompaniments of antithesis'.

[3] *Arte*, p. 11. The time is that of the barbaric invasions. He may have borrowed this observation from Wilson.

rhyme', he warns that 'your clauses in prose should neither finish with the same nor with the like terminants', such as 'nature . . . displeasure'.[1] Incidentally, he restricts paromoion to alliteration, the 'Figure of like letter';[2] but paronomasia is a resemblance of words, covering both 'love . . . live' and 'excuse . . . accuse'.[3] The 'metrical' aspect of prose involves parison, the 'Figure of even', or 'clauses of equal quantity'. But in prose 'there should not be used at once of such even clauses past three or four at the most'.[4] On the whole, Puttenham's doctrine for the figures of schematic prose is more restrictive than that of Wilson; generally he thinks of them as more appropriate to verse. But the elements of late Latin and medieval rhymed prose still required from him some statement of their relation to prose, though his concern was poetry. His motivation, since he was neither pedant nor antiquarian, must have been the 'modern writers in vulgar', though ornament concerned both poetry and prose.

But Puttenham cannot be left at that, for the doctrine involved in his attitude toward prose is of great importance to this study. It is the doctrine of ornament found in his third book, of which the first chapter presents poetical ornament as the figures or colours of poetry. The second chapter, however, deals with the necessity of such figures to eloquence, for they distinguish writing and speeches from 'our ordinary talk'. And it is no accident that he now remarks: 'I have come to the Lord Keeper Sir Nicholas Bacon, and found him sitting in his gallery alone with the works of Quintilian before him; indeed he was a most eloquent man, and of rare learning and wisdom, as ever I knew England to breed'. In the third chapter Puttenham returns to poetical ornament, but more truly to doctrine found in Quintilian.[5]

---

[1] *Arte*, pp. 173-4. Homoioteleuton is achieved 'by using like cases, tenses, and other points of consonance'.

[2] Ibid., p. 174. His definition of *hirmos* (p. 176), '*Irmus*, or the Long loose', is coloured by the character of the period, for it is a 'maner of speach drawen out at length and going all after one tenure and with an imperfit sence till you come to the last word or verse which concludes the whole premisses with a perfit sence & full periode'.

[3] Ibid., p. 203. As a resemblance of words rather than of letters it would cover examples in Wilson that appear at first glance to be cases of alliteration.

[4] Ibid., p. 214. For Puttenham 'cadence' means rhyme (p. 79) and prose is not 'numerous' (p. 8).

[5] For example, *Institutes*, VIII. iii. 61 ff., to which other passages will be added later. But Puttenham makes his own use of Quintilian's distinction between language that impresses only the ears and that which impresses the mind by its graphic quality.

Here he observes that figures have a double efficacy, 'some serving to give gloss only to a language, some to give it efficacy by sense', and some both. 'That first quality the Greeks called *Enargia* . . . because it giveth a glorious lustre and light. This latter they called *Energia* . . . because it wrought with a strong and virtuous operation.'[1] If 'figure breedeth them both', the former is a kind of vividness, and the latter a kind of force, producing 'a stir to the mind'.[2] Scaliger had used the term 'efficacy' (*Efficacia*), which encouraged confusion but pointed to the end of both terms.[3] And rhetorical efficacy is not perspicuity, the requirement of simple communication. These observations serve to introduce Puttenham's discussion of language, style or 'a certain contrived form and quality' of words, and figures. Since the doctrine of energia or enargia connects with Aristotle, the Stoics, Seneca, and Quintilian, it will emerge again in this study, particularly in connexion with Bacon. Meanwhile, it is sufficient to observe that Puttenham stated their difference as a principle for the division of figures, and that he made some of the figures of schematic prose figures of both sound and sense.

Gabriel Harvey's *Advertisement for Pap-hatchet*, written in 1589 but published as part of *Pierces Supererogation* in 1593, plunges us into the rowdier aspects of the stylistic controversy at the close of the sixteenth century.[4] When this former Ciceronian objects to

---

[1] Thus Chapman's dedication of *Ovid's Banquet of Sense* finds the former something more than perspicuity: 'That *Enargia*, or clearness of representation, required in absolute poems, is not the perspicuous delivery of a low invention; but high and hearty invention expressed in most significant and unaffected phrase.' But Sidney's *Apology* (Smith, ii. 201) attributes the failure of love poetry to a failure in the poet to 'feele those passions, which easily (as I think) may be bewrayed by that same forciblenes, or *Energia* (as the Greekes cal it), of the writer'. This distinction, which Puttenham adapts, was frequently obscured. Under 'Illustration' Hoskins (*Directions*, p. 42) connects Sidney with the process which leads to *enargia*, and also deals (pp. 47–8) with the 'animation' which gives *energia*, and invites the Pathetic fallacy.

[2] This summary neglects the 'tunable' quality associated with *enargia*—awkwardly combined with 'outward shew'—though it is important to his division of figures. Founded upon *enargia*, or *energia*, or their combination, these divisions are the 'auricular', 'sensable', and 'sententious' respectively. Of the figures noticed here, homoioteleuton and paromoion are 'auricular', while paronomasia, antithesis, and parison are 'sententious'. Metaphor, for example, is a 'sensable' figure. The 'auricular' is the ornamental class. For Quintilian *energia* is only another way of achieving vividness; it derives from action and lends force to expression.

[3] Cf. Smith, ii. 419, note to p. 148.

[4] Harvey, in his earlier years, lectured on rhetoric at Cambridge, and changed from a strict Ciceronian to the school of Ramus and Erasmus. Yet in style Harvey (*Foure Letters*) admired the 'smooth and clenly and neate and fine elegancy' of Ascham's time.

Euphuism, we are less concerned with the familiar remark about similitudes than with the rather Anti-Ciceronian sentence in which it is couched:

I cannot stand nosing of Candlesticks, or euphuing of Similes, *alla Sauoica*: it might happly be done with a trice; but euery man hath not the guift of *Albertus Magnus*; rare birdes are dainty; and they are queint creatures that are priuiledged to create new creatures.[1]

Having mentioned Lyly's 'pretty sentences', Harvey probably has in mind the sententious aspect of Euphuism when he observes: 'I long sithence found by experience how Dranting of Verses, and Euphuing of sentences, did edify.'[2] But the 'Euphuing of sentences', thus connected with the new versifying, may be pointed at their schematic effect. He declares that 'the finest wits prefer the loosest period in M. Ascham or Sir Philip Sidney before the tricksiest page in Euphues or Pap-hatchet'.[3] It is to be inferred that the 'loosest period' is the lesser evil, not the desideratum, and that *Pap-hatchet* was Euphuistic to him. If he had called Ascham 'noster Isocrates',[4] he had also condemned his excessive use of like-endings.

In *Pierces Supererogation* familiar aspects of the 'tricksiest page' appear in Harvey's question about Nashe: 'Dare the pertest or deftest of you hunt the letter, or hawk a metaphor, with such a Tite-tute-tate?' And he further observes that 'although he be a harsh Orator with his tongue (even the filed Suada of Isocrates wanted the voice of a Siren or the sound of an Echo), yet would he seem as fine a Secretary with his pen as ever was Bembus in Latin'.[5] Nashe's pen at least had an echo for the letter, but

as for a fine or neat period, in the dainty and pithy Veyne of Isocrates or Xenephon, marry, that were a periwig of a Siren, or a wing of the very bird of Arabia, an inestimable relique. . . . It is for Cheeke or Ascham to

---

[1] Smith, ii. 269. Note the short, sharply separated clauses.

[2] Ibid. 272. Since Hoskins connected Lyly with schematic effects rather than with 'sentences', Harvey may intend the former by 'Euphuing', which produced 'prettie sentences'. Otherwise the sententious element in Euphuism connected it with other contemporary styles.

[3] Ibid. 274.

[4] *Marginalia*, ed. Moore Smith, p. 127.

[5] Smith, ii. 276. Harvey soon adds that he has 'seldome read a more garish and pibald stile . . . in any sluttish Pamfletter that denounceth not defiance against the rules of Oratory and the directions of the English Secretary'—which was an epistolary rhetoric published by Angel Day in 1586. Harvey was not peculiar in regarding such a rhetoric as applicable even to pamphleteering.

stand leuelling of Colons, or squaring of Periods, by measure and number: his penne is like a spigot, and the Wine presse a dullard to his Ink-presse.[1]

This 'siren' may remind us that Harvey began by observing that 'surely Euphues was someway a pretty fellow' before he became Pap-hatchet.[2] The loosest period of Ascham evidently falls somewhere between the precision of Isocrates and the spontaneity of Nashe. While the 'leveling of Colons' suggests balance, the 'squaring of Periods by measure and number' points to isocolon, which produced an artificial rhythm and was connected with Isocrates. But 'measure' probably involves cadence. Clearly, if Harvey was no friend of paromoion, he was no enemy of Isocratic structure.

Yet this meant for him a neat and pithy style, which he found in Ascham, Cheke, Isocrates, and Apollonius Tyanaeus or Philostratus. It was an Attic style which even Philostratus could represent. Harvey summed it up when he said, 'A pithy or filed sentence is to be embraced, whosoever is the Author'.[3] The 'Atticism of Isocrates' that he found in Ascham was not his Euphuistic paromoion but rather the neat balance of his periods. Harvey admired neatness of expression; and his taste for the brief member, frequently ordered into short and neat sentences, seems to grow until he is almost what Milton calls a tormentor of semicolons. Nashe, in fact, once called him 'the short shredder out of sandy sentences without lime'.[4] Nor is he quite averse, apart from the iteration of contempt, to the emphasis of parallel sounds; but his neatness never goes so far as Lyly's obvious and persistent balance. The *copia* of invective tends to obscure a basic neatness in Harvey, loosening structure as it releases words.

II

In 1591 Henry Savile completed the story of schematic prose that Wilson had outlined; he also voiced an objection to Senecan

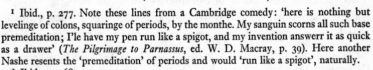

---

[1] Ibid., p. 277. Note these lines from a Cambridge comedy: 'here is nothing but levelinge of colons, squaring of periods, by the monthe. My sanguin scorns all such base premeditation; I'le have my pen run like a spigot, and my invention answerr it as quick as a drawer' (*The Pilgrimage to Parnassus*, ed. W. D. Macray, p. 39). Here another Nashe resents the 'premeditation' of periods and would 'run like a spigot', naturally.

[2] Ibid., p. 268.

[3] Cf. *Marginalia*, p. 152; Smith, ii. 282. Nashe combined Erasmus's *De Copia* and Quintilian on Seneca in his advice (Smith, i. 335) 'to learne to speake many things in few'; neither to say everything, nor to imitate only the appearance of brevity. But he also reflected Seneca (*Ep.* 75).

[4] McKerrow's *Nashe*, i. 317. This is the old gibe at Seneca.

style which Bacon was to modernize in 1623. In brief, he connects the pointed Senecan style with the Gorgian, and in effect discovers a common ancestor for schematic prose and pointed prose. Savile, who achieved distinction in history and classics, and to whose competence Sidney entrusted his brother Robert, appends this final note to the *Life of Agricola* in his translation of Tacitus:

A good Man you would easily think him, &c. (*Bonum virum facile crederes, magnum libenter.*) *Et te Corneli Tacite bonum historicum facile credimus, bonum oratorem crederemus libenter*, were it not for this and some other sayings of the like making. *Fuit illi viro*, saith Tacitus judging of Seneca, as we may of him, *ingenium amaenum, & temporis illius auribus accommodatum.* How that Age was eared, long or round, I cannot define: but sure I am it yielded a kind of Sophisticate Eloquence, and Rhyming Harmony of Words, whereunder was small matter in Sence, when there seemed to be most in appearance. This kind of Rhetorick was induced into *Graecia* by the teachers of Oratory in School, whose Judgments, Use and Experience had not refined: first by *Gorgias*, as it may well appear by that little of his which is left; then by *Isocrates* and his Disciples, and being refused by that judicious Nation found favour in some corners of *Asia*, till at length the use of Eloquence decaying in Commonwealth, and the study thereof remaining in Schools, that bastard Rhetorick returned again, yielding us in stead of the soundly contrived sentences of *Demosthenes*, *Aeschines*, *Hyperides*, the paintings of *Aristides*, *Philostratus*, *Dio Chrysostomus*, and others, though not without opposition of many, as *Dionysius*, *Lucian* and such like. The Ancient *Romans* sucking the best from the *Greeks*, when they were at their best failed not much that way, unless peradventure we may reckon *Hortensius* as one of the number: for so *Tully* in *Bruto* seems to describe him. But of the latter, whom have we almost not infected with that Heresie of Style begun by *Seneca*, *Quintilian*, the *Plinies*, and *Tacitus*, continued in their Successors the Panegyrists, and lastly, conveyed to Christian Religion by *Cyprian*, *Ambrose*, *Augustine*, *Bernard*, &c.[1]

This sketch of the course of Sophistic rhetoric gives perspective to the exponents mentioned by Wilson, and almost coincides with the sketch offered by Croll.[2] But observe that Savile is prompted by the

[1] Of these Church Fathers only Augustine has any claim to be Ciceronian in Erasmus's *Ciceronianus*, but is culpable in Wilson. On Savile's offenders see Eduard Norden's *Die Antike Kunstprosa*, which provides the exposition for his sketch. Cf. also Karl Polheim, *Die Lateinische Reimprosa* (Berlin, 1925); C. S. Baldwin, *Medieval Rhetoric and Poetic* (New York, 1928), chaps. i, ii, iii, ix. Note Savile's contrast between the 'ancient Romans' and the 'latter Romans'.

[2] Cf. *Euphues*, p. xxxiv: 'The source of the medieval use of the schemes is in the

'jingling epigrams' of Tacitus to write this sketch of a bastard rhetoric which Isocrates helped to promote.

One stage in this descent becomes of peculiar interest when we recall the Atticist movement which Brutus represented. Aristeides, Philostratus, Dio Chrysostom, all represent the Atticizing tendency of the New or Second Sophistic.[1] The style of Apollonius Tyanaeus, known only through the *Life* by Philostratus, is described as Attic by Gabriel Harvey:

His oun sentences, were short, & adamantine: vttered like oracles, with A diuine grace: & he spake with A certain dignity, like A prince, or Commander: tanquam autoritatem habens. His wordes, were not pompously affected; but Attique, emphatical, & pithy: euer to ye purpose, & effectual.[2]

Such a style was also called Laconic. A similar description of the style of Tacitus appears in Savile's translation, though it is not by him.

'For a taste of this affectation in Tacitus' Savile gives divers examples of the like sounds that Wilson had described and criticized for English readers. Their jingling character may be observed in a few samples, not unlike the patristic styles here mentioned:

1. *Hist.* pag. 15. Rara temporum foelicitate ubi sentire quae velis, & quae sentias dicere licet. . . . 2. *Hist.* pag. 88. Et Vitellius credidit de perfidia & fidem absolvit. 3. *Hist.* pag. 143. Arserat & ante Capitolium sed fraude privata: nunc palam obsessum, palam incensum, with many more of the same mark.[3]

Gorgianic school of ancient Greece, of which Isocrates was the inheritor and the chief ornament. From him the Gorgianic rhetoric passed on to the sophists' schools of the decadent period, and was thence diffused to Imperial Rome and the founders of Christian eloquence, Ambrose, Augustine, Cyprian; and it was by way of the latter, the church-fathers, especially perhaps through the mediation of Gregory the Great, that it proceeded to its great medieval destinies.' Patristic example was no doubt the chief cause for the cult of the Gorgian schemes.

[1] Cf. introduction to Philostratus, *Lives of the Sophists*, ed. W. C. Wright (Loeb Classical Library), pp. xix, xx, xxiv.

[2] *Marginalia*, ed. Moore Smith, pp. 152–3. Wright (p. xx) describes the style of Philostratus thus: 'His sentences are short and co-ordinated, his allusions are often so brief that he is obscure, and in general he displays the carelessness of the gentlemanly sophist, condescending to write narrative. . . . He was a devoted admirer of Gorgias. . . . In fact he regarded the Atticizing sophists of his day as the true descendants of the Platonic sophists, and scolds Plutarch for having attacked, in a work that has perished, the stylistic mannerisms of Gorgias.'

[3] Tacitus was fond of such word-play as paronomasia and polyptoton, and of alliteration, often to set off antithesis. Croll quotes this bit of Tacitean imitation from the Anti-Ciceronian Muretus: 'Iidem si turpitudinem suam palam esse videant, jam

For Savile the 'Heresy of Style begun by Seneca' had its origin in Gorgias and was distinguished by its 'Sophisticate Eloquence and Rhyming Harmony of Words'. Wilson had alluded to this heresy through Tacitus. It will be interesting to see whether this 'rhyming harmony' finds any place in the analysis of Seneca's style given in modern criticism.

Under the heading 'Ornaments of Style', W. C. Summers discusses the characteristic rhetorical figures of Seneca.[1] These he particularizes as word-play, alliteration, word-contrast, commutatio or antimetabole, and asyndeton. Summers declares that 'in the figures *Word-play* and *Word-contrast* we have two of the most prominent characteristics of the Senecan style'.[2] But these terms, which involve parallelism, cover the widest sense of his synonyms paronomasia and antithesis, for *word-play* includes not only paronomasia but also homoioteleuton and polyptoton. Alliteration is closely related to word-play. He considers antimetabole as a combination of word-play and word-contrast, and deals with asyndeton in connexion with Seneca's cult of brevity. Apart from the regular Latin use of adversative asyndeton, 'again and again', he declares, 'where Cicero or Livy would have had one sentence, with a main clause and a subordinate clause, Seneca gives us two parallel clauses'.[3] In Seneca's use of like-sounds parallelism is a regular accompaniment, although it would be more accurate to say that the paromoion is used to emphasize the parison or antithesis. Paronomasia and balanced antithesis make a kindred appeal in that they contrast likeness of form with difference of meaning. In general, modern criticism may be said to support rather than to refute Savile's charge of rhyming harmony in the style of Seneca.

Since Croll ignores this aspect of Silver Latin style in connexion with Euphuism, let us set two passages from Seneca beside two of his examples from medieval Latin. His example of the use of paro-

---

famae securi, quae palam dici vident, palam quoque faciunt, et famam dum bonam desperant, malam negligunt' (*PMLA*, xxxix. 299 n.). Compare these sentences from Seneca (*Ep.* iii. 3–5): 'Nam quidam fallere docuerunt, dum timent falli, et illi ius peccandi suspicando fecerunt. . . . Sed alterum honestius dixerim vitium, alterum tutius; sic utrosque reprehendas, et eos qui semper inquieti sunt, et eos qui semper quiescunt.'

[1] See introduction, *Select Letters of Seneca* (London, 1910), pp. lxxxi–xc (1929 ed.).
[2] Ibid., p. lxxxii.
[3] Ibid., p. xcii.

moion in a life of St. Guthlac, written by a certain Felix in the time of Bede, runs as follows:

Sic (sc. *Deus*) . . . Guthlacum de tumide aestuantis saeculi gurgite, de obliqu*is* mortal*is* saecul*i* anfract*ibus*, de atr*is* vergent*is* mund*i* fauc*ibus* ad perpetuam beatitudin*is* militia*m*, ad rect*i* itiner*is* calle*m*, ad ver*i* lumin*is* prospect*um* perduxit.[1]

One would not expect Seneca to produce anything comparable while writing on the proper style for a philosopher, but the result is surprising:

Multum praeterea habet inanitatis et vani, plus sonat quam valet. Lenienda sunt, quae me exterrent, conpescenda, quae inritant, discutienda, quae fallunt, inhibenda luxuria, corripienda avaritia; quid horum raptim potest fieri?[2]

Croll calls attention to 'the exact correspondence of final sounds, word by word, in successive members, and also the "syllabic antithesis" (intentional variation of vowels) in *-am* . . . *-em* . . . *-um*, near the end'.[3] Note that Seneca has similar and more insistent repetitions of sound, although his paromoion is much less complicated in pattern and more accidental in appearance.

For a later example Croll cites a passage from Jocelyn of Brakelond:

Vidit et alium cum eo militem, Gilbertum de Cerivilla, non solum quantum ad apparentiam gradu dignitatis inferiorem, sed et ab humeris supra statura minorem. . . . Et jam totus desper*ans*, et rationem in impetum convert*ens*, impugn*antis*, non defend*entis*, assumpsit officium. Qui dum fortiter percussit, fortius percussus est, et dum viriliter impugnabat, virilius impugnabatur. Quid multa? Victus occubuit.[4]

---

[1] *Euphues*, p. xxxi. The italics marking the like-sounds are Croll's.

[2] *Ep.* 40. 5. Cf. *Ep.* 115. 1–2 for a more normal passage on a kindred subject: 'Quaere, quid scribas, non quemadmodum; et hoc ipsum, non ut scribas, sed ut sentias, ut illa, quae senseris, magis adplices tibi et velut signes. Cuiuscumque orationem videris sollicitam et politam, scito animum quoque non minus esse pusillis occupatum. Magnus ille remissius loquitur et securius; quaecumque dicit, plus habent fiduciae quam curae.'

[3] For the connexion of Euphuism with medieval Latin prose Croll (p. xxxviii) finds convincing evidence in 'syllabic antithesis', 'for this characteristic feature of it could not have come from the classics, from the church-fathers, from Apuleius, or from the Greek romances'. But when Quintilian (ix. iii. 78) defines 'like falling' or *similiter cadens*, he says that although it implies a certain similarity, it 'does not necessarily involve identity in termination, since it means no more than similarity of case, even though the words may be differently declined'; and in its use 'any arrangement of correspondences is permissible'. To distinguish this from the 'intentional variation of vowels' is not easy; and approximate rhymes or paronomasia, as Wilson shows, will produce a similar effect in English.

[4] *Euphues*, p. xxxii.

This example from the chronicles illustrates not only like-endings but also polyptoton, which Quintilian treated with paronomasia, and which appeared in Savile's examples from Tacitus. It is hardly fair to match this passage with Seneca's declaration that he would have his epistolary style spontaneous and easy, but it is illuminating:

Quis enim accurate loquitur, nisi qui vult putide loqui? Qualis sermo meus esset, si una sederemus aut ambularemus, inlaboratus et facilis, tales esse epistulas meas volo, quae nihil habent accersitum nec fictum. . . . Etiam si disputarem, nec supploderem pedem nec manum iactarem nec attollerem vocem, sed ista oratoribus reliquissem, contentus sensus meos ad te pertulisse, quos nec exornassem nec abiecissem. Hoc unum plane tibi adprobare vellem: omnia me illa sentire, quae dicerem, nec tantum sentire, sed amare.[1]

In this comparison Seneca proves more surprising, for he is less put to shame; but Jocelyn is simpler than Felix.

If the most prevalent figures of medieval Latin 'are those which are most characteristic of Euphuism, namely, *parison* with the various kinds of *paromoion*',[2] it is not astonishing that Silver Latin should be associated with the rhyming harmony of schematic prose by both Wilson and Savile. Although Seneca does not weave the complicated sound-patterns of Bede, or even of lesser lights, he certainly is not a novice in vocal devices; but his usual method of employing like sounds is in simple parallels or balances.[3]

Since Wilson, Savile, and Hoskins all name St. Augustine in connexion with schematic prose, two specimens of his style may be cited for comparison:

Talia dicite ardenter, dicite leniter. Dicite ardentes fervore charitatis, non tumore dissensionis. . . . Exhibeamus Domino pietatem, fratribus charitatem.

Nec nobis dicetur ut gemamus; quia jam laudamus. Sicut enim caro

---

[1] *Ep.* 75. 1–3. Cf. Cicero's example of his own Gorgian effort—often cited in the rhetorics: 'Est enim, iudices, haec non scripta sed nata lex, quam non didicimus, accepimus, legimus, verum ex natura ipsa arripuimus, hausimus, expressimus, ad quam non docti sed facti, non instituti sed imbuti sumus.'

[2] Croll, *Euphues*, p. xxxiii.

[3] Cf. the following examples of simple schematic balance: 'Nihil adversus haec sapientia promittit, nihil proficit; sui iuris sunt, iniussa veniunt, iniussa discedunt' (*Ep.* 11. 7). 'Observa; videbis eosdem intra exiguum tempus acerrime ridere et acerrime rabere' (*Ep.* 29. 7). 'Contemplationem institutio tradit, actionem admonitio' (*Ep.* 94. 45). All my examples from Seneca come from the *Epistles*, where schematic effects are least appropriate.

mortalis convertitur in corpus angeli; sic et gemitus convertetur in laudes. Hic poenitentia, et pressura, et gemitus: ibi laudes, laetitia, et gaudium.[1]

And since St. Bernard is often cited in this connexion, we may add an example from him:

Monachus enim, qui sui negligens, alios curiose circumspicit, dum quosdam suspicit superiores, quosdam despicit inferiores: et in aliis quidem videt quod invidet, in aliis quod irridet. Inde fit ut pro mobilitate oculorum levigatus animus, nulla utique sui cura aggravatus, modo per superbiam ad alta se erigat, modo per invidiam in ima demergat: nunc per invidiam nequitur tabescit, nunc pro excellentia pueriliter hilarescit. In altero nequam, in altero vanus, in utroque superbus existit: quia et quod superari se dolet, et quod superare se gaudet, amor propriae excellentiae facit.[2]

Now this is both neat and trim in its balance and full of Savile's rhyming harmony. Perhaps even more striking than its like-endings or balances is its paronomasia—the way in which antithetical ideas come together in similar sounds.

St. Bernard's balanced paronomasia, of which this is an extreme example, is rather more typical of Lyly's Euphuism than of the more complicated schemata of the Middle Ages. For comparison with Euphuism, here is Burch's translation of the first sentence brought a little closer to the sound effects of the Latin: 'For the monk who neglects himself to become curious about other men, respects some as superior, rejects others as inferior; and beholds in those cause to desire, in these cause to deride.' But the loss in translation is manifest, and indicative of the limitations to which Euphuism was subject. It was Bernard's paronomasia, no doubt, that associated him with Seneca in Savile's mind, just as it connected Rainolds with Bernard and Augustine for Jackson.[3] Perhaps it was sufficient that all these writers indulged in chimes of one kind or another.

These examples support Croll's conclusion that the Church

---

[1] Cited in illustration of Hoskins, *Directions for Speech and Style*, ed. H. H. Hudson, pp. 87–8.

[2] *De Gradibus Humilitatis*, xi. 39; *The Steps of Humility*, ed. G. B. Burch (Cambridge, Mass., 1940), p. 198. Cf. the much simpler schematic effects in Seneca: 'Nihil tam certum est ex his, quae timentur, ut non certius sit et formidata subsidere et sperata decipere' (*Ep.* 13. 12). 'Qui mori didicit, servire dedidicit; supra omnem potentiam est, certe extra omnem' (*Ep.* 26. 10).

[3] See Chap. IV.

Fathers 'prefer the simpler of the two methods of schematic elaboration described above, namely, the use of parison and homoioteleuton in a row of phrases or clauses, while the more *characteristic* medieval method is the complication of figures within a period.'[1] He adds, however, that this difference is less marked in Cyprian than in Augustine and Ambrose. If we add that other forms of paromoion are found in the simpler method, we may conclude by allowing Seneca a modest claim to practise the lesser method. But the use of parallelism and plays on sound brings both Augustine and Seneca into association with schematic prose, and justifies Wilson and Savile in connecting that prose with patristic and Silver Latin writers. The striking similarity for both critics is the rhyming harmony of their words.

When Bacon, like Savile, finds in this style 'small matter in Sence, when there seemed to be most in appearance', he seems less concerned with the 'Rhyming Harmony of Words' than with their pointed character. In 1623 Bacon added to his criticism of the Ciceronian style this description of the Senecan style:

The labour here is altogether, *That words may be aculeate, sentences concise, and the whole contexture of the speech and discourse, rather rounding into it selfe, than spread and dilated*: So that it comes to passe by this Artifice, that every passage seemes more witty and waighty than indeed it is. Such a stile as this we finde more excessively in *Seneca*; more moderately in *Tacitus* and *Plinius Secundus*; and of late it hath bin very pleasing unto the eares of our time.[2]

The phrase about 'the ears of our time' is an obvious echo of the remark which Savile turned against Tacitus. While Bacon declares that the artifice of this mode makes everything seem 'magis ingeniosa quam revera', Savile said as much, and proceeded to associate the Senecan heresy with the Sophistic style from which the schematic prose of Euphuism descends.

The criticism of Senecan style by Savile and Bacon brings to a focus the problem of the relation of schematic prose to pointed prose. While Bacon returns to Seneca, Savile goes back to Gorgias for the origin of what seems to both primarily a Senecan style. Croll agrees with Norden that rhyme-prose is a development from

---

[1] *Euphues*, p. xxxvi.
[2] *De Augmentis Scientiarum*, translated by Gilbert Wats (Oxford, 1640), p. 29. Bacon's complete statement about Senecan style will be examined later.

Gorgias, but would add the 'medieval schematic mind' as a more decisive factor than the 'imitation of antiquity' in the formation of Euphuism.[1] Lamb, on the other hand, stresses for Renaissance prose the pointed character of the Gorgian heritage.[2] And Summers, in 'The Pointed Style in Greek and Roman Literature', summarizes the contradiction implied in these different views:

> I cannot regard Gorgias and Isocrates as fore-runners of the pointed style. It is true that this owes a great deal to the figures which they had developed, but whereas in e.g. Bion and Seneca the figures are used to give emphasis and clearness to the point which is to be made, in Isocrates they seem to be mainly musical or rhythmical devices, subservient to the run of the period, whilst in both Isocrates and Gorgias antithesis is constantly used for its own sake alone and actually obscures the thought.[3]

This conclusion suggests that the schemes may be either a means to rhythm and sound effects or a means to point. Not the presence of the same figures, but their use, is the criterion here set up to determine the relation of the pointed style to the Gorgian: Are the figures subservient to thought or to sound? Croll has made the same distinction with regard to antithesis as used by Lyly and by Bacon.[4] It is involved in the discussion of Isocrates by Erasmus. But it is a distinction that ought to recognize one limitation, which is that the excessive use of antithesis or any formal pattern is likely to incur, if not to deserve, the charge of subservience to sound.

Aside from the question of origin, Summers's account of the pointed style has much in common with the brief outline of the schematic style by Savile. Summers defines the pointed style as epigrammatic:

> a kind of writing which, without sacrificing clearness or conciseness, regularly avoids, in thought or phrase or both, all that is obvious, direct and natural, seeking to be ingenious rather than true, neat rather than beautiful, exercising the wit but not rousing the emotions or appealing to the judgment of the reader.[5]

---

[1] *Euphues*, pp. xxxvii–xxxviii. [2] *Clio Enthroned*, esp. pp. 308 ff.
[3] *Select Letters of Seneca*, 1929 ed., p. xviii. [4] *Euphues*, p. xvii.
[5] *Select Letters*, p. xv. Here its qualities are given a pejorative emphasis. Blair (lect. XVII) defines 'point' in terms of Pope's antithesis: 'What is called the point of an epigram, consists, for the most part, in some antithesis of this kind; surprising us with the smart and unexpected turn which it gives to the thought; and in the fewer words it is brought out, it is always the happier.' This gives appropriate emphasis to 'What oft was thought, but n'er so well expressed.'

He adds that 'in the Silver age what this Introduction understands by the word *point* is denoted by the word *sententia*'.[1] Observing that the pointed thought was occasional in the writers of the Golden Age, but became a habit in their successors, he compares the ways in which Cicero and Seneca express identical thoughts:

> In two short sentences Seneca gives us the half-paradoxical 'to need no pleasure is itself a pleasure,' the pointing of the antithesis 'old and young' by the use of *senex* and *iuuenis* in an oblique form, so that the words end similarly (homoioteleuton), and the rendering by a brief and alliterative clause of the thought 'Death sends its summons without recognizing such distinctions as *younger* and *older*.'[2]

'For a full list and classification of these neat "points", for which we seem to have no really comprehensive title, though one or another of the words "epigram", "conceit", "turn", and "paradox" will apply to most of them', the reader is referred to his introduction on 'The Language and Style of Seneca's Prose'. Having already enumerated the schematic figures in this section, I will summarize the other ornaments of style to which Summers finds Seneca addicted. Briefly, these appear in his wealth of illustration ('at times the illustrations are rattled off in a string which Euphues himself might envy'); in his passion for point and epigram, for metaphor (including colloquial or technical terms), for personification, for oxymoron and paradox (forms of antithesis); and in his cult of brevity and emphasis with its *sententiae* and *suspiciones*, its 'abruptae sententiae et suspiciosae'. Such was 'that Heresy of Style begun by Seneca' which Savile described as 'a kind of Sophisticate Eloquence' that gave the illusion—as Bacon put it—of being 'more witty and weighty' than indeed it was.

On the important antecedents of this style Savile and Summers are in no real disagreement. Savile sees it as a development from Gorgias and his disciples which found favour in Asia; Summers as a later development which employed Gorgian figures. But Summers

---

[1] *Select Letters*, p. xxxv. Cf. Summers, *The Silver Age of Latin Literature* (London, 1920), p. 12. Here 'point' includes 'epigram, antithesis, paradox, and allusion'. On the pointed style he remarks (p. 15): 'One can hardly conceive a more apposite adjective for it than the *argutus* with which Cicero has labelled one of the Asian styles of oratory (*Brutus*, 325), which he further describes as characterized by the predominance of thoughts neat and attractive rather than deep or dignified, obviously using his epithet in much the same sense as I use mine.' Or, we might add, Bacon his.

[2] *Select Letters*, pp. xvi–xvii.

also associates it with Asia and Hortensius, no doubt because he too gets much of his story from Cicero's *Brutus*. Summers traces the pointed tendency through Timaeus, Bion, early Asiatic oratory —'certainly pointed', the elder Cato, and Hortensius to the schools of declamation in the Empire. In Sallust, who takes Thucydides as his model, the tendency becomes a habit, and anticipates the absolute reign of Point which begins with Ovid.[1]

The declamations of the rhetorical schools, which were the agents of infection for Savile, are represented by the elder Seneca's *Oratorum et Rhetorum Sententiae, Diuisiones, Colores*. The title itself points to the cult of *sententia*, and the contents are thus described by Summers:

> Anyone who reads a page or two of the work itself will find it a collection of close-packed sentences bristling with antithesis and brilliant with such ornaments as alliteration and homoioteleuta, sentences in which every word has to be carefully weighed and a vigilant look-out kept for ingenious hints and mysterious allusions.[2]

Its style is *staccato* in character; the shortness of sentence and marked avoidance of the period seem designed to draw as frequent applause as possible. Cassius Severus, whom Tacitus regarded as the first speaker to desert the old Republican eloquence, seems to have adopted the declamatory mode, for the elder Seneca thus describes his style: 'There was not a clause in which it was safe for the hearer to let his attention go astray: everything had a purpose. The thoughts were more numerous than the words.'[3] These words, which Jonson later applied to Bacon, express the ideal which the Senecan Lipsius took for his own. The elder Seneca's book contains extracts from the declamations of Papirius Fabianus, celebrated more as the master of the younger Seneca than as an important philosopher of the time. 'The style reminds us', says Summers, 'more than does that of any other Latin prose, of the younger Seneca.'[4] In conclusion Summers and Savile are in essential agreement as to the effect of the schools of declamation upon Latin prose,

---

[1] Thucydides, whose cultivation of Gorgian antithesis is well known, has a place of honour among the Anti-Ciceronians of the Renaissance.

[2] *Select Letters*, p. xxxvi. Ten books deal with the *Controuersiae* and one with the *Suasoriae*. Note especially its kind of wit, its *suspiciones*.

[3] Ibid., p. xxxviii. At least he cultivated its pregnant brevity. Jonson knew and borrowed extensively from this work.

[4] Ibid., p. xl.

and Summers likewise is obliged to reckon with the Gorgian figures in his account of the pointed style.

Diodorus Siculus relates how Gorgias the Rhetorician amazed the Athenians 'by his extraordinary *antitheta*, and *isocola*, and *parisa*, and *homoioteleuta*, and other figures of the same kind, which at that time from the novelty of their style were deemed worthy of adoption, but are now looked upon as affected and ridiculous when used in such nauseous superabundance'.[1] Gorgias was a connoisseur in antithetic writing, although his excessive use of these figures produced both strained antitheses and jingling prose. His effect upon rhetorical theory is to be seen in the following statement: 'Antithesis is usually treated by both ancient and modern writers along with parison, paromoion, and paronomasia—the so-called Figures of Parallelism, of which antithesis is in most cases the concomitant, and is considered the chief';[2] it is to be seen in their treatment, from Aristotle down, as a part of periodology. As the elements of Gorgias's rhetoric, these figures are discussed by Cope in his work *On the Sophistical Rhetoric*,[3] where they are 'divided into three classes, which have severally for their object parallelism in sense, structure, and sound'.[4] Since these figures have been associated with Ciceronianism, Euphuism, and Senecanism, they seem to have powers that move between rhythmic balance and expressive form or mere jingle. If they appear in Ascham for the sake of balance, may they not appear in Lyly for the sake of point? At least Webbe thought *Euphues* a 'witty discourse'—not merely an exercise in *schemata verborum*; and Lyly was not without some such prepossession.

For an example of parallelism in sound, specifically paronomasia, Cope observes: 'And this from one of Bp Andrewes' Sermons is quite in the "Sicilian" manner: "If it be so expedient He come, Christ I trust is not impedient but He may come." '[5] Thus Cope,

---

[1] *Bibliotheca Historica*, xii. 53.

[2] J. E. Hollingsworth, *Antithesis in the Attic Orators from Antiphon to Isaeus* (Menasha, Wis., 1915), p. 31.

[3] *Journal of Classical and Sacred Philology*, iii (1857), 69 ff.

[4] Parallelism in sense includes only antithesis, that is, 'an opposition either of words or sense, or both, in two corresponding clauses of a sentence'. Parallelism in structure includes both parison and isocolon. Parallelism in sound includes like-beginnings, like-endings, repetitions, different inflexions of the same word, and similarity of sound with difference of meaning. [5] Ibid., p. 72.

like Lamb, finds an illustration of Gorgian rhetoric in Renaissance style. The appeal which Gorgian rhetoric seems to have had for churchmen may be explained in part by another observation from Cope: 'His measured cadences and artfully balanced clauses bear a close resemblance to the parallelisms of Hebrew poetry.'[1] In the English Bible, whose language preserved the native tradition in prose, similar length, form, and even sounds between successive members could find support. But Isaiah, for example, was not a Euphuist, though Rainolds supervised his translation for the Authorized Version, and though the schemes of symmetry may be found there, even to some 'coursing of the letter', even to a touch of transverse alliteration, 'and they shall beat their swords into plowshares, and their spears into pruninghooks'.[2] None the less Biblical style, especially in the Vulgate, permitted the exploitation, notably with Andrewes, of Biblical texts by Gorgian rhetoric.

Out of this rhetoric two possibilities emerge: either the figures of parallelism can be made subservient to antithesis of thought, as in Seneca and pointed prose; or antithesis of thought can become subservient to the figures for the elaboration of sound effects, as in Gorgias and schematic prose. There is, of course, another use of these figures as a means to rhythm in the period. But Gorgias created what is essentially the antithetic rhetoric, whether correspondence be used to emphasize the opposition of thought, or antithesis be used to elaborate the correspondence of sound. Because Gorgias created this antithetic rhetoric, at least for prose composition, he could be regarded as the forerunner both of schematic prose and of pointed prose. He might, indeed, claim to have created a hybrid form, which may be called schematic point; for his figures are divisible into schemes of rhythm and schemes of point.[3]

[1] Ibid., p. 73. In the eighteenth century Bishop Lowth had made a study of these parallelisms in the Hebrew distichs.

[2] Isaiah ii. 4. If Gorgias borrowed these devices from poetry, others could do the same; but he might claim for prose the pattern in which he combined them. Cf. J. E. Hollingsworth, *Antithesis in the Attic Orators*, appendix: 'Antithesis in the Bible and in English Literature.'

[3] In oratory the schemes are used for sound and rhythm; in the essay for point. The complete absence of symmetry is not essentially Anti-Ciceronian, but rather its use for point. Of course it is avoided by Anti-Ciceronians when following Tacitus rather than Seneca; it is more likely to be absent in the elliptical, hopping style of Lipsius than in the schematic point of Seneca. In making points Tacitus employs figures of repetition that are less dependent on balance for their effect than those of Seneca; in this he resembles the Sallust described by Seneca.

Savile traces the descent of the Gorgian figures to his time; and reminds us, like Wilson, that Gorgian rhetoric is represented by Silver Latin writers and the Church Fathers, who provided secular and religious models. As antithesis could be both a figure of words or scheme and a figure of thought, it was put to both uses in these models. As it became a figure of thought primarily, it tended to discard the superficial symmetries, such as isocolon and paromoion, keeping only enough parison to emphasize the antithesis of thought, and perhaps some alliteration to the same end. Yet the appeal of paronomasia remained; for, like antithesis, it emphasized difference of thought by similarity of form. It is through such a course that antithetic rhetoric passes when it is translated from Lyly to Bacon, when the emphasis passes from words to things; but this does not impose upon Bacon a derivation from Lyly. As a figure of wit, however, antithesis sometimes permitted itself greater licence. In preachers like Lancelot Andrewes it retains many of the original symmetries of sound, by that benefit of clergy of which Dryden spoke and by virtue of patristic imitation. But all of these writers represent variations that derive from the antithetical period which was created by Gorgias and is best described by Demetrius. It should be recalled that the criticism of both Wilson and Savile is directed against the 'Rhyming Harmony of Words' or the superficial symmetries, which are the *differentia* of schematic prose.

4. *Aculeate Style and the Cult of Form*

To allege that Senecan style was a reaction from Euphuism is to depend upon evidence which is ultimately ambiguous. It would be no more difficult to argue that Senecan style was a development from Euphuism. By the turn of the century there was a rather lively contest of styles among Elizabethan writers. As examples of polished style, observes Harvey in rebuke to Nashe, 'few go beyond Cartwright, and the chiefest of his Confuters, furnished writers: and how few may wage comparison with Reinolds, Stubbes, Mulcaster, Norton, Lambert, and the Lord Henry Howarde? whose several writings the silver file of the workman recommendeth to the plausible entertainment of the daintiest Censure.'[1] An interesting addition to this list of elegant writers is Robert Parsons, here represented by his *Resolution*. Quite different is Jonson's later list of writers eminent in eloquence. For him More, Wyatt, Surrey, Chaloner, Smith, Eliot, Gardiner 'began eloquence with us'. It was continued by Nicholas Bacon; and consummated in Sidney, Hooker, Essex, Ralegh, Savile, Sandys, Egerton, and Bacon.[2] But Harvey as well as Jonson was averse to Euphuism, and yet the name of Rainolds in his list might suggest the contrary.

This must be the John Rainolds who was in high repute for his Oxford lectures on Aristotle's *Rhetoric*, who supervised the translation of the Prophets for the Authorized Version, and who has been advanced as the author of Euphuism in its strict sense.[3] At least the Latin lectures of Rainolds seem to have some relation to the

---

[1] *Elizabethan Critical Essays*, ed. G. G. Smith, ii. 280. The chief confuter of Cartwright was Whitgift. On the stylistic extremes which exerted pressure at this time—the current forms of the plain, the mean, and the grand style—see G. P. Krapp, *English Literary Prose*, pp. 382–4.

[2] Cf. *Discoveries*: 'Scriptorum Catalogus.' In his *Grammar* Jonson often quotes from More and 'that excellent oration of Sir John Cheek against the rebels'. For a comparable list see Edmund Bolton's *Hypercritica*, 'Addresse the Fourth'.

[3] See William Ringler, 'The Immediate Source of Euphuism', *PMLA*, liii (1938), 678–86.

sudden efflorescence of Euphuism, though perhaps only as the product of a schematic Ciceronian like Ascham.[1] In 1602, however, John Manningham cannot share Harvey's enthusiasm for Rainolds:

> Though a fashion of witt in writing may last longer than a fashion in a sute of clothes, yet yf a writer live long, and change not his fashion, he may perhaps outlive his best credit. It were good for such a man to dy quickly. (*Of Dr. Reynolds; Th. Cranmer.*)[2]

His lack of enthusiasm is explained by these particulars:

> Reynolds esteemes it his best glorie to quote an author for every sentence, nay almost every syllable; soe he may indeede shewe a great memory but small judgment. . . . He takes a speciall grace to use an old worne sentence, as though anie would like to be served with cockcrowen pottage, or a man should like delight to have a garment of shreeds. (*Cra. and I.*)[3]

If 'cockcrowen' is a malicious allusion to the proverb, 'As the old cock crows so doth the chick',[4] it gives point to the cult of sentences which connects Rainolds with Lyly, but also with many others in that time. For Cicero and Quintilian, indeed, this was a mark of the plain or pointed style.

Further light is thrown upon Rainolds and his time by another contemporary witness. Sir John Harington in his account of Dr. Thomas Dove, whom Harvey called 'eloquent', finds that the ground on which he would build 'his chief praise, to some of the *Aristarchi* and sour censurers of these days [*c.* 1608], requires first an apology'.[5] Therefore he recalls that even in Cambridge about twenty-five years ago 'a question rose among the divines . . . whether rhetorical figures and tropes, and other artificial ornaments of speech taken from profane authors, as sentences, adages, and such like, might be used in sermons'. The 'precise sort' were bitter against the use of such

---

[1] Frances A. Yates, *John Florio* (Cambridge, 1934, pp. 40–1, 50–2), presents a case for Florio, or his *First Fruits*, as the source of Euphuism.

[2] *Diary*, ed. John Bruce (Camden Society, 1868), p. 85. This is, however, a slower rate of obsolescence than Hoskins allows.

[3] Ibid., p. 86. On the cult of 'sentences' see M. P. Tilley, 'Euphuistic Devices of Sentences, Similitudes and Examples', *Elizabethan Proverb Lore* (New York, 1926), pp. 13–32. To each of these devices the popular *Wit's Commonwealth* devoted a volume, published successively in 1597, 1598, and 1599. The purpose of these collections, to which Lyly contributed, is intimated in the address 'To the Reader' of the second part: 'I hold that sentences, similitudes and examples are necessary to uphold a wit.'

[4] Cited under 'Parimia, or Proverb' in Puttenham's *Arte of English Poesie*.

[5] See *Nugae Antiquae*, ed. T. Park (London, 1804), ii. 206–9.

profane helps, 'but the graver and more orthodox were of the other opinion'. The official verdict in favour of rhetoric was rendered by Dr. Fleming, his tutor, in a sermon which made much of the example of St. Paul. About twelve years later the same question arose at Oxford, and was 'determined in the pulpit by Dr. Howse, against Dr. Reinolds, who had held the other opinion', which he then retracted. Thus, finding the opinion sound 'that Eloquence may serve as a handmaid', Harington proceeds to praise Dove, in whom the late queen 'thought the Holy Ghost was descended again'.[1] Here we have a reason for any variation of style in Rainolds on sacred or profane matter.

If neither Harvey nor Manningham suggests the highly patterned writing that Ringler finds in Rainolds, such is not the case with another contemporary critic. When Henry Jackson edited Rainolds's *Orationes Duodecim* in 1614, he defended the schematic structure of Rainolds's style; but, like Bacon, attacked the 'watery' vein of the Ciceronians. Jackson's preface, which is dated 1613, declares, 'Nihil hic dico de Osorij dictione, quam *aqueam* appellat vir eruditus', referring to Bacon's attack in *The Advancement of Learning*; but he does say something about Turner in connexion with Ciceronian 'intemperie'.[2] Jackson defends Rainolds's use of schematic prose by the example of St. Augustine and St. Bernard.

Quid? an non ipse *Martinus* delicatiores paronomasias confectatur, cum ex *Augustino* huiusmodi colligit, *diserti* & *deserti*, *periti* & *perituri*, ista non in *Augustino*, sed ineptissimo *Martino* culpamus. Sunt tamen nonnunquam ridicula, vbi est affectatio. Quis illa in *Augustino* reprehendat, quae habet multis in locis. Etsi in his similiterue desinentibus nimium fuisse *Augustinum* iudicant viri docti.[3]

---

[1] For Rainolds the queen had other thoughts according to Harington (ii. 181–2): 'she school'd Doctor Reynolds, for his preciseness, willing him to follow her lawes, and not to run before them.' Bastard's epigram gives us

> Reynoldes?—religion's oracle most true!
> Mirrour of arte, and *Austen* of our times!

[2] *Orationes Duodecem* (London, 1628), p. 102. Probably Robert Turner. In his dedication of Hooker's *Two Sermons upon Part of St. Jude* (pub. 1614) Jackson has nothing to say about Hooker's style. In the eighteenth century Philip Doddridge describes Rainolds the preacher: 'A most elaborate writer.—He has many surprising similes.—His style is remarkably laconic' (*Works*, Leeds, 1804, v. 429). This suggests a Euphuistic Senecan. If Doddridge refers to Edward Reynolds, this style belongs to the period after Bacon.

[3] Ibid., p. 104. Martinus is Gregory Martin.

Here Jackson refers to Wilson's *Arte of Rhetorique*, in which we have already noticed St. Augustine's connexion with 'similiter desinens'. But Jackson continues,

Habent tamen haec vsum, locumque suum. Quàm pulchrè *Augustinus* distinguit *panem Domini* à *pane Domino*? Quam scité *Bernardus* ait in Curiâ Romana *malos proficere*, *bonos deficere*, Episcoposque sui temporis, non *doctores esse*, sed *seductores*; non *pastores*, sed *impostores*; non *prae-latos*, sed *Pilatos*. Sed si haec in *Rainoldo* reprehensionem mereantur, licèt elegantissima aptissimaque; quid dicemus de nugis *Baronij* cuiusdam, quas in *vindicijs* contra *Rainoldum* confectatur?[1]

In a quibbling age the jingles of Euphuism, of paronomasia, and like-endings could be tolerated if they involved differences of meaning; they could be praised if they were subservient to fine distinctions, pointed sharp oppositions.

Jackson's defence, although made after the hey-day of Euphuism, still finds the Church Fathers a useful bulwark against those who attack the Euphuistic schemes in contemporary writers. Moreover, he can still admire these schemes when in skilful hands they contribute beauty and subtlety to composition. If one of the 'viri docti' was Thomas Wilson, another was Henry Savile, who included St. Bernard in his indictment of Sophistic prose, and insisted that patristic rhetoric came from the schools which produced Seneca.

In the parliament of 1598 Euphuism, it seems, was by no means dead. Sir Roger Wilbraham in his *Journal* bears witness to its life:

Her maiestie came to the house of the Lords and commons; the speker (Yelverton serieant) made a most fine and well filed speche: verie short & manie well couched sentences somewhat imitating, but bettering Euphues . . . this spech was full of elegancies, swetlie delivered: but thought too full of flatterie to curious & tedious. . . .[2]

No doubt part of the flattery lay in the style directed toward a rather antithetic queen, who had read Isocrates with Ascham, and who perhaps supplied the urge Wilson reports out of Tacitus, that 'Serjeants at the law were driven to use this kind of phrase'.[3] But the

---

[1] *Orationes Duodecim*, p. 105.

[2] See *The Camden Miscellany* (London, 1902), x. 10–12. In 1597, as a matter of fact, Lyly had sat as a member of Parliament for the third time.

[3] On Elizabeth's taste for antithesis see Ascham's *Works*, ed. Giles, I. i, pp. lxiv and 192. Ascham testifies that her ears were well attuned to the niceties of style. Perhaps her taste for Isocratic antithesis extended to Senecan antithesis; at least to his matter, according to Harington: 'She did much admire Seneca's wholesome advisinges, when

speech was thought 'too curious and tedious', and Sir Roger describes the response as follows:

> Sir Thomas Egerton L keper: said her maiestie had given him expresse charge to answare to the learned & eloquent oration. . . . He cited some sentences of Jerome &c. of the blessings of a iust prince: prayed for her sentenciouslie & brieflie, & craved pardon for himself. . . .[1]

Of another speech by the Lord Keeper, Sir Roger remarks, 'and so with an eloquent and pithy speech ended'. It is interesting that for Sir Roger 'bettering Euphues' seems to mean, among other things, speaking even more 'sententiously and briefly'; that eloquence for him was at once pithy and elegant in a Euphuistic way. It takes little imagination to see among these associates of Bacon several cultivators of a sententious style that both imitated and surpassed Euphuism in this respect.[2] Wilbraham emphasizes the sententious aspect of Euphuism, which Croll recognizes but does not make a part of its rhetoric; yet Croll observes of Lyly's proverbs that 'he also practises constantly the art of imitating their form and style in his own remarks'.[3] At the same time Francis Meres's preface to *Palladis Tamia*, the second part of *Wit's Commonwealth*, lays down similar requirements for style:

> He that would write or speake pithily, perspicuously, and persuasively must use to have at hand in readinesse, three kinds of ornaments and effectual motives, Sentences, Similitudes, and Examples. . . . What can I desire more, then to see the naked Truth arrayed in Sentences fitting the taste of Phylosophers; invested in Similitudes loved of Oratours; and approved by Examples, the rule and levell of the unstayed and raging multitude? . . . I judge him of an happie wit, who is profound and substantiall in Sentences, eloquent and ingenious in Similitudes; and rich and copious in Examples.

The differentiation of rhetorical effect peculiar to these Euphuistic devices should not be overlooked.

About 1599 John Hoskins wrote his *Directions for Speech and*

---

the soul's quiet was flown awaie; and I saw muche of hir translating thereof' (*Nugae Antiquae*, ed. Park, i. 357). See her translations from Cicero and Seneca in the *Nugae*, and mark her expression of the terser Senecan antithesis.

[1] *Camden Miscellany*, x. 12, p. 12. Egerton is one of Jonson's masters of prose. But, like Rainolds, he cites sentences.

[2] Bacon was associated with Wilbraham, for instance, in the investigation of the Essex plot.

[3] *Euphues*, p. vii.

Style, where he set forth the Lipsian rules 'for penning of letters' that were taken over by Jonson in his *Discoveries*.[1] After this Senecan programme for style rather than speech, Hoskins gives the rhetoric 'for varying', in which he defines Euphuism. The figures of repetition—of word or sound, which we encountered in Wilson's treatment of like-endings, are essential to this definition, for they are the figures by which paronomasia is varied in Lyly.[2]

Under *antimetabole* he treats one of the figures which, according to Wilson, made like-endings especially delightful—'when sentences are turned'.[3] He notes Sidney's fondness for this figure,[4] and seems to recall Wilson in his comment:

And notwithstanding that this is a sharp and witty figure and shows out of the same words a pithy distinction of meaning, very convenient for schoolmen, yet Mr. P. did wrong to tire this poor figure by using it thirty times in one sermon. For use this, or any other point, unseasonably, it is as ridiculous as it was in the fustian oration: *horse-mill*, *mill-horse*, etc. But let discretion be the greatest and general figure of figures.[5]

But this is to regard antimetabole as a figure of wit or point rather

---

[1] Hoskins enjoyed a prolonged reputation for 'polishing' authors, including Ralegh and Jonson; cf. *Directions*, ed. Hudson, pp. xii, xxviii. As a rhetoric related to the letter, his *Directions*, like Day's *English Secretary*, taught a more familiar form of discourse than that of the oration, though he glances at other forms from time to time. His Lipsian rules will be considered later.

[2] On the Sicilian origin of the figures of repetition see Bromley Smith, 'Some Rhetorical Figures Historically Considered', *Quarterly Journal of Speech*, xx (1934), 16–29.

[3] These figures are the same in Hoskins and Farnaby (*Index Rhetoricus*), except that Farnaby puts antimetabole under *Schemata sententiae ad Explicationem* rather than *Schemata Rhetoricae dictionis*, and Hoskins leaves them together but unclassified. In this section, 'For Varying', Hoskins approximates the schematism, but not the view, of Talaeus, whose *Rhetorica* had been abstracted by Dudley Fenner in *The Artes of Logike and Rethorike* in 1584. Cf. Hudson's 'Introduction' on the sources of the *Directions*.

[4] Besides serving Hoskins as a practical rhetoric, the *Arcadia* had a significance like that of *The Faerie Queene*; Cornwallis (Essay 46) calls it 'that Master-peece of English, which in a light History meanes the most grave matter'. Cf. Frances A. Yates (*John Florio*, p. 226): 'The Arcadian style has not been so minutely dissected as has the euphuistic. It employs alliteration, repetition and many of the other devices of euphuistic sound-pattern, but its sentences flow on and lose themselves in curves and involutions instead of being regularly blocked out in parallel clauses of more or less equal length as in euphuism proper.' Sidney is also fond of polyptoton and isocolon; but it is more significant that Hoskins could illustrate most of his rhetoric from the *Arcadia*.

[5] *Directions*, ed. H. H. Hudson (Princeton, 1935), p. 15. Hudson's text should be checked with the text printed by Louise B. Osborn in *The Life, Letters, and Writings of John Hoskyns* (New Haven, 1937), and especially with her collation of the Bodleian MS. (pp. 274 ff.). Neither printed text supplies an altogether satisfactory version.

than as a figure of sound; indeed, to get different meanings out of the same words or sounds was then the chief figure of wit. As Hudson has identified Mr. P. as Thomas Playfere, Hoskins's comment shows how a style could be distinguished by what Wilson called 'overmuch use' of one figure. Nashe complimented Playfere in kind.[1] This 'sharp and witty figure'—sometimes regarded as a form of antithesis—lent itself to 'point' and continued to be popular with poets like Denham.

Under *paronomasia*, 'a pleasant touch of the same letter, syllable, or word, with a different meaning', Hoskins analyses Lyly's style:

In those days Lyly, the author of *Euphues*, seeing the dotage of the time upon this small ornament, invented varieties of it; for he disposed the agnominations in as many fashions as repetitions are distinguished by the author's rhetoric. Sometimes the first word and the middle harped upon one another, sometimes the first and last, sometimes the middle and last, sometimes in several sentences, sometimes in one, and this with a measure. *Compar*, a change of contention or contraries, and a device of a similitude, in those days made a gallant show. But Lyly himself hath outlived this style and breaks well from it.[2]

Lyly cultivated the dotage of his time by inventing varieties of paronomasia. Here Hoskins specifies the Euphuistic measure, balance, antithesis, and simile as the rhetoric which supports the like-sounds.[3] And paronomasia or *agnomination* characterizes not

---

[1] See *Strange Newes* (1592): 'Mellifluous Playfere, . . . where doe thy supereminen gifts shine to themselues, that the Court cannot bee acquainted with them?'
'Few such men speake out of Fames highest Pulpits, though out of her highest Pulpits speake the purest of all speakers.'
'Let me adde one word, and let it not bee thought derogatorie to anie. I cannot bethinke mee of two in England in all things comparable to him for his time. Seldome haue I beheld so pregnant a pleasaunt wit coupled with a memorie of such huge incomprehensible receipt, deepe reading and delight better mixt than in his Sermons' (*Works*, ed. McKerrow, i. 314).

[2] *Directions*, ed. Hudson, pp. 16, 71. I take the alternate reading, which seems to make the better sense and to follow the text printed by Osborn. On paronomasia see John Smith, *Mysterie of Rhetoric Unvail'd* (1665 ed., p. 6): 'If a little unlike, and of divers originals and descents, it is *Paronomasia*. And if of the same original, it is *Polyptoton*.' These figures, having both likeness and difference, lend themselves to rhyming effects and word-play. Like-endings in English are both more difficult and less noticeable: see Wilson's examples and Smith's definitions.

[3] On *compar* see p. 37, quoted later; or *Rhetoricorum ad Herennium* (iv. 27), where it means balance and correspondence of clauses. Henry Peacham's *Garden of Eloquence* includes it among the rhetorical schemes of words. T. W. Baldwin's *Small Latine & Lesse Greeke* has sufficiently demonstrated the dependence of English rhetoric upon its predecessors in the learned tongues; for example, in Peacham and Angel Day we get Susenbrotus; in Rainolde, Aphthonius.

only Lyly, 'but even with Doctor Matthew this figure was of great accompt, and he lost no estimation by it: "Our paradise is a pair of dice, our almës-deeds are turned into all misdeeds, our praying into playing, our fasting into feasting". '[1] This 'kind of breaking words into another meaning is pretty to play with among gentlewomen', but it tends 'nearer to meter than to matter'. Thus Hoskins damns what Jackson defends in Rainolds. For Hoskins the essential figure of Euphuism is paronomasia, since the author's rhetoric merely 'disposed the agnominations'.

This kind of breaking words into another meaning died hard, even after Euphuism was dead; but after Euphuism it tended nearer to matter than to metre. Eighteenth-century criticism may serve to point the ambiguity that has been found in Lyly's style. William Oldys and the *Literary Magazine* respectively had these words to say, chiefly of the dramatist:

[Lyly] thro' an eternal affectation of sententiousness keeps to such a formal measure of his periods as soon grows tiresome, and so by confining himself to shape his sense so frequently into one artificial cadence, however ingenious or harmonious, abridges that variety which the style should be admired for.

His stile is a kind of prodigy for neatness, clearness and precision. . . . He is, it is true, full of antithesis, and he carries the neatness of his language sometimes to a ridiculous affectation; yet a judicious head may receive great improvement by reading his works, which are now scarcely ever mentioned.[2]

Thus a cult of sententiousness may issue, for different critics, either in an ingenious neatness or in an artificial formality of period. But Lyly's style, at least in its earlier form, was less ambiguous for Hoskins. It might be argued that Lyly's parison oscillates between an oratorical use and a pointed use: in the former it operates on the

---

[1] *Directions*, p. 16. On the wit of Dr. Tobie Matthews see Harington's *Nugae Antiquae* (ed. Park, ii. 258 ff.), which substantiates Hoskins. Croll's discussion of 'syllabic antithesis' (*Euphues*, pp. xxxvii–xxxviii) shows the extent to which paronomasia replaced homoioteleuton in English schematic prose. The correspondences which Child called *annomination* include his syllabic antithesis. He observes that 'Child quotes from G. P. Marsh's *Lectures on the English Language*, 1861, p. 567, the statement that this figure "can hardly be distinguished from Euphuism", meaning that it is the characteristic feature of the style.' It may be added that this is also what Hoskins meant.

[2] See *Euphues*, ed. E. Arber (English Reprints), p. 19. The sententious aspect of Lyly is prominent for these critics, and the latter finds that his style still has something to teach in qualities that were rare in Lyly's time.

principle of balance and is conjunctive; in the latter on the principle of antithesis and is disjunctive. It cannot be ignored that in intention *Euphues* was also 'the anatomy of wit', even in the narrower sense.

For Hoskins amplification is not only a rhetoric of emphasis which provokes admiration; it is also a rhetoric of brevity which works by suggestion.[1] Of the five ways to amplification—comparison, division, accumulation, intimation, and progression—all but 'intimation' tend to dilation and are associated with Cicero.[2] Intimation belongs to the rhetoric of emphasis through brevity; it works by Senecan allusion because it 'intimates more to your mind than to your ears'.[3]

His discussion of amplification has an interesting consequence; it is followed not only by a section on 'Figures serving for Amplification' but by another with this heading, 'These figures following serve properly for Amplification'.[4] By separating these figures from the figures of amplification in the preceding section, Hoskins seems to have wished to separate them from less appropriate or less effective means of emphasis. Certainly, he presents in the latter section a short analysis of the antithetic rhetoric which gave force and wit to the Senecan style. In the table of figures as given in the Osborn text, the special heading of this section is followed by these figures:

> Synoeceosis, *quae docet diversas res coniungere,*
> *et communi oppinioni cum ratione adversari*
> Contentio
> Sententia.

[1] *Directions*, pp. 17–24. For a broad treatment of amplification see W. G. Crane, *Wit and Rhetoric in the Renaissance* (New York, 1937).

[2] These forms of amplification, with the addition of division from Bacon's *Colours*, derive from Quintilian (VIII. iv). But intimation is not so much 'reasoning' as a related form, a kind of insinuation (VIII. iv. 21–6); it is related to what is called 'emphasis' in his discussion of ornament (VIII. iii. 83–5). This 'emphasis' intimates a deeper meaning than the words actually express, either by signifying more than is said or by emphasizing a significant omission. Emphasis and intimation differ in their nature and place because the former is an inference from a word, the latter from a thing; and things are more impressive than words.

[3] Intimation (*Directions*, pp. 25–6) 'leaves the collection of greatness to our understanding, by expressing some mark of it. . . . It exceedeth speech in silence, and makes our meaning more palpable by a touch than by a direct handling. . . . It savors sometimes of hyperbole. . . . This fashion of amplification I term intimation because it doth not directly aggravate but by consequence and proportion, and intimateth more to your mind than to your ears.' Cf. Seneca, *Ep.* lix. 5. On its relation to *sententia* see Quintilian VIII. v. 12.

[4] In the Osborn text the concluding table reiterates this heading: 'figures more prop. for Amplifying' (*The Life, Letters, and Writings of John Hoskyns*, p. 166).

G

These are also the last figures under 'Amplification' in Hudson's table as well as the figures under the special head in the body of his text.

This section provides a contemporary rhetorical nexus between Euphuism and the newer Senecan style, for it looks both ways. Hoskins's description of these figures is therefore worth attention.

> *Synoeciosis* is a composition of contraries, and by both words intimateth the meaning of neither precisely but a moderation and mediocrity of both; as, *bravery* and *rags* are contrary, yet somewhat better than both is *brave raggedness*. . . . And one contrary is affirmed to be in the other directly by making one the substantive, the other the adjective, as above in the examples; or indirectly, as in these words following:
>
> > Seeking honor by dishonoring and building
> > safety upon ruin. . . .
>
> This is a fine course to stir admiration in the hearer and make them think it a strange harmony which must be expressed in such discords. . . .[1]

Concluding that 'this is an easy figure now in fashion', Hoskins left this figure of intimation a mixture of oxymoron and synoeciosis or paradox, where Farnaby's *Index Rhetoricus* discriminated.[2] How this *discordia concors* goes to the root of much seventeenth-century wit the observant reader will know even if he has not read Johnson or Courthope.

Antithesis is a related figure: 'Contentio is contrary to the former. That was a composition of terms disagreeing; this is an opposition of them.'[3] How it may be used with antimetabole 'for the turning of sentences back' is illustrated: 'He is a swaggerer amongst quiet men, but a quiet man amongst swaggerers; earnest in idle things, idle in matters of earnestness.' Its effect upon sound-pattern is

---

[1] *Directions*, ed. Hudson, p. 36. No doubt the more indirect way is the more admirable. Another fashionable figure, which Hoskins finds in the 'fine conversants . . . when they strain for an extraordinary phrase', is *catachresis*, which Dryden rebuked in Cleveland. This he defines as 'the expressing of one matter by the name of another which is incompatible with it, and sometimes clean contrary'; it is not, like metaphor, a 'neighborly borrowing', but 'the abuse of a word drawn from things far different' (pp. 11 and 8). It is sometimes hard to distinguish from *ironia*. As another figure—actually trope—derived from incompatibles, it should be added to the fashionable rhetoric that delighted by the ingenuity with which such hidden connexions were perceived or such contraries reconciled.

[2] Under *Schemata sententiae ad Explicationem* Farnaby classifies the figures of contraries found in Hoskins, and later in Walker: antimetabole, antithesis, synoeciosis, oxymoron.

[3] *Directions*, p. 37.

sufficiently obvious. Of antithesis Hoskins remarks: 'This figure Ascham told Sturmius that he taught the Queen of England, and that she excels in practice of it; and indeed it is a figure fit to set forth a copious style.'[1] He adds that this figure serves both for amplification and for *compar* or balance, whether rhythmical or structural.

Antithesis has a natural relation to the schemes of symmetry, and with them Euphuism appears:

Comparison (compar) is an even gait of sentences answering each other in measures interchangeably, such as in St. Augustine but often in Gregory the Divine, such as in the Bishop of W. his books which he hath written in English, and many places of *Euphues*: but that St. Austin, Bilson, and Lyly do very much mingle this figure with *agnominatio* and *Similiter Cadens*. It is a smooth and memorable style for utterance, but in penning it must be used moderately and modestly.[2]

Note those who mingle this figure with like-sounds, and that only now are like-endings ascribed to Lyly. The final remark—one of the many reminders of the difference between speech and style—suggests the reason why the schemes of symmetry did not disappear in preaching when they were decried in the essay style. Hoskins allows that 'a touch of agnomination of the letter is tolerable with a *compar*'. He considers asyndeton as 'a shorter *compar* where substantive to substantive or word to word are joined, and yet without conjunction'.[3] The asyndetic compar is a good oratorical figure, 'smooth and memorable'; and 'it hath been in request ever since the days of Isocrates, whose orations are full of them'.[4] Thus antitheses provide occasions for the symmetrical schemes, which in

---

[1] See Ascham's *Works*, ed. Giles, I. i, pp. lxiv and 192: 'She very much admires modest metaphors, and comparisons of contraries well put together and contrasting felicitously with one another.' The result of this instruction for Theodore M. Stenberg is 'Elizabeth as Euphuist before *Euphues*', *Studies in English: Texas Bulletin*, viii. 65–78. Hoskins, however, does not regard Elizabeth as a Euphuist; knowing this letter to Sturm, he knew also that Elizabeth's 'copious style' had been derived from a study of Cicero, Livy, and Isocrates. Ascham's Latin letters were published in 1576.

[2] *Directions*, p. 37. This supplements Savile's sketch, and provides almost the only mention of *similiter cadens* in Hoskins.

[3] Ibid., p. 38. The symmetrical schemes are supplementary to antithesis, and, except for paronomasia or agnomination, do not appear in Hoskins's table.

[4] It is Wilson's *similia inter se*. 'It fits well', says Hoskins, 'the even pauses and interruptions of an eloquent tongue'; this is the reading that fits the rhythmic consideration or 'measure' which goes with *compar*. Moreover, this figure promotes brevity, for each part 'with a tedious man would make a sentence'; it 'belongs more properly to that part of amplification called division than to accumulation'.

turn may be set off by like-sounds; but the schemes are to be used with moderation in written discourse.

The third figure in this section, *sententia*, 'if it be well used, is a figure'—

if ill and too much, it is a style; whereof none that writes humorously or factiously nowadays can be clear. For now there are such schisms of eloquence that it is enough for any ten years that all the bravest wits do imitate some one figure which a critic hath taught some great personage.[1]

As for example, Queen Elizabeth's antithesis, which, as Hoskins remarked, Ascham had taught her. Ascham had said: 'She especially admires and strives for suitable metaphors and combinations of antitheses aptly matched and happily set in opposition.'[2] Hoskins's apparent dislike of sententia when used so much as to become a style not only reflects Quintilian but gives point to his testimony. For instance, in this passage:

But these short-breathed gentlemen, these judicious minds, will show me in their works interrogations, agnominations, corrections, and all the figures of rhetoric: I yield to it; and yet will they show me nothing but sentences, unless there be some difference betwixt writing all in sentences and writing all sententiously.[3]

In the use of sentences, this is of course the point—the excess makes a style. For Hoskins there is no difference between the cult of aphorisms and an aphoristic style. It should not be forgotten, however, that for him *sententiae* contribute to epistolary style life or

[1] *Directions*, pp. 38-9. It may be observed that Hoskins follows this principle in defining styles. Cf. Seneca, *Ep.* 114, on the final observation.

[2] See *Directions*, p. 86; Ascham's *Works*, ed. Giles, I. i, pp. lxiv and 192. This taste her letters illustrate, but not Euphuism; and in sentences that are longer-breathed and more complicated than either the Senecan or Euphuistic—more Ciceronian. In business she can be more Senecan, but not Euphuistic in figures of sound. Ascham's remark simply points to her liking for symmetry of structure—a liking to which Euphuism could appeal. She employs the entangled period with symmetry of structure rather than of sound. The uninvolved period of Euphuism, as opposed to the involved Ciceronian period, breaks down into more separated parts; the parts are emphasized at the expense of the whole; the union is aggregate rather than composite. Sidney also writes long sentences, even in French; sometimes, like Elizabeth, he is short in business. For the short style in letters see those dated after 1590 in Harington's *Nugae Antiquae*, especially the extreme example written by Robert Markham in 1598-9 (Park ed., i. 239-44).

[3] *Directions*, p. 39. Florio's *Firste Fruites* (1578) offered 'merie Prouerbes, wittie Sentences, and golden sayings'; his *Second Fruits* (1591) recommended them to 'all that would beautify their speech with a not vulgar bravery', for which 'the Greeks and Latins thank Erasmus, and our Englishmen make much of Heywood'. Cf. M. P. Tilley, *Elizabethan Proverb Lore*, p. 33.

sharpness, 'which is the very strength and sinews, as it were, of your penning'.[1]

If the Senecans were 'short-breathed' and 'judicious', the Euphuists were partial to the figures enumerated in this sneer. Hoskins then illustrates the 'sentence' in combination with other figures, partly to reinforce the point he has just made, and partly to show that there is 'slender reason to ground upon any one figure the frame and fashion of your whole style'.[2] The figures treated in this section are prominent in such sentences, being natural accompaniments of sententious writing. Nor should we forget in this connexion the extent to which Lyly and Rainolds employed the sentence and proverb.

Even more sharp criticism appears in Hoskins's closing remarks on sententia:

In our profession there are not many (if two were many) whose speeches rely upon this figure; and in my judgment *sententia* is better for the bench than the bar. Then of all others, why would the writers of these days imprison themselves in the straitness of these maxims? It makes their style like *arena sine calce*, as one saith of such a writer; and doth not he vouchsafe to use them that called them *posies for rings*?[3]

On the susceptibility of the legal profession to sententia Sir Roger Wilbraham, as we have seen, does not agree with Hoskins, who has been thought to allude to Bacon.[4] If 'the writers of these days' included no Euphuists, then the sententious style must have fettered other writers either before or immediately after the publication of

[1] *Directions*, pp. 7 and 2.

[2] A contention that Sidney could illustrate for him. In this exploitation of one figure—of agnomination by Lyly, of antithesis by Elizabeth, of antimetabole by Playfere—Hoskins reveals the individual cult of style in his time. Such extremes marked an unclassical use of the figures. Although many writers used sententiae, it was their exploitation, almost their exclusive use, that marked Bacon's first essays.

[3] Ibid., p. 40. The probable allusion in 'posies for rings' (or simply 'posies' in the Bodleian MS.) is to Puttenham's *Arte of English Poesie* (1589), bk. I, chap. xxx, 'Of Short Epigrames called Poesies', which mentions their use as 'devises in rings'; cf. also bk. II, chap. xii, 'Of the Device or Embleme', where 'devices' are defined as 'short, quicke, and sententious propositions'. Caligula's remark about Seneca's style as 'sand without lime' is for La Mothe le Vayer an imputation of the 'asthmatic' or *coupé* style (*Œuvres*, Dresden, 1756, II. i. 232).

[4] In the Ascham letter, however, Hoskins had before him this testimony to the Queen's earlier taste: 'She cannot endure those foolish imitators of Erasmus, who have tied up the Latin tongue in those wretched fetters of proverbs.' And such imitators may be the objects of his attack. But whatever the Queen thought of her parliament, Wilbraham thought it Euphuistic rather than Erasmian in its sententiousness.

Bacon's *Essays*. But if these writers were imitators of Erasmus in the cult of the proverb, then they ought to include Lyly. Yet as early as 1596 Nashe had criticized the imitation of Lipsian brevity in Richard Harvey. Moreover, the allusion to 'such a writer' refers to Seneca, and connects these remarks with the chief model of sententious style. Erasmus himself had pointed to Seneca as a prime source for such maxims; and Senecan drama, both old and new, also lent authority to them and their rhetoric. If the influence of Erasmus tied up the English tongue in the 'fetters of proverbs', then he assisted the Senecan movement. Hoskins's criticism, however, exempts just what Bacon's first essays pretended to be:

If it be a matter of short direction for life and action, or notes for memory, I intend not to discredit this new trick. But otherwise, he that hath a long journey to walk in that pace is like a horse that overreacheth and yet goes slow. St. Ambrose sanctifies this figure.[1]

His final caveat goes back to Quintilian and forward to other critics of the Senecan style. St. Ambrose is one of the fathers mentioned by Sir Henry Savile in the transmission of Gorgian style as the Senecan heresy. Quintilian, to whom Hoskins is indebted, had observed that the cultivation of sententiae in his time not only was over-emphasized but led to curtness and over-emphasis in expression.[2]

On Euphuism, moreover, Hoskins had concluded that 'Lyly himself hath outlived this style and breaks well from it.' Therefore, it might be presumed that Lyly did not, like Rainolds, 'outlive his best credit'. But how and where did he break from Euphuism? Where but in his plays? Child, who has made the most detailed analysis of Euphuism, supports Hoskins's conclusion about Lyly's style. 'The Euphuism of the plays', he remarks, 'is in a word a simplified Euphuism.' In this simplification the balanced members become shorter, the parisonic form less frequent; the Euphuistic trains of example and similitude disappear; the euphonic devices become 'not only less frequent but less noticeable'.[3]

[1] Evidently it is a new fashion—newer than Euphuism. The gaits of horses were a constant source of metaphor for movement in style. For Senecan drama see H. V. Canter, *Rhetorical Elements in the Tragedies of Seneca*, University of Illinois, 1925.

[2] *Institutes of Oratory*, VIII. v. On other abuses of style see Nashe's 'Preface to Greene's *Menaphon*'.

[3] See C. G. Child, *John Lyly and Euphuism* (Erlangen and Leipzig, 1894), p. 88; and in general chap. iii, 'The Euphuism of Lyly's Plays'.

The late plays, which Hoskins probably had in mind, reveal a still greater change, which Child summarizes as follows:

> If in the later plays we feel that Lyly is still Euphuistic, the explanation is that while abandoning the use of artificial devices he still held to antithesis and parallelism. Even these he employs with anything but his old constancy, and to parison no longer pays careful attention—its occurrence is largely an accident of the use of antithesis.[1]

In these plays Hoskins could feel, by virtue of his more exact definition of Euphuism, that Lyly 'breaks well from it', because he eliminates the essential element of Euphuism, its sound-pattern. If his antithesis invited some use of the schemes, it was no more than might be expected in the antithetic rhetoric that Hoskins considered more proper to amplification. At this stage it would not be easy to distinguish Lyly from Seneca, even for the sober Anti-Ciceronians. The difference disappears completely in Minto's definition of Lyly's style: 'His peculiarity lay not so much in hosts of parallels and instances, as in the sententious pointed way of expressing them. That is the Euphuistic *form*.'[2] It might be urged, with more exactness, that in his late plays such was Lyly's form. If Lyly created a polished speech appropriate to a code of manners, he also taught English a lesson in neat composition, which outlined thought in a clear and distinct form.

Yet Minto was not being obtuse. It should not be ignored that *Euphues* was also 'the anatomy of wit' in this sense: 'It is wit that allureth; when every word shall have his weight, when nothing shall proceed but it shall either savour of a sharp conceit or a secret conclusion.'[3] These are the aims of the pointed style, recalling Seneca's *argutiae* and *suspiciones*. The examples quoted from Seneca, Tacitus, and the Church Fathers are brought to mind when one reads such a passage as the beginning of Lyly's address 'To my very good friends the Gentlemen Scholars of Oxford':

> There is no priuiledge that needeth a pardon, neither is there any remission to be asked where a commission is graunted. I speake this Gentlemen, not to excuse the offence which is taken, but to offer a defence

---

[1] Ibid., p. 100. For Child parison means partial or complete forms of exact balance. Note its relation to antithesis.

[2] William Minto, *A Manual of English Prose Literature* (Boston, 1898), p. 231.

[3] *Euphues*, ed. Croll and Clemons, p. 262. Of course, the schemes also gave every word its weight.

where I was mistaken. A cleere conscience is a sure carde, truth hath the prerogatiue to speake with plainenesse, and the modestie to bear with patience.[1]

Schematic wit may even allure the reader to deal more gently with errata: 'Faults escaped in the Printing, correct with your pens: omitted by my negligence, overslip with patience: committed by ignorance, remit with favor.'[2]

In his first petition to the queen, in 1598, Lyly approaches the obscure brevity and abruptness esteemed by many Senecans:

I dare not pester your Highnes with many wordes, and want witt to wrapp vpp much matter in ffewe; This Age, Epitomyes, the Pater Noster, thrust into the Compasse of a penny; The world into the Modell of a Tennis Ball, All Scyences melted into Sentences: I would I were soe Compendyous, as to expresse my hopes, my ffortunes, my overthwartes into sillables, as Marchantes doe Riches into a ffewe Ciphers; Butt I ffeare to Committ the Error: I discommend tedyousnes, like one that Roveinge to searche out whatt tyme was, spent all his and knewe it not. . . .[3]

From this petition Lyly derived the satisfaction at least of writing its sharp conceits and secret conclusions to a queen who was receptive to rhetoric. In his second petition to the queen, in 1601, the secret conclusions—the 'intimations' of Hoskins—are blunter and the rhetoric more obvious; more play on sound is allowed to sharpen his points; his brevity is clearer and yet more poignant.

Most gratious and dread Soueraigne, Tyme cannot worke my peticions nor my peticions Tyme.

After many yeeres, since yt pleased your Highnes to except against Tentes and Toyles, I wish that for Tentes I might put in Tenementes: Soe should I be eased of courtly Toyles: Some landes, good fines or forfeitures, that shall comme to your Majesty, by that just fall of those false Traytors; That seinge nothinge will come to me by Revells, I may pray vppon the Rebells.

Thirteene yeeres your Highnes servant: but yet nothinge.

---

[1] *Euphues*, 1581 ed.

[2] *Euphues and his England*, 1580: 'To the Gentlemen Readers'.

[3] See Feuillerat, *John Lyly*, p. 556. On the Pater Noster penny see McKerrow's *Nashe* (iv. 455; note to iii. 318, 14–15), which quotes Holinshed on all that Peter Bales, the famous writing-master, wrote 'within the compasse of a penie'. Lancelot Andrewes in a sermon at Hampton Court, 6 Mar. 1594, suggests the taste of the times: 'In coins, they that in smallest compass contain greatest value, are best esteemed: and in sentences, those that in fewest words comprise most matter, are most praised.'

Twenty frendes, that though they saye they will be suer, I find suer to be slowe.

A thousand hopes, but all nothinge, a hundred promises, but yet nothinge. Thus castinge vp the Inventorye of my frendes, hopes, promisses, and tyme: The Summa totalis amounteth in all to iust nothinge....[1]

The antithetic rhetoric of these petitions, products of his later style, has been relaxed but has not lost all of its neat form.

These examples give some idea of the range of Lyly's style from early to late, as well as of its witty intention, which is manifest in his 'jingling epigrams'. From these examples it is possible to see how that style could be regarded as both pointed and schematic—that its general evolution was from emphasis on the schematic to emphasis on the pointed.

Since Hoskins criticized Euphuism for its exploitation of sound by means of the schemes, it would be useful to know, for purposes of comparison, what was then found objectionable in Ciceronian style. Under the date 13 March 1601, John Manningham records the exchange of 'fiery words' between Mr. Watts and Mr. Danvers on Ciceronianism, in which Mr. Watts asserted that Anti-Ciceronianism was only a case of sour grapes.[2] If Mr. Danvers's remarks are unrecorded, those of Sir William Cornwallis are not. Like Bacon, but in 1601, Cornwallis attacked the vanity of words. In his essay 'Of Vanity' he remarks:

Of words first; for it is one of the first things we doe, they are but the Lackyes of reason, of which to send more then will performe the businesse, is superfluous; me thinkes, an *esse videatur*, at the close of a period, is as nice as a Tumbler ending his tricks with a caper: and *Tullies Venit, imo in Senatum venit*, mooues me no more against *Catiline*, then the first *Venit*. Me thinkes this same Rhetorick, the child of words, is but a pickled Herring to bring on drinke, for his diuisions and repetitions are for nothing but to bring his memory acquainted with his tongue, and to make three words of one. How shall a man hope to come to an end of their works, when he cannot with two breathes saile through a period, and is sometimes grauelled in a Parenthesis? I wonder how *Cicero* got the people of *Rome* tyed so fast to his tongue, for were his matter no better then his stile, hee should not perswade mee to looke vpon him? I make as great

---

[1] Ibid., p. 561. The turn in the first sentence is based on antimetabole, the figure for which Playfere was famous. Lyly's hope is staked on the Essex rebellion.

[2] *Diary*, ed. John Bruce (Camden Society), p. 39. On Ciceronianism see A. C. Clark's essay in *English Literature and the Classics*, ed. G. S. Gordon, Oxford, 1912.

difference betweene *Tacitus*, and *Senecaes* stile, and his, as Musitians betweene *Trenchmore* & *Lachrymae*. Me thinks the braine should dance a Iigge at the hearing a *Tullian* sound, and sit in counsell when it heares the other.[1]

'This disease of words let in by Cicero' is the first of vanities, and Cicero must now be saved by his matter, for he is betrayed among pedants and boys because of his style.

Although Seneca and Tacitus were brief where Cicero was copious, it is their gravity that Cornwallis chooses particularly to contrast with Cicero's jigging movement. Of course to 'sit in counsel' is neither to hear a flood of words nor to respond to their rhythm—at least for the brain.

But eloquence (as wee take eloquence) is of no vse, but among such eares as call a Bag-pipe musick, it fits them, and among them must be vsed; but among wisemen, it is to distrust their vnderstandings, loosing time in repetitions, and Tautologies. The vertue of things is not in their bignesse, but quality, and so of reason, which wrapped in a few words, hath the best tang.[2]

It should be observed that Cicero's cadences, emphatic repetitions, divisions, and general copiousness are the objects of attack, not the oratorical schemes that are found in Euphuism—unless we except such repetitions.[3] Cornwallis, moreover, has a Ciceronian in mind when he describes a kind of discourse which he rejects:

There is another Creature that weyes every word and will be sure to turne the *verbe* behind, affects elegancy and to be thought learned; this

[1] *Trenchmore* was a lively dance, and *Lachrymae* a grave piece by Dowland. Cf. the charges brought against Cicero by the Atticists which are summarized in Quintilian, XII. x. 12. One of the main charges was against his rhythm. On the imitation of Cicero's *esse videatur* see Quintilian, X. ii. 18; Erasmus, in Scott's *Controversies*, ii. 48; Montaigne, 'Of Bookes'.

[2] *Essayes*, no. 43. Cf. edition by D. C. Allen (Baltimore, 1946), p. 175. Plutarch (*Morals*, ed. W. W. Goodwin, iv. 243) remarks of 'Garrulity' how much more 'they are reputed to excel in prudence, who deliver their minds in few words, roundly and sententiously, and contract a great deal of sense within a small compass of speech, than such as fly out into voluminous language, and suffer their tongues to run before their wit'; and further that 'the Laconic way of speech has nothing of bark upon it, but by cutting off all superfluity of words, it becomes steeled and sharpened to pierce the understanding of the hearers'.

[3] Nashe (*Works*, ed. McKerrow, iii. 66) charges Gabriel Harvey with the affectation of Ciceronian cadence: 'Some there be (I am not ignorant) that, vpon his often bringing it in at the end of euerie period, call him by no other name but *esse posse videatur*: but they are such as were neuer endenizond in so much arte as *Similiter Desinens*, and know not the true vse of *Numerus Rhetoricus*.' The implication is that Harvey likewise is ignorant of its use, even confuses the two.

fellowe is formall, he robs himselfe of his commendations with this pre-meditated course. Men looke for much where they discerne such a preparation.[1]

And Montaigne, as we shall see, did not find it in Cicero.

Cornwallis's mockery of the Ciceronian style may be compared with Fuller's account of Hooker's periods and their effect upon his audience:

His style was long and pithy, driving on a whole flock of several clauses before he came to the close of a sentence. So that when the copiousness of his style met not with proportionable capacity in his auditors, it was unjustly censured for perplexed, tedious, and obscure.[2]

Later, copiousness was commonly regarded as another way to obscurity. Camden translated Seneca to characterize this style in the language of his own time: 'And some there are that think it a grace if their speech do hover, and thereby hold the hearer in suspense.'[3]

Cornwallis's taste in style deserves some enlargement. He admires the Anti-Ciceronian favourites, Seneca, Tacitus, Sallust, Plutarch, Caesar; he has read 'Lipsius in his *Constantia*'; he knows that 'from Tacitus's concise style there are many Jewels to be gotten'.[4] He is the first to slant the English essay toward Montaigne, or to strike the personal note of Seneca. In Cornwallis the curt style is both more curt and more often relieved by the loose style than in Bacon; he is less given to Senecan balance and to epigram. Like the later Character-writers, he tends to begin with a conceited definition, and is commonly very metaphorical; of course, these traits are not absent from Bacon.

The curt style predominates in the first part of his *Essayes* (1600), and the loose style in the second (1601). This change is no less sharp, but far more sudden, than that of Bacon. In the translation which he read, Cornwallis found Montaigne 'translated into a style admitting

[1] *Essayes*, no. 11.

[2] *Church History of Britain*, ed. Nichols, iii. 141.

[3] See *Remains*: 'Languages.' But it was the abuse of sub-dependence that made sixteenth- and seventeenth-century periods heavy, and the influence of Ciceronian Latin provoked the excess of subordination. No doubt the couplet discipline in verse, which set new requirements for the sentence, helped to lighten English style; stanzas or run-on verse did not impose sufficient limitation.

[4] Cf. *Essayes*, nos. 15 and 32, and references *passim*. His *Discourses upon Seneca the Tragedian* (1601) are really concerned with the moralist.

as few Idle words as our language will endure'; and he could say, 'Montaigne speaks now good English'.[1] Cornwallis is not only the first English essayist to approach Montaigne in manner; he is the first to suggest the Montaigne variety of Senecan style.[2] For in the two parts of the *Essayes*, if he does not run the Montaigne course, he creates a surprising parallel to that course in passing from the 'curt' to the 'loose' style.

Cornwallis also expresses his preference of matter to words, his dislike of 'Rhetoric's Cookery', his agreement with Plato, 'Rhetorica suadet, non docet'.[3] This opposition of two accepted ends of rhetoric came to characterize a common attitude toward rhetoric in the seventeenth century. But the opposition of *suadere* and *docere* gives more than stylistic meaning to the common, Ramistic, definition of rhetoric as the art of speaking ornately; for this was the speech of the affections, of *movere* as well as *delectare*.[4] This opposition, it may be added, made a Stoic separation of ends and appropriate speech.

In the *Advancement of Learning* (1605) Bacon attacks the Ciceronians for the same excesses that annoyed Cornwallis:

For men began to hunt more after words than matter; more after the choiceness of the phrase, and the round and clean composition of the

---

[1] *Essayes*, no. 12. Montaigne's remarks on speech and style in his essay 'Of the Institution and Education of Children' make a compendium of Anti-Ciceronian doctrine which should be compared with the remarks of Bacon and Cornwallis.

[2] Though Cornwallis derived from Montaigne, he declares: 'I hold neither *Plutarches*, nor none of those auncient short manner of writings, nor *Montaignes*, nor such of this latter time to bee rightly tearmed Essayes; for though they be short, yet they are strong, and able to endure the sharpest triall' (Essay 45). True essays (such as his) are trials in expression, attempts to express thought, or what Robert Johnson called his essays, 'Imperfect Offers' (1601). 'It is a manner of writing well befitting vndigested motions, or a head not knowing his strength, like a circumspect runner trying for a start, or prouidence that tastes before shee buyes.' But Bacon's essays were also explorations or imperfect offers, however strong they appeared to Cornwallis.

[3] See *Essayes*, no. 45. Bacon, on the other hand, defended rhetoric against this passage in the *Gorgias*; but he allowed Plato's distinction between the art of persuading and the art of teaching. Rhetoric's 'cookery' was a common slur with those who espoused philosophy rather than rhetoric.

[4] Cicero encouraged this separation by such remarks (*Brutus*, 89) as 'that of the two chief qualities which the orator must possess, accurate argument looking to proof and impressive appeal to the emotions of the listener, the orator who inflames the court accomplishes far more than the one who merely instructs it'; and by his explicit relation (*Orator*, 69) of the three functions of oratory (to prove, please, and move) to the three styles, plain, middle, vehement or grand; and by adding that in moving 'is summed up the entire virtue of the orator'. In Aristotle such ends are integrated; there is no separation in terms of language, except that the function of style is to please; the other functions are aspects of proof.

sentence, and the sweet falling of the clauses, and the varying and illustration of their works with tropes and figures, than after the weight of matter . . . the whole inclination and bent of those times was rather towards copie than weight.[1]

Bacon, like Cornwallis, fails to point his criticism toward any specifically Euphuistic trait—varying their works with figures is too general. But we cannot conclude that he was unaware of the distinction between the classical and the Euphuistic use of the schemes which was drawn by men like Wilson and Savile. This is not less surprising because he emphasizes sentence structure. Yet it must be said that in prose characterized by schematic structure, more or less complicated schematic patterns become distinctions of degree rather than of kind. If patterned paromoion assimilated the Ciceronian and Euphuistic styles to one another, parison gave the pattern. This paromoion was more than the native alliteration, which at best achieved only a very simple pattern; it extended from consonance and assonance to full rhyme. If the purer Ciceronians rejected the paromoion, so did the more severe Senecans; but the Latin sentence figures could still be used by both. It is the schematic Ciceronians who get confused with the Euphuists, and here the difference lies chiefly in periodic structure—whether their schemes are developed in a more involved or a more deployed structure.[2]

To amplify Bacon's criticism, or to set it in the proper frame of reference, we may examine the doctrine of the period as it was currently expounded. This is found conveniently in Farnaby's *Index Rhetoricus* (1625). Although Farnaby does not explicitly distinguish, he obviously thinks of the period in two ways: as an intellectual form and as a rhythmical form. 'The period', he says, 'is composed

---

[1] Everyman ed., p. 24. The 'choiceness of the phrase' was guaranteed by 'Nizolian paperbooks'. No doubt the cult of Ciceronian diction stimulated the feeling against 'ink-horn terms' in the vernacular. It will be remembered that Erasmus's Ciceronian hunted more after the words of Cicero than after the matter for his letter.

[2] A. C. Howell uses *res et verba* (*ELH*, xiii. 131–42) to trace the course of the plain versus ornate style in the seventeenth century. But Bacon directed this contrast against the cult of form, not merely against ornamental diction. And Sprat, like Bacon on the Senecans, stresses another aspect, brevity, which also induced plainness; it is involved in Cicero's words on brevity: 'brevity is attained by using simple words, saying each thing once, and by observing nothing except that you speak with lucidity'. These words (quoted by Howell) also involve, as Bacon and others realized, considerations of form, such as words used for symmetry; they do not make the plain style exclusively a matter of diction. Bacon's criticism is instructive on this point.

of two members, of which the former is called the *protasis* and the latter the *apodosis* or *redditio*.' The protasis signifies tension ahead. But, he continues, the period may be composed of three or four members, 'which are either equal, or in the plain (*acri*) style the latter are shorter, in the grand (*ornata*) longer'. It is the middle style that indulges in isocolon. Here the rhythmic form enters the definition. Both forms are used to define the most beautiful period: 'Pulcherrima tamen est illa Periodus, quae membris quatuor absolvitur, ut quae animum suspendat et aures impleat.' To suspend the mind and satisfy the ears is to meet both requirements of the period. This definition is followed by a consideration of *concinnitas*, for which the Gorgian figures are defined. Then Farnaby gives an account of *numerus*, which means chiefly the measures of clausal cadence, though the movement of speech is said to be quick in short syllables, slow in long, and moderate in their mixture. Here appropriate feet for these measures are discussed. Most interesting, perhaps, in this account of the period is the specification of shorter (abrupt) members for ending periods in the plain style, and longer in the grand style.[1] It is such doctrine that explains Bacon's references to 'the round and clean composition of the sentence, and the sweet falling of the clauses'. There is no such treatment of periodology in Hoskins, but the relation of Gorgian parallelism to oratory is remarked, and speech is suggested as part of his concern.

In his attack on Ciceronianism Bacon was criticizing the preceding generation; in his attack on Senecanism, which was not made until 1623, he was criticizing his own generation. Before examining the latter, however, it will be useful to see how Seneca's style had been praised. In 1604 Justus Lipsius, the great arbiter of Stoic or Senecan

---

[1] Cf. Abbé Batteux, *A Course of the Belles Lettres* (London, 1761), vol. iv, part iii, on the doctrine of rhythm in the eighteenth century. In his chapter 'Of number taken as the *sensible relation between different spaces*', he expounds prose rhythm—on the principle that '*numerus in continuatione nullus est*'—as intervals marked by pauses, analogous to those of verse, and hence kept within certain bounds. He also considers rhythm under the aspects of cadence, movement, and metre. This is the doctrine of Cicero's *De Oratore* (III. xlvii–xlviii), which is echoed by Farnaby, together with material from the *Orator* (212-22). Batteux remarks that 'intervals which have a symmetry of combination are the most agreeable', and that this results sometimes from their equality, sometimes when an irregular interval is followed by two regular ones, sometimes from climax or the continual lengthening of phrases and members, sometimes from the reverse or continual shortening of elements. Cf. Quintilian (IX. iv. 122 ff.) on various kinds of composition or style for various purposes and effects.

style, summarized many of his own ideals in a description of Seneca's style which he wrote for his *Manuductio ad Stoicam philosophiam*. This description is a tissue of the ideas, and even the phrases, about style that are found in Seneca's *Epistles*; some of them had already been used by Lipsius in setting out his own principles of style.

Verba, selecta, propria, significantia: immo quae plus aliquid semper dicunt, quam dicunt. Qui proprius quidam eius Genius videtur, ut in parcimonia verborum more ἐνέργεια atque efficacia sit; in brevitate, claritas et splendor. Sunt allusiones, imagines, translationes, crebrae et paene continuae: quae delectant simul et docent; et in rem animum, atque extra rem mittunt. Est cura, non affectatio; decor, non comptus; tractata oratio, non torta. Est et compositio quaedam et viriles numeri: sed ut structuram agnoscas, mollitiem abnuas; et pugnae atque arenae omnia, non delectationi aut scaenae parata. Iam in ipsa brevitate, et stricto dicendi genere, apparet beata quaedam copia. Fundit verba, etsi non effundit; fluit, non rapitur; amni similis, torrenti dissimilis; cum impetu, sed sine perturbatione se ferens. Denique, ut felices arbores, quarum praecipua dos est fructum ferre, flores et folia tamen habent; sic iste, quem fructus caussa legimus et colimus, oblectationem adfert pariter, et Venerem cum Minerva iungit.[1]

Seneca's special genius is 'that in a parsimony of words he has a wonderful force and efficacy'. Here used to define that genius are both Aristotle's *energeia* and Scaliger's *efficacia*, or the key terms in the cult of expressiveness. A careful reading of Seneca's *Epistles* will reveal the extent to which Lipsius depends upon them for a description of Seneca's style.

By imitation Lipsius exemplifies the virtues which he describes. Antithesis and parallelism are apparent even in the translation, which I subjoin;[2] but the way in which like-sounds reinforce them

---

[1] Cf. Basil Anderton, *Sketches from a Library Window* (New York, 1923), pp. 29–30. Cf. Seneca, *Ep.* 59, for example.

[2] From Anderton: 'His words are choice, suitable and significant; they always mean something more than they actually say. And this seems a special genius of his, that in an economy of words he has a wonderful force and efficacy; in brevity he has clearness and brilliance. Allusions, figures, metaphors, are frequent, almost continuous; and these both please and instruct, directing the mind to the subject, and even beyond the subject. There is carefulness without affectation; ornament without finery (*comptus*); there is close arrangement in what he says, but nothing forced or crabbed. Style also is apparent, and virile harmony and rhythm, yet in such a way that, while you recognise artistic construction, you will admit no effeminate artificiality, and it is for fighting and the arena that the whole equipment is made, not for pleasure and scenic show. Then, too, in his very brevity and terseness of speech there is manifest a certain happy abundance: his words well forth amply, though not wastefully; they flow, not rush; they are

can only be seen in the Latin. How the use of like-sounds for emphasis rather than pattern divides the Senecan style from the Euphuistic may be learned from this imitation of Seneca. Yet the verbal echoes which Savile called a 'rhyming harmony of words', but which here lay stress on the parallel elements, are still too prominent to be overlooked. And this is the emphatic, even 'factious', style described by Hoskins; it is the style whose peculiar kind of *copia* justifies Burton and is condemned by Hoskins.

Croll has remarked of Lipsius: 'He and Montaigne are the chief sources of the Senecan literary mode, and his own style is obviously formed by a slight exaggeration of Seneca's point and brevity, and unfortunately a great exaggeration of his play upon words.'[1] But his play upon words—not easily separated from his point—included not merely paronomasia but other oral devices familiar to schematic writers like the Euphuists and to critics like Savile. It is not surprising that the uses of these oral devices were often undiscriminated except by the rejection of Senecans like Bacon.

In the *De Augmentis Scientiarum* Bacon adds the new Senecan style, although 'paulo sanius', to the vanity of words:

Litle better is that kind of stile (yet neither is that altogether exempt from vanity) which neer about the same time succeeded this *Copy* and *superfluity of speech*. The labour here is altogether, *That words may be aculeate, sentences concise, and the whole contexture of the speech and discourse, rather rounding into it selfe, than spread and dilated*: So that it comes to passe by this Artifice, that every passage seemes more witty and waighty than indeed it is. Such a stile as this we finde more excessively in *Seneca*; more moderately in *Tacitus* and *Plinius Secundus*; and of late it hath bin very pleasing unto the eares of our time. And this kind of expression hath found such acceptance with meaner capacities, as to be a dignity and ornament to Learning; neverthelesse, by the more exact judgements, it hath bin deservedly dispised, and may be set down *as a distemper of Learning*, seeing it is nothing else but a hunting after words, and fine placing of them.[2]

like a river, not a torrent; they move on with strength, but without spate. Lastly, like goodly trees that, whilst their chief property is to bear fruit, have yet flowers and leaves: so Seneca, whom for his fruit's sake we read and admire, brings us delight at the same time, putting Venus beside Minerva.' By these contrasts and antitheses Lipsius defines the peculiarly Senecan qualities and separates them from the Ciceronian. Seneca is artful but not artificial; note his figurative aspect, his rhythm, his sententious but fluent expression.

[1] 'Attic Prose: Lipsius, Montaigne, Bacon', *Schelling Anniversary Papers*, p. 123.

[2] Translation by Gilbert Wats (Oxford, 1640), p. 29. Similar traits are to be found in

'Discourse, in short, rather turned than poured'—*oratio denique potius versa quam fusa*—that is the Senecan style. Savile's query of 'long or round' is answered by 'more round than long'. While it cannot be said that the whole inclination of this style is 'rather towards copie than weight', it can be asserted that it is like the Ciceronian in being 'a hunting after words' rather than matter.[1] If Bacon can be said to include Euphuism in his criticism of either style, it is less likely to be found in the 'sweet falling of the clauses' in the Ciceronian than in the 'fine placing (*concinnitas*)' of words in the Senecan. Though Bacon had misgivings about the pointed style, he allowed, if somewhat grudgingly, that it was bent in the right direction.

In Bacon's succession of styles the course of Roman prose descends to modern times. But Croll observes that Bacon's criticism of Senecan style 'is all directed toward "vain shows" and verbal ornament, the same fault of undue love of concinnity, in short, which was a cause of the revolt against Cicero's form of rhetoric'.[2] Of course, Bacon's criticism of Senecan style is against the vanity of words as an impediment to learning, but this does not mean that its fault is identical with the Ciceronian. 'This is somewhat puzzling,' continues Croll, 'especially in view of the fact that Seneca himself had made current among Anti-Ciceronian critics the phrases they habitually used to express their contempt for the sensuous beauty of the balanced Ciceronian phrase: *non ornamentum virile concinnitas*, and so forth.' It may be observed that Bacon actually emphasizes the studied character of Senecan concinnity: 'cum sit verborum etiam et eorum concinnitatis aucupium quoddam'. The plain answer

Lipsius's description of Seneca's style. In the essay 'Of Anger' Bacon warns against 'extreme bitterness of words; especially if they be aculeate and proper'. Then their effect was not diminished by such 'stings and goads'. See Quintilian (VIII. v) on *sententiae*.

[1] In the Latin text the Senecan style is thus described: 'Illud totum in eo est, ut verba sint aculeata, sententiae concisae, oratio denique potius versa quam fusa; quo fit, ut omnia per hujusmodi artificium magis ingeniosa videantur quam revera sint.' And Seneca differs from Tacitus and Pliny as 'effusius' from 'moderatius'. Bacon's description recalls Cicero's character of one of the two kinds of Asiatic style: 'unum sententiosum et argutum, sententiis non tam gravibus et severis quam concinnis et venustis' (*Brutus*, 325).

[2] *Schelling Anniversary Papers*, p. 140. Such faults in Seneca, it should be observed, are disclaimed by Lipsius. Bacon does not specify concinnity in the Latin text on the Ciceronians: 'plerisque magis comptam phrasim, teretem periodum, clausularum rhythmos, troporum stellulas, quam pondus rerum, rationum nervos, inventionis acumen, aut judicii limam affectantibus.'

is that Bacon specifies concinnity here and not in the Ciceronian; but he probably has Senecan word-play chiefly in mind.

When Bacon says, 'atque nostri temporis auribus coepit esse non ita pridem accommodatum', he is referring not merely to the style found in Seneca but to the style which followed Ciceronianism; therefore he is either overlooking Euphuism, or else he is regarding it either as Senecan or as Ciceronian. But Euphuism was neither easy to overlook, nor could it have been regarded as Ciceronian by Savile; on the contrary, he would have called it Senecan. It may even be asked whether 'such a curious search after words and their concinnity' applies to anything so well as to Euphuism, which certainly was pleasing to meaner wits, and not less because it seemed an ornament to learning. If Bacon does not follow Savile in describing this style, he is at least in agreement on the main points—the weighty appearance and the chiming reality.

But Croll finds that 'the reader of Seneca can reconcile the contradiction' in Bacon's attack:

For that very literary and rhetorical essayist customarily framed his *antitheses* and *argutiae* in a balanced form, different indeed from that of the copious oratorical style, but yet capable of becoming almost as transparently artificial. At its best an excellent literary form for the insinuation of subtle shades of thought and fine distinctions, at its worst it is indeed no more than 'mere words and their concinity.'[1]

While Bacon's own words do not exclude the 'verbal ingenuity and mere pun' which Croll assigns to the imitators of Seneca,[2] this description allows Bacon to find a likeness between Cicero and Seneca in balanced phrasing, though it is not clear that he did. He seems rather to have found Senecan style pointed, concise, antithetic, chiming—even Euphuistic, for 'concinnitas verborum' can mean the 'jingle' of words, as Shaw rendered Bacon's phrase. For Savile concinnity of sound unites Seneca and Tacitus, not Seneca and Cicero. Thus it is more plausible to suppose that Bacon is con-

---

[1] *Schelling Anniversary Papers*, p. 140. Note that at its best the balanced form of his antithesis does not detract from its subtlety. But this admission begins to blur some of Croll's distinctions.

[2] William Rawley, Bacon's chaplain and biographer, makes a pertinent observation: 'Neither was he given to any light conceits or descanting upon words, but did ever purposely and industriously avoid them; for he held such things to be but digressions or diversions from the scope intended, and to derogate from the weight and dignity of the style.'

demning Senecan style for its Euphuistic concinnity than to argue with Croll that he is asserting his preference for Tacitus, who is made only less guilty. It is more probable that he objects to pointed antithesis and word-play, which unite Seneca and Tacitus, than to balanced form, which does not. If symmetry of style—apart from rhythm—is involved, it is the charge against Senecan style, not Ciceronian. If the Senecan style became Anti-Euphuistic in the specific sense of 'anti-jingle', it appeared Euphuistic in so far as it employed the figures of parallelism, though for pointed effects.[1]

When Croll objects to the use of antithesis for purposes of characterization, particularly of Euphuism, he explains that 'it may be a figure of words, or sound, on the one hand, and a figure of thought (*figura sententiae*) on the other', and that 'in the latter use, it is one of the most important *differentia* by which we recognize the style of the Anti-Ciceronian movement'.[2] But that, it may be objected, is having it both ways as a mark of style. Then he distinguishes the use of antithesis among the Anti-Ciceronians:

Without or with similarity of sound between the opposed words or members, it distinguishes the style of Bacon, who usually avoids balance in its use, and the style of Sir Thomas Browne, who likes just so much symmetry of form as will serve to point his artful and rhythmical departures from it, and the style of Montaigne in his latest period. In Lyly's use of it, on the other hand, antithesis is purely a 'scheme', that is, a figure of the arrangement of words for an effect of sound. It is not meant to reveal new and striking relations between things; and it is as different as possible, for instance, from such a use of it as in Bacon's saying that 'revenge is a kind of wild justice'.[3]

[1] Since the *De Augmentis Scientiarum* was prepared for a European audience, it might be argued that his criticism of Senecan style was inserted to balance his Anti-Ciceronianism, which was made less offensive. But in theory any 'vanity' in words was prejudicial to the advancement of learning, and the compulsion to describe varieties must be accounted for in other terms. The special reason here must be such acceptance 'as to be a dignity and ornament to Learning', of which Lipsius was the most conspicuous example.

[2] *Euphues*, p. xvii.

[3] Ibid., p. xvii. Yet of antithesis in Guez de Balzac, who made a cult of form and was often published in English, Gaston Guillaumie has this to say: 'De tous les procédés littéraires, il n'en est pas de plus fécond pour mettre en relief la pensée: de l'opposition des mots naissent des contrastes entre les faits et les idées qui, en soulignant l'expression, lui donnent à la fois plus de finesse et plus de force. Aucun écrivain de l'époque classique n'a su manier l'antithèse avec plus de virtuosité que Balzac. Ce procédé lui est si familier, qu'il fait, pour ainsi dire, partie intégrante de son style et constitue la caractéristique essentielle de sa tournure d'esprit' (*Guez de Balzac et la prose française*, p. 444).

This is on the whole a more guarded statement of the Anti-Ciceronian reaction against symmetry of form than that which Croll later permits himself in the article on 'Baroque Style'. Of course, the imposition of his 'baroque' analogy then makes an asymmetrical factor crucial in his description.

Antithesis, in passing from a Gorgian to a Senecan use, may be said to pass from a figure of words to a figure of thought, but not to relinquish all symmetry of form. In antithesis every word may be made to count either for symmetry or cogency of expression, or else may be made as unobtrusive as possible.[1] Bacon's use of antithesis in the above example, however, is not quite normal; it is rather a use of *synoeciosis*, 'a composition of contraries', or paradox. Antithesis or '*contentio* is contrary to the former. That was a composition of terms disagreeing; this is an opposition of them'.[2] And it is opposition that tends to involve symmetry, as Hoskins observed, or as John Constable suggests in his allusion to Pascal: 'He says, those Authors who to make an *antithesis* force their words, are like those who make false windows for symmetry. Their rule is not to speak accurately, but to make set figures.'[3] Of course, 'to make set figures' was a Euphuistic rule for antithesis, but Pascal is used by Constable to criticize Senecan style.

Let us look at the 'antithesis' in the opening of Bacon's 'Of Revenge', a late (1625) essay: 'Revenge is a kind of wild justice; which the more man's nature runs to, the more ought law to weed it out. For as for the first wrong, it doth but offend the law; but the revenge of that wrong putteth the law out of office.' The initial paradox undergoes an antithetical development, and the contraries

Balzac, who was born about ten years before Browne, cultivated in the letter the various forms of symmetry that belong to oratory. After it ceased to be the mode in England to 'Parley Euphuesime', it became the mode in France to 'parler Balzac'.

[1] Cf. J. E. Hollingsworth (*Antithesis in the Attic Orators*, p. 35): 'As antithetic writing became more systematic, it was natural that every word be made to count either for symmetry or cogency of expression, or should be made as unobtrusive as possible. Hence arose parison, paronomasia, homoeoteleuton, &c. . . . By these means the co-ordinate clauses were elaborated to the utmost degree of artistic symmetry and pleasing euphony. An alternative process was to subordinate one of the antithetical clauses. . . . The possibilities of artistic elaboration here were hardly fewer than with the co-ordinate clauses, particularly with Lysias and Isocrates.' Hollingsworth divides antitheses into two types: clausal and intra-clausal; of the former there are three varieties: co-ordinate, subordinate, and extended antitheses or periodology.

[2] Hoskins, *Directions*, p. 37.

[3] *Reflections upon Accuracy of Style* (London, 1731), pp. 170-1.

which appear to be reconciled are suddenly thrown into opposition, making us realize that revenge is more wild than just. In the antithetic development parallelism has its place, emphasizing the neat point that nature runs to what law weeds out. Less neat, because less salient in form, is the development of that point into a second point: that while crime offends law, revenge puts law out. In short, law must weed out or be put out. Pointed prose cannot forego all parallelism in its antitheses except at the expense of neatness or effectiveness; such antithetic 'form', as Aristotle remarked, is essential to aphorism. The extent to which Bacon could employ parallelism is illustrated in the essay 'Of Studies'.

It is instructive to observe Bacon as he quotes and translates Seneca in his essay 'Of Adversity', another late (1625) essay:

It was an high speech of Seneca (after the manner of the Stoics): *That the good things which belong to the prosperity are to be wished; but the good things that belong to adversity are to be admired. Bona rerum secundarum optabilia, adversarum mirabilia.*

Bacon duplicates Seneca's balance, suggests his transverse likeendings, but adds alliteration to the parallelism of the second member. Again Bacon writes, 'It is a yet higher speech of his than the other (much too high for a heathen): *It is true greatness to have in one the frailty of a man, and the security of a god. Vere magnum, habere fragilitatem hominis, securitatem dei*'. Here he duplicates Seneca's form even more closely: the balanced antithesis, the likeendings of 'frailty' and 'security'. If this form be considered accidental, it may be argued that the similarities could have been, but are not, avoided.

The conclusion of this essay will illustrate Bacon's use of antithesis and balance with perhaps less 'similarity of sound between the opposed words or members':

Prosperity is not without many fears and distastes; and adversity is not without comforts and hopes. We see in needleworks and embroideries, it is more pleasing to have a lively work upon a sad and solemn ground, than to have a dark and melancholy work upon a lightsome ground: judge therefore of the pleasure of the heart by the pleasure of the eye. Certainly virtue is like precious odours, most fragrant when they are incensed or crushed: for prosperity doth best discover vice; but adversity doth best discover virtue.[1]

[1] But notice, for example, the cunning inversion of matching parts in 'a lively work

This neatness of design in a late work is not unrepresentative of the more pointed writing in Bacon's *Essays*. Although it usually stops short of the similarity of form and sound attained in his translation of Seneca, it is a neatness which Bacon may be said to share with Seneca—and with Lyly, who carried the symmetry much farther. And yet Bacon, for example in his dedication of the *Advancement of Learning*, did sometimes go this far: 'But your Majesty's manner of speech is indeed prince-like, flowing as from a fountain, and yet streaming and branching itself into nature's order, full of facility and felicity, imitating none, and inimitable by any.' And he wrote in the same book—in a vein that we do not associate with him because he renounced it much more completely than he did parallel-ism—of Socrates as 'professing to affirm nothing, but to infirm that which was affirmed by another'.[1] It is indeed rare to find Bacon writing like his friend Bishop Andrewes.

If Bacon's essay style can remind us of Lyly, Shakespeare's use of the pointed style in the oration of the stoic Brutus might find its place in the text-book of the elder Seneca. To cite no more, consider this passage:

If then that friend demand why Brutus rose against Caesar, this is my answer: Not that I loved Caesar less, but that I loved Rome more. Had you rather Caesar were living and die all slaves, than that Caesar were dead, to live all freemen? As Caesar loved me, I weep for him; as he was fortunate, I rejoice at it; as he was valiant, I honour him: but, as he was ambitious, I slew him. There is tears for his love; joy for his fortune; honour for his valour; and death for his ambition. Who is here so base that he would be a bondman? If any, speak; for him have I offended. Who is here so rude that would not be a Roman? If any, speak; for him have I offended.[2]

upon a sad and solemn ground . . . a dark and melancholy work upon a lightsome ground'. Note also the tendency to isocolon.

[1] *Advancement*, Everyman ed., p. 118. Note the Tacitean polyptoton, upon which the point turns.

[2] Cf. Falstaff's parody of Euphuism in *1 Henry IV* (II. iv. 443 ff.). Here is an excerpt: 'Harry, I do not only marvel where thou spendest thy time, but also how thou art accompanied: for though the camomile, the more it is trodden on the faster it grows, yet youth, the more it is wasted the sooner it wears. . . . There is a thing, Harry, which thou hast often heard of, and it is known to many in our land by the name of pitch: this pitch, as ancient writers do report, doth defile; so doth the company thou keepest; for, Harry, now I do not speak to thee in drink, but in tears, not in pleasure but in passion, not in words only, but in woes also.' Here the antithetic rhetoric is less neat than Lyly's, and the verbal echoes less schematic; but the 'euphuing of similes'—basic to the parallelism—is obvious enough. Cf. the passage from Cheke in Chap. III.

Here are no sweeping periods; every sentence is pointed—as in the schools of declamation—so as to be as telling as possible. In form the Euphuistic symmetry is apparent, but verbal echoes become obvious only at the close; here the echoes are more Senecan than Euphuistic, less complicated than earlier in the speech. Brutus makes an oratorical use of the pointed style, and yet his verbal ornament may remind one of Lyly.

Two diverse views of this oration may help to emphasize the problem which its style presents. A classical scholar, after distinguishing between the Attic and Asiatic styles, has remarked: 'Shakespeare, by sheer force of genius, has grasped the essential features of the two modes, and contrasted them, in the speeches of Brutus and Mark Antony, in the tragedy of *Julius Caesar*.'[1] But since Rolfe also noted both the copious and the curt varieties of the Asiatic, we may ask whether this is the Attic of a Stoic or the curt Asiatic style. Is it marked by 'naked simplicity' or by 'epigrammatic conciseness'? On the other hand, a Shakespeare scholar also contrasts Brutus's style with 'the free and fluent rhetoric of Antony', and reaches a different conclusion. First quoting Plutarch's character of Brutus's 'Epistles', he remarks:

Thus prompted Shakespeare makes Brutus affect the balanced structure of Euphuism. Not only in his oration. Read his words to Cassius at their first interview. . . . Nothing could be more neat, accurate and artificial than this Euphuistic arrangement of phrases. . . . But it is a style unsuitable to, one might almost say incompatible with, genuine passion. . . . And could the symmetrical clauses of this oration move the popular heart?[2]

[1] John C. Rolfe, *Cicero and his Influence* (Boston, 1923), pp. 33–4. Plutarch, however, had called Antony's oratory 'Asiatic'.

[2] M. W. MacCallum, *Shakespeare's Roman Plays* (London, 1925), p. 252. Plutarch (*Lives*, Temple Classics ed., ix. 244) had remarked that Brutus 'counterfeited that brief compendious manner of speech of the Lacedaemonians. As when the war was begun, he wrote unto the Pergamenians in this sort; I understand you have given Dolabella money: if you have done it willingly, you confess you have offended me: if against your wills, shew it then by giving me willingly. Another time again unto the Samians: Your counsels be long, your doings be slow, consider the end. And in another epistle he wrote unto [of] the Patareians: The Xanthians despising my good-will, have made their country a grave of despair: and the Patareians that put themselves into my protection, have lost no jot of their liberty. And therefore whilst you have liberty, either choose the judgement of the Patareians, or the fortunes of the Xanthians. These were Brutus' manner of letters which were honoured for their briefness.' Thus North's translation provided hints for the basic structure of Brutus's style, but not for the verbal echoes employed by Shakespeare.

Of course, Stoic oratory was deficient in emotional display, to which it made no claim, which it in fact avoided; but restraint may be confused with frigidity, and Laconic speech was famous for its trenchant force. Thus we have Brutus described as an Attic and as a Euphuist, though modelled on a Laconic; and a curt Asiatic may be suggested. Whatever its origin or name, the style is both Sophistic and pointed in character; though most akin to Lyly's in that time, perhaps Harvey would have called it 'Attic'.

In adopting the Senecan style, Bacon rejected its paromoion rather thoroughly, but not altogether its symmetry of form. In general Bacon is still liable to his own description of that style. If pointed prose uses the schemes to make its points neat rather than to make its sounds jingle, it must still be acknowledged to use them. In short, it is not the absence of the figures of parallelism, but the use to which they are put, that differentiates Senecan style from Euphuism. Although Croll has made this point for antithesis, he has not recognized sufficiently the function of parallelism in pointed prose. If Bacon rejected the 'aculeate' style as another vanity of words, he did not find in it the same cult of form that he found in the Ciceronian. He rejected it principally—and this is very revealing—for having the appearance rather than the reality of weight. Yet Lyly's achievement in formal neatness was not lost on his contemporaries. And Lyly had avowed a plain style, for wit—though it might change—was not alien to such a style.

5. *Lipsius his Hopping Style*

Thomas Nashe, always alert to satiric occasion, testifies in 1596 to Lipsian imitation in England. In *Have with you to Saffron-Walden* he remarks, 'and nere a Dick Harvey or cathedral Doctor of them all can read a more smooth succinct *Lipsian* Lecture of short hair, than thou over thy Barber's Chair'; and 'therefore Lipsian Dick, because lamely and lubberly he strives to imitate and be another English Lipsius'.[1] This charge is supported by the reply, *The Trimming of Thomas Nashe*; for this, because of its logical display and succinct manner, seems more appropriate to Richard Harvey, though Nashe had called Gabriel a 'short shredder' of sentences.[2]

In 1615 Nicholas Breton is praised for his Lipsian style by a eulogist of his *Characters upon Essaies*:

> I herein finde few words, great worth involve:
> A Lipsian stile, terse Phrase. . . .

In 1628 John Earle's character of 'A selfe-conceited Man' places a Lipsian style among the new heresies: 'He prefers *Ramus* before *Aristotle* and *Paracelsus* before *Galen*, and whosoever with most Paradox is commended and *Lipsius* his hopping style, before either *Tully* or *Quintilian*.' Earlier, in 1623, Bacon had seen fit to condemn the style of which Lipsius was a modern exemplar.

These allusions outline a reputation which was sustained perhaps less by scholarly work than by a popular exposition of Stoic philosophy in a Senecan style; they outline a fashion which, as Bacon said, conciliated honour to learning. Even in a translation into Restoration English the *De Constantia* of Lipsius can produce this effect:

To conclude, let them understand I have written many other things

---

[1] *Works*, ed. McKerrow, iii. 13, 85.
[2] Certainly, it returns the metaphor with interest, and is the work of no less a barber than Richard Harvey; but its edge is less cutting than that of Gabriel, and its matter closer to Richard.

for others; but this book chiefly for my self; the former for fame, but this for profit. That which one heretofore said bravely and acutely; the same I now truly proclaim. To me a few Readers are enough, one is enough, none is enough. All that I desire is, that whosoever opens this book, may bring with him a disposition to profit, and also to pardon.[1]

Lipsius was the chief contemporary model of pointed prose.[2] Before examining this apostle of the hopping style, it will be necessary to clear the ground a little.

The rise of the Anti-Ciceronian cult which marks the seventeenth century has been traced by Croll to Muretus,[3] and its dissemination to Lipsius, Montaigne, and Bacon. What these men discovered in Seneca and Tacitus, or disliked in Cicero, characterized the new taste in style—a taste that ran to the essay style rather than to the oratorical. In an introductory lecture to a course on Cicero, Muret's style first clearly 'betrays the influence of Seneca's brief antithetical sentences. *Vera et solida eloquentia*, he says, *non tantum in verbis posita est, sed in rebus*'.[4] In Muret's eulogy of St. Bartholomew's Croll notes that the style is of a form exactly opposite to that of the Ciceronian, 'namely a condensed style full of points and aphorisms ... derived from the study of Roman prose of the first century, and especially from Pliny's Panegyric to Trajan'.[5]

In 1580 Muretus had defended Tacitus by going so far as to imitate his pointed brevity and studied asymmetry and to praise his obscurity and asperity of style. The passage which Croll has quoted from this excellent appraisal of Tacitus found its way into late seventeenth-century English from the work of La Mothe le Vayer:

Howsoever it be, it is no wonder if *Tacitus* (having imitated *Thucydides*,

---

[1] 'To the Reader', *A Discourse of Constancy*, translated by Nathaniel Wanley, London, 1670. His style is more sharply defined in the preface. Lipsius's use of that difficult Stoic, Persius, reminds one of the similar use made by Chapman: see the epigraph which defies the audience of *Ovid's Banquet of Sense*.

[2] His Anti-Ciceronian qualities appear in this character by Scioppius, quoted in Thomas Pope Blount's *Censura Celebriorum Authorum* (London, 1690, p. 592): 'In *Justi Lipsii* stylo, Scriptoris aetate nostrâ clarissimi, istae apparent dotes: Acumen, Venustas, Dilectus, Ornatus vel nimius, cùm vix quicquam propriè dictum ei placeat, tum Schemata nullo numero, tandem verborum copia: desunt autem Perspicuitas, Puritas, Aequabilitas, Collocatio, Junctura & numerus Oratorius. Itaque Oratio est obscura, non paucis barbarismis & *Soloecismis*, plurimis verò *Archaismis* & *Idiotismis*, innumeris etiam *Neoterismis* inquinata; comprehensio obscura, compositio fracta & in particulas concisa, vocum similium aut ambiguarum puerilis captatio.'

[3] 'Muret and the History of "Attic" Prose', *PMLA*, xxxix (1924), 254–309.

[4] Ibid., p. 294. This sentence also expresses Senecan doctrine.

[5] Ibid., p. 290.

and both followed *Demosthenes*) retained something of that roughness and austerity, which is observed in the writings of those Two *Graecians*; and which all the Ancients accounted as a virtue, so far is it from deserving to be imputed as a fault, to him that should propose them to himself for imitation. And as some Wines are recommended to our palates by a little bitterness that is in them; and as many persons find that a dusky and obscure light in Churches is most sutable to their exercise of devotion: so others conceive the obscurity of an Author, mixed with a little roughness of Stile, is rather to be esteemed than otherwise; because it disposes the mind to attention, and elevates and transports it to notions, which it would not arrive at in a more easy composition.[1]

Muretus, as Croll remarks, 'stirs the ground about the roots of seventeenth-century style'; for the Jacobean cult of obscurity shares this doctrine with him.

Lipsius first employed the Anti-Ciceronian style in his *Quaestiones Epistolicae*, which appeared just before his edition of Tacitus in 1575. The character of his new style is best described by Lipsius himself in a letter to a friend:

I am afraid of what you will think of this work. For this is a different kind of writing from my earlier style, without showiness, without luxuriance, without the Tullian concinnities; condensed everywhere, and I know not whether of too studied a brevity. But this is what captivates me now. They celebrate Timanthes the painter because there was always something more to be understood in his works than was actually painted. I should like this in my style.[2]

Croll remarks that both the critical terms and the style of this passage come from Seneca; yet it would be hard to show that the stylistic direction differs from that which Muretus discovered in Tacitus. Although Lipsius as a Stoic was eventually associated with the point and brevity of Seneca, he began by admiring the dark implications and studied ellipses of Tacitus.

There is one kind of brevity which Seneca disparaged, and which was more often associated with Tacitus, and that is obscurity, *obscura brevitas*. Seneca approved in Sallust 'abruptae sententiae et suspiciosae', or in Lodge's words, 'abrupt Sentences and suspicious, in which more is to be understood than heard', so long as they were not carried to the point of obscurity. Although Seneca did not

---

[1] *Notitia Historicorum Selectorum*, translated by W. D. (William Davenant) (Oxford, 1678), pp. 217–18. Cf. Croll, *PMLA*, xxxix. 300.
[2] Quoted by Croll, *Schelling Anniversary Papers*, p. 122.

allow *copia* or superfluity, he did allow fluency, because it was un-laboured and because it revealed personality.[1] In fact, to him *fundere* meant to avoid affected and laboured composition, and to achieve the naturalness that he desired, but which was not without artifice.[2] It was this side of Seneca that encouraged the loose style at the same time that his cultivation of *sententiae* stimulated the curt style.[3]

The difficulty of discriminating between Senecan and Tacitean imitation may be suggested by a contemporary criticism of the neo-stoic Lipsius. In Boccalini's *Ragguagli di Parnasso*, first translated into English in 1626, Lipsius is brought before Apollo for his idolatry of Tacitus, and Muretus is one of those who jealousy indict him as follows:

Hee now loved to discourse with no other learned man: no conversation did more agrade him: he commended no other *Historian*: and all with such partiality of inward affection, namely, for the elegancie of his speech, adorned more with choise conceits, than with words; for the succinctnesse of his close, nervous, and gave sententious Oratorie, cleare onely to those of best understanding, with the envy and hatred of other vertuous men of this dominion, dependents of *Cicero*, and of the mighty *Caesarean faction*, who approve it not. And did with such diligence labour to imitate him, that not onely with hatefull antonomasia, hee dared to call him his Auctor, but utterly scorning all other mens detections, he affected no other ambition, than to appeare unto the world a new *Tacitus*.[4]

However, Lipsius is in the end by Apollo 'not only absolved, but highly commended and admired'. In this trial Lipsius, the great Neo-Stoic, is specifically a Tacitean, but generally an Anti-Ciceronian.[5]

---

[1] See *Epp.* 114, 59, 100. Cf. F. I. Merchant, 'Seneca the Philosopher and his Theory of Style', *American Journal of Philology*, xxvi (1905), 57 ff.

[2] Cf. *Epp.* 75, 115.

[3] This ambiguous effect appears in the style of Lipsius; cf. Adrien Baillet, *Jugemens des savans sur les principaux ouvrages des auteurs* (Amsterdam, 1725, ii. 193): 'Son style ne laisse pas d'être fort coulant, éloquent, facile, & plein d'agrémens, quoiqu'il soit concis, serré & tout rempli de pointes. Et c'est ce qui paroît avoir été presque sans exemple jusqu'à present. Cette brièvetè singuliére de style n'a ni ténèbres ni obscurités. Son ordinaire est de dire beaucoup de choses en peu de mots, & le sens de ses pensées s'étend avec d'autant plus d'effusion & d'abondance, qu'il paroît d'abord serré dans un petit nombre de paroles.'

[4] *The New-found Politicke*, translated by Florio, W. Vaughan, and another (London, 1626), p. 15 (part I, *Rag.* 86).

[5] For a review of contemporary opinion of his style see A. Baillet, *Jugemens des savans* (Amsterdam, 1725), vol. ii, art. 437.

If we were to distinguish Lipsius the Tacitean from Lipsius the Senecan, we should have to distinguish where the seventeenth century often confused; yet as a Tacitean he could find merit in obscurity, as a Senecan he might condone word-play. Lipsius was the standard-bearer of Senecan style; his 'contagion spread very far'; and we are told that those who despaired of achieving the happy abundance of Cicero turned to the dry and meagre style of Lipsius. These are the epithets that Cicero always applied to the Stoics; they appear in *De Oratore* (III. xviii) when he allows the Stoics a kind of eloquence, delicate and acute, but useless to the orator. Lipsius proved very offensive to the Ciceronians because of his 'manner of breaking his sentences and darting his maxims'.[1] But if his Anti-Ciceronian taste culminated in an edition of Seneca in 1605, it had begun with an edition of Tacitus thirty years before.

In 1591 the first English translation of Tacitus, the work of Sir Henry Savile, was recommended to the reader by A. B. (probably Anthony Bacon) in these words:

For Tacitus I may say without partiality, that hee hath writen the most matter with best conceyt in fewest wordes of anie Historiographer ancient or moderne. But he is harde. *Difficilia quae pulchra*: the second reading over will please thee more then the first, and the third then the second.[2]

In the second and enlarged edition of 1598 Richard Grenewey declared in his dedication that there is in Tacitus 'no word not loaden with matter, and as himself speaketh of Galba, he useth *Imperatoria brevitate*: which although it breed difficulty, yet carrieth great gravity'. Thus the words of Muretus came to partial fulfilment in recommendations to the readers of Tacitus in English, who received the sixth edition of this work in 1640.

[1] On this manner cf. Seneca, *Ep.* 100. His 'Secte nouvelle' is described in Baillet's *Jugemens des savans* (Amsterdam, 1725, ii. 195): '. . . cette manière de briser le style & de composer sans période & sans liaison, fut embrassée par ses Ecoliers avec une avidité assès peu discréte.' At best they achieved the defects of his qualities; learned 'de parler bref, de couper leur style, de ne point faire de période, & de ficher même quelques pointes & quelques subtilités au hazard'.

[2] Jonson and Bolton make Essex the author of these words. Jonson (Epigram XCV) says that Savile has rendered Tacitus 'in all his bounds, And all his numbers, both of sense and sounds'. On 'Difficilia quae pulchra' see the interesting comment of F. L. Schoell, *Études sur l'humanisme continental en Angleterre*, pp. 59–60. This Platonic dictum, which is found in the *Adages* of Erasmus, Schoell relates to an aesthetic theory which he finds in the doctrine of difficulty expressed by Chapman in his preface to *Ovid's Banquet of Senses* (1595).

When Thomas Lodge revised his translation of Seneca in 1620, he apologized to the reader for his own shortcomings:

My businesse being great, and my distractions many; the Authour being seriously succinct, and full of *Laconisme*; no wonder if in somthings my omissions may seeme such, as some whose iudgement is mounted aboue the Epicycle of Mercurie, will find matter enough to carpe at, though not to condemne.[1]

Seneca was above all 'Laconic'; to Lipsius also was attributed 'cet air Laconique'; and English rhetorics began to name, besides the three characters of style, four ancient schools—Asiatic, Laconic, Attic, and Rhodian.[2] Thus Seneca and Lipsius could be classified, among the ancient kinds, as Laconic, which included the modern *style coupé*.[3] But W. R., in his eulogy of Lodge, found other qualities to commend:

If his matter held not still the Romane Majestie, I should mistake him one of Ours; he deliuers his mind so significantly and fitly. Surely, had hee chosen any other Tongue to write in, my affection thinkes, it had beene English; And in English, as you haue taught him in your Translation; you expresse him so liuely, being still the same Man in other garments . . . retaining still the natiue grauitie of his countenance. . . .[4]

Although the praise goes to Lodge, it is for catching the qualities of Seneca, to whom he becomes the 'Senec-Sibyl (or rather Mercury) of his oraculous Discourses'. And thus Seneca emerges with qualities that are difficult to discriminate from those of Tacitus, for he, too, is succinct, majestic, grave, and oraculous; moreover, Lodge has taught him a second native language, or so it seems to W. R. in Jacobean days. Whatever the origin, whether in the pregnant brevity of Seneca or in the obscure brevity of Tacitus, the virtue of difficulty suggested gravity of style to Anti-Ciceronian ears; weight rather than *copia* now translated the Roman majesty.

While there is evidence for saying that gravity and obscurity were more commonly associated with Tacitus, and point and ingenuity with Seneca, these qualities are not very certain differentia

---

[1] *Workes of Seneca* (London, 1620): 'To the Reader.'
[2] Cf. Baillet, *Jugemens des savans* (1725), ii. 194; Thomas Farnaby, *Index Rhetoricus*, 1625 (1672, p. 43 n.); Charles Butler, *Oratoriae Libri Duo* (1629), I. ii. 3.
[3] Cf. La Mothe le Vayer, 'L'Éloquence française', *Œuvres* (Dresden, 1756), II. i. 291.
[4] *Workes of Seneca* (London, 1620), sigs. b2ʳ–b2ᵛ.

for writers who were celebrated for their succinctness. It is well to
remember such differentia, but it is more historical to accept the
general identity of the two styles as Anti-Ciceronian or fundamentally Senecan in character. In Hakewill's *Apologie or Declaration of
the Power and Providence of God*, first published in 1627, we find
a recapitulation of Savile's identification of the two styles:

> Sr *Henry Savill* sharply censures (Tacitus) for his style. . . . *Fuit illi
> viro*, saith Tacitus, (judging of *Seneca* as we may of him) *ingenium
> amaenum, & temporibus illius auribus accommodatum*: How that age was
> eared long or round I cannot define, but sure I am it yeelded a kinde of
> sophisticate eloquence and riming harmony of words; where-under was
> *small matter* in sense, when there seemed to be most in appearance, and
> divers instances he brings out of *Tacitus*. . . .[1]

These important remarks from the first English translator of Tacitus
are essentially Bacon's indictment of the Senecan fashion, which
we have examined. And this turning of the tables upon Tacitus, to
which Hakewill subscribes, emphasizes the resemblance, even in
vices, between Seneca and Tacitus as they sounded to English ears.
Particularly in the disciple Lipsius, their imitation constituted the
Senecan mode of the Renaissance.

But Croll has preferred, for appropriate reasons, to call this mode
'Attic', although he describes its rhetoric as largely Stoic. Again he
identifies, not without justification, the Stoic and the 'pointed' style,
and so mingles what Cicero describes as an Attic–Stoic and an
Asiatic style; but he neglects some of the consequences for ornament of this mixture of sententious styles. He equates 'Attic' to the
plain or essay style, and 'Asiatic' to the florid oratorical style; he
opposes them as the cult of 'expressiveness' versus the 'cult of
form'.[2] Gabriel Harvey, the erstwhile Ciceronian, has left us some
idea of this conception of Attic by so describing Philostratus, a
writer of the Second Sophistic condemned by Savile: 'His words
were not pompously affected; but Attic, emphatical, and pithy.'[3]

---

[1] *Apologie* (London, 1635), p. 285. Of course, 'long or round' refers to styles, like
Bacon's 'copious' and 'round' or *versa*. In *Rerum Anglicarum post Bedam* (1596) Savile
had also anticipated Bacon on the deficiencies of English history.

[2] Cf. ' "Attic" Prose in the Seventeenth Century', *Studies in Philology*, xviii (1921),
96 and 101 ff. The 'pointed' oratory which issued from the 'love of expressiveness' he
considers a later meaning of 'Asiatic', although it was one of the varieties described by
Cicero.

[3] *Marginalia*, ed. Moore Smith, p. 152. Said nominally of Apollonius Tyanaeus as
presented in the *Life* by Philostratus.

Thus the Atticizing Sophists could be described by the term 'Attic' just as the Stoics could mingle their virtues with the Attics for Erasmus.

But the Stoic manner in its strict character was later defined, on the authority of Cicero, by Thomas Stanley. Distinguishing between the logical and the rhetorical manner of discourse, he remarks:

> The first way was peculiar to the Stoicks, short, acute, and spinous, called likewise Logick, most worthy of Philosophy; for this useth definition, divisions, and the lights which they afford, as likewise similitudes, dissimilitudes, and the nice acute distinction of them.[1]

It is the logical requirement that determines the stricter character of Stoic style; once that is relaxed, its rhetorical virtues are simply those of the plain style. The Stoic style, with its logic retrenched and its 'point' increased, would be difficult to distinguish from the Senecan.

The suggested affiliations of the Senecan style are curiously mixed. Stoic, Attic, or terse Asiatic, one or another has been suggested by critics from Savile to Croll. It is not easy to distinguish the Attic style from the Stoic, since they merely assert different associations for the plain style. Cicero used similar terms to describe the styles of Atticists and Stoics.[2] In theory Aristotle's *Rhetoric* was important for the plain style, and so for the Stoics, whose influence established the plain ideal for philosophic style.[3] The style of the philosophers, said Cicero, is designed for instruction rather than persuasion, 'and some think they exceed due bounds in aiming to give even a little pleasure by their style'.[4] For Cicero, among plain styles, the Attic was distinguished by finish and urbanity, the Stoic by dialectic. Comparing the Stoic and the Academic or Peripatetic styles, he held that 'Stoic oratory is too closely knit and too compact for a popular audience; theirs is too free and discursive for the usage

---

[1] *History of Philosophy* (1655–62), 2nd ed. (London, 1687), p. 452. 'There are two kinds of disputation: One, when the truth it self is subtilly polished in the dispute: The other, when every expression is accommodated to the vulgar opinion.' The 'dissimilitudes' involve their antithetic rhetoric.

[2] See Cicero on the Atticists, *Brutus*, 285, 289, 291; and on the Stoics, *Brutus*, 114, 119, 120. Cf. J. F. D'Alton, *Roman Literary Theory and Criticism* (London, 1931), pp. 217 ff., 323 ff.

[3] Cf. D'Alton, pp. 69–70, 139–40.   [4] *Orator*, 63.

of court and forum'.[1] Implicitly he describes Brutus as a combination of Attic and Stoic, for Brutus has followed 'that school of philosophers in whose teaching and precepts the method of logical discussion is joined with charm and fullness of presentation'.[2] To take these schools broadly, it is the loose rather than the close philosophic style that Seneca finds in Fabianus, from whom he derived his idea of *fundere*.[3]

To the four Theophrastian virtues of style, the Stoics added a fifth virtue, brevity.[4] But making brevity a prime virtue of style brings the Stoics, willy-nilly, into possible confusion with both the Attics and the terse Asiatics, who also put a premium on brevity. All of these styles could claim some of the distinctive rhetoric of the schools of declamation, with which Croll has connected the *genus humile* or his 'Attic' style.[5] The Stoic virtues of style, as set forth by Diogenes of Babylon, were 'correctness of language, clearness, conciseness, aptness, and ornament that rose above the level of vulgar speech'.[6] Naturally, when applied to a particular style, the Theophrastian virtues of clearness, correctness, ornateness, and appropriateness were subject to definition; and the Stoic, being a plain style, was at odds with ornament, which remained its most controversial element. On this score also, as in its concern for

---

[1] *Brutus*, 120.

[2] Ibid. This school (cf. note in Loeb ed.) professed to be a revival of the Old Academy, but 'was a rather loose synthesis of Platonic, Peripatetic, and especially Stoic ideas'.

[3] *Ep.* 100.   [4] Cf. D'Alton, pp. 77, 163.

[5] See *Studies in Philology*, xviii. 119. Cf. D'Alton (p. 553): 'Even in Cicero's time, there were some who found his oratory unpalatable, and who appealed against his advocacy of rhythmical prose to the simplicity and naturalness of the Ancients. . . . But, in the age following Cicero, there was a new form of reaction against Ciceronian prose. With changed conditions there came a stirring of new impulses. The schools of declamation, where in a measure was witnessed a rebirth of the Sophistic spirit, began to set the fashion. From the speaker were especially demanded greater brilliance, pointedness, and terseness, as well as the play of paradox and epigram that would add a new sparkle to his oratory. The stateliness and formal structure of the Ciceronian period were out of harmony with the spirit of the time. The Younger Seneca found Cicero's prose too lumbering in its march, while its cadences had evidently begun to pall upon him. A taste was engendered for a style of greater pregnancy and allusiveness, a style that was more broken and spasmodic, that showed a less obvious pattern than of old, and that seemed deliberately to despise rigid syntax and fixed rules.'

[6] See D'Alton, p. 36. For G. L. Hendrickson (*AJP*, xxvi. 259) the ornament is only an avoidance of the vulgar; for C. N. Smiley (*Wisconsin Studies in Language and Literature*, iii. 52) it is a form of embellishment that rejects inaccurate or imprecise colloquialisms; for E. V. Arnold (*Roman Stoicism*, p. 149) it is 'neatness', or the Stoic 'graces of style' are 'becomingness' and 'neatness'. For Hendrickson all the Stoic virtues are designed 'to make language an *exact* vehicle of expression'.

truth rather than victory, the Stoic style came into conflict with Sophistic oratory, not less sharply because it represented philosophy.[1]

Ornament was the one Theophrastian virtue that Cicero found restricted in the Attic plain style; the others he defined in more or less Stoic terms.[2] For Quintilian all that exceeds the requirements of perspicuity and propriety may be considered ornament. As the Stoic interest in language was motivated by the need for precision as well as the desire to follow nature, their ornament may have been intended to supply deficiencies in the conversational idiom, such as the lack of neatness. In Stoic theory correctness was applied to the conversational idiom, for the plain style kept close to 'sermo cotidianus'; and, since 'to speak the truth was to speak well', appropriateness was restricted to that of word to thing.[3] The stylistic virtues, in short, were interpreted according to the Stoic end, which was to instruct (*docere*). Erasmus took a not unlike view of the Attic style when he emphasized its severity.

Seneca of course was a Stoic in philosophy, and likewise an exponent of the Stoic doctrine of style, particularly for philosophic purposes.[4] The basic doctrine for his theory of style is set forth in *Epistle* v. Language should be employed according to nature, 'secun-

[1] Basic doctrines for the Stoics which governed their theory of style were that 'to speak well is to speak the truth' and that speech as well as conduct must be in harmony with nature.

[2] *Orator*, 79. See the passage in Chap. I and cf. R. C. Jebb's summary (*Attic Orators*, i. 159): 'According to Cicero, the chief marks of the "genus tenue" are these:—1. In regard to composition—a free structure of clauses and sentences, not striving after a rhythmical period. 2. In regard to diction—(a) purity, (b) clearness, (c) propriety. 3. Abstemious use of rhetorical figures.' Jebb notes (i. 167) that Lysias deserts the character of the plain style in his delight in artistic parallelism.

[3] See G. L. Hendrickson, *American Journal of Philology*, xxvi. 258–9; and D'Alton, *Roman Literary Theory*, pp. 35–7, 69–70, 161–3. Quintilian (XII. x. 40–2) presents a Stoic view in this passage: 'Some think there is no *natural eloquence* but such as is of a character with the language of conversation . . . which is intended only to express our thoughts, and requires no foreign or elaborate ornament; they say that all that is super-added to such language is mere affectation, and vain ostentation of style, at variance with truth, and invented only with a view to a display of words, to which, they assert, the only office attributed by nature is to be instrumental in expressing our thoughts. . . . They contend that the most ancient speakers were most in conformity with nature.' Quintilian admits some foundation of truth in this argument, and concludes that we ought not to depart too far from 'exact and ordinary language'.

[4] Cf. D'Alton, *Roman Literary Theory*, p. 139; F. I. Merchant, *American Journal of Philology*, xxvi. 44–59; C. N. Smiley, *Wisconsin Studies in Language and Literature*, iii. 50–61.

dum naturam'.[1] To follow nature is to seek the 'mean'. It is contrary to nature to dispise unlaboured elegance; we may be plain and neat at the same time.[2] As elaborated in *Epistle* cxiv, the great law of style is to avoid extremes. Seneca's chief caveat against Stoic style, in which for once he agreed with Cicero, concerns the Stoic devotion to dialectics which made their style over-subtle and even obscure. His own style, which seems to conflict with Stoic doctrine, has seldom been described better than by Jortin in the eighteenth century: 'The style of *Seneca* is abrupt, concise, unconnected, and moving by leaps and bounds; quite different from the coherent style of the most approved authors, who have rounder and better-turned periods, and less sudden transitions.'[3] It is thus described by D'Alton in our time:

Seneca, in fact, embodied in his own prose many of the faults of his contemporaries. His love of short phrases, antitheses, balanced clauses, word-play, alliteration, and the jingle of similar syllables, shows how closely allied he was to the traditions of the schools. Ovid, a typical product of the rhetorical school, is for him 'poetarum ingeniosissimus'. Seneca was fond, too, of a pregnant brevity dear to certain declaimers. It was, however, above all in his love of paradox and epigram, that he showed himself a characteristic Modern.[4]

While the former is concerned wholly with structure, the latter raises the vexing problem of ornament.

Thus we come back to the question of ornament in Stoic style, on which Seneca and the Stoics have been thought to diverge. This, the main problem discussed by Smiley,[5] is important for any consideration of Senecan influence. Cicero tells us that Zeno liked to round off an argument with a simile; he describes the style of Cato of Utica as 'pointed'. But for Seneca's style the real question is whether the Stoics made use of Gorgian figures.[6] In reply Smiley

[1] The words of Fabianus, for instance, are 'nec huius saeculi more contra naturam suam posita et inversa' (*Ep.* 100. 5).

[2] Cf. *Ep.* 5. 4–5. Fabianus, again, is neither careless nor anxious in his choice of words; his style is neither elevated nor low.

[3] *Tracts* (London, 1790), ii. 337.

[4] *Roman Literary Theory*, p. 333. Fronto's word (ibid., pp. 351–2) for jingle in Seneca is 'tinnulas'.

[5] See 'Seneca and the Stoic Theory of Literary Style', *Wisconsin Studies in Language and Literature*, iii (1919), 50–61.

[6] Cf. Fronto the master to Marcus Aurelius the pupil and Stoic: 'In fact, is there one among former Emperors—I prefer to compare you with Emperors that I may not

points out that Zeno's masters, Heracleitus and Antisthenes, were both exemplars of the Gorgian style; and argues, not too cogently, that certain Gorgian figures were inevitable by-products of the Stoic dialectic. The writing of syllogisms naturally produced various kinds of parallelism and accented the tendency towards a paratactic style. Thus the Gorgian aspect of Seneca's style is not at odds with Stoic style, and Seneca 'wrote, as he professed to write, not for the ears but for the minds of men'.[1] Yet Smiley cannot call Seneca an Atticist, since 'his literary form is obviously more closely related to the Asianism of Hierocles of Alabanda, whose style Cicero characterizes as "genus sententiosum et argutum" '. This similarity poses a problem in the associations of Stoicism, and we are left in some confusion about the plain Stoic style, which may be both pointed and Asiatic.

Plutarch, however, reports that Chrysippus the Stoic 'defines Rhetoric to be an art concerning the ornament and the ordering of a discourse that is pronounced'.[2] This makes it equivalent to the third book of Aristotle's *Rhetoric*. Then he quotes Chrysippus as writing, 'And I am not only of opinion that a regard ought to be had to a liberal and simple adorning of words, but also that care is to be taken for proper delivery, as regards the right elevation of the voice and the compositions of the countenance and hands.' Whereupon Plutarch chides him for contradiction:

Yet he, who is in this place so curious and exact, again in the same book, speaking of the collision of the vowels, says: 'We ought not only to let these things pass, minding somewhat that is better, but also to neglect certain obscurities and defects, nay solecisms also, of which others, and those not a few, would be ashamed.'

Thus rhetoric for Chrysippus apparently included ornament, if modest ornament; but expression, at least in its trivial aspects, was not to concern one at the expense of more important matters. If some regard were to be given to the adorning of words, you were not, as Bacon objected, 'to hunt more after words than matter'.

compare you with contemporaries—is there one who used these rhetorical figures which the Greeks call *schemata*?' (*Correspondence*, ii. 41).

[1] Smiley, *Wisconsin Studies in Language and Literature*, iii. 60-1. Many things, no doubt, are inevitable by-products of syllogisms, but not the Gorgian figures; certainly, repeated terms provide them, if at all, on a very elementary level.

[2] 'The Contradictions of the Stoics', *Morals*, ed. W. W. Goodwin, iv. 456.

The extent to which the negligence of the Stoic might go should also be observed.

Two kinds of Asiatic style are differentiated by Cicero.[1] The first, to which Smiley refers, was the sententious and pointed, characterized less by weight and dignity than by symmetry and neatness. This type is represented by Timaeus in history, and by Hierocles and Menecles in oratory. The second was the swift and impetuous, and yet it was not merely flowing but refined and ornate in diction. This manner in Aeschylus of Cnidus and Aeschines of Miletus had rush and rhythm, but lacked elaborate symmetry of sentence. In the words of Jebb, 'Asianism oscillates between bombast and importunate epigram'.[2] Cicero remarks that Hortensius enjoyed a more brilliant reputation in his youth, when he made a cult of the pointed style of Menecles, but that in him as in the Greek the pointed phrases were rather graceful and charming than either necessary or useful. Yet, in the dialogue, Brutus admires the Asiatic Hortensius.

With this distinction in mind, let us turn to what Cicero has to say about Hegesias, who became the antithesis of Attic. In the *Brutus* (286–7), while discussing the Attics, he remarks that Charisius and Demochares are wholly unlike and yet both thoroughly Attic, and that Charisius appears to have made Lysias his model. Then he adds:

It was Charisius whom Hegesias strove to be like, and he regarded himself so thoroughly Attic that he considered the native Attic writers almost uncouth rustics in comparison with himself. But where will you find anything so broken, so minced, anything so puerile as that balance and antithesis which he cultivated?[3]

---

[1] Cf. *Brutus*, 325.

[2] Cf. D'Alton (*Roman Literary Theory*, p. 214): 'the one aiming at epigrammatic effects, at prettiness of diction, at symmetry and balance of clause, the other copious and florid, with a tendency to bombast.' Hegesias is an example of the first type, 'for he made at times puerile efforts after symmetry'. On the connexion of this 'neat' Asiatic type with the Gorgian see E. Norden, *Die Antike Kunstprosa*, pp. 138–9.

[3] Cf. Quintilian's criticism of Seneca, *Institutes*, x. i. 130. Of Lysias writes J. E. Hollingsworth (*Antithesis in the Attic Orators*, p. 43): 'The characteristic simplicity of his style, and the habitual avoidance of figures yield to his love of antithesis and parallelism. His style is not fundamentally antithetic like that of Antiphon or Isocrates. He systematically employed synonyms in developing a regular symmetry in the members of his antitheses; in this he resembled Gorgias. And Gorgianic embellishment is not lacking; it is only a secondary feature of his style however. The antitheses often further the argument and pleasantly relieve the ordinary plainness of his writing.' The Atticizing tendency of the Second Sophistic, therefore, was not without precedent for its use of the schemes, especially if we add their exaggeration by Hegesias.

If Hegesias did not succeed in being Attic, he apparently did achieve the first type of Asianism. In the *Orator* (226), while arguing for the rhythmical period, Cicero once more alludes to him: 'Hegesias perversely avoids this, and while he, too, tries to imitate Lysias, who is almost the equal of Demosthenes, he hops about, cutting his style into little fragments.'[1] This is not only a dig at the Atticists who imitated Lysias, but an insinuation about their dislike of the full periodic style. Yet again (*Orator*, 230) he returns to Hegesias: 'Some also in the vicious manner which stems chiefly from Hegesias, cutting and breaking up their rhythms, fall into an insipid style that resembles verselets.' Here we may recall that he has already condemned the style of the Sophists in similar terms. It is hard to avoid the conclusion that, however malicious, Cicero regarded the style of some of the Atticists as akin to the sententious and pointed Asiatic style, to which he ascribes Gorgian traits. He might have said as much about the Atticizing tendency of the Second Sophistic.

Among the Gorgian figures to be avoided in the plain style, according to Cicero (*Orator*, 84), is the 'studied charm produced by the change of a letter' or paronomasia. This is illustrated in his *De Oratore* (II. 256) from Cato the Censor; e.g. 'nobiliorem mobiliorem'. But it may be said that, as illustrated, Cato uses paronomasia in sharp retorts. If this makes him seem less studied, it does not relieve him of a Gorgian figure; but it does suggest how the Stoic might employ such a figure in the interest of wit, since verbal wit is the subject under discussion. Furthermore, it is this Cato that Cicero (*Brutus*, 63–9) proposes as a substitute for Lysias, the model of the Atticists; for, he begins, 'both are acute, precise, clever, brief'.[2] If the juxtaposition is ironical, the epithets in which they meet nevertheless give little promise of keeping apart such concise styles as the Attic, Stoic, or pointed Asiatic.

---

[1] Cf. his comment on Cato (*Paradoxa Intr.* 2): that in him the cult of brevity resulted in 'minutis interrogatiunculis quasi punctis'. Cf. Quintilian on Seneca, and 'Lipsius his hopping style'.

[2] Cf. Quintilian (XII. x. 39): 'Were not Scipio, Laelius, and Cato, the Attics of the Romans, as it were, in eloquence?' Cf. Erasmus on the Attic qualities in Chap. I. W. C. Summers (*Silver Age of Latin Literature*, p. 16) says: 'The fragments of a typical Roman like Cato show that Cicero was fully justified in claiming for him the title *argutus*.' Cf. *Brutus*, 65, where Cicero asks, 'Whom will you find . . . *in sententiis argutior*?' Summers (p. 15) holds that the pointed style was 'obviously adapted' to the Roman temperament and language.

The possibility of a nexus between these styles, which Cicero certainly does not contradict, explains their apparent confusion in the schools of declamation and in Silver Latin. As we have seen, Seneca can appear both Stoic and Gorgian, but not Attic; Hegesias can pretend to Atticism but achieve Asianism. And both names can balance one another in a critical proportion:

Abandoning the long periods of Demosthenes as involving too great a strain on his audience, Hegesias substituted short sentences, simple in their structure and depending for their effect on antithesis, metaphor, and play on words. He stands to Demosthenes as Seneca stands to Livy, and Macaulay to Gibbon, and the ancient critics strongly disapproved his staccato style.[1]

It is the play on words, as well as 'importunate epigram', that is not Attic. But although there are different ways of being 'acute, precise, clever, brief', all belong in some degree to the 'genus sententiosum et argutum'. And for Croll's 'Attic' this is a more appropriate *genus* than the broader *genus humile*.

In the seventeenth century the best statement of the Stoic aims in style is that given by Thomas Stanley. For the Stoics, he says on the authority of Diogenes Laertius,

There are five excellencies of speech, Propriety, Perspicuity, Succinctness, Decorum, Elegance. Propriety is a proper phrase, according to Art, not after the common expression. Perspicuity is, when that which is intended is delivered clearly. Succinctness is, when that only is comprised, which is necessary to the thing. Decorum, is a conformity to the thing. Elegance is an avoiding of vulgar phrase.[2]

Although correctness and aptness are given other names, the qualities are the same, and the definitions are illuminating. Most striking is the way in which ornament as elegance tends to merge with propriety or correctness; almost as striking is the definition of decorum or aptness solely from the demands of subject matter. In fact, the only demands that are not related to subject matter come in elegance and correctness, for which common expression does not supply the

[1] F. A. Wright, *A History of Later Greek Literature* (New York, 1932), p. 79. La Mothe le Vayer (*Œuvres*, Dresden, 1756, II. i. 233) explains the vogue of the *style coupé* by the fact that figures like antithesis and paronomasia acquire in it an unequalled brilliance.

[2] *History of Philosophy* (1687), p. 436. So 'amongst the faults of speech is *Barbarism*, a phrase not in use with the best persons; and *Solaecism*, a speech incoherently framed'. But of these Chrysippus held that the Stoic was not to be too careful.

standard, but rather the best speech according to art. Obviously, neat and elegant speech is here the Stoic definition of ornament. More than common expression, but nothing in excess of matter, is required. Chrysippus probably had no more in mind.

Now let us examine the Stoic and Senecan doctrine of style that Lipsius formulated for the Renaissance, especially in view of its currency with Hoskins, Jonson, and others. This formulation, as set down in his *Epistolica Institutio* in 1590, is found both conveniently and significantly in Castelain's edition of Jonson's *Discoveries*.[1] It was first adapted to English by Hoskins, and then borrowed from him by Jonson. The fact that it concerns epistolary style not only gives it general utility but brings it closer to moral Seneca or Bacon's model in the essay. While it particularly concerns epistolary style, it also represents the general theory and practice of Lipsius.

But its nature will be understood a little better if we recall the rhetorical range of Elizabethan Letter-writers.[2] *The Enimie of Idlenesse* by William Fulwood defines the formal letter as 'nothing else but an Oration written', and so states the conception which led to the rhetoric proper to the oration but prescribed for the letter by the Latin formularies.[3] Angel Day's *English Secretorie*, on the other hand, borrows Erasmus's definition of the letter as 'the familiar and mutual talk of one absent friend to another'. This talk reflects Erasmus's addition, in the *Modus Conscribendi Epistolas*, of the 'familiar' to the three oratorical kinds, which Day likewise employs.[4]

---

[1] *Discoveries*, ed. M. Castelain (Paris, 1906), pp. 110-16. The *Oratoria Institutio* published under the name of Lipsius in 1630 defines the three general styles and their uses; divides *elocutio* into perspicuity, ornament, and arrangement; and then relates the figures to these distinctions. The virtues of the plain or familiar style, found in letters and comedies, require that it be pointed, distinguished by frequent 'sentences', neatly disclose the recondite, be witty, dissolved, brief. Appropriate to it are these figures of words: *contentio, membrum, agnominatio, traductio*; and these figures of thought: *divisio, ratiocinatio, sententia*.

[2] See Katherine Gee Hornbeak, 'The Complete Letter-Writer in English 1568–1800', *Smith College Studies in Modern Languages*, vol. xv, nos. 3-4, chap. i; T. W. Baldwin, *Small Latine & Lesse Greeke*, vol. ii, chap. xxxviii.

[3] More properly, by the *ars dictaminis* or rhetoric of letter-writing; the formularies taught by means of specimens. Cf. C. S. Baldwin, *Medieval Rhetoric and Poetic*, chap. viii, 'Dictamen'. Preaching and letter-writing were important Renaissance as well as Medieval fields for the ancient lore of persuasion.

[4] Cf. Hornbeak, *Letter-Writer*, pp. 20-1. Cicero had said of philosophic style (*Orator*, 64): 'Consequently it is called conversation rather than oratory', though all speaking

Of course the familiar is not an oratorical kind but rather a manner or style. Between these two definitions lay the gamut of rhetoric through which the letter could run. But Day was too much concerned with the 'Oratory parts in an Epistle' to develop the final implications of his definition, though he did provide illustration in a section of familiar letters. It must be added that his 'familiar speech of the absent' recalls the famous epistolary ideal expressed by Seneca in *Epistle* lxxv.

Lipsius prescribes five qualities for epistolary style: brevitas, perspicuitas, simplicitas, venustas, decentia. The prime quality is brevity, which—with Demetrius—he thinks proper to the letter.[1] Brevity must be regarded in matter, composition, and words. 'Compositionis, ut structuram et periodum longiorem omnem fugias: membris utare, et asyndetis saepe.' To avoid all longer periods in favour of unconnected members is, of course, to be Senecan as well as epistolary. Hence perspicuity is treated as a necessary restraint upon the cultivation of brevity.[2]

Simplicity requires epistolary style to resemble conversation. Demetrius, Cicero himself, and Seneca all support this requirement.[3] 'Quod feminas ornare dicitur, non ornari: hoc epistolam', adds Lipsius, permitting himself a touch of paronomasia or word-play. Simplicity of thought appears in naturalness.[4] At this point it should be observed that although simplicity replaces correctness in the Stoic scheme, it preserves the reference to everyday speech; simplicity is the essence not only of that speech but of the plain style itself.

With another paronomasia Lipsius introduces the last two

is oratory. Day's requirements in 'framing an Epistle'—aptness, brevity, and comeliness or decorum—may be compared with those of Lipsius and Hoskins.

[1] 'Prima illa, prima mihi sermonis virtus est: adeoque epistolae propria, ut, si longior, (cum Demetrio sentio) Libri jam nomen assumat, Epistolae amittat.' Demetrius, *On Style*, provided Lipsius with a treatment of epistolary style.

[2] 'Clarè ergo scribito, si potes, et breviter, sed ita, ut hoc laudis esse scias; illud necessitatis.' Lipsius, like Seneca, stresses clearness in brevity. But the Lipsian is more Tacitean than Senecan in telescoping members or colons to phrases or commas; his elliptical members become semicolons or little more than commas in appearance, and are properly separated by semicolons rather than by commas. This is the extreme development of the 'cut' style, by which its hopping effect is intensified.

[3] 'Itaque Demetrius, ut Dialogum, Epistolam scribi vult: et ipse Cicero, "texi eam quotidianus verbis". Seneca apposité: "Qualis sermo meus esset, si una sederemus aut ambularemus, illaboratus et facilis: tales volo esse epistolas meas." '

[4] 'Nulla enim ex re magis natura cujusque et certa indole, elucet (Demetrio verè scriptum) quam ex epistola.'

qualities: 'Reliquae mihi duae virtutes, Venustas et Decentia: etsi vix reliquae.' The former derives from wit or ingenuity; the latter from judgement; both defy rules. Here *venustas* implies liveliness or neatness of expression; *decentia* is decency or appropriateness.[1] 'Venustatem appello', says Lipsius, 'cum sermo totus alacer, vivus, erectus est.' Although nature commonly gives wit, some advice may be offered: that you mix in adages, allusions, verses, or epigrams, and season with jokes or anecdotes; for these are the life and soul of letters.[2]

It is not by chance that ornament could mean for the Stoic what it meant for Cicero's description of the Attic style—wit and neat expression, or what it meant for Hoskins, 'life and sharpness'. We may recall that Aristotle's *Rhetoric* (III. x–xi) gives unusual attention to liveliness in general and epigram in particular. Here the important elements of style are metaphor, antithesis, and animation or *energeia*; the last is found in 'expressions which set things before the eyes', such as animating metaphor. 'So far as the style is concerned, it is the antithetical form that appeals to us.' The element of surprise, especially in metaphor, is also important, and extends even to plays on words. 'The liveliness of epigrammatic remarks is due to the meaning not being just what the words say'; and 'the more briefly and antithetically such sayings can be expressed, the more taking they are'.[3] But the saying is most lively if 'its wording is metaphorical, metaphorical in the right way, antithetical, and balanced, and at the same time it gives an idea of activity'. Thus

[1] For Quintilian (VI. iii. 17–21) *venustas* is one of the names of wit, defined as 'that which is said with grace and charm'; and 'brevity in wit gives greater point and speed' (ibid. 45). The Euphuistic devices of sentence, similitude, and example contribute vigour or *energia* (life and quickness) to epistolary style for Hoskins and Jonson; the *venustas* of Lipsius includes similar products of wit. On 'sharpness' or point cf. Hoskins *Directions*, p. 2.

[2] Lipsius found in Demetrius a discussion of epistolary style under the plain style, or rather as one of the hybrids. The *venustas* or charm of this style, as set forth by Lipsius, is found in Demetrius under the plain and elegant style. To the plain style in Demetrius belong especially 'vividness' and the 'persuasiveness' that depends on 'lucidity and naturalness'. To this persuasiveness may be added the virtue indicated by Theophrastus, that something 'should be left to the comprehension and inference of the hearer', whereby he 'becomes not only your hearer but your witness'. This 'something left unsaid' is the *suspicio*, hint, or allusion of Seneca; the 'intimation' of Hoskins; and a general motive to pregnant brevity.

[3] The *Rhetoric to Alexander* gives an extensive treatment of *sententiae*, distinguishing two kinds, the received opinion and the paradox. The second requires reasons to prevent incredulity; but for Aristotle it would be the smarter saying (cf. his *Rhetoric*, II. xxi).

Aristotle gives particular emphasis to the smart formulation of thought.[1] Whether such doctrine helped to define ornament for the plain style or not, it is clear that support for this definition was not lacking when wit and neatness had been part of the idea of Attic style for Cicero, when the acute and subtle Stoics had been given to the use of paradox and aphorism, or when Seneca had outdone himself in illustrating these precepts for liveliness.[2]

Decentia or appropriateness has two relations: to person and to thing. That of person is twofold: what fits yourself, and him to whom you write.[3] Appropriateness to thing requires that everything be said for the sake of argument; even the form of sentence and phrase should fit the thing described. On this form of propriety Lipsius is most specific, for it is fundamental to the Stoic subordination of expression to thought. Of course it not only excludes padding for the sake of rhythm or symmetry—in which Lysias indulged— but it severely limits the play of persuasion which makes thought agreeable to another. Thus propriety to the audience, which justified Sophistic oratory, is virtually excluded in Stoic doctrine; and here, where it has a special epistolary importance, it is barely mentioned or but scantly treated. Propriety to the writer or speaker, however, was another matter, since the Stoic insisted that the orator was 'sapiens' and 'vir bonus'; but it too is less important here.[4] In short,

[1] Hobbes's *Briefe* (III. ix–x) of Aristotle translates this doctrine into contemporary terms. Quintilian, in one of Jonson's favourite books (VI. iii), also supplied important doctrine on the kinds and uses of wit. Hoskins refers to Aristotle's *Rhetoric* and reports Sidney's translation of the first two books. In the latter half of the seventeenth century Tesauro and Bouhours translate Aristotle into their treatment of the rhetoric of wit.

[2] On the development of the idea of ornament in the plain style, and especially the Stoics' 'gradual recognition of the psychological justification of considerations of a sensuous and emotional character', see G. L. Hendrickson, 'The Origin and Meaning of the Ancient Characters of Style', *American Journal of Philology*, xxvi. 289.

[3] This division is found in Cicero's discussion of propriety (*Orator*, 70–4), from which Lipsius quotes one sentence—in Lipsius thus: 'nec immerito Cicero monuit, ut in vita, sic in oratione, nihil difficilius esse, quam quid deceat, videre'. In Cicero the discussion precedes his description of the Attic style. In Cicero's doctrine of propriety Aristotle's three kinds of artificial proof are translated from the realm of persuasion to the realm of propriety: the propriety of thought as well as language to subject, speaker, and audience. In Aristotle, where the three proofs apply to thought, the three proprieties apply to style (*Rhetoric*, III. vii).

[4] Seneca refers to the speaker as well, for language reflects the speaker, including his moral character. Cf. F. I. Merchant (*AJP*, xxvi. 47): 'Following nature is an approximation varying in degree and kind with the individual. If, then, excellence in writing depends on conformity to nature, it follows that a man's style is determined by his character. And this is what Seneca teaches . . . the style is the man.'

in this treatment of propriety, as in the Stoic interest in language, we may observe 'one of the chief aims of the Stoic theory of style, namely the use of words which precisely and exclusively correspond to the objects described'.[1]

This summary of Lipsius is limited by the text relevant to Hoskins's condensation; hence it represents Hoskins better than it does Lipsius. In fact, it makes Lipsius more Senecan than he appears in the text-book treatment of the original, where he is hampered by convention. But if this comparison gives Hoskins's English a bolder character, it does not make Lipsius himself any less Senecan. Hoskins's abstract of this doctrine 'For Penning of Letters' is both his directions for style and his antithesis to speech as oratory. Its kind simply and usefully represented the plain style; its presence is as significant in the *Directions* as the doctrine of the period is in Farnaby's *Index Rhetoricus*.

There is another aspect of Stoic doctrine, however, that involves propriety to the writer as well as to the thing, and at the same time provides a means of persuasion. This is the Stoic criterion of truth as it concerns the doctrine of clearness: 'The true mind-picture is a stirring of the soul, which reveals both what is taking place in the soul and the object which has caused this. . . . The distinctive note of a true mind-picture is its "clearness" (enargeia). . . . To this clearness the mind cannot but bow.'[2] Thus truth, the Stoic end of expression, becomes involved with the mind of the conceiver, and the vividness of any mental event becomes a measure of its persuasion.

Smiley has developed the rhetorical implication of this doctrine, which may be set forth briefly.[3] Perspicuity of an intensified sort is found in vividness or distinctness. When Zeno introduced *enargeia* as an attribute of the Stoic criterion of truth, the idea probably affected his theory of style. For in speaking of *narratio*, Quintilian (IV. ii. 117) cites the authority of Zeno for requiring that the words be distinct and imbued with sense (*sensu tincta*);[4] he translates

[1] E. V. Arnold, *Roman Stoicism* (Cambridge, 1911), p. 148.

[2] Ibid., pp. 131–2, 141 ff. This is the 'comprehension-picture'. This psychological test supports Croll's view that the Stoic way to impress the audience was 'to render one's own experience in the encounter with reality as exactly, as vividly, as possible' (*Studies in Philology*, xviii. 115–16).

[3] See C. N. Smiley, *Wisconsin Studies in Language and Literature*, iii. 52–3.

[4] Quintilian probably means that the words should be particular and expressive, even

'enargeia' as 'evidentia' or palpability (IV. ii. 63-4), and says that it is no doubt a great virtue 'when a truth requires not merely to be told, but to some extent obtruded'. Still, he thinks, it may be included under perspicuity. Thus it appears that perspicuity was projected by Zeno into vividness of style.

This virtue of style, which the Stoics associated with the psychological basis of truth, seems to be the quality that Seneca finds in the use of metaphor and simile by the ancient Roman prose writers, evidently Stoics:

> For those writers, whose eloquence was simple and directed only towards proving their case, are full of comparisons; and I think that these are necessary, not for the same reason which makes them necessary for the poets, but in order that they may serve as props to our feebleness, to bring both speaker and listener face to face with the subject under discussion (*ut et dicentum et audientum in rem praesentem adducant*).[1]

If this is only another way of being imbued with sense or of making things seen, and not the chief way, certainly metaphorical vividness is justified in the interest of subject or the obtrusion of truth; and is, as Croll has observed, one of the great resources of the essay style. This doctrine as it relates to style seems to be an extension or development of the *energeia* of Aristotle's *Rhetoric* (III. x-xi).

Quintilian develops *enargia* in his doctrine of ornament, and in a form which illuminates several passages of Renaissance rhetoric.[2] In Book VIII, where the qualities of style are specified as correctness, propriety, perspicuity, and ornament, he makes enargia (iii.

sententious; when discussing *sententia* (VIII. v. 1-2) he remarks that the older meaning of *sensus* related to the bodily senses, 'but a custom has now become prevalent of calling the conceptions of the mind *sensus*, and those striking thoughts . . . *sententiae*'. This suggests the possible range of meaning.

[1] *Ep.* lix. Seneca has just praised Lucilius for his brevity, for meaning still more than he says; and has excused his use of metaphor and simile by the example 'of our ancient prose writers, who had not yet learned to affect a style that should win applause'. No doubt it is not merely brevity but the virtue of being 'steeped with meaning' that he has in mind when he tells Lucilius, 'et plus significas quam loqueris'. Cicero, we may recall, says that Zeno liked to round off an argument with a simile; immediately before this remark in his *De Natura Deorum* (2. 22) both Cleanthes and Chrysippus are reported in arguments which conclude with similes.

[2] *Enargia* is what Cicero called *evidentia* or 'illustration'. See Quintilian (IX. i. 27, and ii. 40-4) for the relevant passage from Cicero's *De Oratore* (III. liii) and a discussion of *evidentia* as a figure, which he associates with Cicero, Seneca the Rhetor, and modern declaimers. Various elements in this discussion derive from Cicero's *De Oratore* (III. lii-liii).

61 ff.) basic to his discussion of ornament, which is defined as something added to perspicuity and propriety. Its requisites are vigorous conception and expression and a final attractiveness which is properly called embellishment. Enargia, distinctness or lively representation, is something more than mere perspicuity, and hence must be numbered among the ornaments of style.

Ornament thus includes anything that gives effectiveness to style; it is not limited to the usual sense of adornment.[1] Therefore Quintilian proceeds to emphasize vigorous expression. If perspicuity merely lets itself be seen, enargia forces itself on the attention. It is a great merit to set forth objects so that they may be seen; it is not enough to impress only the ears; hence concreteness or graphic expression is necessary. There are various means to this vividness, which is an excellence of the highest order; they include all the ways of reducing abstract or general statement to concrete or particular expression. Similes are a main resource in the lively representation of things, but as they strengthen proof they are numbered among arguments; yet even argumentative similes (v. xi) contribute to the ornament of style. Significant brevity, which comprises much in few words, is a happy contribution to vividness of style; likewise the 'emphasis' or suggestion that intimates a deeper meaning than the words actually express.[2] Of force there is more than one kind; and one of these, *energia*, has its name from *action*; its chief virtue is to keep what is said from being ineffective—a virtue that carries us back to the vividness of *enargia*.

The related chapter on external proofs (v. xi) embraces comparisons of like with like, especially examples resting on the authority of history, poetry, or fable, and *judgements* resting on similar authority. Comparison or similitude, which includes analogy, follows example in importance. Proofs of authority also include judgements

---

[1] So, too, in chap. vi of Book VIII tropes are given two functions: to add significance or force, and to provide ornament; and these functions divide tropes into two classes. In tropes used for significance 'there is also embellishment; but the reverse is not the case' (VIII. vi. 3). On 'the utmost possible significancy' as a peculiar kind of propriety see VIII. ii. 9–10.

[2] Chap. v of Book VIII is devoted to *sententiae*, and Book XII (x. 48) describes their effect very favourably: 'They strike the mind of the hearer, they frequently produce a great effect by one impulse; they impress themselves, from being short, more effectually on the memory; and they persuade while they please.' These elements of vivid expression are also found in the doctrine of Seneca.

of all sorts, maxims of poets or philosophers or other eminent persons, even proverbs or common sayings that are received as true. External proofs are artificial proofs because they must be utilized by the ingenuity of the speaker.

It is by enargia and energia that Puttenham's *Arte of English Poesie* (III. iii) explains the double efficacy of figures: the first quality gives them lustre or external appeal, the second works a stir to the mind. Hence some figures serve the ear only, some serve the conceit only, and some both. Thus Puttenham adapts Quintilian to account for a function in figures beyond mere embellishment; it is really the old division of figures of words (*enargia*) and figures of thought (*energia*). One of enargia's chief forms of expression, the similitude, crosses in Puttenham as in Quintilian from ornament to argument. In the third Book (chap. xix) we find the 'Figures sententious, otherwise called Rhetorical', which both stir the mind and adorn, or 'beautify language with eloquence and sententiousness'. Both to the poet and 'to an excellent persuader in prose, the figure of *Similitude* is very necessary, by which we not only beautify our tale, but also very much enforce and enlarge it. I say enforce because no one thing more prevaileth with all ordinary judgements than persuasion by *similitude*.' Thus it belongs to persuasion by way of amplification. Three varieties of resemblance derive from the bare similitude: the image (*Icon*), parable (*Parabola*), and example (*Paradigma*). These comparisons of like to like contribute both to ornament and to persuasion.[1]

The doctrine of ornament as found in Hoskins is even less restricted to pure embellishment, perhaps because Quintilian is even more influential.[2] After his section of figures for varying expression, there are two sections which are summarized by this sentence: 'To amplify and illustrate are two the chiefest ornaments of eloquence, and gain of men's minds two the chiefest advantages, admiration and belief.'[3] The end of amplification is to gain admiration 'by telling us it is extraordinary'. The end of illustration is to gain

[1] Similar doctrine is found in the treatise *Ad Herennium* (iv. 45–9), where similitudes are 'to be employed either for the sake of ornament or of proof or of making more clear what one is saying or of placing the matter before the eyes'.

[2] Quintilian, however, may have encouraged the aggrandizement of *elocutio*, not by his definition of oratory as 'the art of speaking well' (II. xv. 38), but by his emphasis on eloquence as the supreme achievement of the orator (VIII, introd. 13 ff.).

[3] *Directions*, ed. Hudson, p. 17.

belief 'by showing us that it is evident'.[1] Under these headings figures are grouped according to their main function. But 'division' appears under both amplification and illustration; in the former its function is to magnify, not to prove, and it involves the particularization of the general; further consideration is promised in 'the art of invention'. Under illustration it is related to logic and finds its place among logical figures; it is the 'division which logicians use'.[2] Here there are suggestions for invention and indications of the logical ways of making something 'evident'. Illustration as it involves rhetorical figures is concerned with giving life or lustre to discourse. If to illustrate means to give clarity, life, and lustre to something in order to make it evident or persuasive, illustration as ornament becomes a rather comprehensive term.[3]

Such a doctrine of ornament, which is 'rhetoric' for Bacon, is exemplified in varying degrees by Puttenham and Hoskins; it is related to Quintilian and the doctrine of *enargia* or *evidentia*, which had a Stoic value. It is present in the meaning of *venustas* for Lipsius, which exceeds but does not contradict the conception of ornament that is proper to the Stoic view. The animation of *energia* is, as Quintilian saw, another form of the vividness which exceeds perspicuity but is not mere embellishment. In fact, Quintilian merely uses two terms for what Aristotle included under *energeia* (*Rhetoric*, III. xi), and the other term is probably coloured by Stoic use. The qualities of style for Quintilian are the same as those required by Aristotle, with greater difference in the definition than in the content of ornament. The only quality that separates the Stoics from either is brevity, to which both Aristotle and Quintilian make tacit subscription.

[1] On presenting images to the imagination Quintilian (VI. ii. 32) remarks: 'Hence will result that *enargeia*, which is called by Cicero *illustration* and *evidentness*, which seems not so much to state as to exhibit; and our feelings will be moved not less strongly than if we were actually present at the affairs of which we are speaking.'

[2] Cf. L. Osborn, *Hoskyns*, p. 275; variant for p. 137.

[3] It is not the restrictive doctrine of the Ramistic Thomas Horne, *Rhetorices Compendium, Latino-Anglice* (1648, 1651), p. 39: 'To help the invention of learners, who may adorn a discourse, by drawing it through the several Tropes or Figures.' For Horne (p. 26) the logical places are both 'very helpful for understanding the Tropes in Rhetoric' and 'very useful to help invention' of matter. A logical analysis of the tropes had been suggested for metaphor by Aristotle in *Poetics*, 21. For logical analysis metonymy is made to order: see John Smith's analysis of that trope, *Mysterie of Rhetorique Unveil'd* (1665), pp. 11 ff.

Lipsius's requirements for epistolary style, and especially those which he emphasizes, may be compared with the qualities he found in Seneca and desired in himself. But just as Lamb has found an antithetic and a loose style in Lysias and Thucydides, or the contemporaries of Lipsius found in him both clipt and flowing effects, so Croll has found a curt and a loose style in the Anti-Ciceronians deriving from Seneca. These he analyses in detail in 'The Baroque Style in Prose', where his baroque analogy lends undue weight to 'deliberate asymmetry' of form.[1] Their differences must now engage our attention.

The characteristics that Croll assigns to the curt style or *style coupé* and its typical sentence are as follows: short members; an associative rather than a logical order; asymmetry of members in length and form; the omission of syntactic ties. They derive from or are related to a co-ordinate or appositive grouping of members.[2] The loose style and sentence, though related to the curt, is marked by greater length of member and group, a loose use of connectives, an emergent order with an unforeseen syntax (the curt shows artful compression), and a dislike of formality.[3] This style employs both the co-ordinate and the complex structure of members, but, unlike the curt, is not obliged to begin with the main idea.[4] Its order derives from thought, not rhetoric, to which the curt is more indulgent. While retaining the lax structure of the curt, the loose moves away from the discrete and abrupt aspects toward connexion and rhythm. It may, as in Browne, move far enough to achieve an orotund effect within a looser form which suggests the period, though its progress

[1] See *Studies in English Philology*, ed. Malone and Ruud, pp. 427–56.

[2] In its hopping or discontinuous mode of progression, members may be connected by *and*, *or*, *nor*, and still be in the curt style because the conjunction has no logical force, but merely connects two efforts to realize the same idea.

[3] Croll enumerates these syntactic links for the loose style: the loose co-ordinating conjunctions, the absolute-participle construction, the parenthesis. These all permit a free, emergent development. While the loose style uses relatives and subordinating conjunctions for logical progression, it loosens their rhetorical connexion—usually indicated by disjunctive punctuation. It may be added that the present participle splices 'a loose organization into a semblance of continuity'; it may substitute for a co-ordinating verb in a compound predicate. This co-ordinating use derives from its appositive use. These means do not connect a premeditated form, but produce a linked or trailing period by successive proliferation.

[4] The loose style favours the co-ordinate form to the extent of treating subordinate structure in a similar fashion; for even with relative pronouns and subordinating conjunctions it 'relaxes at will the tight construction which they seem to impose' (Croll, *Baroque Style*, p. 445).

is not cumulative but culminative. While the two styles are essentially the same, the loose modifies the traits of the curt so as to produce a more flowing speech, appropriate to the forum rather than to the arena. At bottom Senecan style is the development of thought by an analytic rather than synthetic arrangement of members.

Croll's analysis, of which this is a modified summary, gives us a more subtle account of the Senecan style than that which satisfied the contemporaries of Lipsius. If you take Croll's summary of the curt style as basic for his analysis of Senecan style, and then compare it with the contemporary descriptions already given, you can perceive the difference. That summary, in Croll's words, includes four marks of the curt style: 'first, studied brevity of members; second, the hovering, imaginative order; third, asymmetry; and fourth, the omission of the ordinary syntactic ligatures.'[1] Or you may compare it with another description given by Croll to illustrate one variation of the curt style. He quotes Balzac, 'De Montaigne et ses Escrits', on the imitation of Seneca:

Nous demeurasmes d'accord que l'Autheur qui veut imiter Seneque commence par tout et finit par tout. Son Discours n'est pas un corps entier: c'est un corps en pieces; ce sont des membres couppez; et quoy que les parties soient proches les unes des autres, elles ne laissent pas d'estre separées. Non seulement il n'y a point de nerfs qui les joignent; il n'y a pas mesme de cordes ou d'aiguillettes qui les attachent ensemble: tant cet Autheur est ennemy de toutes sortes de liaisons, soit de la Nature, soit de l'Art: tant il s'esloigne de ces bons exemples que vous imitez si parfaitement.[2]

The lack of connexions is here the primary feature, but various consequences are suggested. For example, if in Balzac's words the imitator of Seneca 'commence par tout et finit par tout', in Croll's scheme he puts the main idea first and follows it by various realizations of the idea. They are the same consequence of a *coupé* style. But not all of Croll's distinctions are so easily derived from this primary feature.

Croll, however, directs our attention to Balzac's style, which he calls Anti-Ciceronian:

But by several means, and chiefly by the kinds of repetition illustrated in this passage (*c'est . . . ce sont; il n'y a point . . . il n'y a pas mesme; tant . . .*

[1] *Studies in English Philology*, ed. Malone and Ruud, p. 435.
[2] Ibid., p. 438; *Entretiens* XVIII.

tant), he succeeds in introducing that effect of art, of form, of rhythm, for which Descartes and so many other of his contemporaries admired him. He combines in short the 'wit' of the seventeenth century with at least the appearance of being 'a regular writer', which came, in the forties and fifties, to be regarded in France as highly desirable.[1]

This mixed effect has been described by Guillaumie with a different conclusion:

C'est dans *Sénèque* que Balzac a puisé l'habitude de ces jeux d'esprit, de ces raccourcis vigoureux d'expression, de ce style à facettes, où l'antithèse, constamment renouvelée, permet à l'idée de s'avancer par gradations savantes, jusqu'à un dernier choc de mots, où elle s'arrête enfin, lumineuse et définitive. C'est à l'école de Sénèque que Balzac a pris l'habitude de la phrase courte, qu'il a su associer à la période cicéronienne, par un jeu raffiné de symétries et d'oppositions, qui font de lui un des plus grands artistes de la prose française.[2]

Guillaumie is discussing here the subject 'De l'antithèse à la pointe', to which his first statement refers; the question raised by his second statement is treated in his chapter on harmony.[3] There, while discussing grammatical symmetry or verbal parallelism, he quotes the passage from Balzac on the necessity of 'liaisons'—the connexions by which Balzac built, with the aid of Gorgian symmetry, the 'phrase courte' of Seneca into the Ciceronian period. Thus Balzac's 'liaisons' are found to be something more than Croll's 'reiterated introductory formula', by which symmetry is introduced only to be broken.[4] Guillaumie suggests not only how an antithetic style advances but how it may be built into the period.

It is not amiss to recall that symmetry is associated with Seneca in the description quoted from D'Alton. It should be added that he recognizes in the Senecan manner a 'tendency towards obscurity, and at times towards a studied asymmetry', but also that it was Tacitus 'who learned to exploit its potentialities to the full'.[5] And

---

[1] Ibid., p. 439. But these are the means to symmetry, with which Balzac is obviously concerned.

[2] Gaston Guillaumie, *J. L. Guez de Balzac et la prose française* (Paris, 1927), p. 455.

[3] There he considers various elements of Gorgian symmetry in Balzac: antithesis, parison, isocolon, paromoion, and the like. For expressiveness also the parallelism of ideas is made apparent by verbal parallelism. But he is especially concerned with rhythmic symmetry and cadence.

[4] Ibid., p. 475.

[5] J. F. D'Alton, *Roman Literary Theory*, pp. 334, 553.

Croll himself once found balance the principle in Seneca. In short, it is in Tacitean rather than Senecan imitation that Croll's 'asymmetry' should arrive at the dignity of a principle. The 'hopping' of Lipsius, for example, suggests the more extreme appositive style of Tacitus, which is more elliptical than Seneca's, less given to balanced phrasing, more like Sallust as described by Seneca.

But—to return to Balzac's statement—if a 'cut' style is likely to produce the traits enumerated by Croll, even the metaphor in the contemporary phrase 'Lipsius his hopping style' may suggest most of them. Indeed these traits are implicit in a 'hopping style': the members are hops in size, and hopping in their discontinuous movement. Discontinuity is the essence of a hopping style: it includes the lack of connectives, the broken effect, the abruptness, the quickness, the lack of coherence in order.[1] To begin with the main idea does not promote coherence; but it does promote brevity as well as speed, because it permits elliptical development, which may or may not defeat symmetry. To make a sentence out of a succession of epigrams, and yet preserve unity, is to make successive statements of the same idea; if there is any movement, it must be in the variation; if there is any rise in emphasis, it must derive from increasing vividness of statement. Thus studied brevity, hovering order, asymmetry, and lack of connexion may all be consequences of hopping from one facet of the idea to another, or of the characteristic mode of progression. But where the Lipsian 'hop' stresses the discontinuous movement, the Senecan 'amble' stresses the antithetic movement; and yet both movements can meet in one, as Shakespeare knew, for 'the skipping king, he ambled up and down'.[2]

Desire for speed of communication, for returns on one's time, is sufficient to explain most of these effects. What prompts Montaigne to say that he would have Cicero 'begin at the last point', with the conclusions, is impatience with his long-winded style. 'To confess the truth boldly', says Montaigne, 'his style of writing appears to me tedious, like the style of others that resemble him.'[3] No doubt a craving for dramatic effect could be added to this desire. 'I like reasons', Montaigne adds, 'that charge at once into the heart of the

---

[1] The omission of connectives is often an effort to condense; participial constructions are a common way of effecting this economy.

[2] See *I Henry IV*, III. ii. 60.

[3] *Essays*, bk. II, chap. x, 'Of Books'.

question; his keep on feebly beating about the bush.' And there you have the Anti-Ciceronian feeling and suggestions of its consequences for style. The Anti-Ciceronian wanted his sentence to be unlike the period of Cicero—not to put off conclusions, but to begin at the last point. And this is reason enough for brevity and inverse Ciceronian emphasis, for preferring the hopping style to the periodic, for imitating the 'succinct Lipsian Lecture'.

Montaigne himself, who was annoyed by the ceremony of Cicero —'what there is of pith and marrow is smothered by these lengthy dressings', not only reinforced the example of Lipsius but provided another model of Anti-Ciceronian style. Of this model Gustave Lanson remarks:

Montaigne makes his style speak like himself. That is why he does not mould his form to the rhythms of Cicero and Livy, too solemn and not lively enough. That is why he voluntarily gathers into it the turn and antithesis of Seneca, the massed turns which give nerve to a style.[1]

The result, says Lanson, is that he is enabled, by the contour of his sentence, to register all the sallies and somersaults of his thought, his humour, his accent. Thus Montaigne created in French the subjective phrase, the dramatic sentence of a mind thinking, or what Croll calls Libertine or 'loose' prose.

We may observe in Jacobean style a parallel to the movement which Lanson remarks in Rabelais and Montaigne: that it oscillates between the antithetic nervousness of Seneca, who groups ideas in vibrant oppositions, and the periodic amplitude of Cicero, who displays them in large patterns; that it combines the two manners and injects sharp sentences into moving perorations.[2] But Jacobean style also relaxed the formal architecture of the oratorical period in the interest of subjectivity just as it renounced Ciceronian parade in the interest of point. Yet it turned between these two poles. These rhetorical manners suggest the wit and *gravitas* that Shaftesbury found in Seneca, or the wit and magniloquence that T. S. Eliot finds in the seventeenth century.

[1] *L'art de la prose*, p. 49.
[2] Ibid., p. 39. These are the two manners with which Bacon found it necessary to deal.

6. *Bacon and Stoic Rhetoric*

Seneca, when he spoke of style, always preferred things to words—a bias which the seventeenth century remembered to his credit. And Bacon, the chief native critic of prose style, was among the first to sound the seventeenth-century preference for things rather than words. That is the burden of his attack on Ciceronian style in 1605: 'the whole inclination and bent of those times was rather towards copie than weight'.[1] This Renaissance delight in style was furthered, as Erasmus had suggested, by hatred of the schoolmen, 'whose writings were altogether in a different style and form'.[2] That form was related to their method of crumbling knowledge into subtle distinctions and 'vermiculate questions':

so that as was said of Seneca, *Verborum minutiis rerum frangit pondera* (that he broke up the weight and mass of the matter by verbal points and niceties); so a man may truly say of the schoolmen, *Quaestionum minutiis scientiarum frangunt soliditatem* (they broke up the solidity and coherency of the sciences by the minuteness and nicety of their questions).[3]

If this was another way of preferring 'copie' to 'weight', the reproof might be extended to the Senecan style; what was deplored in method was deplorable in style.

In the essay 'Of Seeming Wise' Bacon applies the remark about Seneca to those who 'are never without a difference, and commonly

[1] *Advancement of Learning*, Everyman ed., p. 24.

[2] In style they sacrificed Ciceronian qualities to a concern for exact brevity, 'taking liberty', says Bacon, 'to coin and frame new terms of art to express their own sense, and to avoid circuit of speech, without regard to the pureness, pleasantness, and, as I may call it, lawfulness of the phrase or word' (ibid., p. 23).

[3] Ibid., pp. 26–7; *Philosophical Works*, ed. J. M. Robertson (London, 1905), pp. 55–6. The remark about Seneca comes from Quintilian, x. i. 130. Bacon continues after a similitude: 'And such is their method, that rests not so much upon evidence of truth proved by arguments, authorities, similitudes, examples, as upon particular confutations and solutions of every scruple, cavilation, and objection.' When Bacon discusses method he declares that 'another diversity of method, which is likewise of great weight, is the handling of knowledge by assertions and their proofs, or by questions and their determinations'. The latter method, which is likely to be 'prejudicial to the proceeding of learning', is the method criticized in the schoolmen.

by amusing men with a subtilty blanch the matter'. But this comparison, which again associates the Senecan defect with subtlety at the expense of matter, does not imply that Senecan style is less appropriate to philosophy than Ciceronian rhetoric. The same problem of propriety occurs in Erasmus's discussion of Ciceronian versus scholastic style; there the Ciceronian rejects the style of Sir Thomas More because it 'tends rather to Isocratic structure and dialectic subtlety' than to the *copia* of Ciceronian eloquence. The work of Nizolius, who became an epithet for Sidney, represents this quarrel between Ciceronian and scholastic style. While the *Advancement of Learning* brings us once more face to face with the feud between philosophy and rhetoric as it affects style, Cicero himself had made it quite clear that among ancient philosophers the Stoics compromised least with rhetoric.

When Bacon makes the first disease of learning an affected study of eloquence and copiousness of speech, he promptly damns the Ciceronian cult:

This grew speedily to an excess; for men began to hunt more after words than matter; more after the choiceness of the phrase, and the round and clean composition of the sentence, and the sweet falling of the clauses, and the varying and illustration of their works with tropes and figures, than after the weight of matter, worth of subject, soundness of argument, life of invention or depth of judgment.[1]

In short, they sought all the resources of elocution and neglected those elements which were provided by Bacon's first two intellectual arts, Invention and Judgement. This opposition of words and matter may be said to separate the rhetorical from the logical in his four intellectual arts. The stylistic elements belong to what he calls rhetoric or 'illustration' in his Art of Tradition. Of this 'first distemper of learning, when men study words and not matter', he has 'represented an example of late times'.[2]

Nearly twenty years later he adds another example, the Senecan cult, presumably of still later times. The passage need not be quoted again. Aside from its historical importance, it simply places in the rhetorical vanity the same tendency to subtlety in excess of matter

---

[1] *Advancement of Learning*, Everyman ed., p. 24, or pp. 23–5.
[2] Pygmalion's frenzy supplies him with a good emblem of this vanity: 'for words are but the images of matter; and except they have life of reason and invention, to fall in love with them is all one as to fall in love with a picture'.

that he had criticized in the dialectical method of the schoolmen, and by means of the objection to Seneca. Thus Bacon recognized that matter or things could suffer from the Senecan defect either in method or in style. But so far as this style was guilty of unjustified 'point' rather than *copia* it was a little more healthy, *paulo sanius*.

'Yet notwithstanding', Bacon continues in 1605, 'it is a thing not hastily to be condemned, to clothe and adorn the obscurity even of Philosophy itself with sensible and plausible elocution.' His great examples of such eloquence include both Seneca and Cicero. 'If a man be to have any use of such knowledge in civil occasions, of conference, counsel, persuasion, discourse, or the like; then shall he find it prepared to his hands in those authors which write in that manner' —that is, the rhetorical manner. And to illustrate obscurity, as we shall see, is an admissible use of rhetoric even in philosophical style.

But eloquence as a hindrance to progress in philosophy—'because it is too early satisfactory to the mind of man'—is augmented by two of the peccant humours of learning. The first 'is the over early and peremptory reduction of knowledge into arts and methods':

knowledge, while it is in aphorisms and observations, it is in growth: but when it once is comprehended in exact methods, it may perchance be further polished and illustrate and accommodated for use and practice; but it increaseth no more in bulk and substance.[1]

This methodizing involves an error in the manner of delivery, 'which is for the most part magistral and peremptory, and not ingenuous and faithful; in a sort as may be soonest believed, and not easiliest examined'. One should 'propound things sincerely with more or less asseveration, as they stand in a man's own judgment proved more or less'.[2] The fact that time has found Bacon to be 'magistral' suggests why these two humours, which anticipate some of the matter in Book II, have their connexion with style.

Yet, although the schoolmen may have sacrificed style to thought, and the Ciceronians thought to style, that is not the real issue for Bacon; he is concerned with the end of discourse, whether it looks toward the progress of knowledge or the use of knowledge. While the advancement of learning has been hindered both by the rhetoric of the Ciceronians and by the dialectics of the schoolmen, the logical

[1] *Advancement*, Everyman ed., p. 32.　　　　[2] Ibid., p. 34.

vanity of the latter is akin to the rhetorical vanity of Seneca rather than of Cicero. Here the hindrance concerns a subtilizing, not a methodizing, rhetorical procedure; it begins to pose a problem of style that turns upon the functions of logic and rhetoric as defined by Bacon.

In matters of style Bacon's first and chief distinction is that eloquence is a hindrance to the advancement of learning, but not to the use of learning. It is from this point of view that he condemns both the Ciceronian and the Senecan cult of style, for both set words above matter or rhetoric above philosophy. The relation of words to matter—'for words are but the images of matter'—is brought to a focus by his four intellectual arts. As he introduces these arts in the *De Augmentis Scientiarum* he makes reason the soul of discourse and words its body. Among the arts themselves reason is covered by the first two, Invention and Judgement; words or discourse is covered by the last, Tradition; and the results of invention and judgement are preserved for delivery by the third, Memory.[1] The last two arts involve other faculties besides reason: memory of course is involved in the third, and imagination in the fourth.

When we follow thought from discovery to expression we pass through the acts in which Bacon's four rational arts originate. For the arts of invention, judgement, memory, and expression arise from the acts of finding thought, judging its validity, keeping it for use, and communicating it. The invention of speech and argument, which is not true invention for Bacon, properly belongs to memory, and includes commonplaces and topics.[2] While topics provide a method of exploring the memory for arguments, commonplaces provide a digest of arguments and expressions; the former are proper to logic, and the latter appropriate to rhetoric. Under memory a digest of commonplaces appears again as its chief aid; under 'illustration' or rhetoric, the third part of Tradition, commonplaces receive extended treatment. There sophistic arguments, otherwise treated under Judgement, appear as 'colours', which involve effec-

[1] Ibid., pp. 122 ff. In the introduction to Book II (ibid., p. 66) he says that logic and rhetoric, 'rightly taken, are the gravest of sciences, being the arts of arts; the one for judgment, the other for ornament: and they be the rules and directions how to set forth and dispose matter'.

[2] Cicero, commenting on Stoic oratory in *De Oratore* (II. xxxviii), says that the Stoics were addicted to logic, which gives 'no rule for the invention of truths, but only how to discern them by judgment'.

tive forms of expression.[1] Commonplaces have an aspect of form
and style that does not belong to logic; they can provide *copia* as
well as argument, both 'furniture of speech and readiness of
invention'.

The two ends of learning, when related to these arts, result in
two different kinds of discourse. Bacon allows the term 'invention'
to be used for discourse only on condition that it be recognized
'that the scope and end of this invention is readiness and present
use of our knowledge, and not addition or amplification thereof'.[2]
Real invention produces an addition to matter, not to the images
of matter; words can amplify matter only in the rhetorical sense, but
therein lies their danger for philosophy. The method or organization
of discourse can point either to the advancement or to the use of
knowledge: 'Neither is the Method or the nature of the tradition
material only to the use of knowledge, but likewise to the progression
of knowledge.'[3] Hence the basic diversity of method: 'And therefore
the most real diversity of method, is of Method referred to use, and
Method referred to progression: whereof the one may be termed
Magistral, and the other of Probation.' As he admitted particular
topics—'being mixtures of Logic with the matter of sciences'—so
he admits particular methods of tradition, lest 'multiformity' of
matter be sacrificed to 'uniformity' of method. It is necessary to
know not only what subjects require persuasion, and what require
demonstration, but also the kind of argument required by different
subjects. The kinds of discourse proper to the basic diversity are
called Aphorisms and Methods, and will be considered in due
course.

The Art of Elocution or Tradition has three parts: the organ, the
method, and the illustration.[4] His discussion of the organ, which
includes more than words, is interesting chiefly for its possible suggestions to the Royal Society, especially in connexion with a 'Real
Character'.[5] His discussion of method, however, is related to his

---

[1] Hoskins remarks (*Directions*, p. 22) that division—his second way of amplification—
'Bacon in his fifth "color" took out of the rhetoricians'. In *De Augmentis* it is the twelfth
sophism or colour, but still expresses the sophistic idea that multiplicity of parts is a
sign of greatness.

[2] *Advancement*, Everyman ed., p. 127.

[3] Ibid., p. 140.   [4] Ibid., pp. 136 ff.

[5] Here he notes (pp. 137–8) as particularly worthy of inquiry both 'characters real,
which express neither letters nor words in gross, but things or notions', and are of wider

objection to Ciceronianism, since method affects the character of style. 'The doctrine of Method containeth the rules of judgment upon that which is to be delivered; for judgment precedeth Delivery, as it followeth Invention.'[1] This kind of invention, says Bacon, is 'but a remembrance or suggestion, with an application'; under memory he adds that 'the disposition and collocation of that knowledge . . . consisteth in a good digest of commonplaces . . . which assureth copie of invention, and contracteth judgment to a strength'.[2] By this means judgement may be concentrated on the problem of application, which is primarily a question of method.

Although Bacon moved method from Judgement to Elocution, he continued to think of it as judgement rather than disposition. Under Judgement, of course, method would be related to the kinds of demonstration; for it is of great moment to know when to require the more severe proofs and when to be content with the more remiss proofs. 'The application of the differing kinds of proofs to the differing kinds of subjects' depends upon the 'four kinds of demonstrations, that is by *the immediate consent of the mind or sense*, by *induction*, by *syllogism*, and by *congruity*' or analogy.[3] In method these would entail an order as well as form of statement, of induction, of deduction, and of analogy.

The fundamental diversity of method, pointing to the use of knowledge or to the progress of knowledge, involves the delivery of knowledge as it may be best believed (the Magistral way) and as it may be best examined (the way of Probation). Since knowledge is now delivered as it may be best believed, not as it may be best examined, 'there is a kind of contract of error between the deliverer and the receiver', because the deliverer does not reveal and the

acceptance than the languages which employ them; and also a philosophical grammar 'examining the power and nature of words, as they are the footsteps and prints of reason', or the analogy between words and things.

[1] Ibid., p. 140. Ramus treated method under Judgement, and in the problem of method Bacon is very much aware of Ramus. He observes that 'it hath moved a controversy in our time' and that 'Method hath been placed, and that not amiss, in Logic, as a part of Judgment'. Under the diversities of method he inadvertently introduces one by saying, 'Another diversity of judgment', but corrects it in the Latin text.

[2] Ibid., pp. 127, 135.

[3] Ibid., p. 135. On the relation of Methods to Ramist logic see George Hakewill, *An Apologie* (1635), bk. III, chap. ix, sect. 1. He declares that the logic of the Schoolmen has been reduced to essentials, and the doctrine of Methods added or developed, thereby increasing its utility.

receiver does not inquire how the knowledge was derived.[1] This is the way of persuasion and the oratorical style; the way of probation and the philosophical style is quite different, for 'knowledge that is delivered as a thread to be spun on, ought to be delivered and intimated, if it were possible, *in the same method wherein it was invented*; and so is it possible of knowledge induced'. Thus in the inductive method invention and disposition coincide; the consequence for philosophical style is that matter ought to pass from invention to delivery with the least possible alteration by rhetoric. This method to 'so transplant it into another as it grew in his own mind' provides a basis for the essay style as well as for probation.[2] In the Magistral way, which merely elaborates the results of inquiry, one cannot see the thought grow, for it has been 'polished and illustrated and accommodated for use and practice'.

The consequence of this diversity is another diversity of great importance for style—'the delivery of knowledge in Aphorisms, or in Methods'. Here Bacon begins by observing that 'it hath been too much taken into custom, out of a few Axioms or observations upon any subject to make a solemn and formal art; filling it with some discourses, and illustrating it with examples, and digesting it into a sensible Method; but the writing in Aphorisms hath many excellent virtues, whereto the writing in Method doth not approach'.

For first, it trieth the writer, whether he be superficial or solid: for Aphorisms, except they should be ridiculous, cannot be made but of the pith and heart of sciences; for discourse of illustration is cut off; recitals of examples are cut off; discourse of connexion and order is cut off; descriptions of practice are cut off; so there remaineth nothing to fill the Aphorisms but some good quantity of observation: and therefore no man can suffice, nor in reason will attempt, to write Aphorisms, but he that is sound and grounded. But in Methods,

Tantum series juncturaque pollet,
Tantum de medio sumptis accedit honoris

[1] *Advancement*, Everyman ed., p. 141. Here Croll (*Studies in English Philology*, ed. Malone and Ruud, pp. 441–2) uses Bacon's sentence to support the asymmetrical tendency of Anti-Ciceronian prose. But antithetic symmetry is still the most striking aspect of the sentence, although it is neither Ciceronian in progression nor inductive in method, for the conclusion comes first. 'Symmetrical development' is often encountered in the sentences of Bacon.

[2] Book II of the *Advancement of Learning* exhibits the great Ramistic method of division, proceeding from the most general to the most particular, but with less sacrifice of the multiformity of matter to the uniformity of method.

(the arrangement and connexion and joining of the parts has so much effect), as a man shall make a great shew of an art, which if it were disjointed would come to little. Secondly, Methods are more fit to win consent or belief, but less fit to point to action; for they carry a kind of demonstration in orb or circle, one part illuminating another, and therefore satisfy; but particulars, being dispersed, do best agree with dispersed directions. And lastly, Aphorisms, representing a knowledge broken, do invite men to enquire farther; whereas Methods, carrying the shew of a total, do secure men, as if they were at furthest.[1]

The implications for expression and its effect are fundamental; in criticism they appear in his remarks on Senecan style—its aphorisms are not solid; or on the Stoics—their aphorisms are not fit to win consent. But the contrast in general suggests the Stoic Zeno's distinction between logic and rhetoric, 'the one close, the other at large'; and on the level of expression the parallel is not invalid.[2]

Translated to sentences, 'a kind of demonstration in orb or circle' might characterize the Ciceronian period as well as Ciceronian discourse. Though not by intention, Bacon has pointed to the basic diversity between Ciceronian and Senecan style or discourse; in both aspects it is a contrast between the continuous and the discontinuous. Certainly, writing in aphorisms, which relies upon nothing but content, approaches the method of inducing knowledge; and the Senecan style, which is given to aphoristic expression, ought to be less guilty of the 'contract of error between the deliverer and the receiver'. Here, of course, Methods present knowledge as it may be best believed, and Aphorisms as it may be best examined, with a view to future inquiry.[3] The way of probation is not one of the methods of persuasion; rather it belongs, with aphorisms, to induction and the essay style.[4]

[1] *Advancement*, Everyman ed., p. 142; *Works*, ed. Robertson, p. 125. Note (Ev. 135) 'congruity, which is that which Aristotle calleth *demonstration in orb or circle*'—by which Bacon means analogy. Dr. Johnson, according to Boswell, once expressed the bias to which Bacon and Montaigne were inclined: 'I fancy mankind may come, in time, to write all aphoristically, except in narrative; grow weary of preparation, and connection, and illustration, and all those arts by which a big book is made.'

[2] This contrast is supported by Quintilian's statement (II. xx. 7) of the Zeno position: 'there are two kinds of speech, therefore, the *continuous*, which is called *oratory*, and the *concise*, which is termed *logic* (which Zeno thought so nearly connected that he compared the one to a clenched fist, and the other to an open hand) . . .'. To Ramus also the difference was chiefly in the manner of expression.

[3] Cf. *De Augmentis*, VI. ii.

[4] In connexion with methods Bacon once contemplated a larger discussion of style

Another diversity of method which ought to be noticed is that according to subject matter; 'for there is a great difference in delivery of the Mathematics, which are the most abstracted of knowledges, and Policy, which is the most immersed'.[1] Machiavelli, for example, is praised for his form of writing in an 'immersed' subject; 'namely, discourse upon histories or examples. For knowledge drawn freshly and in our view out of particulars, knoweth the best way to particulars again.'[2] In general, uniformity of method is detrimental to learning—the way to reduce it to barren generalities. Likewise, if the subject matter is new or beyond popular opinion, it must be understood before it can be argued, and therefore one must resort to simile and metaphor; 'for it is a rule, That whatsoever science is not consonant to presuppositions, must pray in aid of similitudes'.[3] Elsewhere Bacon remarks that 'it is not a thing so easy as is conceived to convey the conceit of one man's mind into the mind of another without loss or mistaking, specially in notions new and differing from those that are received'.[4] This justifies the use of simile in the philosophical style. After such evidence of concern with the problem of communication, these diversities of method should not be ignored in any consideration of Bacon's theory and practice of style.

Bacon had introduced the intellectual arts by observing that the rational part of human philosophy

is of all knowledges, to the most wits, the least delightful; and seemeth but a net of subtilty and spinosity. . . . So generally men taste well knowledges that are drenched in flesh and blood, civil history, morality, policy, about the which men's affections, praises, fortunes do turn and are con-

(*Valerius Terminus*, cap. 18): 'That the very styles and forms of utterance are so many characters of imposture, some choosing a style of pugnacity and contention, some of satire and reprehension, some of plausible and tempting similitudes and examples, some of great words and high discourse, some of short and dark sentences, some of exactness of method, all of positive affirmation, without disclosing the true motives and proofs of their opinions, or free confessing their ignorance or doubts, except it be now and then for a grace, and in cunning to win the more credit in the rest, and not in good faith.' These 'characters of imposture' belong to the rhetorical style, not to the style of probation, which demands both intellectual and formal candour.

[1] *Advancement*, Everyman ed., p. 143.
[2] Ibid., p. 186.
[3] Ibid., p. 144. Cf. his remarks on the use of parable in the preface to *The Wisdom of the Ancients*: 'And every man, of any learning, must readily allow that this method of instructing is grave, sober, or exceedingly useful, and sometimes necessary in the sciences, as it opens an easy and familiar passage to the human understanding, in all new discoveries that are abstruse and out of the road of vulgar opinions.'
[4] *Valerius Terminus*, cap. 18.

versant; but this same *lumen siccum* doth parch and offend most men's watery and soft natures.[1]

It is this fact of human nature that limits the power of the intellectual arts, though they are the keys of all other arts; it is this fact that gives rhetoric its power, 'though in true value it is inferior to wisdom'.[2] In the art of elocution, although method belongs to logic, illustration belongs to rhetoric and enjoys the advantage of the less abstract knowledges, to which method must also accommodate itself. Of the accommodation of method to the relative abstractness or concreteness of subject matter we have already taken notice.

'The duty and office of rhetoric', says Bacon, 'is to apply reason to imagination for the better moving of the will.'[3] This definition involves the three powers and arts which concern the rule of reason: reason itself, which pertains to logic; imagination, which pertains to rhetoric; and will or affection, which pertains to morality. Men are wrought and undermined by these powers: by the cunning of reason, by the importunity of imagination, and by the vehemency of passion. Imagination solicits 'by impressions or observations'. By this definition, then, reason uses rhetoric for a moral or civil end, not being able to achieve it directly because of the nature of the affections. When the moving of the will is not involved, logic alone suffices. The end of these arts is not to disturb reason but to establish and advance it, and Bacon proceeds to demonstrate this function in rhetoric.

Plato was wrong to consider rhetoric 'a voluptuary art', because it has a psychological function. And Bacon uses Plato himself to prove it.

And therefore as Plato said elegantly, *That virtue, if she could be seen, would move great love and affection*; so seeing that she cannot be showed to the sense by corporal shape, the next degree is to show her to the imagination in lively representation: for to show her to reason only in subtilty of argument, was a thing ever derided in Chrysippus and many of the Stoics; who thought to thrust virtue upon men by sharp disputations and conclusions, which have no sympathy with the will of man.[4]

When rhetoric supplies lively representation it is not filling a voluptuary function. Logic alone cannot affect the will of man; it requires

---

[1] *Advancement*, Everyman ed., pp. 121-2.   [2] Ibid., p. 146.   [3] Ibid., pp. 146 ff.
[4] Ibid., p. 147. Stoic rhetoric fails in a rhetorical function because it is too logical. Yet for philosophy Bacon agreed with Chrysippus in subordinating words to matter.

the aid of imagination, and this is necessitated by the nature of the affections. For they are not pliant and obedient to reason, but are governed by immediate impressions and observations, which fill the imagination and frequently conflict with reason. But rhetoric by its power over imagination can make the 'remote appear as present' and so impose the ends of reason upon the affections or will. Rhetoric thus becomes a mediating art by virtue of its control over a mediating power.[1] Thus Bacon shows why 'naked proposition and proofs' are insufficient where the will is involved, since they have no direct power over the affections. The power of imagination in this psychology is crucial to Bacon's conception of rhetoric and the place of style therein.

But logic and rhetoric differ also in their use of reason.

It appeareth also that logic differeth from rhetoric, not only as the fist from the palm, the one close, the other at large; but much more in this, that logic handleth reason exact and in truth, and rhetoric handleth it as it is planted in popular opinions and manners. And therefore Aristotle doth wisely place rhetoric as between logic on the one side, and moral or civil knowledge on the other, as participating of both: for the proofs and demonstrations of logic are towards all men indifferent and the same; but the proofs and persuasions of rhetoric ought to differ according to the auditors.

Thus they differ not merely in a closer or looser form of language, but also in kind of argument, or the bases of argument; popular reasons owe their force to associations with the will of man. Rhetoric not only adds imagination to reason, or provides an imaginative form of reason; it also employs another sanction for reason, the sanction of popular belief and habit. In a right use of rhetoric reason should not only be true in itself, but supported by 'popular opinions and manners'; this is the persuasive form of reason.

The adaptation of speech to audience, however, has been insufficiently pursued, since it applies to individuals as well as to classes.[2] In 'this politic part of eloquence in private speech' even

---

[1] Imagination (cf. p. 120) is a mediating power because it is a messenger between sense and reason and reason and will; reason is separated from will by imagination, and hence its importance to reason where will is concerned.

[2] If this criticism is prompted by Aristotle, it is not justified by him. For Aristotle an art, such as rhetoric, deals with generals. Bacon may have Plato or Quintilian (II. xxi. 4) in mind: 'In the *Phaedrus* he plainly shows that oratory has place, not only in judicial proceedings and political deliberations, but also in private and domestic matters.' It certainly has place in Bacon's architecture of fortune.

orators are deficient: they are so committed to 'well-graced forms of speech' that they lack adaptability. But here Bacon seems to be moving from the realm of persuasion to the realm of propriety.[1] He says that this application 'ought to extend so far, that if a man should speak of the same thing to several persons, he should speak to them all respectively and several ways'. If he intends the varying of argument as well as the varying of language, he seems to neglect the former, which provided his point of departure. No one was more conscious than Bacon of the force of Cicero's remark on the propriety of words: 'Although a word has no force apart from the thing, yet the same thing is often either approved or rejected according as it is expressed in one way or another' (*Orator*, 73). Here Bacon is concerned with the defect of formal speech for the informal occasions of persuasion, with the difference that obtains between the oration and the familiar letter.

Under policy, where this deficiency may also be placed, he discusses the kind of argument appropriate to such occasions. In ancient times men collected prudential wisdom in the form of parable, aphorism, or fable. But fables merely supplied the lack of historical examples. 'And therefore the form of writing which of all others is fittest for this variable argument of negotiation and occasions is that which Machiavel chose wisely and aptly for government; namely, discourse upon histories or examples.'[2] Here at last 'variable argument' is made explicit. Parable, aphorism, fable, and example are proper sources of argument in the art of 'prudential conversation', but they are also the kinds of illustrative proof that Quintilian associated with *enargia* or effective vividness.

Bacon's conception of rhetoric is given point by what he has to say elsewhere about imagination. Since rhetoric uses imagination

---

[1] In language the relation to the audience is for Aristotle an aspect of propriety (*Rhetoric*, III. vii), not of proof. The persuasive force of style derives from the contribution which language makes to the object of the speaker through the pleasure of the audience.

[2] *Advancement*, Everyman ed., p. 186. Bacon has been engaged in making some brief observations on the 'sentences politic of Salomon', which 'might have received large discourse', he says, 'if I would have broken them and illustrated them by deductions and examples'. One example receives an Anti-Ciceronian turn that is found in Montaigne: '*Melior est finis orationis quam principium*. Here is taxed the vanity of formal speakers, that study more about prefaces and inducements, than upon the conclusions and issues of speech' (p. 183). Thus Bacon suggests how Aphorisms may be turned into Methods.

to a rational end, the function of imagination in rhetoric may be compared with its function in 'Poesy Parabolical', which is directed by a rational purpose. Of course the poetic power of imagination lies in the fact that it is 'not tied to the laws of matter': in respect to matter, poetry is 'feigned history'; in respect to words, 'a character of style'.[1] But parabolic poetry as applied narrative is largely a character of style, 'for that tendeth to demonstrate and illustrate that which is taught or delivered'; at most, it is an imaginative form of argument. Parables still 'retain much life and vigour; because reason cannot be so sensible, nor examples so fit'. Recall the power of rhetoric 'to clothe and adorn the obscurity even of Philosophy itself with sensible and plausible elocution',[2] and you will observe the persuasive addition to reason that imagination makes in rhetoric and parabolic poetry.

In this function of imagination 'sensible' is a key word; in representation hieroglyphics have the advantage over letters. Thus in the field of expression or imagination the power of creating images has a large place:

For we see that, in matters of Faith and Religion, we raise our Imagination above our Reason; which is the cause why Religion sought ever access to the mind by similitude, types, parables, visions, dreams. And again, in all persuasions that are wrought by eloquence, and other impressions of like nature, which do paint and disguise the true appearance of things, the chief recommendation unto Reason is from the Imagination.[3]

Its analogical power is important where logical statement is impossible; and in persuasion or similar impression, which alters the appearance of things, the chief appeal to reason derives from imagination. Hence the faculty of rhetoric is 'Imaginative or Insinuative Reason', or a rational use of imagination like that in parabolic poetry. Such is the work as opposed to the play of imagination, for here imagination performs a useful function. If the matter of rhetoric is rational, reason acquires a large part of its efficacy in rhetoric from the character of style in which imagination clothes it—from 'sensible and plausible elocution'. While rhetoric is to the imagination what

---

[1] *Advancement*, Everyman ed., pp. 82–3. In the Latin text lyric poetry is turned over to philosophy and the arts of speech as having its source in reason.

[2] Ibid., p. 25. If 'it is not good to stay too long in the theatre' (p. 85) it is because of our susceptibility to the 'idols of the theatre' (*Nov. Org.* i. 62).

[3] *Advancement*, Everyman ed., p. 121. These, too, are 'not tied to the laws of matter'.

logic is to the understanding, imagination is the special power of reason in rhetoric. Here, speaking of imagination, Bacon is concerned with the effect of eloquence; later, speaking of rhetoric, he is concerned with the cause of eloquence. In rhetoric as a cause imagination is subject to the direction of reason; in rhetoric as an effect it is not.

Bacon's definition of rhetoric as the 'illustration of tradition' or the 'doctrine of ornament' is not Aristotelian;[1] nor is it merely stylistic. It involves all that may be added to bare argument or logic in order to make it persuasive, including the turn or shape of the argument itself; ornament is not decorative, but persuasive; it is, or gives, a persuasive form of proof. Hence the office of rhetoric is to illustrate reason by imagination for the better moving of the will. The function of tropes and figures as imaginative means to the moving of the affections, even as persuasive forms of proof, is sometimes forgotten in our conception of the so-called stylistic rhetoric; but is never forgotten, for example, by Hoskins. Even in its most ornamental aspect, for varying expression, stylistic rhetoric presupposed the necessary concern for invention and disposition. Part of Erasmus's ridicule of the Ciceronians was that they began with elocution and invented afterwards, found meaning for fine phrases; not that they ignored invention, but overrated elocution. For Bacon the power of rhetoric to create illusion, especially by means of images in the fancy, derives from the imagination, which shapes things to the mind of man where reason bends the mind to things. And this power was recognized in the rhetorics, but most completely, in Bacon's terms, by Quintilian.

Quintilian (VI. ii. 29–33) presents the basic doctrine on moving the feelings by presenting images to the imagination. Since our feelings are not in our own power, by what means can we be affected? Images have this power. Their effectiveness depends upon imagination—the lawless faculty of the mind which in day-dreaming makes images so real that we confuse thinking and acting. By applying reason to imagination Quintilian would turn this power to advantage in rhetoric. 'Whosoever shall best conceive such images, will have the greatest power in moving the feelings.' The result will

---

[1] Ibid., p. 146; cf. the Latin text. Aristotle's *energeia*, however, defines the ways of expression that bring an image to the mind.

be 'that *enargia*, which is called by Cicero *illustration* and *evidentness*, which seems not so much to state as to exhibit'. Hence the utility of illustrative proof from example and similitude (v. xi) and all the concrete means which, as Seneca remarked, bring us face to face with the subject under discussion. Enargia moves the feelings for Quintilian; it supports truth for the Stoics;[1] for both it has a psychological basis.

Though unnamed, enargia has its place in Bacon's doctrine of illustration—likewise founded upon a psychological basis—for he, too, would have elocution 'sensible', or *sensu tincta*, and endowed with 'lively representation'. The place of enargia in ornament is elaborated, as we have seen, by Quintilian in Book VIII. Ornament as conceived in that book was illustrated by Erasmus's collections of sentences, similitudes, and examples;[2] and Quintilian's conception of ornament gave elocution as found in Hoskins and Bacon a significance beyond embellishment. Thus illustration, the more comprehensive term, includes *evidentia* and defines the relation of imagination to rhetoric for Bacon.

The rhetorical function of imagination emerges for Bacon in the problem of style offered by Stoic moral instruction. He agrees with Plato that if virtue could be seen, she would be loved; but since virtue cannot be seen, lively representation must be substituted.[3] This is to realize why, as Quintilian said in discussing enargia, 'it is a great merit to set forth the objects of which we speak in lively colours, and so that they may as it were be seen', and why similes 'are adapted to give a lively representation of things'.[4] This problem centres attention upon the function of rhetoric as illustration; but the nature of the will or affections of man explains its necessity.

Finally, in the consideration of rhetoric, Bacon descends to its deficiencies.[5] These are not the deficiencies of rhetoric for philosophic style—the rhetorical hindrances to the advancement of learn-

---

[1] Quintilian (IV. ii. 117) connects it with the Stoics when he says, 'every word ought to be expressive, and, as Zeno says, tinctured with perception (*sensu tincta*)'.

[2] *De Copia Verborum ac Rerum* was based on Quintilian's introduction to that book; cf. T. W. Baldwin, *Small Latine & Lesse Greeke*, ii. 182.

[3] Bacon probably derived this Platonic idea not from the *Phaedrus* but from Cicero's *De Finibus* (II. xvi. 52), which raises the problem of rhetoric in the Stoics.

[4] *Institutes*, VIII. iii. 62 and 72. See Bacon's remarks on emblems in the *De Augmentis*, v. v.

[5] *Advancement*, Everyman ed., pp. 148 ff.

ing particularized in the cult of style, the delivery for belief, or the rhetorical form of deceptive completeness. Rather they are various collections which he has already suggested as useful to rhetoric. There is 'a collection of the popular signs and colours of good and evil'; a collection of *antitheta* or '*theses* argued *pro et contra*'; and a collection of *formulae* or appropriate phrases for recurrent situations.[1] In the Latin text the first two are illustrated by collections of his own making; the third is best represented by his *Promus of Formularies and Elegancies*, although that work is something more.

Antitheta in the Latin text are treated as 'the places of common use, whether for proof, confutation, persuasion, dissuasion, praise or dispraise'. In this compilation Bacon finds himself anticipated by Cicero and Seneca the Elder, and we may extend the anticipation by remarking that his collections are related to the scheme of Seneca's *Oratorum et Rhetorum Sententiae, Diuisiones, Colores*. For this furnishes counterparts to Bacon's colours, antitheta (*sententiae*), and 'lesser forms' (formulae), which are related to divisions; it could be added that his colours are related to the *Suasoriae* and his antitheta to the *Controversiae*.[2] In antitheta the arguments should be 'cast up into some brief and acute sentences; not to be cited, but to be as skeins or bottoms of thread, to be unwinded at large when they come to be used; supplying authorities and examples by reference'. But the editors of Bacon's *Essays* have found his own 'sentences' frequently cited therein, and their suggested use may remind us how 'aphorisms' were developed rhetorically for Bacon. Both uses were observed by Quintilian.[3]

In the *De Augmentis* (VI. iii) Bacon enlarged his criticism of Aristotle's conception of topics—'for their use is not only in probation, but much more in impression'—by incorporating his own 'Colours

---

[1] Formulae, including those of *dispositio*, have a prominent place in Farnaby's *Index Rhetoricus*. In Hoole's *New Discovery* formulae are related to *dispositio*: 'in what order they are to dispose the Parts, and what Formula's they are to use in passing from one to another'; cf. T. W. Baldwin, *Small Latine & Lesse Greeke*, ii. 292.

[2] Plutarch (*Morals*, ed. Goodwin, iv. 434) reports that Chrysippus the Stoic allowed such antitheta, if used with caution, to dissolve the probability of contrary arguments; and that the Stoics themselves affirmed that Carneades said nothing but 'those arguments which Chrysippus alleged for the contrary opinion'. Plutarch regards Chrysippus as something of a sophist, if superior to the schools of declamation.

[3] *Institutes*, v. xi. 36 ff., and VIII. v. On the place of maxim in rhetoric see Bromley Smith, 'Some Rhetorical Figures Historically Considered', *Quarterly Journal of Speech*, xx. 16–29; Farnaby, *Index Rhetoricus* (1672), pp. 21 ff.

of Good and Evil', published with the *Essays* in 1597.[1] This addition included the doctrine which explained these 'appearances of good and evil, and their degrees as places of persuasion and dissuasion', as well as Aristotle's failure to conceive 'a part of the use of them'. Bacon had already observed that 'many forms are equal in signification which are differing in impression'; now he calls these colours the 'stings and goads of speech', and proceeds to differentiate their functions as probation and as impression.[2]

Persuasion, argues Bacon, 'may be performed by true and solid reasons, or represented by colours, popular glosses, and circumstances of such force as to sway an ordinary judgment; or even a wise man that does not fully and considerately attend to the subject.' This distinguishes the use of 'popular signs' from the use of 'true and solid reasons'. There is, however, another aspect of rhetorical colours, not to be confused with their probative use:

> But besides this power to alter the nature of the subject in appearance, and so lead to error, they are of use to quicken and strengthen such opinions and persuasions as are true; for reasons nakedly delivered, and always after one manner, enter but heavily, especially with delicate minds; whereas, when varied and enlivened by proper forms and insinuations, they cause a stronger apprehension, and often suddenly win the mind to a resolution.[3]

Here they perform the function of impression by virtue of their form—different expressions of the same essential reason; the power to employ apparent reasons is replaced by the power to vivify true reasons. Here they illustrate the 'doctrine of ornament in speech' not by deceiving the reason but by impressing the imagination.[4]

---

[1] Gibert criticizes Bacon's appendixes to rhetoric, declaring that for such aids there is no other repertory but a good mind, that Aristotle has foreseen sufficiently the requirements of refutation, that Bacon's samples are only commonplaces treated probably, that Aristotle did not fail to see that 'turned in a certain fashion, they serve to move' as well as to prove, for he has ignored nothing that serves to excite the passions. Gibert summarizes Bacon's view of rhetoric as follows: 'Il avouë que l'Art Oratoire parle à l'imagination'; that one abuses it either to disguise the truth or persuade the bad; finally, that it moves the passions. Cf. Baillet, *Jugemens des savans* (Amsterdam, 1725), viii. 237–8.

[2] Popular signs or reasons derive their impressiveness from an appeal to experience or general knowledge. Forms of expression vary the power of reasons to please and affect. Bacon illustrates the same idea or reason expressed in different popular or proverbial forms.

[3] This emphasizes again the shortcomings of 'naked proposition and proofs' as well as the virtue of varied style.

[4] The persuasive function of figures is indicated by Thomas Wright in *The Passions*

Earlier, under the Art of Judgement and in connexion with sophisms, Bacon mentions the seducement of reason by the strength of the impression or imagination, but postpones its discussion as proper to rhetoric.[1] He then treats the fallacies or 'false appearances' imposed on us by his famous 'Idols'—as yet incomplete. Those of the market derive particularly from words, and are only to be corrected by exact definitions.[2] Rhetoric, however, has a power of distortion that can be put to beneficent use.

Colours create 'appearances' either for reason or imagination, and so embrace the rhetorical modes and figures from argument to ornament. The familiar battery of sentence, similitude, and example is implicit in these requirements, and is copiously illustrated in his *Promus of Formularies and Elegancies*. Similitude or analogy supplied the images by which reason could employ appearance in his rhetorical theory and practice.[3] These 'resemblances' have become the stamp of wit which associates him with his time, even as he constantly associated time with a river. Analogy is related to colours as a kind of proof, to parable as a kind of discourse, to simile or metaphor as a means to conception; it is the imaginative means to impression. Similitude also leads to one universal science or *philosophia*

of the minde in generall (1604 ed., pp. 192–3): 'Thirdly, our reasons should be largely declared, and yet with sharpe, and short varietie interlaced: resembling a volley of shot speedily delivered, but not without bullets to batter downe the walles of wilfull affections. And for this cause we may use pithie short descriptions, compounded of some metaphor annexed with some proprietie, which is most usuall with orators: as *Cicero* commendeth histories: for saith he, Histories are the witnesses of times, the light of truth, the life of memorie, the mistress of life, the messenger of antiquitie, &c. so may we in like manner describe man to be a shadow of pleasure, a glorious flower, a fading rose, an unsatiable appetite, a circle of fancies, a running river, a mortall angell, a reasonable beast, a vitious monster declining from his nature, &c. Many similitudes or disimilitudes, examples, contrarities, effects repugnant, may easilie be invented, readily delivered, and in a moment understood; so that by this meanes profound conceit shall be facilitated, and therewith the auditors instructed, delighted, and moved.' Thus tropes and figures secure the ends of rhetoric.

[1] *Advancement*, Everyman ed., p. 132.

[2] *De Augmentis* adds terms of art as a remedy.

[3] It was related to his fourth kind of demonstration, by *congruity*; it underlay myth as he saw it in the *Wisdom of the Ancients*. See his preface to the *Wisdom* on the use of analogy when minds were 'unpractised in matters of subtilty and speculation, or even impatient, and in a manner uncapable of receiving such things as did not directly fall under and strike the senses. For as hieroglyphics were in use before writing, so were parables in use before arguments. And even to this day, if any man would let new light in upon the human understanding, and conquer prejudice, without raising contests, animosities, opposition, or disturbance, he must still go in the same path.' For this is essentially the rhetorical situation.

prima: 'Neither are these only similitudes, as men of narrow observation may conceive them to be, but the same footsteps of nature, treading or printing upon several subjects or matters.'[1] How the faculty of seeing resemblances may be developed is suggested in the essay 'Of Studies': 'if he be not apt to beat over matters, and to call up one thing to prove and illustrate another, let him study the lawyers' cases.'[2] Sentences provide another collection in 1625, the *Apophthegms New and Old*, bearing further witness to the sententious tendency in Bacon. Apothegms add the salt of wit, but they may serve the same functions as aphorisms and antitheta.

Certainly they are of excellent use: they are Mucrones Verborum, pointed speeches. Cicero prettily calls them salinas, salt pits, that you may extract salt out of, and sprinkle it where you will. They serve to be interlaced in continued speech: they serve to be recited upon occasion of themselves: they serve, if you take the kernel of them, and make them your own.[3]

He could have added that they may serve even as the staple of discourse, for he had called such discourse 'aculeate', and Hoskins had anticipated his charge. Clearly they are places of wit as well as places of argument.

Bacon's separation of the aspects of proof into the different functions of probation and impression is not unlike the separation made by Farnaby. But Farnaby's division of proofs, although supported by Aristotle, is not Aristotelian in its division of labour: proofs that turn on belief (*Fidem*) are probation; proofs that turn on affection (*Affectus*) are amplification.[4] Farnaby points his divergence by remarking that Cicero comprehends amplification under elocution.[5]

---

[1] *Advancement*, Everyman ed., p. 87.

[2] On the place of the figures of similitude in rhetoric see Bromley Smith, 'Some Rhetorical Figures Historically Considered', *Quarterly Journal of Speech*, xx. 24–9.

[3] See Preface. Quintilian (VI. iii. 17–21) defines *salsus*, one of the varieties of wit, as 'a simple seasoning of language, a condiment which is silently appreciated by our judgment'.

[4] *Index Rhetoricus* (London, 1672), p. 21.

[5] Ibid., p. 23. '*Cic. de Orat. comprehendit Amplificationem sub Elocutione.*' For probation he cites Quintilian, v. xi; for amplification Quintilian, VIII. iv; 'Eras. lib. de copia rerum' appears for both. Cf. Aristotle on amplification as argument, *Rhetoric*, I. ix. and II. xxvi. Obadiah Walker (*Instructions for Oratory*, 1659, sect. vi), following Quintilian, includes amplification under elocution or 'Ornaments of Speech'; this section, according to Walker (p. 24), deals with 'the several *figures*, and *modes* of livelier and more passionate expression'.

The means of proof are enthymeme, example, or induction by enumeration, but he notes that *Exempla illustrant, potius quam probant*; the kinds of amplification are those enumerated by Quintilian, and found in Hoskins together with 'division' from Bacon.

Now Bacon's colours are probation in the first sense and amplification in the second: as they turn on belief they are true or sophistic; as they turn on affection they are more or less forceful. As amplification the colours depend upon imagination to give them affective form, both from words and from things; as probation they make use of common opinion. Cicero's *De Oratore*, which includes in Book III both the *amplificatio* and the *elocutio* of Farnaby,[1] also represents the larger doctrine of ornament or illustration found in Quintilian and Bacon. For his collections Bacon may have in mind Cicero's 'magazine of materials', looking especially to the exaggeration and extenuation of *amplificatio*, as well as his general topics of argument or 'theses argued *pro et contra*', already cited in the art of invention.[2] For antitheta also, in the *De Augmentis*, are to be 'exaggerated or degraded with the utmost effort of genius', even beyond all measure of truth, and thus given the aspect of amplification, or greater force as 'impression'. In short, the forms of amplification are involved both in colours and in antitheta.

Likewise Bacon's conception of rhetoric as illustration or ornament is not unlike that of Hoskins, who appears to write of *elocutio* but involves persuasion. For him the functions of varying, amplifying, and illustrating expression have different ends, which are delight, admiration, and belief respectively.[3] He probably has in mind Cicero's three ends of rhetoric, to please, to move, and to prove; but figures will not divide that neatly. For him amplification impresses or causes admiration; illustration makes evident or induces belief.[4] Division, his second way of amplification, is taken from

---

[1] Ibid., p. 25. For Farnaby *elocutio* consists in elegance, composition, and dignity. *Dignitas* requires ornate, apt, and varied expression; the tropes and figures supply ornateness. Yet the *schemata sententiae* are classified according to the ends they serve: explication (which includes *enargia*), probation, amplification, excitement, or fullness. Elegance and dignity derive from the requirements of style: elegance from purity and perspicuity; dignity from ornateness and propriety. Composition concerns the arrangement of words from euphony to periodology.

[2] Cf. Cicero, *De Oratore*, III. xxvi–xxvii; *Orator*, 46.

[3] Cf. *Directions*, ed. Hudson, pp. 12, 17, 42.

[4] Figures and their effectiveness are related to these ends. Comparison as a way of amplification involves similitude. Amplification in reverse is called diminution.

Bacon's *Colours*, where it also appears as 'a way to amplify anything'.[1] When Hoskins says that Bacon took this colour out of the rhetoricians, he probably has Quintilian in mind, for he proceeds to illustrate this method of amplifying 'according to several circumstances' in a way that recalls Quintilian on enargia.[2] But where this way of amplifying statements such as 'he put the whole town to the sword' led to vivid representation for Quintilian, it has for Hoskins effects belonging to several functions, including the aspect of proof, or his concern with division under illustration.[3] If to amplify by circumstance was the way to lively representation for Bacon as well as Quintilian, amplification was also the way to impression for Hoskins. Thus the 'ornaments of eloquence', no less than proofs, may turn on 'admiration and belief', or so affect men's minds.

Bacon's attitude towards rhetoric is most sharply defined by his criticism of the Stoic deficiency in rhetoric. In the *De Augmentis* this criticism is not limited to 'many of the Stoics', but applies to all. He then declares that virtue must be shown 'to the imagination in as lively representation as possible, by ornament of words':

For the method of the Stoics, who thought to thrust virtue upon men by concise and sharp maxims and conclusions (*concisis et argutis sententiis et conclusionibus*), which have little sympathy with the imagination and will of man, has been justly ridiculed by Cicero.[4]

If 'concise and pointed sentences' were before implied in 'sharp disputations and conclusions', they are now made explicit; but are still involved in the logical method of the Stoics, which makes no appeal to the imagination. The Stoics do not use rhetoric 'to fill the imagination to second reason', so as to move the will in favour of virtue; they make no attempt 'to procure the affections to obey reason'. If the theory of 'lively representation' suggests the enargia of the Stoics, it should be remembered that Quintilian had developed enargia not in connexion with Stoic truth, but in relation to the affections; not as a vivid perspicuity, but as affective speech. Thus

---

[1] *Directions*, p. 22. When Hoskins adds that this way does not 'betray itself in method and order' but 'rather adorneth itself', he misrepresents Bacon, who actually says that order weakens its power of amplification.

[2] Cf. *Institutes*, VIII. iii. 67 ff.; *Directions*, pp. 22 ff.

[3] His conception of illustration seems to make Cicero's '*illustratio et evidentia*' involve proof in the act of making clear or evident. Of course, 'distinctness' appears to have had persuasive value for the Stoics.

[4] *De Augmentis*, VI. iii.

the similitude of enargia had a different function for each; for the Stoics it did not belong to the 'ornament of words'. And it did not belong to that category for Bacon when learning 'prayed in aid of similitudes'; then it resembled the use made of simile and metaphor by the early Roman or Stoic writers.[1]

To use Cicero for authority is not without its irony, though not uncommon with Anti-Ciceronians; but the allusion is to *De Finibus*, where it is argued that the playing with words found in Stoic syllogisms is powerless to convince or fortify: 'Would those concise epigrams which you say give you so much pleasure make any man alter his opinions?'[2] The Stoics, declares Cicero, neglected rhetoric.[3] Cato had said: 'This principle might be amplified and elaborated in the rhetorical manner, with great length and fullness and with all the resources of choice diction and impressive argument; but for my own part I like the terse and pointed syllogisms of the Stoics.'[4] This preference reminds us of the quarrel between philosophy and rhetoric; and the alternative that is rejected by Cato was not embraced by Bacon, who described it as Methods and denounced it as Ciceronian. Nevertheless, rhetorical occasions demand rhetorical speech, and a purely logical appeal is insufficient to change the will. It is noteworthy that Cato's contrast does not involve any such distinction, but rather Zeno's contrast of the fist and the palm, 'the one close, the other at large'.[5]

[1] See Seneca, *Ep.* 59.

[2] *De Finibus*, IV. xix. 52; see esp. xviii and xix. Particular criticism is made (IV. xxvii. 74) of Stoic paradoxes, which prove not to be 'startling truths', and of Stoic similitudes or analogies, which prove to be false (75-6). These are common devices of Stoic dialectics. Later (IV. xxviii. 78) censure is made of the uncouth terminology and 'asperities of style' of the Stoics, which Panaetius strove to ameliorate.

[3] Ibid. IV. iii. 7; cf. IV. xxviii. 78-9. It is true, admits Cicero, that Cleanthes and Chrysippus wrote rhetorics, 'but they furnish a complete manual for anyone whose ambition is to hold his tongue; you can judge then of their style, coining new words, discarding those approved by use'. The Stoics are more likely to extinguish than to arouse enthusiasm. Even their maxims are bald rather than 'neatly rounded off'. 'Their meagre little syllogisms are mere pin-pricks; they may convince the intellect, but they cannot convert the heart, and the hearer goes away no better than he came.'

[4] Ibid. III. vii. 26.

[5] Cf. Thomas Baker's view at the other end of the century (*Reflections upon Learning*, 1700, p. 54): 'The Logic in use among the Romans was rather a sort of Rhetoric than Logic. . . . It was first borrowed from the Stoics, who were in vogue at Rome, before Aristotle was much known there; and their Logic having been rather Specious than Solid, as consisting much in pomp of words, and in giving plausible colours to improbable things, was best fitted to that People, who were little farther concerned for that Art, than as it was of use in point of Eloquence. And tho Cicero takes in Aristotle, especially

As Bacon qualified the Stoic Zeno's definition of rhetoric by the more adequate one of Aristotle, so he found occasion to compare Aristotle and the Stoics on the affections. Under moral knowledge, as it belongs to moral culture, he criticizes Aristotle for including knowledge of the nature of man in rhetoric rather than in ethics, to which it essentially pertains.[1] Although rhetoric participates in moral knowledge, it is not concerned with the affections themselves but with the means of moving them by speech, a function of the imagination. For Bacon the participation of rhetoric in both logic and moral or civil knowledge is made possible by imagination, which mediates between the powers of the two realms. If rhetoric handles reason 'as it is planted in popular opinions and manners', it does so through the office of imagination, which finds its materials in this more concrete or 'immersed' knowledge. It is in recognizing these materials that Aristotle surpasses the Stoics for Bacon; his matter has greater sympathy with the will of man, though his topics neglect 'impression'.

Bacon allows that the Stoics probably paid more attention to the affections than Aristotle, who handled them only in a collateral capacity, not as they relate to ethics.[2] 'But yet it is like it was after their manner, rather in subtilty of definitions (which in a subject of this nature are but curiosities) than in active and ample descriptions and observations.' Thus it is the Stoics rather than Aristotle who were concerned with the passions in their proper place, but with the wrong method; the right method is not logical definition, but observation and description, which provide more effective know-

in the Topical part, that has most affinity with Rhetoric, yet it is plain, he has likewise followed the Stoics, tho it was not reputable enough to be own'd.'

[1] *Advancement*, Everyman ed., pp. 169–72. Moral knowledge relates to the appetite and will of man, and in this field these things have been neglected: 'the several characters of natures and dispositions'; the manners which are determined by nature or by fortune; the infirmities of mind that derive from the affections; the factors within our control that affect the will or appetite and alter manners. This is the inquiry into man, rather than nature, that his *Essays* pursue; this is the knowledge which they try to reduce to precept.

[2] Ibid., p. 171: 'And yet in his Rhetorics, where they are considered but collaterally, and in a second degree, as they may be moved by speech, he findeth place for them, and handleth them well for the quantity; but where their true place is, he pretermitteth them.' Thomas Wright had attempted a wider treatment of the affections, including both their rhetorical and their ethical aspects. In *The Passions of the minde* (1604 ed., p. 4) he considers the various purposes to which a study of the passions may contribute, referring to Aristotle in connexion with rhetoric.

ledge. Bacon concludes that the poets and historians, who follow the better way, are 'the best doctors of this knowledge',[1] which is essential to moral persuasion but futile without affective speech. In rhetoric Aristotle fails to treat the chief means; in ethics the chief end; the Stoics mistake the means in the former, but not the end in the latter.

But in moral inquiry Bacon condemns those who 'have compounded sciences chiefly of a certain resplendent or lustrous mass of matter, chosen to give glory either to the subtilty of disputations, or to the eloquence of discourses'.[2] This disposes of both the schoolman and the Ciceronian. Eloquence no less than logic can defeat the end of such discourse. 'But', he adds, 'Seneca giveth an excellent check to eloquence; *Nocet illis eloquentia, quibus non rerum cupiditatem facit, sed sui* (eloquence does mischief when it draws men's attention away from the matter to fix it on itself).'[3] On the detection of sophisms, Bacon likewise refers to Seneca's comparison of sophistry to juggler's tricks, by which he had criticized the wiredrawn ingenuity of Stoic dialectics.[4] It is significant of Seneca's position that Bacon should turn to him, despite his style, when considering manifestations of the two distempers of 'vain words' and 'vain matter'. Although Seneca was a Stoic, Bacon could not charge the Stoics with erring on the side of eloquence; and despite any subtlety, Seneca did not share their fault of logic.

There is some reason to believe that the problem of Stoic rhetoric, and indeed of the relation of rhetoric to philosophy, may have been focused in Bacon's mind by Cicero's *De Finibus*. In that work the proper style of philosophy is a recurring issue, and both Stoic and Peripatetic rhetoric are subjected to criticism. In Book II Cicero begins by adopting the dialectical rather than the rhetorical mode of discussion, specifically the Socratic method; but he is presently stopped by objections from the Epicurean, who exclaims, 'Why, just as if continuous discourse were proper for orators only, and not for

---

[1] *Advancement*, Everyman ed., p. 172: 'where we may find painted forth with great life, how affections are kindled and incited . . . and other the like particularities: amongst the which this last is of special use in moral and civil matters; how, I say, to set affection against affection, and to master one by another. . . .' These doctors answer the 'how' of expression as well as the 'how' of psychology.

[2] Ibid., pp. 153-4.

[3] Cf. *Works*, ed. Robertson, p. 133; Seneca, *Ep.* lii. 14.

[4] *Advancement*, Everyman ed., p. 131; Seneca, *Ep.* xlv.

philosophers as well!' Cicero, after rejoining that such was the view of Zeno the Stoic, agrees to alter his style, to speak 'in the rhetorical manner, but with the rhetoric of the philosophers, not with the sort which we use in the law-courts', for the latter is 'a little lacking in subtlety'.[1] In this exchange the Epicurean objects to the dialectic of question and answer with its logic-chopping and quibbling, but Cicero refuses the oratorical manner for a rhetoric more appropriate to philosophy.

What this rhetoric is in his opinion Cicero makes clear when he opposes the style of the Peripatetics and Academics to that of the Stoics. Here are the appropriate virtues:

In the first place, even the topics that required close reasoning they handled in a neat and polished manner, employing now definition, now division; as indeed your school does also, but your style is rather out-at-elbows, while theirs is noticeably elegant. Then, in themes demanding ornate and dignified treatment, how imposing, how brilliant is their diction . . . no hair-splitting like that of the Stoics, no niggling minutiae, but the loftier passages studiously ornate, and the minor topics studiously plain and clear.[2]

Here and elsewhere in Cicero the style of the Stoics is regarded as terse, subtle, bald, and rather crabbed. But neither the dialectical mode which he found in the schoolmen nor the rhetorical mode which he found in Cicero was acceptable to Bacon in the advancement of learning, though persuasion had its place in the use of learning.[3] None the less, on the propriety of continuous discourse to the orator rather than the philosopher he was inclined to agree with Zeno the Stoic.

[1] *De Finibus*, II. vi. 17. Thomas Stanley (*History of Philosophy*, 1687, p. 452) observes relative to Stoic method: 'There are two kinds of disputation: One, when the truth it self is subtilly polished in the dispute: The other, when every expression is accommodated to the vulgar opinion; for, we must use popular and usual words, when we speak of popular opinions, which *Panaetius* in the like manner hath done. . . . The vulgar way of dispute is likewise twofold: One by continued oration; The other by question and answer.'

[2] *De Finibus*, IV. iii. 6. The Stoic, however, finds the Peripatetic 'style of discourse somewhat deficient in cogency' (III. xii. 41). Cicero in the *De Oratore* (II. xxxviii) characterizes the Stoics as addicted to logic and 'a kind of language that is not clear, diffusive, and fluent, but thin, dry, concise, and minutely intersected'.

[3] When urging a Socratic method in 'catechizing', George Herbert (*A Priest to the Temple*, chap. xxi) observes: 'This practice exceeds even sermons in teaching; but there being two things in sermons, the one informing, the other inflaming; as sermons come short of questions in the one, so they far exceed them in the other. For questions cannot inflame or ravish, that must be done by a set, and laboured, and continued speech.'

A conspicuous feature of the Stoic discipline, as Croll has observed, which gave a special value to brevity, was the art of condensing experience into aphorisms; so that Stoic style in its most characteristic form tends toward the *sententia*. Seneca remarked that 'such thoughts as one may extract here and there in the works of other philosophers run through the whole body of our [i.e. Stoic] writings'.[1] Meric Casaubon in his preface to the *Meditations* of Marcus Aurelius argues for the integrity of his copy by observing that the method and composition of the book is such 'that it doth for the most part consist of certain Aphorisms and Canons . . . without any certain order or series, either in regard of the whole (but that they all tend to one purpose;) or in regard of the parts themselves'.[2] This 'independence of matters', he argues, is not peculiar to Marcus Aurelius, but involves others besides Epictetus, 'the Pattern of all latter Stoicks'. Indeed, it was a consequence of the cult of aphorisms and aphoristic style. Thus *sententiae* had an important place both in the style and in the moral discipline of the Stoics. In both respects they were brilliantly illustrated in Seneca. Since Bacon included Senecan style in the category of vain words when he published the *De Augmentis*, it is important to know whether he altered his remarks about aphorisms. There is, of course, the addition of his collection of antitheta, but no change in the doctrine of aphorisms.

To apothegms as an appendix to history, however, he adds this remark:

Neither are Apophthegms themselves only for pleasure and ornament, but also for use and action. For they are (as was said) 'words which are as goads,' words with an edge or point, that cut and penetrate the knots of business and affairs. Now occasions are continually returning, and what served once will serve again; whether produced as a man's own or cited as an old saying.[3]

Apothegms, like Colours, are now 'goads'; that is, have rhetorical efficacy. It is clear that it was not the *sententiae* of the Stoics to which Bacon objected, but their syllogistic deployment. Here their

[1] *Ep.* xxxiii. 3.

[2] *Marcus Aurelius Antoninus, his Meditations*, translated by Meric Casaubon (London, 1663), p. 15. To Shaftesbury this was the Senecan pattern. Fronto (*Correspondence*, ii. 41) mentions the use by Marcus Aurelius of the 'rhetorical figures which the Greeks call *schemata*'.

[3] *De Augmentis*, II. xii. The allusion is to Ecclesiastes, xii. 11. This 'edge' was also attributed to the 'form' of Colours.

propriety to essays as well as to history is apparent, and they are obviously described as 'aculeate'. If they are recognized as ornament, they are emphasized for rhetorical effectiveness, especially the use which concerned the *Essays*.

In the *Advancement* Bacon registers chiefly disappointment with extant collections. Perhaps his own *Apophthegms New and Old* was connected with this deficiency. His preface lays stress on the use of aphorisms for ornament or rhetoric rather than for the advancement of learning.[1] *Dicta*, maxims, aphorisms, *sententiae*, although a feature of Stoic dialectics, Lipsius treated under *venustas* or ornament. They might be called Stoic salt. But it is precisely the cultivation of *sententiae* to which Quintilian objects in Seneca and the schools of declamation, and finds responsible for their disjointed style—the antithesis of Cicero's. In the days of Euphuism they were still one of the chief titles to wit. If Bacon's allusion to the 'verbal points' of Seneca does not involve *sententiae*, he nevertheless describes them in his criticism of Senecan style.

Yet it is not too much to say that in rhetoric Bacon was more sympathetic to Stoic elements than to Ciceronian elements. Many of the items comprehended under *venustas* for Lipsius or Seneca are found in the doctrine and style of Bacon. Let it not be forgotten that Seneca observed in the Stoics, and Bacon cultivated, not only *sententiae* but also the similitudes of 'lively representation'. In practice Bacon is not above some discreet word-play,[2] and is certainly given to balanced antithesis. Among the varieties of *sententiae* or epigram Quintilian (VIII. v. 9) includes the enthymeme of two thoughts in opposition, which 'seems to be as pre-eminent among other thoughts as Homer among poets and Rome among cities'. Quintilian, who is reflected in Hoskins's discussion of *sententia*, describes various kinds of 'fine thoughts', including those which turn upon plays on words, but counsels neither rejection nor excessive cultivation. Erasmus, who had also echoed Quintilian, found Cicero deficient in them.

Neither can it be ignored that for Bacon logic differed from

---

[1] Aphorisms are regarded by Bacon as the basic style for science, as the form of moral wisdom, as ornament, and as commonplaces for the elaboration of methods.

[2] Note this example from the essay 'Of Great Place': 'The rising into place is laborious, and by pains men come to greater pains; and it is sometimes base, and by indignities men come to dignities.' Moreover, this has the form of what Bacon, in 'Of Unity in Religion', calls 'cross clauses', that is, antithetic.

rhetoric in Zeno's terms as well as Aristotle's: 'as the fist from the palm, the one close, the other at large.' He certainly knew Cicero's remark, among others, that Zeno

used to say that the faculty of speech in general falls into two departments; as Aristotle had already laid down; and that Rhetoric was like the palm of the hand, Dialectic like the closed fist; because rhetoricians employ an expansive style, and dialecticians one that is more compressed.[1]

While Bacon admits this as the stylistic difference—which now stresses brevity rather than cogency—he also admits a logical difference with Aristotle. Since rhetoric has wisely been placed between logic and moral or civil knowledge, rhetoric also requires special or particular topics, here being mixtures of logic with moral or civil knowledge. And this mixture justifies his defence of commonplaces. But psychologically rhetoric for Bacon harmonizes reason and passion by means of imagination, which manifests itself in style. These two differences, logical and stylistic, distinguish the philosophical and the rhetorical style in his theory of communication. In philosophy the schoolmen and the Stoics were at fault not in style but in logic.

It may be observed that the proper connexion for aphorisms, in their essential character, arrived with the *Novum Organum*, in which Bacon faced the problem of philosophical expression.[2] There he returned to the opposition of methods and aphorisms: he observed that sciences are set forth with 'such ambition and parade' that it is not strange if men regard them as 'long since perfect and complete'. With such methods he contrasts the way of candour in the inquisition of truth:

But the first and most ancient seekers after truth were wont, with better faith and better fortune too, to throw the knowledge which they gathered from the contemplation of things, and which they meant to store up for use, into aphorisms; that is, into short and scattered sentences, not linked together by an artificial method; and did not pretend or profess to embrace the entire art.[3]

[1] *De Finibus*, II. vi. 17.
[2] In the *Advancement* Bacon includes apothegms among the valuable appendixes to history, and comments upon the need of reducing to precept the 'wisdom of business' —a need to which his *Essays* ministered.
[3] *Novum Organum*, i. 86. The rhetorical significance lies in the 'short and scattered sentences' versus 'artificial method' or elaborated discourse. The use contemplated here is not rhetorical but scientific, in the broad sense of knowledge meant to be stored up for use.

Among these ancient seekers, who pointed the way, Bacon no doubt included Hippocrates, whom he liked to praise, and Heraclitus, whom he liked to quote. For the aphoristic style was popular with the early medical writers, who apparently owed something to the oracular manner of Heraclitus.[1]

In taking this view of how science should be written, Bacon confirms his sympathy with pre-Socratic times, and again anticipates the Royal Society. That body cannot have been unaware of his *Sylva Sylvarum*, and particularly of 'A Set of Aphorisms for compiling a just History of Nature and Art'. Here, in Section I, Aphorism III, Bacon urges that natural history should avoid all things that merely 'swell the bulk of the Work':

The first Particular is, that all Antiquities, Quotations, and Authorities of Authors, be laid aside; all Contests, Controversies, and contrary Opinions; together with all philological Ornaments: and let no Author be cited, but in doubtful Cases; nor Controversy mention'd, but in Subjects of great Consequence: and as for embellishments of Style, metaphorical Expressions, and studied Eloquence, with the like lighter matters, they should be wholly rejected. And let whatever is received, be delivered closely and concisely; that words may have the least share in it.[2]

Thus Bacon anticipates most of the requirements set forth in the Society's statute on reports and in Sprat's description of their style of discourse. He disliked elaborated structures both in science and in expression, since both reflected an unjustified completeness. His demands for science upheld his bent toward aphoristic style, and this bent inclined him more to the Stoics and Senecans than to the Ciceronians.

Aphoristic writing and methodical writing are different styles for different purposes, and so Bacon used them. It should not be forgotten, however, that aphorisms not only offer the form in which all knowledge can be preserved for use but that they can be developed

---

[1] See Hippocrates, ed. W. H. S. Jones (Loeb Classical Library), i. 309, 337; iv. 453, 463.

[2] Peter Shaw, the eighteenth-century editor of Bacon's *Philosophical Works*, annotates this passage: 'The Business is not now to gain upon Men's Affections, or win them over to *Philosophy*, by Eloquence, Similitudes, or the Art of Writing; which the Author practised in the *De Augmentis*; but carefully to enquire into, and justly to copy, and describe, Nature, as she is in herself; and here the Style cannot well be too plain and simple.' Bacon does, however, approach this style in Book II of the *Advancement*. On the *Sylva* see Joseph Glanvill, *Plus Ultra* (1668), p. 75.

into method. Bacon wrote his severest philosophical work, the *Novum Organum*, in Aphorisms; but when he conciliated honour to learning, he clothed his *Advancement*, chiefly Book I, in the rhetoric of persuasion or Methods. And yet the 'artificial method' of Book II is generally rather bare, being more 'initiative' than rhetorical in purpose.[1] It would be a mistake to say that Bacon always cut off 'illustration' or 'example' or 'connexion and order' or 'descriptions of practice' in his Aphorisms and never economized on them in his Methods. By the standards of his time Bacon was frugal not only in words but in rhetoric. Perhaps the habit of aphorism and the urge to persuade were too strong in him always to be kept apart;[2] but they were none the less limited by the demands of subject and audience—demands that his theory recognized.

When his use of aphorisms seems to approach contradiction, it is probably accommodation, for his aphorisms do adjust their theoretical character to the requirements of subject and audience. In general a popular audience or an 'immersed' subject demands more concreteness of style; a learned audience or an abstract subject requires a logical rather than a rhetorical style; an audience at odds with the subject or a subject above the audience requires further adjustment of style. Such accommodations explain in part the differences of style found in the *Essays* and the *Novum Organum*;[3] but these differences do not obscure the aphoristic basis of both works. Although Bacon's later style is generally less close than his earlier style, in the *Essays* for instance, it never ceases to be close. The *De Augmentis* is less cryptic than the *Advancement*, though comparison is hazardous; but in the former we find a treatise in aphorisms which was only promised in the latter.[4] And the last edition of the *Essays* offers new examples of the earlier manner. But in both instances it is more a manner of discourse than an earlier style that is resumed. In narrative Bacon writes in the loose style, but not without devices of point

[1] In opening Book II he says, 'I propose to speak actively without digressing or dilating'. He makes clear that Book I is addressed to a popular audience.

[2] At the close of the *Advancement* he insists that his purpose has been to state his positions and reasons rather than to persuade.

[3] The end of discourse may also affect the use of aphorisms. The *Advancement* suggests that the subjects of the *Essays* had a place in the progress of knowledge, but the *Essays* themselves were also directed toward the use of knowledge.

[4] *De Augmentis*, VIII. iii: 'Example of a Treatise on Universal Justice or the Fountains of Equity, by Aphorisms.'

and antithesis. In the *History of Henry VII*, for example, he opens in the periodic style, but his basic manner is the loose style, from which he moves toward the periodic rather than the curt. In his periodic structure here subordination interposed between subject and predicate is conspicuous. But while he inclines toward the periodic for weighty or dramatic effects, he still employs the pointed rhetoric of the curt style for smart and incisive turns in the Tacitean manner.

In the *Essays* wherever method is involved it is like that described in the *Valerius Terminus*: 'a method not the same whereby it was invented and induced, but such as is most compendious and ready whereby it may be used and applied.'[1] In this method the antitheta, which are 'antitheses of things' and aphoristic in form, are elaborated more or less, but the whole remains compendious. Although his collection of antitheta was a collection of materials for invention, aphorism or antitheta provided the mode wherein much of his knowledge was not only invented but delivered. Of course, no one in that time had to be urged to cite *sententiae*; they had indeed contributed much to Euphuism. The tremendous vogue of the *Adages* and other collections of Erasmus is sufficient evidence not only of this taste, to which collections like *Wit's Commonwealth* continued to minister, but also of the 'sentence's' place in the rhetoric of that time. But some notion of how Bacon unwinds them is given by his expansions of various proverbs of Solomon, where he speaks of expression by simile as 'lively representation'.[2]

Apart from sententious fashion, personal bent, or Senecan influence, one reason why the *Essays* appeared in aphoristic style was no doubt that Bacon thought aphorisms not only the best way to reduce wisdom to precept, but the proper mode for works that did not pretend to finality. Two tendencies in the *Essays* have often been pointed out: one toward greater concreteness of style and one toward more organized structure.[3] This development seems to have been achieved by an increasing use of the elements which Bacon says are cut off

[1] Cap. 18. Of the 'magistral' method he remarks elsewhere in the *Advancement* (Everyman ed., p. 34): 'It is true, that in compendious treatises for practice that form is not to be disallowed.'

[2] See *De Augmentis*, VIII. ii.

[3] See E. Arber's *Harmony of the Essays* (London, 1871) for parallel versions. For a close study of changes in the *Essays* see R. S. Crane's article in *Schelling Anniversary Papers* (New York, 1923), pp. 98 ff.

in aphorisms; hence the inference that his last essays surrender aphorisms for methods. But the 1625 volume as a whole fails to reveal any general surrender, for both casual impression and close inspection tell us that the essays remain predominantly aphoristic in style or Senecan in mode. Though many of the essays added in 1625 have relaxed the bare aphoristic form, some retain it almost as strictly as ever.[1]

Here we ought to remind ourselves that for Bacon cutting off connexion and order does not mean surrendering to disorder; rather it means not introducing more order than there is in the thought itself, or not elaborating a deceptive appearance of connected and finished discourse. Though rhetoric justifies such an appearance, the form of the essays remains an index to the state of their wisdom. But discourse of connexion and order involved the logical deployment which for Bacon defeated the end of moral persuasion in the Stoics. The rather sparing introduction of connective elements that has been observed in the *Essays* will not be found to violate this principle, by which style reflects the evasion of logical method; but it does lessen the curt effect.[2]

None the less Bacon's *Essays* do reveal a change from aphorisms to methods, which no doubt was affected by Stoic example. If we recall that aphorisms are composed of nothing but the pith and heart of sciences, that they cut off illustration, example, connexion, order, and description, which methods employ, we can observe this change with some precision. It should be added that change can be observed most surely where it is most free—in the new essays found in each of the later editions. Now the general course of this change may be summarized as follows: to the stark aphoristic form of 1597 the essays of 1612 add some connective elements and some ornament or illustration; the essays of 1625 add most, if not all, of the elements that belong to methods. Let us not forget that lack of con-

---

[1] Crane finds that the increase in planned (coherent and organized) essays is in the progression 1–4–9 for the three editions, making fourteen out of the final fifty-eight essays, not counting a few partly planned. Out of the twenty new essays in the final (1625) edition, five are of the old planless (aphoristic) type; they are *Revenge*, *Adversity*, *Delays*, *Innovations*, and *Suspicion*. Thus even the last edition remains preponderantly aphoristic or Senecan.

[2] As Bacon became less disconnected he naturally became less abrupt. Truncating clauses to phrases and putting semicolons for commas might be taken as the badge of the Lipsian.

nexion and order, which largely characterizes the Baconian essay, was the commonest charge against Seneca. Thus the essays of 1612 are still essentially aphoristic in manner and curt in style; only in the 1625 essays do we find the aphoristic character submerged in methods or the curt style truly relaxed.

It is then that the increase in organized structure really modifies the character of the essay. It is not change in that pith or matter has been increased, but in that expression has been articulated and multiplied. In style the essays of 1597 and 1612 are not only more curt, but they employ more parallelism and balance, which they retain in their 1625 form; the new essays of 1625 demonstrate the real increase in loose style and the real decrease in balance.[1] An exceptional case, the essay 'Of Friendship', as written in 1612 and rewritten in 1625, presents this change of character in its most startling form. But the essays of 'Revenge', 'Adversity', 'Delays', 'Innovations', and 'Suspicion', which appear in 1625 for the first time, show that the aphoristic tendency is still operative in Bacon; they reflect the more curt Senecan fashion of the earlier essays, and provide a late contrast between aphorisms and methods.

When Bacon praises Machiavelli for drawing knowledge out of particulars, and declares that 'it hath much greater life for practice when the discourse attendeth upon the example, than when the example attendeth upon the discourse',[2] he is praising a method which induces knowledge in an effective form, but it is hardly the method of the *Essays*. There his use of example and illustration is of the sort depreciated here: 'the examples alleged for the discourse's sake are cited succinctly and without particularity, and carry a servile aspect toward the discourse which they are brought in to make good.' This is no doubt the way of supplying 'examples by reference' which belongs to the use of antitheta. But so long as aphorisms are not organized or elaborated by what the *De Augmentis* calls 'deduction and connexion' they do not lose their initiative character, even though they are amplified rhetorically. If the examples and illustrations of the *Essays* carry this servile aspect, the simile and metaphor are used to secure the reception of ideas or

---

[1] Cf. the use of balance in his speeches for the Gray's Inn revels, where he is doing another kind of thing.

[2] *Advancement*, Everyman ed., p. 186. Incidentally, here is Playfere's antimetabole.

the 'impression' of counsels civil and moral, so that they may come home to men's bosoms as well as business, and thereby avoid the failure of Stoic rhetoric. For Bacon rhetoric by definition was directed against the force of the passions, which were involved in many of his subjects, and the rhetorical tropes and figures were important means of affecting them.

It is probable that Bacon's antipathy to scholastic logic influenced his view of Stoic rhetoric, although he had other grounds for disagreement. But however different their views of means to ends, they shared some of the means; and these means, pointed to rhetorical ends, were prominent in Seneca. Yet Bacon rejected the Senecan style even though he claimed Seneca's *Epistles* as the prototype for his *Essays*. If he accepted the method but rejected the style of Seneca, did he find contemporary reasons for both actions? Why he should adopt the rather formless method of Seneca has sufficiently appeared; to his rejection of Senecan style we may turn once more.

This pointed and turned style, in Bacon's account, followed close upon the Ciceronian, and might therefore have been the Euphuistic. The antithetic structure of Euphuism could be described as 'rather rounding into itself than spread and dilated'—*potius versa quam fusa*; certainly it seemed more witty and weighty than it was. When Bacon adds that this kind of expression has been deservedly despised by the 'more exact judgments', we may recall that Savile criticized the Senecan heresy in terms that touch Bacon's charge against its wit on the one hand and Sidney's charge against the chime of Euphuism on the other. The *concinnitas* of Euphuism, like the wordplay of Senecanism, was more suited to 'meaner capacities'; and when Bacon concludes that this style also 'is nothing else but a hunting after words and fine placing of them', it is difficult to believe that he did not connect this style with the chiming artifice of Euphuistic prose.[1]

Should it be objected that 1623 was too late for such an attack, it may be answered that 1605 was not early for an attack on the style of Ascham's generation, which this style followed. Of course, the

---

[1] Furthermore, *concinnitas* as the 'fine placing' of words has no real parallel in his description of Ciceronianism, which does not suggest the schemes. His Senecanism and Ciceronianism are related because they are both 'a hunting after words' rather than matter; they are differentiated by *copia* versus brevity, and both 'point' and 'fine placing' are associated with the latter.

date of publication does not establish the date of composition, though it would admit a later fashion than that of strict Euphuism. Certainly 'concinnitas verborum' is easier to find in the style of the Euphuists than in that of the Senecan essayists and character-writers for whom Bacon provided a model—though not in word-play. Out of this dilemma the simplest escape is to conclude that for Bacon the Senecan style and Euphuism were not unrelated. Their sententiousness produced an appearance of weight, which was at least 'paulo sanius', but their sound-patterns destroyed the illusion. Having rejected the word-play, Bacon had rejected the distinctive as well as reprehensible aspect of this style, and had therefore no reason to identify it with his own. Bacon may be said to reveal a later bias by regarding the Senecan style as pointed, just as Savile reveals an earlier bias by regarding it as schematic or at least rhyming; but the two critics unite in their conclusion.

The problem of style for Bacon is posed in another form by Spedding's preface to the *De Augmentis Scientiarum*. Speaking of the Latin form of the *Advancement of Learning*, Spedding remarks that long ago Bacon had asked Dr. Playfere to do it, 'who (according to Tenison) sent him a specimen, but "of such superfine Latinity, that the Lord Bacon did not encourage him to labour further in that work, in the penning of which he desired not so much neat and polite, as clear masculine and apt expression" '.[1] But Playfere's failure, says Spedding, may be sufficiently accounted for by another fact:

A memorandum in the *Commentarius Solutus* dated 26 July, 1608—'Proceeding with the translation of my book of Advancement of Learning—hearkening to some other if Playfer should fail,'—shows that at that time it was still in his hands; and he died at the beginning of the next year.[2]

This may explain the failure of Playfere, but not the real problem set by Tenison—the apparent incongruity of Bacon's choice.

Does Tenison's opposition of styles betray the bias of a different age? At least 'superfine' is not inappropriate to 'Mellifluous Play-fere' as Nashe called him, perhaps thinking of St. Bernard, the

---

[1] *Works*, ed. Robertson, p. 416. The Tenison reference is to *Baconiana*, p. 26.

[2] This fact suggests that his criticism of Senecan style may have been written by 1608, especially since it comes early in the work.

'Mellifluous Doctor'. Playfere was famous for his antimetabole, one of the figures which according to Wilson made like-sounds most delightful. But in asking Playfere to translate the *Advancement*, Bacon wrote: 'for by that I have heard and read, I know no man a greater master in commanding words to serve matter.' If what Bacon had read was Playfere's own work, then he engaged him with his eyes open; and, if his phrase is not empty flattery, for the very gift that he esteemed above all in style—for the very antithesis of Ciceronianism.

The answer to this problem—as Burnet later said in effect—is that in style Bacon was closer to Playfere than to Tenison. Of the figure which Playfere tired out, Hoskins had remarked 'that this is a sharp and witty figure and shows out of the same words a pithy distinction of meaning, very convenient for schoolmen'. In short, it could be 'aculeate'; it was in fact often regarded as a kind of antithesis, and Bacon had used it. But it was also, for Hoskins as for Wilson, one of those delightful figures of repetition—'sundry correspondences of each of their places, one to another'—which accounted for the Euphuists, and marked others as schematic Ciceronians. If Bacon later discovered his aversion to Playfere's style, did he call it Senecan or Ciceronian? The probabilities are that he did not call it Ciceronian. For if Bacon once included Euphuism in Ciceronianism, but later discriminated between two kinds of *concinnitas*, he still found the Senecan pointed.

It might be concluded that Bacon preferred the Senecan style without its cult of word-play, which brought it too close to the chime of Euphuism—but not into identity with Ciceronianism. Perhaps he felt that without this—or as he wrote it—Senecan style could indeed be as 'witty and weighty' as it seemed. For so Jonson described him, with words borrowed from Seneca the Elder, who had used them to describe the style of a 'pointed' speaker.

7. *Pointed Style after Bacon*

As the reign of Elizabeth drew to an end, English prose style yielded to the pressure of a new movement. No sooner had the Ciceronian movement reached a proud eminence in the formal periods of Hooker than the Anti-Ciceronian movement found a leader in Bacon, whose terse manner of expression became the hallmark of style among the later essay and character writers. In 1610 Bacon wrote to Tobie Matthew: 'They tell me my Latin is turned Silver, and become current.' By this time his English had in fact turned Silver and become current among the Senecan essayists.[1] Even Polonius was a Senecan in theory when he observed that 'brevity is the soul of wit', and in practice when he recognized Hamlet's 'points' by remarking, 'How pregnant sometimes his replies are!' Bacon's mother was less percipient, for she wrote to Anthony, 18 April 1593: 'I send herein your brother's letter. Construe the interpretation. I do not understand his enigmatical folded writing.' No bad example itself of concise and discrete phrasing!

But this is not history, and we may well ask to what extent the English seventeenth century was critically aware of the Senecan style.[2] In retrospect Francis Thompson could recognize Silver Latin imitation in Sir Thomas Browne:

> Browne was more idiomatic in structure than the Ciceronian Hooker. But the admirable knitting of his sentences was not due merely to a better study of English idiom. He was steeped in classic models more compact and pregnant than Cicero. Like his French contemporaries, he was influenced by the great Latin rhetoricians, Lucan, Ovid, and Seneca; whose rivalry it was to put an idea into the fewest possible words.[3]

[1] Before the edition of 1612 Bacon's *Essays* were represented by that of 1597 and 1598, not counting the manuscript of about 1607; Cornwallis's *Essays* had appeared in 1600 and 1601, and had been reprinted, part one twice, before 1612. But in influence there is no reason to alter the balance in favour of Cornwallis; besides, they differ more in manner than in style.

[2] Croll's studies of 'Attic' or Senecan prose afford but a partial answer to this question.

[3] *Works* (London, 1913), iii. 166–7. On the significance of Jacobean translation from

But how many of Browne's contemporaries recognized this influence or this rivalry in their own time? Was Jonson merely translating Horace or was he also expressing himself when he wrote:

> Myself for shortness labour, and I grow
> Obscure. This, striving to run smooth, and flow,
> Hath neither soul nor sinews.[1]

For Erasmus, it may be recalled, these lines introduced the Attic style as well as the Rhodian style, to which Cicero belonged.

Three tendencies of Anti-Ciceronian style have been associated by Croll with three important names: the *curt* with Lipsius, the *loose* with Montaigne, and the *obscure* with Bacon.[2] The curt and the loose tendencies, as Croll observes, were both Senecan in pattern; but the curt and the obscure tendencies, which he is anxious to discriminate, were commonly confused in seventeenth-century Senecanism. And this is not unnatural, since the peculiar quality of Tacitus is brevity pushed to the verge of obscurity; moreover, his style offers more likeness than difference when compared with 'Seneca's own style—disconnected, pointed, antithetic, metaphorical and piquant'.[3] Here is Tacitus as seen by Montaigne:

He always pleads with strong and solid reasons, in pointed and subtle fashion, in accordance with the affected style of that age; they were so fond of inflated language that when they could find no point or subtlety in things they borrowed them of words. He writes not unlike Seneca;

Silver Latin see H. B. Lathrop, *Translations from the Classics into English from Caxton to Chapman* (Madison, 1933), chap. iv, esp. pp. 235, 244, 252, 304. For Browne's taste in such writers see *Works*, ed. Keynes, vi. 108, 206. Hooker is thus characterized by John Earle (*English Prose*, p. 438): 'It is in Hooker's style that we see the effect of classical studies at once in its most pronounced and in its most favourable aspect. Here we must note that straining after the long and pregnant sentence which classical eloquence suggests as the ideal of high discourse.'

[1] Jonson echoes these words in 'An Epistle to Master John Selden':
> I know to whom I write. Here, I am sure,
> Though I be short, I cannot be obscure:
> Less shall I for the art or dressing care,
> Truth and the Graces best when naked are.

Aubrey (*Lives*) remarks of Selden: 'In his younger yeares he affected obscurity of style, which, after, he quite left off, and wrote perspicuously.' Logan Pearsall Smith's *Treasury of English Aphorisms*, which does not explore the byways, shows these seventeenth-century writers taking as large a place as Pope: Bacon, Browne, Fuller, Halifax, Jonson, Selden, Taylor.

[2] See 'Attic Prose: Lipsius, Montaigne, Bacon', *Schelling Anniversary Papers*, New York, 1923.

[3] J. W. Duff, *A Literary History of Rome in the Silver Age* (London, 1927), p. 198; cf. pp. 228-9 and 593 ff.

he appears to me more muscular, Seneca more pointed (*plus charnu . . . plus aigu*).[1]

Both differed from Cicero's finished and flowing amplitude chiefly in the abrupt terseness and jerky strength of their sentences.

In English criticism, moreover, it will be erring on the right side to regard Senecan style in its most obvious character—as the cultivation of sententious brevity and all the qualities that go with rhetorical *sententiae*. In general, the curt Senecan style is an essay style marked by the cultivation of brevity, staccato form, and point; its rhythm is spasmodic: in particular, the Tacitean variety is an extreme development of this style. For both Seneca and Tacitus brevity meant Sallust, and in the seventeenth century all three were distinguished for similar qualities. To the curt Senecan style our investigation will be restricted, since the English writers of this period were much less conscious of the loose Senecan style, largely because it was only a relaxed form of the other. But occasionally the loose form, though less distinct from the native tradition, also will be noticed.

It is necessary to remark, however, that the curt style was generally supplemented or relieved by the loose style. The two were commonly intermingled in the expression of Bacon or Browne. Both styles have been analysed by Croll in 'The Baroque Style in Prose', where he has summarized them as 'the concise, serried, abrupt *stile coupé*, and the informal, meditative, and "natural" loose style'. Both styles have in common a disjunctive form, secured either by omitting or by relaxing the syntactic ligatures; and an order of members that is emergent rather than premeditated. The loose style was the more natural, and the curt style the more artful, for it did have to make its 'points' show. While the loose period may suggest the Ciceronian, its *concinnitas* or symmetry of structure is more evasive; while it may adumbrate a Latin climax, it follows a more organic order of thought. Where Ciceronian periods build climaxes, Senecan sentences make points, and the loose period combines the two functions; hence the loose period does not rise and fall in its movement, but rises from point to point. The curt style pre-empts attention before the Restoration, and the loose style predominates after; but both forms prepare the way for modern English prose. In general, the separation or opposition of the curt style and

[1] *Essays*, bk. III, chap. viii.

the loose style distinguishes the Restoration from the first half of the century.

Among seventeenth-century prose forms the witty or pointed style finds its natural place in the essay, character, letter, paradox, and problem. For example, both in style and in form the Character succeeded, in Overburian words, by 'in little comprehending much'. Although pointed wit was a general ambition, these prose forms were subject to distinction, if not always distinguished. Flecknoe, in his *Epigrams and Characters* of 1673, explains his mixture: 'Epigrams, which I aptly couple with the Characters, since these are only Epigrams in Prose, as the others are only Characters in Verse.' Then he makes distinctions: Characters 'differ from Portraits, in that they are only Pictures of Mind, abstracting from the Body, and from Essays, in that they discourse not, but give you only the heads of things in general'. But as all these forms strove in some way to be 'epigrams in prose', they were all, in their way, 'wit's descant on any plain song', and therefore often associated in publication. And to 'discourse not, but give you only the heads of things in general' was the ambition of the Baconian essay as well as of the Character.

Although it is historically difficult to separate the three forms of Anti-Ciceronian style defined by Croll, it is necessary to make the attempt for the sake of nicer analytic discriminations. In the characters assigned to them, the *curt* and the *loose* have formal differences, but the *obscure* does not. The first two, says Croll, derive from Seneca, but the last from Tacitus. It might be more illuminating to regard the curt as the norm, from which style could move in two opposite directions. If toward the loose, it would add length and connexion to its members; if toward the obscure, better called the truncated—for Tacitus sought to abridge, not defeat, expression—it would become more compressed and asymmetrical.[1] The curt and the truncated are essentially brief styles, while the loose is not; they are all related by their disjunctive composition, which may be either asyndetic or loosely syndetic. For the brief styles it seems necessary,

---

[1] Cf. *The Annals of Tacitus*, trans. G. G. Ramsay (New York, 1904), p. lxi: 'Some of his most compact sentences may be described as truncated periods; several subordinate ideas are introduced under one principal verb, but they are expressed by single words, usually Ablatives or Participles, loosely connected, sometimes without any connexion at all, instead of by complete subordinate sentences.' Thus the interests of compression lead to less co-ordinate structure in Tacitus than in Seneca.

therefore, to distinguish the kind of brevity involved. In terms of their models, the curt has brief members, but not obviously abridged expression; the truncated has both, and hence less balanced phrasing and less patterned word-play. Both are curt in the sense of being short and abrupt in movement. These traits account for the fact that Tacitus was often criticized as strange and obscure in expression, while Seneca was often criticized as short but prolix.

Some basis for such discriminations is provided by Jonson's *Discoveries*. In a passage on style Jonson begins by setting up a norm for stylistic economy: 'A strict and succinct Style is that, where you can take away nothing without loss, and that loss to be manifest.'[1] This is a style in which nothing is superfluous. Next he associates a briefer style with Tacitus: 'The brief Style is that which expresseth much in little.' Here the thought is compressed into fewer words. Next comes a still briefer style, associated with the Laconic: 'The concise Style, which expresseth not enough, but leaves somewhat to be understood.' This implies rather than expresses part of the thought. Then there is the abridged style, with its decided effect on movement: 'The abrupt Style, which hath many Breaches, and doth not seem to end, but fall.'[2] This is associated with Suetonius, Seneca, and Fabianus; as a style it is brief, broken, and uneven in movement.[3] Such a style is set off by Jonson's next words: 'The congruent, and harmonious fitting of parts in a sentence, hath almost the fastning, and force of knitting, and connexion.' Thus correspondent structure and euphony give the connexion which the abrupt style lacks, and lead into Jonson's next topic, the period.

[1] See 'De stylo', *Discoveries*, ed. Castelain, pp. 100–1. The names associated with Jonson's scale of brevity suggest degrees of culpability that would be questioned by others. This was no doubt Jonson's norm for terse style.

[2] This echoes Seneca, *Ep.* 100, in which he discusses the style of Fabianus. Compared with Cicero's smooth composition—in Lodge's words—'Asinius Pollio's discourse is uneven and skipping, and such as will leave thee when thou least expectest it. To conclude, in Cicero all things end, in Pollio they fall, except a few which are tied to one certaine kind of custome and example'. In *Ep.* 114 the same style is associated with Sallust, in whose imitators 'the Sentences were curtalled, and words had their unexpected cadence, and obscure brevitie with the rest was reputed Elegancie'. Jonson draws upon Vives; cf. Castelain ed., pp. 100–1. Cf. Quintilian, IV. ii. 40–7, for this passage is reflected in the discussion of brevity by Hoskins and Jonson (on epistolary style) as well as by Walker in his *Instructions concerning Oratory*.

[3] On the style of Suetonius Everyman's *Smaller Classical Dictionary* remarks: 'His language is very brief and precise, sometimes obscure, without any affectation of ornament.'

It should also be remarked that clearness or perspicuity is not a trustworthy guide to the ideals or affinities of styles, since perspicuity is the constant of language as a vehicle of communication. It is rather the variants, or the qualities associated with perspicuity, that give styles their peculiar character. Thus when John Hughes tells us, in his essay *Of Style*, that the qualifications of a good style are propriety, perspicuity, elegance, and cadence, it is the propriety, elegance, and cadence that are significant. When Jonson likewise names perspicuity, but in connexion with other qualities, it is the other qualities that differentiate the ideals of Jonson from those of Hughes. The difference will tell us much of the evolution of style between Jonson and Hughes. Of course, an emphasis upon brevity endangers perspicuity, and obscurity all but eliminates this constant of communication;[1] yet even what Bacon calls the 'concealment of the cryptic' involves some audience. Otherwise, the presence or absence of perspicuity is not in itself very significant. It was in this knowledge that John Selden declared, 'Brevity, and Plainness (as the one endured the Other) I have joined'.[2] With this reminder, we may turn to the seventeenth-century awareness of Senecan style and its consequences for prose.

Both Seneca and Tacitus were great favourites of the first half of the seventeenth century. Seneca appealed as a moralist who could put even the Christian to shame, and Tacitus rivalled Machiavelli for shrewd political wisdom. The Ciceronian view may be represented by the words attributed to Cardinal du Perron, who made a derogatory comparison of Seneca to Cicero.

We ought not to say, that *Seneca* is full of Sentences, for there are a 100000 Times more in *Cicero*. All that *Seneca* says, he speaks as a Sentence, but they are not always Sentences that he says, and he often says the same Things in different Expressions, and he himself writes against too concise a Stile.

This also bears witness to the taste for 'sentences'. Perron concludes that 'there is more in two Pages of Cicero, than ten of Seneca: Nay there is more in one Epistle of Cicero, tho' it be plain, and quite

---

[1] As Thomas Wright remarks in *The Passions of the minde* (1604, p. 141): 'Who of purpose writeth obscurely, perverteth the naturall communication of men; because we write to declare our minds, and he that affecteth obscurity, seemeth, not to be willing that men should conceive his meaning.'

[2] 'From the Author of the Illustrations', Drayton's *Poly-Olbion* (1613).

naked of any artificial Ornaments, than in ten of Pliny with all the curious Dress you would wish.'[1] And Tacitus fares no better at the hands of Perron:

The most wretched Stile in the World is that of *Tacitus*, and the Worst of all those who have written History. All the Art of his Stile consists in a few Things, such as Antitheses and Aposiopeses, whereby a Word is sometimes conceal'd: But one Page of *Quintus Curtius* is worth Thirty of his.[2]

Perron, furthermore, does not believe that Tacitus will make a good statesman; 'but he may make a good Courtier, for he will inform him of the Tricks of the Court'. While ''tis the easiest Thing in the World to imitate his Style', one quickly tires of it.[3] But Bacon's criticism of these writers was much less extreme; certainly it was not balanced in favour of Cicero.

Jonson's 'New Cry' mocks 'ripe statesmen', who 'carry in their pockets Tacitus'. One of the first essayists, Robert Johnson, finds Tacitus the perfect historian and remarks his 'judicial, but strangely brief sentences'.[4] In a Latin letter to Sir John Harington—the younger of Exton—who had posed a difficult passage in Tacitus, Prince Henry replies: 'Do you believe me to be a person capable of untying knots, explaining riddles, and illustrating the obscurities of difficult authors?' He explains that, finding himself unable 'to comprehend any thing but what is low and contracted (*nisi tenue, humile, & angustum*)', he 'never dared to look into Tacitus, whom I had heard represented by every one, as a writer of admirable sagacity, and full of short and pointed sentences, but too obscure in his style for my capacity'.[5] Seneca and Tacitus were the Jacobean

---

[1] *Perroniana*. See *The Miscellaneous Remains of Perron, Thuanus, St. Evremont, &c.* (London, 1707), p. 22. This is another statement of Bacon's complaint that Senecan style presented only the appearance of weight. Jonson criticized Perron in the *Conversations*.

[2] Ibid., p. 96. Aposiopesis is one of the chief figures by which to obtain Hoskins's 'intimation'.

[3] Perron (p. 97) also sets down a principle: 'These Things which require Demonstration, must be written in a proper Stile without a Metaphor, such as Medicine, Theology and History; but an Orator may sometimes use Ornaments and Flowers of Rhetorick.'

[4] *Essaies, or rather Imperfect Offers* (London, 1601), 'Of Histories'.

[5] See Thomas Birch, *Life of Prince Henry* (London, 1760), pp. 121, 421–2. It is interesting that the style in which Prince Henry feels competent is the plain, low, and brief. His father had directed him in *The Basilicon Doron* (Scottish Text Society, ser. 3, vol. xvi, pp. 179, 185): 'In your language be plaine, honest, naturall, comelie, cleane, short, and sentencious . . . use a plaine, shorte, but statelie stile.'

models for such sentences, and many others besides Campion could have written the first sentence of his *Observations*: 'There is no writing too brief, that without obscurity comprehends the intent of the writer.'

As the Senecan style took hold of the seventeenth century it revealed two tendencies, one toward pointed brevity and the other toward plain brevity. On the basis of *sententia* or antithesis, however, the curt styles were all more or less pointed. The first tendency paid allegiance to Seneca's practice, and the second to his theory, in so far as that theory and practice were in conflict. Bacon espoused plain brevity, and Andrewes cultivated pointed brevity, being under the influence of Church Fathers of that persuasion. Burton, who is more loose than curt, nevertheless turns to Seneca's *Epistles* for the defence of his style, finding support not only in the doctrine of plainness but also in the unlaboured flow of Fabianus. The devotees of brevity, on the other hand, could turn to the famous passage in which Seneca tells what delighted him in the style of Lucilius:

All your words are compact, and suited to the subject. You say all that you wish, and you mean still more than you say. This is a proof of the importance of your subject matter, showing that your mind, as well as your words, contains nothing superfluous or bombastic.[1]

And to continue with Seneca was to answer the question whether metaphor and simile were inconsistent with the curt style:

I do, however, find some metaphors; not, indeed, daring ones, but the kind which have stood the test of use. I find similes also; of course, if anyone forbids us to use them, maintaining that poets alone have that privilege, he has not, apparently, read any of our ancient prose writers, who had not yet learned to affect a style that should win applause.

Thus spoke the Stoic theorist who had learned to affect a style not unrelated to applause. Thus Seneca could furnish authority for either pointed wit or plainness, for either sententious brevity or unlaboured fluency.

The English Seneca, later Bishop Hall, in 1608 introduced into English

a new fashion of discourse, by Epistles; new to our language, usual to others: and (as Novelty is never without som plea of use) more free, more

---

[1] *Ep.* 59. 5. This style gave Bacon's appearance of weight.

familiar. Thus, we doe but talk with our friends by our pen, and expresse our selves no whit lesse easily; some-what more digestedly.[1]

His new fashion of discourse was Seneca's mode for the essay; but Hall echoes, after Erasmus and Angel Day, Seneca's conception of the familiar letter. The form is altered, but the content remains, when Bacon describes his *Essays* of 1612 in the cancelled dedication to Prince Henry:

> Certain brief notes, set down rather significantly than curiously, which I have called *Essays*. The word is late, but the thing is ancient. For Seneca's Epistles to Lucilius, if one mark them well, are but *Essays*, that is, *dispersed meditations*, though conveyed in the form of Epistles.

In both the old and the new it is implied that the effect is expected to be rather disconnected and abrupt. For Hall, too, brevity of style is appropriate to the new fashion:

> I grant, Brevitie, where it is neither obscure nor defective, is very pleasing, even to the daintiest judgements. No marvaile therefore, if most men desire much good counsell in a narrow roome; as some affect to have great personages, drawne in little Tablets; or, as we see worlds of Countryes described in the compasse of small Mappes: Neither doe I unwillingly yeeld to follow them; for both the powers of good advise are the stronger, when they are thus united; and brevity makes counsell more portable for memorie & readier for use.[2]

This is equally valid for Bacon's *Essays*. If Hall renewed Seneca's practice of writing essays as epistles, he also renewed his style both in the *Epistles* and in the *Characters of Virtues and Vices*.[3]

But Seneca was also a model of another sort—the kind that Burton found in him. When Burton explains his own style in

---

[1] *Epistles in Six Decads*: Epistle Dedicatory to Prince Henry. In the eighteenth century Bishop Hall is described by Philip Doddridge (*Works*, 1804, v. 429) as follows: 'The most elegant and polite writer of his age. He abounds rather too much with antitheses and witty turns. In some of his writings he seems to have imitated Seneca and Austin. His sermons are much the worse for a compliance with the taste of the age in which he lived.'

[2] *Epistles*, Decad. 6, Ep. 10. These comparisons remind one of Lyly's first petition to the queen.

[3] See Croll's note (*Studies in English Philology*, p. 434) on Hall's style in 'What if they be unpleasant? They are physic; it is enough if they be wholesome': 'Note how exactly this reproduces a movement characteristic of Seneca: "Quid tua, uter vincat? Potest melior vincere: non potest non peior esse qui vicerit".' Note the antithetic rhetoric of Seneca (*Ep.* 14. 13) and compare Tacitus (*Hist.* i. 50): 'inter duos quorum bello solum id scires, deteriorem fore qui vicisset'. For the quotation from Hall see *Heaven upon Earth*, sect. 13.

'Democritus to the Reader', he comments on the difference of tastes in style: 'He respects matter, thou art wholly for words; he loves a loose and free style, thou art all for neat composition, strong lines, hyperboles, allegories.'[1] To Burton the alternatives are the 'loose' style, which respects matter, and the 'neat' style, which affects rhetoric; for both of which Seneca provided a model. By 'strong lines, hyperboles, allegories' Burton suggests the bold rhetoric of his time, which is best defined by the first of these terms. The cult of 'strong lines', which I have outlined in another place,[2] was a cult of expressiveness in which an effort to write with too much point often produced obscure brevity or bombast. Before giving our attention to Burton's 'loose' style, it is necessary to examine this alternative of 'neat composition', at least in its major aspect, which is related to brevity.

'Strong lines', when successful, were the products of a search for vigorous, pregnant, or exciting expression; when unsuccessful, they were merely crabbed, riddling, or bombastic. Feltham described their effect in that produced by a 'rarely sententious man': 'I cannot read some parts of Seneca, above two lines together. He raises my soul to a contemplation, which sets me a thinking, on more than I can imagine.'[3] Brathwaite's dedication of *Whimzies* (1631) says that character-writing has 'relished more of Aphorisme than Character' and suggests that strong lines were connected with this relish:

> *Strong lines* have beene in request; but they grew disrelishing, because they smelled too much of the Lampe and opinionate singularitie. *Clinchings* likewise were held nimble flashes; but affectation spoyl'd all, and discovered their levitie.

He redresses the balance by his plainer and more prolix manner, but common means to strong lines were paradox, hyperbole, and catachresis, or even the pun. Yet Brathwaite observes that the character style is current enough, 'so it be not wrapt up in too much ambiguity. He writes best that *affects* least; and *effects* most.'

When Meric Casaubon was a boy in the university, 'strong lines' designated language that sought 'to find somewhat that is extraordinary, and may relish of some rapture or Enthusiasm'.[4] And

---

[1] *Anatomy of Melancholy*, Everyman ed., i. 27.
[2] See 'Strong Lines', *English Studies*, xviii (1936), 152–9.
[3] *Resolves*, First Century, no. xiv.
[4] *Treatise of Enthusiasme* (London, 1655), p. 142. He relates the term to Longinus

Casaubon observes that it is Seneca's manner 'to be very high and tumid in his expressions'.[1] For Hobbes in 1650 the 'ambitious obscurity' of trying to say more than you think or of expressing less than you think was responsible for strong lines.[2]

They were associated with strength in another way, by a masculine style, even roughness of expression; and they were cultivated both in poetry and prose. In prose an abrupt style, 'hopping' in the manner of Lipsius, obviously could not be a smooth style, though it might be forceful or obscure;[3] nor could Bacon's 'enigmatical folded writing' make easy reading. The association of strong lines with a cult of obscurity is made sufficiently clear by Quarles in apology for his verse:

> In this Discourse, I have not affected to set thy understanding on the Rack, by the tyranny of *strong lines*, which (as they fabulously report of *China* dishes) are made for the third *Generation* to make use of, and are the meere itch of wit; under the colour of which, many have ventured (trusting to the Oedipean conceit of their ingenious Reader) to write *non-sense*, and feloniously father the created expositions of other men; not unlike some painters, who first make the picture, then, from the opinion of better judgements, conclude, whom it resembles.[4]

This is also testimony to what we call the conceits of Metaphysical poetry.

More than one allusion suggests that strong lines were connected with the cult of *sententiae* in drama:

> I know you in your hearts
> Hate serious plays, as I do serious parts,
> To trouble us with thoughts and state-designs—
> A melancholy plot tied with strong lines.[5]

They were even connected with those dramatists, in Bentley's words, 'who aspired after the sublime Character, and by Metaphors

(iii. 3) on tumidity or bombast, who associates it with Hegesias, and makes it a consequence of aiming at grandeur 'in trying to avoid the charge of being feeble or arid'. It might be a consequence of using imagery in prose 'to present things vividly', or with *enargeia* as Longinus (xv. 2) defines its object in prose.

[1] *Treatise of Enthusiasme*, p. 145.

[2] 'Answer to Davenant', *Critical Essays of the Seventeenth Century*, ed. J. E. Spingarn, ii. 63.

[3] Cf. Jonson's *Discoveries*, 'Ingeniorum Discrimina', nota 4.

[4] 'To the Reader', *Argalvs and Parthenia* (London, 1629). On the other side, Richard Whitlock (*Zootomia*, p. 251) declares in 1654 that the affectedly ignorant 'call contracted Sense *Obscurity*'. Another opposite is Carew on Donne.

[5] Sir Robert Howard, Epilogue to *The Duke of Lerma*, 1668.

and Epithets and Compound Words made all their Lines strong and lofty'.[1] But the writers of strong lines did not seek the sublime style so much as what Demetrius calls the forcible style. Many of the means to force were employed by Seneca and strong lines; for example, brevity, abruptness, and the covert allusion. For Demetrius the Laconic is a type of the forcible style.[2] Seneca's phrase 'abruptae sententiae et suspiciosae' points to the cultivation of *suspiciones* or 'ingenious hints and mysterious allusions' in connexion with *sententiae*. In fact, this phrase suggests the main directions of strong lines, that is, vigour of movement and sharpness of wit or sense— often associated with roughness of style and *catachresis*, the tumour of this time.

The only critical treatment of strong lines is found in a French work on true and false wit that Bouhours published in 1687.[3] In the Second Dialogue he discusses a variety of sublime thoughts which he calls 'pensées fortes'; they derive their significance from some remarks by Demetrius on Laconic style.[4] John Oldmixon's version of Bouhours, called *The Arts of Logick and Rhetoric*, presents these 'Strong Thoughts' to English readers as 'Thoughts that are Just, expressed in a few Words, and in so lively a Manner, as to have a quick and powerful Effect'.[5] In short, 'the Strength of Expression very often contributes to the Dignity of Thought'.[6] No author is richer than Tacitus in these 'Masculine and concise Thoughts'; those of Tertullian are 'perhaps the stronger for that the Style is so rough and barbarous'.[7]

But brevity may contribute to obscurity, as Horace has remarked; hence one should not be too sparing of words 'on Pretence of rendring a Sentiment the stronger'.[8] This is the peculiar defect of

[1] Richard Bentley, *Dissertation upon Phalaris* (London, 1699), p. 297.
[2] Cf. *On Style*, v.
[3] *La Manière de bien penser dans les ouvrages d'esprit.*
[4] Cf. *On Style*, 7: 'For there is greater force and intensity when much meaning is conveyed in a few words.'
[5] *The Arts of Logick and Rhetoric* (London, 1728), p. 123. This is Bouhours's definition.
[6] The examples provided by Bouhours exhibit the style that Croll finds in the expressions of the 'strong wits'; cf. 'Muret', *PMLA*, xxxix. 299.
[7] *The Arts*, p. 125. Bouhours illustrates not only the strong thoughts of Tacitus, but the subtle thoughts of Pliny and the mysterious thoughts of Seneca. The rhetoric of 'point' and 'turn' provides the lively means of expression for all.
[8] Ibid., pp. 399 ff.

Tacitus. Though Bouhours merely cites the criticism that Seneca and Quintilian had made of Sallust, Oldmixon adds, 'yet how often do we hear this Sallust cried up by modern Critics, as more Eloquent even than Cicero'. As *Hudibras* has it,

> For Brevity is very good,
> If 'tis or 'tis not understood.

But 'Sallust is generally a Pattern to all Writers for Brevity, when he is not too sparing of his Words'. Thus Oldmixon comments on a writer in whom Seneca found a special variety of *sententiae*, which may be called strong thoughts or strong lines.[1]

The opposition of plain brevity to pointed brevity, or to strong lines, may be seen in Peter Heylin's apology for his style in 1621:

If itching eares which commonly follow shallow iudgements expect contradictory epithites, fustian phrases or a stile which no common capacity can goe ouer, I professe no satisfaction for them. I had rather informe the minde then please the hearing, and could wish my booke were laid rather next my readers heart then hung like a Iewell in his eare. Againe the brevitie which I vse, and the subiect concerning which I write are not capable of strong lines, and elegant raptures.[2]

Here the antithetic rhetoric of Hoskins receives at least negative testimony, but Heylin's brevity and subject exclude rhetorical ornament. Seneca, too, professed to write for the mind, and so earned the allegiance of Burton. It is not surprising, particularly if we remember Euphuism, to hear books condemned for a vocal intention that is 'hung like a jewel in the ear'. If Lancelot Andrewes complained that sermons were enjoyed for the same reason, he also satisfied by leaving an *aculeus* behind. But while the essay in its pedestrian uses sought its proper style in plain brevity, the Character and paradox, or the more witty forms, cultivated pointed brevity.

Burton, respecting matter rather than words, calls upon Seneca

---

[1] Long ago Cheke told Ascham (Smith, i. 40) that in Sallust there 'was more art than nature, and more labour than art. And in his labour also too much toil, as it were with an uncontented care to write better than he could; a fault common to very many men.' If this was also said of Jonson, he put the case against Sallust in modern terms (*Timber*, cxvi): 'And as it is fit to read the best authors to youth first, so let them be of the openest and clearest, as Livy before Sallust, Sidney before Donne.'

[2] Preface to *Microcosmus* (London, 1621). For Demetrius (*On Style*, iv. 209–20) the plain style requires clearness, vividness, and naturalness, from which persuasiveness is derived. It inclines toward brevity rather than prolixity. A special quality of the plain style is vividness or *enargeia*, which includes not only vivid representation but repetition, cacophony, and onomatopoetic words.

to support his 'extemporean' style. Nor did the seventeenth century forget this other side of Seneca, which encouraged the 'loose' style, though his curt style proved more attractive. Burton's apology for the plain style testifies to the fashionable rhetoric, but also to the authority of Seneca in behalf of the plain style. Condensed to these aspects, the apology appears as follows:

[*The Anatomy of Melancholy* is] writ with as small deliberation as I do ordinarily speak, without all affectation of big words, fustian phrases, jingling terms, tropes, strong lines, that like *Acestes'* arrows caught fire as they flew, strains of wit, brave heats, elogies, hyperbolical exornations, elegancies, &c. which so many affect. I am . . . a loose, plain, rude writer. . . . I call a spade a spade, *animis haec scribo, non auribus*, I respect matter, not words . . . seeking with *Seneca, quid scribam, non quemadmodum*, rather what than how to write. . . . Besides, it was the observation of that wise *Seneca, when you see a fellow careful about his words, and neat in his speech, know this for a certainty, that man's mind is busied about toys, there's no solidity in him. Non est ornamentum virile concinnitas*. . . . I am therefore in this point a professed disciple of *Apollonius* a scholar of *Socrates*, I neglect phrases, and labour wholly to inform my reader's understanding, not to please his ear; 'tis not my study or intent to compose neatly, which an Orator requires, but to express myself readily and plainly as it happens.[1]

Here Seneca speaks to the tune of Heylin; and Apollonius, who was Attic for Harvey, joins in the chorus; but Seneca had also contributed to the fashionable rhetoric which Burton avoids. Although fundamentally, of course, the opposition is between the essay style and the oratorical style, in Burton's time Senecan 'point' had affected both, and might be discovered not only in the jingling terms, strong lines, and strains of wit in his catalogue but in the Character and sermon. Somewhat later a more elaborate Latin mould engaged the attention of Browne; it cannot be called loose in the same sense that Burton is loose, for it endeavoured to achieve *concinnitas*. The loose period in Browne realizes an orotund effect within a laxer form than that of the Ciceronian period; in Burton, on the other hand, it pro-

---

[1] *Anatomy of Melancholy*, Everyman ed., i. 31–2. For comparison this is the *humilis* style as described by Farnaby (*Index Rhetoricus*, 1672, p. 43): 'elegans, pressa, verecunda, leniter fluens, simplex munditiis: non tamen inculta aut sicca, non enervis aut arida'; or 'correct, concise, decorous, smooth flowing, simple in its elegance: not, however, unpolished or dry, not weak or meagre'. The negative qualities were often assigned to the Stoics, as by Cicero. Burton's criteria derive from Seneca and are often echoed in this period.

duces a conversational effect; but in both it remains emergent in form, unlike the Ciceronian period.[1]

Burton also defends himself by reciting the attacks made on Seneca. For not even Seneca could escape censure, and by 'Lipsius himself, his chief propugner!' His '*sermo illaboratus*, too negligent often and remiss', is thus criticized by Lipsius:

> *In partibus spinas et fastidia habet* [he is very involved and stilted in parts], saith Lipsius; and, as in all his other works, so especially in his epistles, *aliae in argutiis et ineptiis occupantur, intricatus alicubi, et parum compositus, sine copia rerum hoc fecit* [some are full of idle subtleties; sometimes he is involved and ill arranged, and this without any great wealth of matter], he jumbles up many things together immethodically, after the Stoics' fashion, *parum ordinavit, multa accumulavit,* &c.[2]

Thus Burton might have claimed the example of Seneca and the Stoics for the jumble which he accumulated, but ordered in general with great ceremony. For his style he claimed the authority of Seneca. In practice Burton alternates between clipped and tumbling expression, cutting his speech into short clauses, 'foaming out synonymies' —the amplification which Hoskins calls 'accumulation'. These manners, which are allied in effect, are relieved by a more connected, but still loose, type of discourse. Burton runs the full gamut of Senecan style, to which he adds his own exuberant amplification.

Thus, having seen some of the forms which the new style took, we may resume our concern with its historical progress. In 1615 when Nicholas Breton, a belated Elizabethan, wrote *Characters upon Essaies*, he dedicated the work to Bacon, but it was a feeble imitation. Nevertheless, it received significant praise in the verse of I. B. *In Laudem Operis*, for there he finds 'a Lipsian style, terse Phrase'. About the same time Thomas Adams uses a Lipsian allusion in his sermon on 'The Two Sons': 'He was no talkative fellow; that to every short question returns answer able to fill a volume; with as many parentheses in one sentence as would serve Lipsius all his life.'[3] Less flattering is another reference to Lipsian style which

---

[1] The loose period, owing to its emergent form, may treat suggested patterns or syntactic commitments as loosely as its connectives.

[2] *Anatomy*, Everyman ed., i. 29. These epistles provided Burton with his stylistic doctrine. Note in this Lipsian criticism the association of lack of order and method with the Stoics.

[3] *Sermons*, ed. J. Brown (Cambridge, 1909), p. 197. This makes the parentheses of Lipsius famous for their scarcity; cf. Croll, *Revue du seizième siècle*, ii. 225.

appears in John Earle's character of 'A selfe-conceited Man' as set forth in 1628:

His tenent is alwayes singular, and aloofe from the vulgar as hee can, from which you must not hope to wrest him. He ha's an excellent humor, for an Heretique, and in these dayes made the first Arminian. He prefers *Ramus* before *Aristotle*, & *Paracelsus* before *Galen*, and whosoever with most Paradox is commended & *Lipsius* his hopping stile, before either *Tully* or *Quintilian*.[1]

In later editions the Lipsian passage is deleted; perhaps Earle felt that this allusion had lost its point. At any rate, he shows that the abrupt or 'hopping' style of Lipsius was the smart modern fashion as opposed to the correct Ciceronian. These references to Lipsius give us the cardinal features of the Senecan style as it appeared to the seventeenth century: it was terse in phrase and abrupt in movement.

Owen Feltham, who bears the clear imprint of Baconian imitation, speaks of style in his essay 'Of Preaching', which was added to his *Resolves* in 1628. His preferences in style are plainly Senecan:

A man can never speak too well, where he speaks not too obscure. Long and distended clauses, are both tedious to the ear, and difficult for their retaining. A sentence well couched, takes both the sense and the understanding. I love not those *cart-rope* speeches, that are longer than the memory of man can fathom. . . . The weighty lines men find upon the stage, I am persuaded, have been the lures, to draw away the pulpit-followers.[2]

Sententious but not obscure, such is the good style; apparently the pulpit had not been Senecan enough. Feltham feels that besides the advantage of action, the stage has the benefit of a 'more compassed language: the *dulcia sermonis*, moulded into curious phrase'. Though speaking of oratory, Feltham echoes Seneca: 'And this is *Seneca's* opinion: Fit words are better than fine ones. I like not those that are injudiciously made, but such as be expressively significant; that lead the mind to something besides the naked term.'[3] Again we encounter the central doctrine of expressiveness. But judgement is

---

[1] *Micro-cosmographie* (London, 1628), 'Character 12'.

[2] *Resolves*, First Century, xx. The potential defect of speaking too well is significant, but virtue lies in weighty or strong lines. Seneca's influence on drama had spread the cult of *sententiae* over the stage; cf. Jonson's 'Preface to *Sejanus*'.

[3] Ibid.; cf. Seneca, *Ep.* lix. 5–6.

necessary for pregnant speech: as 'Saint Augustine says, Tully was admired more for his tongue, than his mind'. And yet studied language is not vain, for 'he that reads the Fathers, shall find them, as if written with a crisped pen'. Fit words do not preclude study, but rather enjoin it. 'He prodigals a mine of excellency', cautions Feltham, 'that lavishes a terse oration to an aproned auditory.'

If Feltham's own style is a little 'curled', what he lavished on his audience may be observed by continuing the passage which draws upon Seneca:

> And he that speaks thus, must not look to speak thus every day. A combed oration will cost both sweat, and the rubbing of the brain: and combed I wish it, not frizzled, nor curled. Divinity, should not lasciviate. Un-worm-wooded jests I like well; but they are fitter for the tavern, than the majesty of a temple.

Here is that violence of metaphor which stamped the character-writers and which was later criticized in Feltham. Otherwise, his ornament derives from Senecan antithesis, with some parallelism and a touch of alliteration to set it off; again he is like the character-writers.

If we have any doubt of Feltham's Senecanism, Thomas Randolph sets it at rest. His *Conceited Peddler* (1630), which W. C. Hazlitt calls 'a shrewd satire on the follies and vices of the age', makes much of 'points' and 'a sovereign box of cerebrum' produced by alchemy, 'the fire being blown with the long-winded blast of a Ciceronian sentence, and the whole confection boiled from a pottle to a pint in the pipkin of Seneca'.[1] Of course 'points' were the favourite form of Senecan wit, and the brevity of Seneca appeared intellectual by contrast with Ciceronian length. Randolph supports the conclusion that for his age the Senecan and the Ciceronian were the two poles between which style turned. His verses 'To Master Feltham on his book of Resolves' place Feltham accordingly—'Nor doth the cinnamon-bark deserve less praise'—

> I mean, the style being pure, and strong and round;
> Not long, but pithy; being short-breath'd, but sound,
> Such as the grave, acute, wise Seneca sings—
> That best of tutors to the worst of kings.

[1] *Works*, ed. W. C. Hazlitt (London, 1875), i. 40, 44.

Not long and empty; lofty, but not proud;
Subtle, but sweet; high, but without a cloud.
Well-settled, full of nerves—in brief 'tis such,
That in a little hath comprised much.[1]

Little could be added to this character of Senecan style, for such it appeared to that age; pithy, short-breathed, grave, acute, and nervous—such was Seneca and such Feltham. It is a style, as Bacon described it, 'rather rounding into itself than spread and dilated', *potius versa quam fusa*; antithetic, not fluent like the Ciceronian.

Jonson pauses in his *Discoveries* (1641) to condemn all the essayists, but he makes a familiar criticism: 'These in all they write, confess still what books they have read last; and therein their own folly, so much, that they bring it to the Stake raw, and undigested.'[2] Here Jonson glances at the cult of sentences and consequent lack of coherence in the Senecan essay. Sir John Daw in *The Silent Woman* (II. ii) is more explicit on Seneca and Plutarch, who 'have such credit with gentlemen': 'Grave asses! mere essayists: a few loose sentences, and that's all. A man would talk so his whole age. I do utter as good things every hour, if they were collected and observed, as either of them.' Both Jonson and Bacon collected such sentences, but did not confess their own folly so patently.[3]

A few pages later Jonson eulogizes Bacon in a description inspired by Seneca the Elder:

Yet there hapn'd, in my time, one noble *Speaker*, who was full of gravity in his speaking. His language (where hee could spare, or pass by a jest) was nobly *censorious*. No man ever spake more neatly, more pressly, more weightily, or suffer'd lesse emptinesse, lesse idlenesse, in what hee utter'd. No member of his speech, but consisted of his owne graces. His hearers could not cough, or looke aside from him, without losse.[4]

---

[1] Ibid. ii. 575. Here the epithet 'strong' has the qualities that went with strong lines. This crisp antithetic phrasing is common in verse and prose alike from Jonson to Denham.

[2] *Discoveries*, ed. M. Castelain (Paris, 1906), p. 39. Jonson has explained how they and 'even their Master *Mountaigne*' fall into contradictions: they 'turne over all bookes and . . . write out of what they presently find or meet, without choice'. This was not Jonson's method.

[3] Dallington in his *Aphorismes* (1613) speaks of 'Lipsius soder', or the sentences that knit together his quotations, as in Montaigne and Burton.

[4] *Discoveries*, ed. Castelain, p. 47. Cf. the sententious declamatory manner of Cassius Severus as described by the elder Seneca: 'There was not a clause in which it was safe for the hearer to let his attention go astray: everything had a purpose. The thoughts were more numerous than the words' (W. C. Summers, *Select Letters of Seneca*, p. xxxviii).

Bacon, like Seneca, was nobly censorious 'where he could spare, or pass by a jest'. Of course, Jonson is speaking of Bacon as an orator, but it was for speaking thus 'pressly' that Cicero condemned the Stoics.[1] For Jonson, however, Bacon may 'stand as the mark and acme of our language', and of the style which Jonson favoured. His own *Discoveries*—a triumph of his theory of imitation, of converting other men's substance to his own use—is stamped with a studied brevity, a 'fine and neat language', a distinctness of form only to be attained by disciplined art. But his triumph, like his theory, is secured by the doctrine taught by Seneca, *oratio vultus animi est*, and expressed by Jonson thus, 'Language most shows a man: speak that I may see thee'.[2]

When Jonson advised Drummond 'that Petronius, Plinius Secundus, Tacitus, spoke best Latin; that Quintilian's 6.7.8. books were not only to be read, but altogether digested', he was advocating the newer taste in prose to one whose verses 'smelled too much of the Schools, and were not after the fancy of the time'. These books of Quintilian provided instruction in invention, disposition, and elocution with an emphasis on elements that appealed to Jonson's time, and therefore appear in the rhetorical aspects of this study.[3] But these elements were not unknown to the schools, for they were represented by the academic works of Erasmus, which still competed with the Ciceronian emphasis of Ascham,[4] despite his dislike of 'those foolish imitators of Erasmus, who have tied up the Latin tongue in those wretched fetters of proverbs'.[5] Erasmus had implemented the Quintilian doctrine of ornament—'curam ergo verborum, rerum volo esse solicitudinem'—which was explained in *De Copia Verborum ac Rerum* and is found in the 'illustration' of Bacon. In this doctrine the sentence, example, similitude or analogy—all provided with collections by Erasmus—were not so much ornamental as functional in matter and argument. Not only had Lyly accepted

[1] Cf. *Brutus*, 120. 'Cette façon d'écrire pressée', says La Mothe le Vayer in *L'Éloquence françoise*, is called after its ancient name, the Laconic.

[2] Cf. Seneca, *Epp.* 114 and 115; *Discoveries*, ed. Castelain, p. 104. Here Jonson seems to have derived it from Vives. Cf. F. I. Merchant (*AJP*, xxvi. 55): 'The relation between character and style . . . received from Seneca a more energetic treatment than from any one else in antiquity.'

[3] It is worth noting how often the citations of Quintilian are to these books.

[4] Cf. T. W. Baldwin, *Small Latine & Lesse Greeke*, ii. 308.

[5] Ascham, *Works*, ed. Giles, I. i, p. lxiv: here attributed to his pupil, Elizabeth.

'those wretched fetters of proverbs' but more recently Bacon had tied up the English tongue in the fetters of *sententiae* and illustrated it with Erasmian ornament.

Much of Jonson's most personal stylistic doctrine derives from Seneca's famous *Epistles* and from similar matter in Vives's *De Ratione Dicendi*. Out of Vives comes his summary of the varieties of sententious style:

A strict and succinct style is that, where you can take away nothing without losse, and that losse to be manifest. The briefe style is that which expresseth much in little. The concise style, which expresseth not enough, but leaves somewhat to bee understood. The abrupt style, which hath many breaches, and doth not seeme to end, but fall.[1]

Against this passage, as we have seen, Jonson sets the names Tacitus; the Laconic; Suetonius, Seneca, and Fabianus. Vives refers to Seneca for the remark that Fabianus inclines to the abrupt style but Cicero ends everything. Elsewhere Jonson describes out of Seneca the abrupt style which does not round out.[2] For Jonson perhaps Bacon also illustrated the first variety; certainly he illustrated the weight which he opposed to Ciceronian *copia*. Jonson's own kind of brevity is perhaps best expressed in a later sentence: 'We should therefore speak what we can the nearest way, so as we keep our gait, not leap; for too short may as well be not let into the memory, as too long not kept in.' Terse, not concise, is the proper brevity. On the other hand, while Jonson echoes Bacon's words on Ciceronian style, he removes the opposition between the ends sought by the Ciceronians and those sought by Bacon.[3]

---

[1] *Discoveries*, ed. Castelain, pp. 100–1. Sections 120–2 derive in large part from Vives's *De Ratione Dicendi*, which offered a doctrine that emphasized brevity. For the Senecan doctrine see especially *Epp.* 100, 114, 115. Quintilian (x. i. 106) says that 'from Demosthenes nothing can be taken away, to Cicero nothing can be added'.

[2] *Discoveries*, ed. Castelain, p. 38; Seneca, *Ep.* 114: 'Others, that in composition are nothing, but what is rough, and broken. *Quae per salebras, altaque saxa cadunt.* And if it would come gently, they trouble it of purpose. They would not have it run without rubs, as if that stile were more strong and manly, that stroke the eare with a kind of unevennesse.' Here strong lines should not be forgotten.

[3] *Discoveries*, ed. Castelain, pp. 108–9. Jonson (pp. 44–5) describes another speaker out of Seneca the Elder, and again brings the *Controversiae* close to this time: 'Nor was hee onely a strong, but an absolute *Speaker*, and *Writer*: but his subtilty did not shew itselfe; his judgement thought that a vice. For the ambush hurts more that is hid. Hee never forc'd his language, nor went out of the highway of *speaking*; but for some great necessity, or apparent profit. For hee denied *Figures* to be invented for ornament, but for ayde; and still thought it an extreme madnesse to bend, or wrest that which ought

Jonson also follows Vives—again with a significant liberty—in describing the forms of language, which relate to periodic structure.

> The next thing to stature, is the figure and feature in Language: that is, whether it be round, and streight, which consists of short and succinct *Periods*, numerous and polished, or square and firme, which is to have equall and strong parts, everywhere answerable, and weighed.[1]

Here 'round' seems to derive its chief meaning from number or rhythm; 'square' from symmetry of structure. These forms may be differentiated a little more sharply by the definitions given in a study of Balzac's prose:

> The square period is that which has its members of so nearly equal length that they seem to form a square. The rounded period is that which is composed of four members, so well joined and so correspondent that those which follow can be put in the place of those which precede without impairing either the sense or the beauty.[2]

Thus the 'round' adds correspondent parts to equal members; its symmetry is not purely linear. This is Vives's rather than Jonson's 'round', which is separated from Gorgian symmetry of structure, but associated with the 'short and succinct'.

On epistolary style Jonson borrows a thoroughly Senecan programme. It represents his most integrated statement on style; and although drawn from Hoskins's *Directions for Speech and Style*, it derives from the *Epistolica Institutio* of Justus Lipsius.[3] In the Lipsian scheme, as we know, five qualities were necessary: *brevitas*,

to be right.' Note that figures are not in the ordinary way of speaking, but can be useful rather than ornamental.

[1] *Discoveries*, ed. Castelain, pp. 105–6. Vives does not make this sharp separation between rhythm and symmetry, nor dispose the elements quite as Jonson does. Perhaps 'opposition' is a better word, since Jonson puts 'numerous' against 'equal' parts or isocolon.

[2] G. Guillaumie, *Guez de Balzac et la prose française*, p. 481; relative to syllabic symmetry and length of periods. The square period also has four members or parts. Another variety of period involved 'a certain demy-period call'd by the Greeks, *ergasia*, which modern Authors do call the tail of a Period, and 'tis express'd by a Participle almost in this manner: *Being certain that*, &c. *Nothing being more advantagious than*, &c.'. See *The Rules of Civility* (Antoine de Courtin's *Nouveau traité de la civilité*), London, 1678, p. 195. Bacon often employed this absolute construction.

[3] Hoskins's *Directions* was edited from manuscript by Hoyt H. Hudson (Princeton, 1935). Though not printed by Hoskins, it was given to the public partially, and posthumously, by Jonson; and almost completely, but still unacknowledged, by Blount. The section 'For Penning of Letters', which Hoskins adapted from Lipsius, is found almost verbatim in Jonson, but with some modification in Blount.

perspicuitas, simplicitas, venustas, and *decentia.* These were sub-
sumed under four heads by Hoskins, whose statement is retailed by
Jonson.

Of these qualities 'the first is brevity':

Brevity is attained in matter, by avoiding idle Complements, Prefaces,
Protestations, Parentheses, superfluous circuit of figures, and digressions:
In the composition, by omitting Conjunctions (*Not onely; But also; Both
the one, and the other, whereby it commeth to passe*) and such like idle
Particles, that have no great business in a serious Letter, but breaking of
sentences; as often times a short journey is made long, by unnecessary
baits.[1]

These means to brevity, especially in composition, are scarcely
limited, though here justified, by the requirements of the letter. But
where Hoskins had particularized the two means by which the disjunctive Senecan style was achieved, Jonson telescopes, whether
intentionally or not, the two into one.[2] Hoskins had said that brevity
in composition is attained 'by omitting conjunctions' and 'by breaking of sentences'; in Lipsius these correspond to practising asyndeton and avoiding periods. Either Jonson misunderstood the text
or altered it in view of the next remark. Hoskins remembers that
Quintilian says 'there is a briefness of the parts sometimes, that
makes the whole long'; and then comments: 'This is a fault of some
Latin Writers, within these last hundred years, of my reading, and
perhaps Seneca may be appeacht of it; I accuse him not.' It would
be awkward, to say the least, to accuse Lipsius; but for Hoskins to
borrow is no mean compliment.

'The next property of Epistolary style is Perspicuity', and with
this Jonson combines 'Plainness', which is *simplicitas* in Lipsius.
Following Lipsius, who quotes Seneca's wish that his epistles might
be 'illaboratus et facilis', Jonson counsels informality or 'a diligent
kind of negligence'. The third quality is *vigor* or 'Life and Quickness'; Lipsius says, 'Venustatem appello; cum sermo totus alacer,
vivus, erectus est.' Here Lipsius names and Jonson translates the
'argutae sententiae' of Senecan style—the sayings, similitudes, conceits, and allusions that give 'life or sharpness' to writing. The last

---

[1] *Discoveries,* ed. Castelain, p. 113. Jonson departs from the Hoskins text here: 'by
breaking of sentences, as oftentimes a long journey is made shorter by many baits.'
[2] Suetonius (*Cal.* liii) records Caligula's contempt for Seneca's style as 'sand without
mortar'.

quality, the *decentia* of Lipsius, becomes *discretio*, 'respect to discern', which signifies propriety for Jonson. In all these matters, of course, Jonson was merely repeating Hoskins, who noted with some disapproval the new tendency toward a 'sententious' or Senecan style.

Now this hierarchy of stylistic qualities, with brevity heading the list, is Senecan; and perspicuity, being a constant in communication, is less significant than vigour or *energia*, which gets a Senecan definition. While Jonson is given to quoting Quintilian, his own practice shows that Senecan doctrine was more persuasive in moulding his style.[1] It may be added that Jonson restricts the Lipsian doctrine to letters even less than Hoskins. Where Hoskins begins, 'In writing of letters there is to be regarded the invention and fashion', Jonson begins, 'In writing there is to be regarded the invention and the fashion'. Though his margin names epistolary style, something more is indicated by the sentence with which Jonson introduces his Hoskins material: 'Now that I have informed you in the knowledge of these things, let me lead you by the hand a little farther, in the direction of the use, and make you an able writer by practice.' These things are various matters relating to language and style in the antecedent discussion. Once more we are reminded that epistolary style was not the restricted style which its name may suggest, but more nearly equivalent to the plain style.

James Howell not only reminds us that the letter was the great rival of the oration as a prose form and style, but distinguishes between them in terms that might have described Seneca and Cicero.

It was a quaint difference the ancients did put betwixt a letter and an oration, that the one should be attired like a woman, the other like a man. The latter of the two is allowed large side robes, as long periods, parentheses, similes, examples, and other parts of rhetorical flourishes: but a letter or epistle should be short-coated, and closely couched; a hungerlin becomes a letter more handsomely than a gown. Indeed we should write as we speak, and that's a true familiar letter which expresseth one's mind, as if he were discoursing with the party to whom he writes in succinct and short terms.[2]

[1] Cf. Dryden's character of Jonson in the *Essay of Dramatic Poesy* (text of 1684): 'If there was any fault in his language, 'twas that he weaved it too closely and laboriously, in his comedies especially: perhaps too, he did a little too much Romanize our tongue, leaving the words which he translated almost as much Latin as he found them: wherein, though he learnedly followed their language, he did not enough comply with the idiom of ours.'

[2] *Epistolae Ho-Elianae*, i. 1. 'In the development of English style', says Joseph Jacobs

The last sentence, if it does not echo Seneca, at least gives a Senecan definition of the letter. Both in this letter, which was provoked by a copy of Balzac's letters, and in his verses 'To the Knowing Reader touching Familiar Letters', Howell so emphasizes the range of letters as to leave even the essay wanting. But he finds French letters

cobweb compositions, where there is no strength of matter, nothing for the reader to carry away with him, that may enlarge the notions of his soul. One shall hardly find an apothegm, example, simile, or anything of philosophy, history, or solid knowledge, or as much as one new created phrase, in a hundred of them.

And Balzac is no exception. It is interesting to see what Howell expects from letters rather than essays; to the reader he remarks the philosophical character of Seneca's letters and the political character of Cicero's.

The 'English Seneca', Bishop Hall, was criticized by the eighteenth century because 'he abounds rather too much with antitheses and witty turns';[1] but his Senecanism had already been criticized by Milton. In the Smectymnuan controversy Hall referred to his own style in his *Answer to Smectymnuus's Vindication*: 'In the sequel, my words, which were never yet taxed for an offensive superfluity, shall be very few; and such as, to your greater wonder, I shall be beholden for, to my kind adversaries.' While defending the authors of Smectymnuus in his *Apology*, Milton declares that Hall's design was 'with quips and snapping adages to vapour them out', and that he could not endure that they 'should thus lie at the mercy of a coy flirting style; to be girded with frumps and curtal gibes, by one who makes sentences by the statute, as if all above three inches long were confiscate'.[2] Although his opponent was anonymous (Hall's son?), Milton was here answering Bishop Hall directly, and criticizing his style for its Senecan traits. Milton returns to the attack in a stronger vein when he declares that the Remonstrant

sobs me out half-a-dozen phthisical mottoes, wherever he had them, hopping short in the measure of convulsion-fits; in which labour the

(Howell's *Familiar Letters*, 1892, vol. i, p. lxi), 'the decisive and critical moment is the introduction of the easy short sentence.' But the curt style brought pointed shortness rather than extempory ease, although Howell, like Seneca, suggests their combination.

[1] Cf. W. F. Mitchell, *English Pulpit Oratory*, p. 367.

[2] *Prose Works* (Bohn ed.), iii. 99; *The Student's Milton*, ed. F. A. Patterson, p. 542. There is now a prescription for 'The Trimming of Thomas Nashe'.

agony of his wit having escaped narrowly, instead of well-sized periods, he greets us with a quantity of thumb-ring posies.[1]

Milton, who believed in well-sized periods, thus condemns 'Lipsius his hopping style' or 'this tormentor of semicolons', who employs the proper punctuation of the 'cut' style.[2] But he rightly feared the wit of this 'factious' style.

Milton's own taste comes out more clearly in a later statement about the clerks of the university who are to be ministers:

How few among them that know to write or speak in a pure style; much less to distinguish the ideas and various kinds of style in Latin barbarous, and oft not without solecisms, declaiming in rugged and miscellaneous gear blown together by the four winds, and in their choice preferring the gay rankness of Apuleius, Arnobius, or any modern fustianist, before the native Latinisms of Cicero.[3]

Here is clear disapproval of the 'modern fustianist', who was commonly an Anti-Ciceronian. In 1622 Archbishop Abbot, in a letter to All Souls College, had found fault with the general deterioration of Latin style at Oxford: 'The style of your letter is somewhat abrupt and harsh, and doth rather express an affected brevity than the old Ciceronian oratory. And I am sorry to hear that this new way of writing is not only become the fault of the College, but of the University itself.'[4] Likewise to Milton a pure style meant Cicero, and neither 'the knotty Africanisms, the pampered metaphors, the intricate and involved sentences of the fathers', nor the Senecan style

---

[1] *Prose Works* (Bohn ed.), iii. p. 135; *Student's Milton*, p. 556. This passage does not refer directly to Hall, but it repeats the charges already made against his style. Yet for history Milton preferred—and, as Firth remarked, even imitated—the sententiousness of Sallust: see his two letters to Henry de Brass.

[2] In complaining of Hall's treatment of his text Milton (*Student's Milton*, p. 550) remarks that 'this tormentor of semicolons is . . . good at dismembering and slitting sentences'. This is apt criticism as well as complaint.

[3] *Prose Works* (Bohn), iii. 155; *Student's Milton*, p. 565. Witness the mixture in Samuel Person's character of 'A Rhetorician, or an Orator': 'A rhetorician, or orator, is one whose speech is elevated to the height of the Ciceronian pole, whose stile is copious, flexible and eloquent: he has gotten Erasmus's Copia verborum; He has a very well-uned Genius, (as I may call it) for his words are sweet Harmony that charms men; He is one that minds the cadency, and chiming of words, as much as the density of the matter, his words are genuine and masculine; He is very sententious, yea, as that famous Seneca, and he seems to have read Gabriel and Camaracensis Books of Sentences.'

[4] Quoted from the *Archives of All Souls* by Montagu Burrows, *The Register of the Visitors of the University of Oxford, 1647 to 1658* (Camden Society, 1881), p. xcvii. Earle's university character of 'A selfe-conceited Man' is thus substantiated.

condemned by Abbot.[1] As a humanist Milton scorned not only those who confused 'the ideas and various kinds of style in Latin barbarous', but also those who introduced Senecan style into English prose.

The Latin mould of Milton's style, while not excluding a colloquial element, is so obvious that we may pause to consider the contemporary awareness of such a mould in English. In 'A Discourse of Languages' Richard Flecknoe attributes the variations of English style 'to the several Inclinations and Dispositions of Princes and of Times':

That of our *Ancestors* having been plain and simple: That of Queen *Elizabeths* dayes, *flaunting* and *pufted* like her *Apparell*: That of King *Jame's*, *Regis ad exemplum*, inclining much to the *Learned* and *Erudite*, as (if you observe it) in the late Kings dayes, the *Queen* having a mayne *ascendancy* and *predominance* in the Court, the *French style* with the Courtyers was chiefly in *vogue* and Fashion.[2]

Flecknoe goes on to say that the inclination of the times has corrupted their metaphors with military terms; 'much of the *Chican* having likewise entred for its part, even to the Scripture style amongst the common Rabble, who are our Rabbies now, and Gypsies cant it in the Hebrew phrase'. The consequence of all this appears in another passage:

For the differencing of *Stiles* (to go on with this matter, since we have begun) wee may divide them into the *Vulgar*, or that of the *Time*, and the *Learned* and *Erudite*: which he, who writes for *Fame* and *lasting*, should principally affect: It bearing Translation best, being cast in the *Latine mould*, which never varies: whilst that of the Time changes perpetually, according to the various humors of the *Time*.[3]

---

[1] *Prose Works*, ii. 388; *Student's Milton*, p. 453. The effect of academic Latin composition upon English prose should not be neglected; both Lipsius and Muretus were read in the schools. But we should be chary of trying to explain style only in terms of education.

[2] *Miscellania* (London, 1653), p. 77. Tyndale offers a good example of the 'plain and simple' style. In him it is generally short of phrase and directed with precision, inclining to co-ordinate structure and unencumbered by sub-dependence. The short sentence, to which he is no stranger, is handled with incisive effect. His sense of idiom and colloquial discourse is at the centre of English speech; it is combined with a sense of form that seems not to give shape to thought but to reveal it; in reality of course it comes from a rare sense of the accidental which obscures the essential and must be removed if the native form is to be exposed. In this he had a surer sense—although he also knew Isocrates—than his great rival, Sir Thomas More. John Earle (*English Prose*, pp. 425–6) assigns him the role of preserver of the native tradition of prose through the Bible.

[3] Ibid., p. 78. In 1890 John Earle (*English Prose*, chap. xii) recognized a similar

Those who would write for posterity must now write less in Latin than in the learned and erudite style that is cast in the Latin mould.

Since the Jacobean style was of this persuasion, we might expect that a Jacobean writer would offer a suitable model; and in the refinement of English no name stood higher than that of Bacon at this time. In 1644 the writer of *Vindex Anglicus* tells us that 'the renowned Lord Bacon taught us to speak the terms of art in our own language';[1] in 1650 Dr. Walter Charleton links Browne with Bacon in the '*Carmination* or refinement of English';[2] and in 1653 S. S. (probably Samuel Sheppard) praises Bacon for being 'so succinct, elaborate, and sententious' that the best foreign wits think it the highest honour to translate him into their native languages.[3] If Bacon set a popular example in his *Essays*, he set a more learned example in his *Advancement of Learning*; for his terms of art carried from Jonson to Browne, and his period supplied an Anti-Ciceronian but Latin mould for more elaborate writing.

Sir Thomas Browne seems to have been of Flecknoe's mind when he explained why he wrote the *Pseudodoxia Epidemica* in English rather than Latin, and how the 'paradoxology' of his subject sometimes carried him into 'expressions beyond mere English apprehensions':

And, indeed, if elegancy still proceedeth, and English pens maintain that stream we have of late observed to flow from many, we shall, within few years, be fain to learn Latin to understand English, and a work will

division of styles in this period. Following a suggestion in Johnson's *Life of Dryden*, he defines a learned style and a popular style which developed in the Renaissance out of the conflict of the native tradition and the classical tradition. Of the sixteenth century Earle remarks (p. 425): 'But now within the vernacular itself began to appear a classical, learned, scholastic style; and the full significance of this new incident will not develop itself until we come to the Seventeenth century.'

[1] *Harleian Miscellany* (London, 1810), v. 431. Thus Bacon made the language more erudite.

[2] Epistle Dedicatory to Helmont's *Ternary of Paradoxes* (London, 1650). Charleton himself was obviously indebted to Browne's 'carmination'.

[3] *Paradoxes or Encomions* (London, 1653), p. 10. Of Bacon's *Essays* Earle (p. 442) takes this view: 'As English prose it is indeed a very remarkable book, especially as it lets us see through the now prevailing and rampant Classicism to some select retreat where the true English tradition flourishes with its native vigour.' When he reviews the nineteenth century he observes (p. 472): 'We have seen above that the short sentence had already in the seventeenth century begun to raise the standard of rebellion against the classical construction in long periods.' This is the contest that we are observing. But while Earle welcomes the progress of the short sentence, he warns against another 'snappy' manner which threatened his time.

prove of equal facility in either. Nor have we addressed our pen or style unto the people, (whom books do not redress, and [who] are this way incapable of reduction,) but unto the knowing and leading part of learning.[1]

Thus, in Milton's time, Browne suggests that there was an unusual effort to cast English into a Latin mould, or to bring Latin terms into English, at least when a writer was not addressing the vulgar.[2] But where Browne went to extremes in the terms of art, Milton went to extremes in the Latin mould, setting his Latin constructions against the idiom of the loose period in English.[3] This more elaborate

---

[1] *Works*, ed. Wilkin (Bohn ed.), i. 3. How Browne addressed his style unto the other audience may be seen in his familiar letters. See Hobbes's *Briefe* (III. iii) of Aristotle's *Rhetoric* on things that make an oration flat: '*Foreign words*. As for example, such as are newly derived from the Latin; which though they were proper among them whose tongue it is, are foreign in another language; and yet these may be used, so it be moderately.' Cf. Obadiah Walker (*Instructions concerning Oratory*, 1659, pp. 25–6) on the requirements of diction: 'Again, such words rather, as are less common (so they be not obsolete, or new-forged); which, for their rarity, are more observed (for we look on words, as men; admire strangers, pass by domesticks) . . . so those derived from the *Latine*, if first made familiar by some use, are to be pre-chosen; being mostwhat far smoother, than the *Saxon-English*; and, (by reason of all Sciences delivered chiefly in that tongue) more adapted for many discourses.'

[2] See Johnson's *Life of Sir Thomas Browne* (Bohn ed., vol. i, p. xxxiii): 'He fell into an age, in which our language began to lose the stability which it obtained in the time of Elizabeth; and was considered by every writer as a subject on which he might try his plastic skill, by moulding it according to his own fancy. Milton, in consequence of this encroaching licence, began to introduce the Latin idiom: and Browne, though he gave less disturbance to our structures and phraseology, yet poured in a multitude of exotick words.'

[3] The use of abnormal or excessive inversion as a means to the imitation of classical effects is often criticized in Milton and others by eighteenth-century rhetoricians like Blair. But compare C. E. Vaughan on Milton's prose (Everyman ed., p. xi): 'In style the *Areopagitica*, like the other prose works of Milton, marks the last stage of that Latin influence which, half a century earlier, had been stamped on English by the genius of Hooker. The long sentence, the sonorous cadence, of Milton's prose could hardly have been what they were, had not he, like Hooker before him, steeped his mind in the writings of the great Latins, and particularly of Cicero. Yet there is a palpable difference between Hooker's way of treating the Latin period and that in which it is adapted by Milton. In Hooker the periodic structure—the "architectural pile", in which the subordinate clauses are grouped symmetrically and with strict logical sequence around the principal sentence—is taken over bodily, or only with such modifications as the nature of an uninflected language, like the English, imperatively requires. The result is magnificent, but it is undeniably an exotic. In Milton the long sentence remains; on occasion, it becomes even longer. But the subordination of clause to clause is largely broken through. Its place is taken by a far looser structure, of which the guiding principle is co-ordination. The style of Milton, if technical terms may be forgiven, is in the main not syntactic but paratactic; not a synthesis of clauses, but an agglomeration.' If this contrast appears in Milton, it is much more apparent and pervasive in Browne. The chief evidence of change is that subdependence 'is largely broken through'. Bacon, however, managed the loose period with much greater discipline; he seldom allows it to sprawl incoherently.

Latin mould, which sought *concinnitas*, may have been in part, and especially with Milton, the result of an effort to stem the idiomatic current of the time exemplified in the pamphlet literature.

While writers of the 'loose period' are 'more idiomatic in structure than the Ciceronian Hooker', the knitting of their sentences still owes much to the formal supports of prose. What Milton achieves by inversion in the arrangement of words, after classical models, others achieve without such inversion—'that appearance of strength, dignity, and varied harmony' which belongs to periodic structure. Where Milton's syntactic Latinism helps him to produce the 'cumulative' effect of Cicero, their more idiomatic structure does not prevent them from producing a 'culminative' effect. In the 'loose period' there is less sacrifice of the thinking or conversational order to effective rhetorical order, especially that of the cumulative period; but the formal resources are still rhythmic and structural balance. The contrast in structure between Hooker and Milton on the one hand and Bacon and Browne on the other is more striking than the difference in their artistic effects. But this is not to say with Croll that writers of the looser period surrender the formal supports of prose and develop their oratorical effects out of an exaggeration of the traits of 'pointed' prose. Neither did their Asiatic parallel, for oratorical tumour does not rise out of the figures of wit unassisted by the figures of sound.

With the problem of obscurity, to which the pointed style contributed, and to which criticism became increasingly sensitive, Hobbes was especially concerned. He first encounters the problem in an Anti-Ciceronian favourite, Thucydides. In the preface to his translation of Thucydides he argues that although Thucydides has pithiness and strength of style, his difficulty springs from profundity rather than obscurity. An occasional sentence may be too long, and that is a positive fault:

For the rest, the obscurity that is, proceedeth from the profoundness of the sentences; containing contemplations of those human passions, which either dissembled or not commonly discoursed of, do yet carry the greatest sway with men in their public conversation. If then one cannot penetrate into them without much meditation, we are not to expect a man should understand them at the first speaking.[1]

---

[1] *English Works*, ed. Molesworth (London, 1843), vol. viii, pp. xxix, xxiii.

For Hobbes there could have been no more persuasive defence, but he did not encourage length in sentences.

On the formal side, the issue of propriety had been raised against Thucydides, to which Hobbes replies:

> Dionysius further findeth fault with his using to set word against word: which the rhetoricians call *antitheta*. Which, as it is in some kind of speech a very great vice, so is it not improper in characters: and of comparative discourses, it is almost the only style.[1]

If this suggests another aspect of Bacon's 'antitheta', it also suggests another resource for the character-writers. But the issue of obscurity returns in connexion with the problem of propriety:

> But yet was this his eloquence not at all fit for the bar; but proper for history, and rather to be read than heard. For words that pass away (as in public orations they must) without pause, ought to be understood with ease, and are lost else: though words that remain in writing for the reader to meditate on, ought rather to be pithy and full.[2]

Of this propriety Bacon, by the testimony of Jonson, was not observant enough; but, as we know, Jonson borrowed his praise.

It is recalled now because Hobbes quotes a similar observation about Thucydides. It is Cicero's comment in the *De Oratore*:

> Thucydides, in the art of speaking, hath in my opinion far exceeded them all. For he is so full of matter, that the number of his sentences doth almost reach to the number of his words; and in his words he is so apt and so close, that it is hard to say whether his words do more illustrate his sentences, or his sentences his words.[3]

Compare the passage which Jonson borrowed from the elder Seneca to adorn Bacon: 'There was not a clause in which it was safe for the hearer to let his attention go astray: everything had a purpose.

---

[1] Ibid., p. xxx. Dr. Johnson was not the only one who demonstrated the last remark.

[2] Ibid., p. xxxi. Then Hobbes calls Lipsius to witness: 'Lastly, hear the most true and proper commendation of him from Justus Lipsius, in his notes to his book *De Doctrina Civili* in these words: "Thucydides, who hath written not many nor very great matters, hath perhaps yet won the garland from all that have written of matters both many and great. Everywhere for elocution grave; short, and thick with sense; sound in his judgments; everywhere secretly instructing and directing a man's life and actions. In his orations and excursions, almost divine. Whom the oftener you read, the more you shall carry away; yet never be dismissed without appetite." ' This may also suggest the style of Lipsius.

[3] Ibid., p. xxiii; *De Oratore*, II. xiii. 56. Hobbes's 'sentences' mean 'thoughts', for Cicero's words are, 'ut verborum propie numerum sententiarum numero consequatur'.

The thoughts were more numerous than the words.'[1] The ratio of words to thoughts is elsewhere used by Jonson, for it serves to measure the proper degree of brevity and to distribute praise or blame. It is a relevant criterion for an age of 'point'. Tacitus writes 'in an age which affects sentences that "contain more thoughts than words" '; his 'dislocated' style is developed from his model, Sallust, who imitated Thucydides.[2] Seneca finds in Sallust that 'at other times one meets with phrases that are disconnected and full of innuendo, into which one must read more meaning than was intended to meet the ear'.[3] To Jonson's tribute must be added the complaint of Bacon's mother about his 'enigmatical folded writing'.

Hobbes, however, became less patient with obscurity. In his *Answer to Davenant*, after attacking the use of 'terms to charm the weak and pose the wise', he derides other failures in perspicuity: 'To this palpable darkness I may also add the ambitious obscurity of expressing more than is perfectly conceived, or perfect conception in fewer words than it requires.'[4] In the first kind of obscurity there are more words than thoughts, at least, clear thoughts; in the second, more thoughts than words. The one is a failure in thought, the other a failure in expression. For Hobbes these are the sources of the so-called strong lines, or their counterfeits, which are, and prove, nothing less than riddles. But without the contempt he had resolved, in the same terms, a similar problem in Thucydides.

In 1654 Richard Whitlock, in his preface to *Zootomia*, declared that Plutarch's discourses most invite imitation for the form, and are not behind any for matter, 'if mixt sometimes with those *Mucrones Sermonum*, Enlivening Touches of Seneca, full of smart Fancy, solid sense and accurate reason'. The wit of Seneca was for Whitlock still a desirable addition to the essay;[5] but 'Exactness of

---

[1] See W. C. Summers, *Select Letters of Seneca*, p. xxxviii; Seneca the Elder, *Contr.* 3, pr. 7; Seneca the Younger, *Ep.* 114. 1.

[2] Cf. W. C. Summers, *The Silver Age of Latin Literature*, p. 190.

[3] *Ep.* 114. 1: 'alias abruptae sententiae et suspiciosae, in quibus plus intellegendum esset quam audiendum?'

[4] *Critical Essays*, ed. Spingarn, ii. 63. In his *Briefe* (III. x) of Aristotle's *Rhetoric* Hobbes does not pervert his text by declaring that in metaphor 'the more unlike and unproportionable the things be otherwise, the more grace hath the metaphor'. But his *Briefe* was closer to his defence of Thucydides than to his *Answer to Davenant*.

[5] A year earlier Flecknoe (*Miscellania*, 1653, p. 99) had defined '*wit*, whose *purlews* are chiefly *words*, as *matter* is of *wisdome*', so that clenches, quibbles, jingles, bulls, 'although properly they be not *Wit* . . . yet they declare the copiousnesse of a *Language*'.

writing on any Subject in Poetic heights of Fancy, or Rhetorical Descants of Application' he left to others.

For my own part I may say, as Lipsius *in his Epistle*; Rationem meam scribendi scire vis? fundo, non scribo, nec id nisi in Calore & interno quodam Impetu, haud aliter quam Poetae. *Would you know (saith he) my manner of writing? it is a kind of voluntary* Tiding of, *not* Pumping for; Notions flowing, *not* forced; *like* Poets unconstrained Heats *and* Raptures: *such is* mine, *rather a* running Discourse *than a* Grave-paced Exactnes....[1]

Fundere, if we remember, was the aim of Seneca's 'loose' style; and Lipsius here echoes Seneca no less than when he subscribed to the curt style in his *Quaestiones*. To an unusual, if not unique, degree Lipsius managed—as contemporaries observed—to combine a broken style with flowing movement. But Whitlock's subscription to this aim suggests that the loose rather than the curt variety of Senecan style was proving congenial to the essay as the product of 'a mind thinking'. Informality is the effect of this style and the aim of the personal essay.

If Whitlock points to the triumph of the loose style in the Restoration, Thomas Blount's *Academie of Eloquence* shows that the curt style yet has some life before it. This rhetoric, which adopts almost in full the *Directions* of Hoskins and also borrows from Bacon, ran through five editions between 1654 and 1684; in fact, no other rhetoric of that time seems to have been quite so popular. If we examine a passage in the *Academie* on *sententia*—borrowed with some modernization from Hoskins—we shall discover that the ideal form of the curt style is still presented as if it were current:

Sententia, if it be well used, is a Figure; if ill and too much, a Style, of which none that write humorously and factiously, can be clear in these days, when there are so many Schismes of Eloquence. We study now-a-days according to the predominancy of Criticall fancies. Whilst *Moral Philosophy* was in request, it was rudeness, not to be sententious; whilst *Mathematics* were of late in vogue, all similitudes came from *Lines*, *Circles* and *Angles*; But now that *Mars* is predominant, we must *recruit* our wits, and give our words a new *Quarter*.[2]

---

[1] Preface to *Zootomia* (London, 1654), sig. a5ʳ; cf. Seneca, *Ep.* 100. Whitlock, like Montaigne, liked a desultory manner of discourse; but he was also influenced by Cornwallis, whom he quotes on the nature of the essay.

[2] *Academie of Eloquence* (London, 1654), p. 34. Cf. Hoskins, *Directions*, pp. 38–40. Although Hoskins retailed Senecan doctrine, he was not uncritical; and Blount adapted this criticism to his own time.

The criticism of sententious style remains the same, but 'critical fancies' have altered a little. Its association with moral philosophy, and so with the moral essay, is still specified. It might be added that mathematical fancy had not yet deserted poetry. But such wariness toward the pure form of the curt style does not prevent Blount, any more than it prevented Hoskins, from retailing Senecan instructions for an epistolary style.

Blount, who repeats the instructions of Hoskins and Jonson, begins with their opening remark on the fashion of this style: 'Now for Fashion, it consists in four qualities of your Style. The first is Brevity.'[1] To illustrate Blount's borrowing, let me quote the passage which I have already cited from Jonson:

> Brevity is attain'd upon the matter, by avoiding idle complements, prefaces, protestations, long Parentheses, supplications, wanton circuits of Figures, and digressions, by composition, omitting conjunctions, *Not onely but also*, *the one and the other*, *whereby it comes to passe*, *etc.* and such like particles, that have no great business in a serious Letter; By breaking off sentences; as oftentimes a short journey is made long by many baits.[2]

In the last means to brevity Blount, like Jonson, makes nonsense of Hoskins's consequence by interchanging 'short' and 'long'. It corresponds to Lipsius's advice to write in members rather than periods, and derives from Demetrius, to whom Lipsius refers under *Brevitas* and *Simplicitas*.[3] Both Jonson and Blount assign a contrary effect to this means to brevity—an effect that Hoskins introduces only as a qualification made by Quintilian. But 'omitting conjunctions' and 'breaking off sentences' are still precise enough phrases with which to describe the disconnected 'curt period' that Croll has analysed.

Blount, however, looks ahead when he adds a remark that is more explicit than any comparable idea in Jonson, not to mention Hoskins; in fact, it is contradictory to the demands of brevity: 'Under this Notion somewhat may be said of Periods, which ought not to be too long, nor yet too short.' Which ought not to be used, said Lipsius; nor did he suggest 'a certain Geometrical mediocrity' in

---

[1] *Academie*, p. 142; cf. *Discoveries*, ed. Castelain, p. 112.

[2] *Academie*, p. 143; cf. *Discoveries*, p. 113. This text is more confused than Jonson's. Oratory was less restricted.

[3] Cf. Demetrius, *On Style*, ii. 46–7. On this point Hoskins's expression is closer to Demetrius, and he may have derived it for himself, as he did the following remark from Quintilian.

length of sentence. This 'vertue' certainly threatens the reign of brevity. Again reflecting his time, Blount quotes Longinus in support of another requirement which threatens the reign of abruptness: 'There ought likewise to be a special regard had to the cadence of the words, that the whole contexture of the Period may yield a certain kind of harmony to the ear.'[1] The doctrine of the period has no place in this programme, but Longinus is a new influence in Blount's rhetoric.

The next requirement carries Blount back to the text of Hoskins and Jonson: 'The next property of Epistolary Style, is, Perspicuity, which is not seldom endangered by the former quality.' And 'under this vertue', echoes Blount, 'may come Plainness, which is, not to be too curious in the order', but to use 'a diligent kind of negligence'.[2] Blount likewise frowns upon 'perfumed moding terms', but goes beyond Hoskins and Jonson by referring explicitly to Seneca:

Besides, a vain curiosity of words hath so scandalized some Philosophers, that *Seneca* (in one of his epistles) says, Had it been possible to make himself understood by signes, he would rather serve himself of them, then of discourse, to the end he might the better avoid all manner of affectation.[3]

Blount's third and fourth qualities are identical with those of Hoskins and Jonson, the third being 'Life' or wit, and the fourth 'Respect' or propriety.

Thus Blount fulfils the promise of his Epistle Dedicatory 'with some particular Instructions and Rules premised, for the better attaining to a Pen-perfection'. As this Senecan scheme of style, appropriately associated with the letter, passed from Hoskins and Jonson to Blount it received important though slight alterations;

---

[1] *Academie*, pp. 143–4. Among Blount's *Common Places* (p. 66), under 'Eloquence', we find a not insignificant entry: 'Eloquence is a way of speech prevailing over those whom we design it prevail; That is, if we will take it in the short or Laconick way, a distilling our notions into a quintessence, or forming all our thoughts in a Cone and smiting with the point, &c. Mr. *Hall* in his Epistle before *Longinus*.' The reference is to John Hall's translation, *The Height of Eloquence*, 1652; and Blount's quotation omits the definition of 'the more spacious or Asiatic' way. Blount seems at least to tip the balance toward brevity.

[2] *Academie*, p. 145; cf. *Discoveries*, p. 115. Thus plainness concerns *dispositio* or order, which in the Hoskins programme is mentioned before 'fashion' or style.

[3] *Academie*, pp. 145–6; cf. *Discoveries*, p. 116. See Seneca's well-known *Ep.* 75. John Wilkins's *Essay towards a Real Character and a Philosophical Language* (1668) sought to avoid this scandal.

and the *Academie of Eloquence*, partly no doubt because of its bias toward a 'modish' audience, renewed the life of Senecan doctrine, as well as the Hoskins rhetoric, in the early days of the Royal Society. This fact is not quite negligible, particularly when this programme could command the authority of Ben Jonson.

In 1655 Meric Casaubon provides another kind of background for the course of style by including 'Rhetoricall Enthusiasme' in his *Treatise of Enthusiasme*. Here he treats 'of the strange, but natural effects of Speech', or the natural causes of strange effects. This rationalistic intention, which is motivated by the 'enthusiasm' of Commonwealth times, relates the effects of speech not only to rhetorical causes but also to contemporary views. Casaubon's attitude toward rhetoric, which is common to the Restoration, turns upon the idea that rhetorical speech is 'dressed with certain devices and allurements' and directed toward the affections.

However, it is a very disputable point, whether bare speech, if well handled, be not sufficient, nay most available to perswade, in things of most weight. For those actions are best grounded, that are grounded upon judgement, upon which bare Speech hath most direct influence; as Rhetorick hath upon the Affections. . . .[1]

'But it is an ample subject', concludes Casaubon, 'upon which Seneca is very copious, and in my judgment hath done very well', though Aristotle has been more expeditious. Casaubon often quotes Seneca against rhetoric or vain words, though he finds Seneca inconstant to himself. But Casaubon's emphasis on bare speech has nothing to do with the Royal Society.

The 'strange effects' of speech are explained as the sensuous 'allurements' of rhetoric, which is a creator of illusion or, as Bacon would say, impression or appearance. First he deals with the pleasures of the ear in rhythmic and harmonious composition; but, though highly regarded by the ancients, 'there is not any part of Rhetoric more subject to scorn and contempt, and not without cause'.[2] For it seems incompatible with a concern for subject-matter. The pleasures of the eye bring us to 'such Figures and Ornaments' as metaphor, similitude, allegory: for 'every metaphor that is proper and natural', according to Cicero, 'exposeth the things

---

[1] *A Treatise of Enthusiasme* (London, 1655), p. 140
[2] Ibid., pp. 172 ff.

that are spoken of to the senses; especially to that of the eyes'.[1]
This is its advantage over plain speech. 'But this very reason that
makes them so pleasing in ordinary language, hath brought Metaphors out of credit with Philosophers, that seek not the pleasures of
the senses, but the naked truth of things.' Plutarch disapproves of
them. 'Seneca allows them to Philosophers . . . because of human
infirmity, that by the help of such figures, the teacher may bring
his hearers to the knowledge of those things, by a kind of present
sight, which otherwise they cannot understand.'[2] To Seneca this
was the practice of early Roman or Stoic writers; it was part of the
theory of Bacon.

Next the pleasures of the eye bring us to 'a certain propriety of
speech' which is commonly called *enargeia* or *energeia*, though they
are sometimes distinguished; it is a 'lively representation' or 'a
representation of shapes and images'.[3] Casaubon observes that 'of
this property or faculty, common Rhetoricians treat largely'; and
we may recall its treatment by Puttenham. Finally, such pleasures
bring us to the Sophistic style: 'It is a very pleasing kind of language, it cannot be denied, to any that have either ears, or eyes, or
souls sensible of any kind of harmony or symmetry; whether in
point of Sounds, or of Structures.' While bare speech is directed to
the judgement, these are the allurements of rhetoric that play upon
the affections, and cause the 'enthusiasm' which is produced by
speech. It is no exaggeration to say that the 'true old Enthusiastick
Breed' disturbed Wilkins more in language than in doctrine. Although the allurements of Canting speech usually did not attain
these refinements, its 'mystical kind of phrase' was just as remote
from bare speech, and became an early object of reform in sermon
style.

While Casaubon recalled Seneca as the advocate of plain speech,
Richard Flecknoe in 1658 spoke of pointed style in the form in
which it had achieved fame:

It gives you the hint of discourse, but discourses not; and is that in
mass and ingot, you may coin and wire-draw to eternity; 'tis more *Seneca*
than *Cicero*, and speaks rather the language of oracles than orators: every
line a sentence, and every two a period. It says not all, but all it says is

---

[1] Ibid., pp. 180 ff. Cf. Sprat on 'Wit' in Chap. IX.
[2] Seneca, *Ep.* 59.   [3] *Treatise*, pp. 182–3.

good, and like an air in Musick is either full of clozes, or still driving towards a close: 'tis no long-winded exercise of spirit, but a forcible one, and therefore soonest out of breath; 'tis all matter, and has nothing of superfluity, nothing of circumlocution; so little comporting with mediocrity, as it or extols to Heaven, or depresses unto Hell, having no mid' place for Purgatory left.[1]

Here Flecknoe defines and illustrates both the Character and the Senecan style, meanwhile suggesting its word-play and violence of metaphor. He not only reminds one of Cornwallis's conception of the essay, but exemplifies the repetitive movement of the curt style. A few years later Dr. John Worthington, in a letter to Dr. Henry More, writes about the *Miscellanea* (1662) of Edmund Elys: 'He hath read Seneca much, and imitates his concise style, which is not so good as Tully's, though more easy to attain to.'[2] Thus had spoken the critics of the Lipsians. Seneca is not yet quite outmoded, either in the Character or in Latin prose.

Dr. Ralph Bathurst, President of Trinity College and a member of the Royal Society, was also a Senecan. It was to Bathurst that Samuel Parker, another member of the Society, dedicated his *Free and Impartial Censure of the Platonick Philosophie* (1666), in which he attacks 'enthusiastic' language as dangerous to philosophy. The prose of Bathurst is thus described by Thomas Warton, his biographer:

His latin orations are wonderful specimens of wit and antithesis, which were the delight of his age. They want, upon the whole, the purity and simplicity of Tully's eloquence, but even exceed the sententious smartness of Seneca, and the surprising turns of Pliny. They are perpetually spirited, and discover an uncommon quickness of thought. His manner is concise and abrupt, but yet perspicuous and easy. His allusions are delicate, and his observations sensible and animated. His sentiments of congratulation or indignation are equally forcible: his compliments are most elegantly turned, and his satire is ingeniously severe.[3]

It would seem that the Royal Society did not affect the 'state of academical literature', at least as Warton finds it in one member of

---

[1] 'Of the Authors Idea, or of a Character', *Enigmaticall Characters* (London, 1658).
[2] *Diary and Correspondence*, ed. R. C. Christie (Chetham Society, 1886), II. ii. 291.
[3] *The Life and Literary Remains of Ralph Bathurst* (London, 1761), pp. 216–17. Warton gives a similar character to Bathurst's verse, observing (significantly) that 'Ovid was the principal pattern of his latin poetry, and his favourite classic'. Dryden's endeavour might be summed up as the effort to replace the wit of Ovid and Lucan by the wit of Virgil.

that society; but perhaps Latin set one free. In short, Bathurst had a talent for the Senecan style; and we may recall that another member of the Society, Glanvill, began to write with a talent of the same sort. No doubt, Senecan 'shortness' was not a serious handicap for a working member of that society.

When Glanvill describes the style of Sprat's *History of the Royal Society*, he might be expected to explain that style in terms of the Royal Society's manner of discourse. This is what he says:

... That the *Style* of that Book hath all the *properties* that can recommend any thing to an *ingenious relish*: For 'tis *manly*, and yet *plain*; *natural*, and yet not *careless*: The *Epithets* are *genuine*, the *Words proper* and *familiar*, the *Periods smooth* and of *middle* proportion: It is not *broken* with *ends* of *Latin*, nor *impertinent Quotations*; nor made *harsh* by *hard* words, or *needless terms* of *Art*: Not rendred *intricate* by long *Parentheses*, nor *gaudy* by *flanting Metaphors*; not *tedious* by *wide fetches* and *circumferences* of *Speech*, nor *dark* by too much *curtness* of *Expression*: 'Tis not *loose* and *unjointed*, *rugged* and *uneven*; but as *polite* and as *fast* as *Marble*; and briefly, avoids all the *notorious defects*, and wants none of the *proper ornaments* of Language.[1]

Is this to reject all ornament and redundance for close, naked, natural expression? Or is it to recognize a more complex set of extremes between which prose may now find its proper character? In this description Sprat appears to steer a course between the Ciceronian and the Senecan, or between the curt and the loose style, avoiding the excesses of both as well as the limitations of 'Artizans, Countrymen, and Merchants'. It is interesting chiefly as a catalogue of prose virtues and vices as the Restoration saw them—a catalogue which the programme of the Royal Society could not rationalize into this division of notorious defects and proper ornaments of language. Glanvill's own clipped and antithetic style is reminiscent of

---

[1] *Plus Ultra* (London, 1668), pp. 84–5. With reference to this work Thomas Birch (*History of the Royal Society*, ii. 197, n. *d*) quotes a letter from Oldenburg to Boyle on 1 Oct. 1667: 'There is a certain gentleman, a florid writer, one of our royal collegiates, who intends to print shortly some paralipomena relating to the history of our society; wherein he means to take more notice of the performances of some eminent members thereof, than hath been done by Mr. Sprat, and farther to recommend and vindicate the modern experimental philosophers, by representing the advantages of this way of trials, both for light and use, above that of former times.' Sprat had not satisfied Oldenburg on all counts, but it does not occur to him that 'a florid writer' might be inconsistent with the achievements of the Royal Society. Cf. Glanvill's *Essays* (1676), Essay III, pp. 34–5, where this description again anticipates his charges against sermon style.

the style in which Lipsius described the style of Seneca. A study in variations upon the same basic pattern is provided by the foregoing passages from Flecknoe, Warton, and Glanvill, which exhibit various degrees of the antithetic Senecan mode.

Ten years later Glanvill made his chief statement of the plain style, but it was related to the sermon, about which the controversy over the plain style centred. As a member of the Royal Society, Glanvill may seem especially qualified to speak for this style, and his general theme is that 'plainness is for ever the best eloquence'. Heretofore, 'plainness' and 'eloquence' usually have not been regarded as synonyms. After such works as Eachard's *Grounds and Occasions of the Contempt of the Clergy* (1670) and Arderne's *Directions concerning the Matter and Stile of Sermons* (1671),[1] Glanvill gave vigorous expression to the doctrine of plainness in *An Essay concerning Preaching* and *A Seasonable Defence of Preaching and the Plain Way of it*, both published in 1678. Plainness is the watchword at this time, and Glanvill would have sermon style plain, natural, adequate, familiar but not mean, 'obvious' rather than 'Cryptic'.

Glanvill knew what the terse Senecan style was, for he had practised it; hence the significance of his remarks on wit. While 'some Sermons lose their efficacy and force by being too full, and close', he would not go so far as 'what M. Cowley saith of Wit in Poetry,

Rather than all be Wit, let none be there.'

Associating wit with 'closeness', he concludes that the right course is to seek a mean between prolixity and brevity.[2] For Glanvill, who would not be dull, the 'proper, grave, and manly wit' still includes 'sharp, and quick thoughts' set out in lively colours; his wit still comes under the head of 'vigour' or 'life'.[3] And it must not be for-

---

[1] Arderne (p. 38) remarks that the practice of an open plainness 'is oft difficult by reason of the other rule joyned to it, it being certain, that he who labours to be short is in danger of obscuritie in discourse'. Here—where plainness means perspicuity—we find the dual allegiance that is found in Jonson and Selden.

[2] *An Essay concerning Preaching* (London, 1678), p. 63. Cowley included in what was not wit 'the dry chips of short lung'd Seneca'. On the relation of 'full' and 'close' cf. Hobbes on Thucydides and Wilkins 'Concerning Expression' in *Ecclesiastes*. In his *Essays* (VII) Glanvill connects Solomon's House with Browne's *Garden of Cyrus* by way of 'the old *Quincuncial, Lozenge* Figures'.

[3] Ibid., p. 72. Glanvill's plainness was opposed not only to affectation but also to dullness. If his flowers are pruned in the *Essays*, the reason may be conviction or it may be necessity. When he brings some of his writings 'together into a small Collection' as the *Essays* (1675), he makes it quite clear that his chief labour has been one of reduction;

gotten that his wit involves 'a quickness in the fancy to give things proper Images', a talent which probably led Oldenburg to call him a 'florid writer'. Thus Glanvill's doctrine resembles his praise of Sprat, except perhaps for his concern about wit, still a proper ornament of the plain style; yet even Sprat appealed to an 'ingenious relish'.

For the essay style Dryden spoke in his *Life of Plutarch*, written in 1683, when he characterized the two ancient models of Montaigne, Seneca and Plutarch. Since Dryden had condemned the wit which marked the curt Seneca, we should not expect him to favour Seneca over Plutarch:

The style of Plutarch is easy and flowing, that of Seneca precipitous and harsh: the first is even, the second broken. The arguments of the Grecian, drawn from reason, work themselves into your understanding, and make a deep and lasting impression in your mind; those of the Roman, drawn from wit, flash immediately on your imagination, but leave no durable effect: so this tickles you by starts with his arguteness, that pleases you for continuance with his propriety.[1]

Seneca is given his typically curt character, but Plutarch is given the loose character, which Seneca was also called upon to support. For this double authority Seneca suffered when his curt manner became the object of criticism, even at the hands of writers who were fundamentally Senecan. Dryden's distinction is primarily one of movement; and, although the abrupt and the flowing had distinguished the Senecan and the Ciceronian, it is clear that he did not have that opposition in mind. For 'easy' there was also a Senecan meaning—to write without labour or ceremony.

While Dryden writes with unusual symmetry in this passage, he is not thinking of Plutarch as a Ciceronian but rather as a writer of the loose style. When the curt style was rejected, Plutarch remained a proper authority for Anti-Ciceronian style, as he had been with Cornwallis. Significantly Seneca is damned for his 'arguteness'— now anglicized—while Plutarch is crowned with 'propriety', to which Dryden had given new importance. The qualities in which

and reduction was necessary to his new form. In altering the *Vanity* he has even felt cramped, unable to express himself with 'that ease, freedom, and fullness' which he might have commanded amid fresh thoughts. Instead he had to prune his fullness. Yet Glanvill remained rather partial to short *cola* or members.

[1] *Prose Works*, ed. Malone (London, 1800), ii. 419. Remember Hobbes on antithesis: 'of comparative discourses, it is almost the only style.'

Dryden believed in 1683, after he had renounced 'sharpness of conceit', are all given to Plutarch, none to Seneca. Yet Dryden is devoted to the 'unexpected' period of the Anti-Ciceronians, which derived more from Bacon's 'aculeate' writers than from Plutarch. But for Dryden, at any rate, being pleased by continuance with propriety has won over being tickled by starts with 'arguteness'.

Obviously the style of this passage seems to refute Dr. Johnson, but it is exceptional. If we recall Dryden's argument that even in verse one word should seem to beget another as in the negligence of prose, we shall better appreciate the significance of Dr. Johnson's classic description of Dryden's style in the prefaces:

They have not the formality of a settled style, in which the first half of the sentence betrays the other. The clauses are never balanced, nor the periods modelled: every word seems to drop by chance, though it falls into its proper place. Nothing is cold or languid; the whole is airy, animated, and vigorous; what is little, is gay; what is great, is splendid. . . . Though all is easy, nothing is feeble; though all seems careless, there is nothing harsh; and though since his earlier works more than a century has passed, they have nothing yet uncouth or obsolete.

In Dryden that other aspect of plainness or simplicity which Hoskins called 'a diligent kind of negligence' has come to fruition; it is now considered the art of being 'easy'. The antithesis to Dryden's style, as set up in Johnson's opposition, is illustrated in the style of this description, or in that which opposes Seneca and Plutarch; it has the formality that betrays what is to come.[1]

If in Dryden 'every word seems to drop by chance', it is because each word seems to beget the next, and no phrase provides an obvious cue to the syntax. The essential characteristic of Dryden's style is, therefore, none other than the organic or trailing structure which belongs to the 'loose period' in Senecan prose. Another such stylist is the later Montaigne, from whom Dryden declares that he learned the art of rambling, which is incident to the desultory

[1] Hazlitt's description of Johnson's style places it unwittingly in the Sophistic tradition: 'The structure of his sentences, which was his own invention, and which has been generally imitated since his time, is a species of rhyming in prose, where one clause answers to another in measure and quantity, like the tagging of syllables at the end of a verse; the close of the period follows as mechanically as the oscillation of a pendulum, the sense is balanced with the sound; each sentence, revolving round its centre of gravity, is contained within itself like a couplet, and each paragraph forms itself into a stanza' (*Works*, ed. P. P. Howe, vi. 102).

Senecan mode. Once in a letter to Etherege, dated Feb. 16th, 1687, Dryden declared, 'for I will never enter the lists in Prose with the undoubted best Author of it which our nation has produced'. Let this be flattery and it is still revealing, for Dryden makes too much of polite conversational prose for us to mistake the direction of the compliment. His admiration for Congreve supports this praise; and, if Congreve reports him correctly, the two admirations suggest what he saw in Tillotson.

When in 1684 Gilbert Burnet adorned the language with a translation of More's *Utopia*, he sketched anew the progress of English style. While his reproof must have seemed ironic to Dryden, it affords another prospect to us. The succession of styles now appears from a later point of view, and Bacon himself has begun to suffer from the change:

The English Language has wrought it self out, both of the fulsome Pedantry under which it laboured long ago, and the trifling way of dark and unintelligible Wit that came after that, and out of the coarse extravagance of Canting that succeeded this: but as one Extream commonly produces another, so we were beginning to fly into a sublime pitch, of a strong but false Rhetorick, which had much corrupted, not only the Stage, but even the Pulpit; two places, that tho they ought not to be named together, much less to resemble one another; yet it cannot be denied, but the Rules and Measure of Speech is generally taken from them: but that florid strain is almost quite worn out, and is become now as ridiculous as it was once admired. . . . We are now so much refined, that how defective soever our Imaginations or Reasonings may be, yet our Language has fewer Faults, and is more natural and proper, than it was ever at any time before. When one compares the best Writers of the last Age, with these that excel in this, the difference is very discernable: even the great Sir *Francis Bacon*, that was the first that writ our Language correctly; as he is still our best Author, yet in some places has Figures so strong, that they could not pass now before a severe Judg. I will not provoke the present Masters of the Stage, by preferring the Authors of the last Age to them. . . . Their Language is now certainly properer, and more natural than it was formerly, chiefly since the correction that was given by the *Rehearsal*. . . .[1]

[1] Preface to Burnet's translation of *Utopia*, London, 1684. The metaphor of the 'canting crew' had been castigated by Simon Patrick in *The Friendly Debates*. For another survey of English prose see 'The Preface of the Publisher' to *The Whole Critical Works of Rapin*, London, 1706. The publisher, Basil Kennet, mentions for style in oratory, Sidney, Hooker, Bacon; in history, Bacon, Herbert, Daniel, Temple,

Here Burnet adds another threat to English style—the reaction from a low to a high style—which was checked by *The Rehearsal*; but he reaches the same conclusion that Dryden had reached with respect to the writers of the last age. Perhaps one ought to conclude that Dryden was ejected from the Royal Society for his heroic plays rather than his failure to pay his dues. One cannot escape the suggestion that the strong rhetoric of recent time associates this latest abuse of language with the cult of strong lines, which Casaubon had related to false sublimity or bombast. It is clear that the latest extravagance had corrupted both the stage and the pulpit.

While the last quarter of the century was still young Sir George Mackenzie, who taught Dryden to observe 'turns', again defined the two poles of style on which the controversies of the century turned:

Before I propose what Phrase or Stile is fit for a Pleader, 'tis fit to tell, That the Two usual Stiles, known by distinct Names, are, the *Laconic*, or short sententious Stile, and the *Asiatic*, or profuse and copious Stile: The First was us'd by the old *Roman* Legislators, as is clear by reading the Digests; but when the Empire was transferr'd to *Constantinople* in *Asia*, the Empire chang'd its Stile with its Seat; and we find that *profluvium Asiaticum* in the *Codex* and Novels: Yet all the *Grecian* and *Roman* Pleaders, even in their Purity, us'd a full copious Stile, as is clear by *Demosthenes*, *Cicero*, and others; and tho' Legislators or Judges should use the *Laconic*, yet the other must still reign at the Bar.[1]

In 1652 John Hall had also defined eloquence in relation to these two poles: 'the short or LACONICK way' and 'the more spacious or ASIATIC'.[2] Still earlier Hoskins—also a lawyer—had said that '*sententia* is better for the bench than the bar', while Bacon apparently

---

Clarendon; in philosophy, Bacon, Sprat; in the essay, Bacon, Temple, Cowley, Collier. In Bacon, for example, he notes 'that bold Expressiveness, and strong significancy of Language.' He concludes that when the English Tongue 'shall be further improv'd upon the Ancient Models, and be made capable of that bold Transposition of Words, and those Powerful Elegancies in Prose, which Mr. Milton, with his happy Second, have so nobly display'd in Verse, it may then attain its last Perfection and Growth.' This conclusion, however, reflects an emulator of Rymer, not the ideal of the time, except for Shaftesbury. White Kennet, in his Preface to *A Complete History of England*, contrasts Daniel and Milton: 'his English is much more Modern than Milton's, tho' he liv'd before him: But Mr. Milton chose to write (if the Expression may be allow'd) a hundred Years backward,' or 'with the Majestick Air of old Greece or Rome.'

[1] 'What Eloquence is fit for the Bar', *Works* (Edinburgh, 1716), i. 16; *Idea Eloquentiae Forensis Hodierna*, 1681. Mackenzie was also a Senecan essayist.

[2] 'Dedication', *The Height of Eloquence*, 1652: a translation of Longinus.

had thought otherwise. Hobbes, too, had found the sententious style in Thucydides 'not at all fit for the bar'; it was not the style for oratory. Laconic or Asiatic, Senecan or Ciceronian, short or copious, this is the great opposition of the century; these are the two vanities of style that Bacon criticized as hindrances to philosophy. But of course they represent a great simplification of the varieties of style involved in the controversies that raged around them.

In retrospect we may attempt to place the curt Senecan style by comparing the stylistic aims expressed by Jonson, Blount, and Glanvill. Although such a comparison is open to some obvious objections, nevertheless, in these aims we can find a simple outline of the changes in prose style during the century. The requirements of particular types need not obscure the general aims, to which all in their measure aspire. Jonson follows Hoskins in advocating brevity, perspicuity (and plainness), vigour, and propriety; but to these Blount adds the inconsistent requirements of cadence and medium length in the period. By placing brevity first, both testify to the reign of the terse Senecan style; but by advancing cadence and 'mediocrity' in the period, Blount looks beyond that style. For the Royal Society to suggest a return to 'the primitive purity and shortness' was, in one respect at least, not to suggest progress. In the quality of plainness, which Jonson and Blount place under the head of perspicuity and relate to disposition as well as diction, we find the aim of style that becomes dominant after the reign of brevity. It is by these watchwords that we can discern movement in style or the schools of style.

Glanvill, though inclined to brevity, emphasizes Blount's new requirement of a mean between brevity and prolixity—Senecan and Ciceronian extremes—but elevates the subordinate plainness of Jonson and Blount to first place in the hierarchy of style. With Glanvill the reign of brevity has given way to the reign of plainness; and plainness, 'the best Character of Speech', is not 'Bluntness', but rather a simplicity in which there are no 'words without sense'. Of the other qualities specified by Jonson and Blount, vigour outweighs propriety with Glanvill. If he believes that the wit which consists in 'playing with words' is 'vile and contemptible fooling', he points out that 'there is a vice of Preaching quite opposite to this, and that is a certain road-dulness, and want of wit', which only philosophy will relieve.[1] For Glanvill at least it is possible to be too plain. In propriety we find the aim of style that becomes dominant after the reign of plainness, which was disposed to neglect it.

'So many things almost in an equal number of words' meant a bare report for the Royal Society; but as a stylistic criterion, echoed from Cicero, it provides a way of distinguishing the brief and the prolix, or the plain and the ornate, styles. The requirement that the words shall not exceed the things or thoughts prevents elaboration and ornament, or words not necessitated by the thought, words devoted to the end of pleasure or efficacy rather than instruction. If it discourages rhetorical ornament, it encourages brevity by eliminating all but functional words.[2] It thus becomes not only a measure of the relative plainness of any style but also a measure of its relative brevity.

Jonson's scale of succinct styles illustrates the application of this principle in determining relative brevity. It has been applied to various writers by various critics; it often appears in the seventeenth century. In one form or another, as we have seen, it has been related to such writers as Thucydides, Sallust, Seneca, Tacitus, Lipsius, or Bacon; it has even distinguished between Demosthenes and Cicero. Sprat's formula in its aspect of brevity was an echo of the past; in its aspect of plainness, if it had literary significance, it was a passing discipline. For Dryden, in his propriety of thoughts and words, emphasized considerations of literary elegance in proportioning words to thoughts; with him the criterion is propriety rather than plainness—the Aristotelian rule for distinction beyond the needs of perspicuity. Though brevity did not remain the soul of wit, it did not cease to be an important attribute; but Senecan point was rejected by Dryden.

[1] *An Essay concerning Preaching* (London, 1678), pp. 72–3. Glanvill's criticism of preaching bears a resemblance both to that of Wilkins, a pillar of the Royal Society, and to that of South, an enemy of the Society. His last remark concerns the more illiterate Nonconformist preaching.

[2] Even Lysias had to resort to synonyms or padding to fill out his occasional symmetrical patterns. Such exigencies constantly beset the cult of form. It is not symmetry but such indulgence that divides the Ciceronian and the Anti-Ciceronian. The proportion of words to thoughts involves both simplicity and brevity, or their opposites.

8. *Scheme and Point in Pulpit Oratory*

It so happens that we know of Lyly's admiration for Lancelot Andrewes, who did not change his style when he became 'stella predicantium' for later audiences. Nashe supplies us with the evidence in *Have with you to Saffron-Walden*, published in 1596, when he acknowledges that Lyly first taught him to admire the sermons of Andrewes, in whom he found both orator and poet:

By Doctor *Androwes* own desert, and Master *Lillies* immoderate commending him, by little and little I was drawne on to bee an Auditor of his: since when, whensoeuer I heard him, I thought it was but hard and scant allowance that was giu'n him, in comparison of the incomparable gifts that were in him.[1]

Lyly's 'immoderate commending' of Andrewes when scant allowance was given him speaks for itself, but the fact that Lyly was instrumental in drawing Nashe to an appreciation of Andrewes is a little ironical, for thus he repudiated his admiration of Euphuism only to have it return in another form.

It should be recalled that Nashe also admired Playfere, who has a place among the 'witty' or 'metaphysical' preachers.[2] Andrewes lived to be almost embarrassed by the allowance that was given him for his style of preaching: 'the Music of a song, and the Rhetoric of a sermon, all is one', he complained rather bitterly.[3] For, although he indulged in the figures of parallelism which he found in the patristic writers, he devoted them to emphasizing antitheses of thought rather than to displaying sound effects.[4] But it was not unnatural that Euphuistic taste should relish the effects of patristic rhetoric on the vernacular sermon.

[1] *Works*, ed. R. B. McKerrow (London, 1910), iii. 105, 107.
[2] See W. Fraser Mitchell, *English Pulpit Oratory from Andrewes to Tillotson* (London, 1932), pp. 170 ff.
[3] Sir John Harington, who was devoted to epigram, later remarked of a sermon by Andrewes that even in 'courtiers eares . . . it left an *aculeus* behind' (*Nugae Antiquae*, ed. Park, ii. 193).
[4] Andrewes set a style of preaching; and Bishop Felton is reported, in Fuller's

The 'hard and scant allowance' actually came to Andrewes later, but long before the commonplace verdict of Thomas Birch that 'the great corruption of the oratory of the pulpit may be ascribed to Dr. Andrews'.[1] In retrospect Birch could declare 'that from the beginning of the seventeenth century as false a taste had infected the pulpit, as had prevailed after the corruption of the Roman eloquence, from the time of Seneca till the lower empire'; that this infection tainted Donne and even Bishop Hall, who, like many others, in his sermons sinks below his other performances, 'wherein he shows himself no ill copier of Seneca's sententious manner'; and finally that Tillotson 'brought back both purity of language and force of reasoning'. Needless to say, the Andrewes censured by Birch is a more familiar figure than the Andrewes admired by Nashe. Before we can examine sermon style from the point of view of Nashe, we need to recall some of the theory for an alliance of scheme and point. With that in mind we can proceed to inspect Andrewes and others with more understanding, and even to distinguish varieties of pointed style.

The patristic sound-play to which Wilson called attention made its most obvious appearance in pulpit oratory, and left its mark on Andrewes, who in turn left it on a long line of preachers. Yet these 'witty' preachers were not schematic in the usual oratorical sense. To their rhetoric Hoskins provides an easy introduction.

Among the figures of repetition Hoskins, like Farnaby, includes paronomasia and polyptoton. After defining paronomasia as 'a pleasant touch of the same letter, syllable, or word, with a different meaning', he associates the repetition of letter with Sidney's 'dictionary method' and Lyly's invention of varieties of patterned agnomination. Of the agnomination of syllables he finds a few examples in the *Arcadia*, such as,

> And whilst he was followed by the valiantest, he
> made a way for the vilest.
> Who went away repining but not repenting.[2]

He recalls the 'posy' affixed to Lyly's book, 'Commend it or Amend

Worthies, to have said: 'I had almost marred my own natural Trot by endeavouring to imitate his artificial Amble.' This metaphor for Andrewes's movement is later connected with the Senecan fashion. Felton points Fuller's notice of Andrewes.

[1] See *Life of Tillotson* (London, 1752), pp. 18–20.
[2] *Directions for Speech and Style*, ed. Hudson, p. 16.

it', and then looks toward the clergy, for 'even with Doctor Matthew this figure was of great accompt, and he lost no estimation by it': 'Our paradise is a pair of dice, our almës-deeds are turned into all misdeeds, our praying into playing, our fasting into feasting.' It is pretty enough wit to amuse gentlewomen or 'tuftaffeta orators', but 'Sir Philip Sidney would not have his style be much beholding to this kind of garnish'. Sidney had of course condemned it in his *Apology*, and for preachers too. Polyptoton, upon which Hoskins looks with favour, brings us the pleasant touch of the same word, for it is 'a repetition of words of the same lineage, that differ only in termination'.[1] For Hoskins paronomasia and polyptoton are not random word-play.

Although like-endings are involved in Hoskins's examples of paronomasia, they are not treated directly; for he does not treat the period, with which the Gorgian schemes were traditionally associated. But he does treat *compar* as incidental to antithesis, and there mentions *similiter cadens*. Where Farnaby connects like-endings with the period, Hoskins associates them with paronomasia; for Quintilian had made all of these figures forms of verbal resemblance. Among the figures in Quintilian that appeal to the ear 'by some resemblance, equality, or contrast of words', Hoskins finds most of Lyly's invention.[2] Of Lyly's paronomasia 'with a measure, *compar*, a change of contention, or contraries, and a device of a similitude', only the last is not accounted for in this class, and it is not a figure.

In Hoskins's treatment of antithesis, under the figures proper for amplification, it will be recalled that when compar is defined he observes not only that Lyly and others use this figure of balance, 'but that St. Austin, Bilson, and Lyly do very much mingle this figure with *agnominatio* and SIMILITER CADENS'.[3] Then he illustrates it with and without 'consonancy of fall' and 'harping upon letter or syllable'. His verdict, however, is that it is much more appropriate to speech than to writing. But he has already made sufficiently clear the association of verbal resemblance with wit as well as oratory.

It should be remarked that 'consonancy of fall' is difficult in

[1] Ibid., p. 17.
[2] Cf. Quintilian, *Institutes*, IX. iii. 66. Puttenham (ed. Willcock and Walker, p. 174) called paromoion simply 'the Figure of like letter'.
[3] *Directions*, p. 37.

English, owing to its poverty of endings; and the rhetoricians from Wilson to Walker were aware of this. In treating like-endings John Smith's *Mysterie of Rhetoric Unvail'd* is quite explicit on the difficulty, and his illustrations would entitle Harvey to criticize Ascham for indulgence in them.[1] As adapted to English, like-endings are likely to be unnoticed, or at least much less noticeable than in the classical tongues. This is already obvious in Wilson's examples, many of which Hoskins would classify under paronomasia, for this was sometimes a comprehensive term. Of course, paronomasia and like-endings are not the same thing, but both play upon likeness of sound, and may serve the same function. It is not surprising that Lyly's contemporaries should think of him primarily as one who schematized the native alliteration.

But Hoskins evidently regarded paronomasia both as a figure of sound and as a figure of wit, however low. As such a dual figure it describes Lyly's style, and Rainolds's, and is found in the Church Fathers. In the use of paronomasia you may, like Savile, be struck by the sound pattern; or, like Hoskins, also by the breaking of words into different meanings. Again, it may be the same style that strikes Savile by the repetition of sounds and Bacon by both the pointed and the chiming disposition of words.[2] It may be significant that in Sidney's digression on oratory *similiter cadens* is mentioned, after alliteration, in the text of the *Defence* but not the *Apologie*. Since in Euphuistic practice the chime is found less often in the endings, it is logical that it should fall primarily under Hoskins's definition of paronomasia.

Quintilian long ago pointed out that verbal resemblance has greater elegance when it is used to distinguish meanings, and his illustrations remind us both of Seneca and of the Church Fathers.[3] Schematic point, if we may so call it, was in fact no newer than Gorgias. Its incidence in the Church Fathers was used, as we have seen, to defend the Latin style of Rainolds, and was justified on the grounds mentioned by Quintilian. In the use of paronomasia it

---

[1] First published in 1657, the *Mysterie* owes its Ramistic cast to Dudley Fenner's *Artes of Logike and Rethorike*, 1584. Smith begins with Fenner's Ramist scheme of dichotomies, but breaks it by restoring the figures which that scheme eliminated.

[2] Obadiah Walker, in his *Instructions concerning Oratory*, treats such correspondence as the 'artificial placing' of words.

[3] *Institutes*, IX. iii. 71 ff.

should be observed, however, that schematic effects are more likely when resemblance is sought, not in different forms or senses of the same word, but in two different words; in jingle rather than quibble. Even then the jingle may serve to set off 'point'. But its conjunction with some kind of design, which Hoskins noticed, is essential to schematic effect, for the jingle must be patterned. And it should be remembered in reading Hoskins that Quintilian, while recognizing the contribution of such devices to smart expression, wondered why some of them should have found their way into the manuals.

Yet no one had provided a better manual for smartness of style than Aristotle in his *Rhetoric* (III. x–xi). In exploring resources of smart sayings, he uncovers all of the devices of pointed prose. Smart sayings depend upon antithesis, metaphor, and actualization (*energeia*); smartness requires brevity and even difficulty; it is nullified by obviousness. Other elements of smartness are apothegms, riddles, paradoxes, jokes, plays on words, proverbs, and hyperbole. 'As to style, popularity of form is due to antithetical statement'; and 'the more concisely and antithetically they are expressed, the greater is their popularity'. Moreover, 'the more special qualities the expression possesses, the smarter it appears; for instance, if the words contain a metaphor, and a metaphor of a special kind, antithesis, and equality of clauses, and actuality'. It may be assumed that 'special qualities' would include the paromoion already associated with antithesis and equality of clauses in the period; word-play is definitely included.[1]

Confronted by these chapters, it would be hard to say that Gorgias did not contribute to the cult of expressiveness as well as to the cult of form. Though Seneca was condemned by Quintilian, he could have appealed to Aristotle. Addison, in his speculations on wit, objects that Aristotle sanctions punning, the most universal of all false wit. But he concludes the same paper with unconscious tribute to Aristotle:

On the contrary, one may represent true Wit by the Description which *Aristinetus* makes of a fine Woman, When she is *dressed* she is Beautiful,

---

[1] Hobbes's *Briefe* (III. x) of Aristotle renders the wit that turns on words or 'a change of letter' into these terms: 'And paragrams, that is, allusions of words, are graceful if they be well placed, and in periods not too long, and with antithesis; for by these means the ambiguity is taken away.' If this suggests the ambiguity of *paronomasia*, it also provides another description of Euphuism or the Senecan style criticized by Bacon.

when she is *undressed* she is Beautiful: Or, as *Mercerus* has translated it more Emphatically, *Induitur, formosa est: Exuitur, ipsa forma est.*[1]

What he calls 'more emphatically' Aristotle would have called 'more smartly'; and it is to be feared that he would have pointed out the 'mixt wit' which carried the resemblance in words to Gorgian proportions, and took Addison unawares by its smartness. Before closing these papers Addison suggests another source of wit already observed by Aristotle and employed by Seneca: 'For not only the *Resemblance*, but the *Opposition* of Ideas does very often produce Wit; as I could show in several little Points, Turns, and Antitheses.' He might have shown in the example above how the resemblance in words may point the opposition of ideas. But in opposition too, no doubt, the true would turn upon ideas and the false upon words; Dryden had suggested as much in his discussion of 'turns'.

Aristotle indicates, and Addison illustrates, how various forms of resemblance and opposition combine to express wit. For scheme and point come together when some parallelism of structure and sound is used to set off the points of antithesis. Paronomasia which gathers up the antithesis in two words of a common root or sound is typical of schematic wit. As Bain observed, 'sameness of form in difference of matter' produces the surprise of wit;[2] it has always added to the pleasure of antithesis. Rhyme in Pope's verse performs a similar office for his 'points'; and chime in prose, even though unpatterned, may heighten point by a figure of sound. While these figures are devoted to euphony in oratory, in pointed prose they are devoted to wit. Formal parallelism, without the verbal echoes, is used in pointed prose to make antithesis 'neat' or emphatic, not euphonic. In this way 'sameness of form in difference of matter' also contributes to point; and so Bacon uses it. But he avoids schematic point or verbal ingenuities, and thus separates himself from the more artful cultivators of point. This suggests that in pointed prose as in oratory there are degrees of symmetry, marked not only by the end but also by the means and manner of its employment.

If pointed prose depends structurally upon more or less balanced

---

[1] *Spectator* 61. In Andrewes the like-sounds would probably have been called 'false wit', like his puns.

[2] Alexander Bain, *Rhetoric* (New York, 1890), p. 139.

antithesis, and if all the curt writers were to some extent pointed, it
is still possible to distinguish varieties of point and degrees of curtness. Perhaps some types can be suggested. There was a plain
brevity—Attic or Stoic—which still cultivated antithesis, typified
by the Attic Lysias or the Stoic Brutus. There was an excessively
pointed brevity which indulged in schematic wit, typified by Seneca.
There was an obscure brevity which abridged its point or contracted
epigram into dark innuendo, typified by Tacitus. If Senecan point
is taken as the norm, then the first is a plainer variety, and the last
a more obscure one; this is partly a difference between less and more
curtness. If the Senecan indulges most widely in the Gorgian
schemes, formal parallelism is not avoided by the first, nor repetition
of sound by the last. Finally, in pointed oratory the schemes contribute both to wit and to euphony; its point is made both telling
and euphonious.

Now the sermons of Andrewes, which provide excellent examples
of schematic wit, are certainly pointed oratory. When Nashe listened
to Andrewes he heard effects like these in Latin,

Hodie multi episcopi malunt esse morosi quam bene morati. . . .
Majorem fere rationem habemus nummorum quam morum,

and like these in English,

All along His life, you shall see these two. At His birth: a *Cratch* for
the *Childe*; a *Starre* for the *Sonne*: A company of *Shepheards* viewing
the *Child*; A *Quire* of *Angels* celebrating the *Son*. In His life: *Hungry*
Himselfe, to show the nature of the *Child*; yet *feeding five thousand*, to
show the power of the *Sonne*. At His *death*: dying on the *Crosse*, as the
Son of Adam; at the same time disposing of *Paradise*, as the *Sonne of God*.[1]

Andrewes leans toward the patristic rhetoric, but he carries the
Senecan cult of brevity much farther than Lyly. His Latin reminds
us of the fathers whom Jackson invoked in defence of Rainolds, and
his English employs the schemes of parallelism which Hoskins
remarked in Bilson and Lyly.[2] Nashe does not call Andrewes a

---

[1] These are the illustrations of W. F. Mitchell, *English Pulpit Oratory*, pp. 151 ff.
[2] Cf. Fénelon, *Dialogues concerning Eloquence*, 'Dialogue III'—devoted largely to
the style of the fathers. On St. Augustine, for instance, he asks, 'Is he not the most
jingling quibbler that ever wrote?' and replies that 'it was the reigning fault of his time'.
Then he offers an apology often made for Andrewes and Donne: 'I must own there is
one thing in him that I never observed in any other writer: I mean, that he has a moving
way, even when he quibbles. None of his works are more full of jingling turns, than his

Lipsian, as he called one of the Harveys; but Andrewes was a virtuoso in the short sentence. His relation to that style can be appraised by Baillet's report that the Lipsians 'embraced his manner of breaking up style and composing without periods and connection; learned to speak briefly, to cut their style, to avoid periods, and to force points and subtleties at random'.[1]

It might be supposed that Bacon would have found the greatest vanity of Senecan style in the sermons of his friend, Bishop Andrewes. As we have already observed, Bacon suggested, perhaps unintentionally, the propriety of Senecan style to the scholastic mind: 'as was said of Seneca, *Verborum minutiis rerum frangit pondera*; so a man may truly say of the schoolmen, *Quaestionum minutiis scientiarum frangunt soliditatem*'. Bacon fell upon the schoolmen's 'digladiation about subtilties', since all their thirst for truth proved only 'fierce with dark keeping', and 'their pride inclined to leave the oracle of God's word, and to vanish in the mixture of their own inventions'.[2] Similar charges were brought against preachers like Andrewes. Bacon also remarked that in contrast to the Ciceronian the scholastic 'writings were altogether in a different style and form; taking liberty to coin and frame new terms of art to express their own sense, and to avoid circuit of speech, without regard to the pureness, pleasantness, and, as I may call it, lawfulness of the phrase or word'.[3] In short, the schoolmen, when measured by Ciceronian standards, were guilty of Senecan faults.

Bacon's remarks on the schoolmen contain suggestions of two charges later brought against the sermon style of Andrewes; both charges have a curious relevance to Quintilian's criticism that Seneca broke the weight of his matter by cultivating *sententiae*. One of these charges relates to Andrewes's practice of 'division', of 'crumbling' his text; and the other to his 'wit' or levity in serious matters.[4] These two aspects of 'rerum pondera minutissimis sententiis fregit' are implied in Quintilian on Seneca; they suggest the propriety of the Senecan style to the scholastic habit of mind. In

confessions, and soliloquys: and yet we must own they are tender, and apt to affect the reader.' See the interesting translation by William Stevenson, with illustrative passages; here cited in the Foulis imprint (Glasgow, 1760), pp. 165–7.

[1] *Jugemens des savans* (Amsterdam, 1725), ii. 195.
[2] *Advancement*, Everyman ed., p. 27.
[3] Ibid., p. 23.
[4] Cf. W. F. Mitchell, *English Pulpit Oratory*, pp. 351–65.

discussing partition Quintilian lends point to these aspects of his criticism of Seneca:

Minute sections, which instead of being *members*, are *bits*, detract greatly from the weight of a speech; and those who are eager for the praise of such distinction, are apt, that they may be thought to have made nice and numerous divisions, to introduce what is wholly superfluous, and to cut asunder what is naturally united; they make their parts, not so much *more in number*, as *less in bulk*; and, after a thousand partitions, fall into that very obscurity against which partition was invented.[1]

This passage develops the Senecan parallel to the method found both in the schoolmen and in Andrewes.

Andrewes and Donne were not only scholastic in their turn of mind but also Senecan in their traits of style; they were both influenced by Church Fathers who had a Senecan bent, such as Tertullian.[2] Perhaps the most striking trait of 'metaphysical' style, which has an affinity to the Senecan, is the opposition or combination of ideas and images so as to exploit their ambiguous, compatible, or contentious aspects; it entails the antithetic rhetoric of Hoskins that I have summarized. This is present in Andrewes when he crumbles a text to pieces; it finds a place in the ingenious explorations of Donne; and it is not absent from the work of the character-writers. Senecan brevity, abruptness, and point characterize the sentences of Andrewes, and affect those of Donne, though less obviously.

Andrewes can be characterized, though incompletely, in terms of the counts on which 'witty' preaching was subsequently indicted. So characterized, he was addicted to far-fetched metaphor or catachresis; wit or formal ingenuities, jingle, quibble, and the like; learned quotations; and minute divisions of the text. Rhetorically the Latin and Greek quotations were made to play a part in the formal ingenuities, and the division not only displayed cleverness but broke up style in a Lipsian fashion, though its purpose was to amplify the 'intendment' of the text. Of catachresis or the abuse of metaphor Hoskins complained and Dryden was still complaining in his time; of the play of antithesis and paradox, which also belongs

[1] *Institutes*, IV. v. 25; cf. X. i. 130. Quintilian is quoted here, as elsewhere, from the translation by Watson in the Bohn edition.
[2] On the Senecan in sermon style see W. F. Mitchell, *English Pulpit Oratory*, places indexed under *Senecan* and *Tertullian*.

to this 'wit', Hoskins has praise where Dryden has blame. Oldmixon quotes some verses which preserve Andrewes's reputation as it had descended to his time:

> The Reverend Prelate, who St. *Swithin's* Chair
> So fairly fill'd, wou'd Pun ye out a Pray'r.
> At Visitation he'd instruct his Sons,
> In Sermons made of nothing else but *Puns*.
> The Court itself so tickled with his Chimes,
> They call'd him the *best Preacher of his Times*.[1]

But Andrewes is not given to quibbles so much as to balance or structural parallelism, either with or without an opposition of ideas, and even here jingles have a minor place.

Andrewes can imitate the Church Fathers, or suggest the Euphuists, as in this passage:

And this word [*concipiet*] is the bane of divers heresies. That of the Manichee that held He had no true body. That had been *virgo decipiet*, not *concipiet*; not—conceive Him, but deceive us. And that of the Valentinian, revived lately in the Anabaptist, that held He had a true body, but made in Heaven and sent into her. That had been *recipiet*, but not *concipiet*; received Him she had, conceived she had not.[2]

But he can also write in a vein more peculiarly his own:

Signs are taken for wonders. 'Master, we would fain see a sign,' (Mat. xii. 38), that is a miracle. And in this sense it is a sign to wonder at. Indeed, every word here is a wonder. Τὸ βρέφος, an infant; *Verbum infans*, the Word without a word; the eternal Word not able to speak a word; 1. a wonder sure. 2. And the σπαργανισμός, swaddled; and that a wonder too. 'He,' that (as in the thirty-eighth of Job (v. 9) He saith), 'taketh the vast body of the main sea, turns it to and fro, as a little child, and rolls it about with the swaddling bands of darkness;'—He to come thus into clouts, Himself! 3. But yet, all is well; all children are so. But *in praesepi*, that is it, there is the wonder. Children lie not there; He doth. There lieth He, the Lord of glory without all glory. Instead of a palace, a poor stable; of a cradle of state, a beast's cratch; no pillow but a lock of hay; no

---

[1] *The Arts of Logick and Rhetorick* (London, 1728), p. 20; Bouhours's *La Manière de bien penser*, 'Englished' by John Oldmixon. Oldmixon set these verses in a context of Bouhours to which Addison is indebted in his essays on wit, for Addison's account was already rather shop-worn.

[2] *Seventeen Sermons on the Nativity*, the Ancient and Modern Library of Theological Literature (London, n.d.), p. 137. As the editor of this volume observes (p. viii), 'in common with the men of his day he had a quick ear to detect similarities of sound, and made use of this skill to display similarities and dissimilarities of sense'.

hangings but dust and cobwebs; no attendants, but *in medio animalium*, as the Fathers read the third of Habakkuk. (Hab. iii. 2.) For if the inn were full, the stable was not empty we may be sure. A sign, this, nay three in one, able to amaze any.[1]

While the qualities displayed in the first passage are not absent in the second, they are modulated into his own teasing, sometimes flashing, eloquence. If the 'pithy, balanced phrases' are less in evidence here, they have been sufficiently illustrated in the other quotations, for they cannot escape attention. This is the kind of orator and poet that Nashe heard in Andrewes, to the appreciation of whom an earlier taste for Euphuism was certainly not an unhappy preparation. But Andrewes, like the later Lyly, has broken well from that style, and his schemes are turned to the benefit of point.

The 'new style' takes another form in the sermons of Thomas Adams, where the Euphuistic style passes into the Character style. His brief antithetic sentence, often set off by chiming sounds, finds its most congenial place in the Character, into which his sermons are always developing.[2] Though devoted to the short, crisp sentence, and inclined to the schematic point of Andrewes, he is simpler and less elliptical than Andrewes, being inclined also to the Character style of Hall. His schemata are confined chiefly to effects of point; as sound they contribute less to oratorical pattern than those of Lyly, and seldom develop the effects of teasing continuity that one finds in Andrewes.

While Adams is more Senecan than Euphuistic, he runs the gamut from Lyly to Hall:

They ruffle in the robes of preferment, and ride in the foot-cloths of reverence.

For this sad sequel is, if not a relative, yet a redditive demonstration of their misery; for after the infection of sin follows that infliction of punishment.

We tread those flowers under our disdainful feet, which, mured from us, we would break through stone walls to gather. The liberty of things brings them into contempt; neglect and dust-heaps lie on the accessible stairs.[3]

[1] Ibid., pp. 200–1. This illustrates Andrewes's gift for *enargia*. The learned languages contribute to make every word here a wonder. One of the most striking parts of T. S. Eliot's 'Gerontion' is indebted to this passage.

[2] Personification, allegory, and moral *descriptio* are stages in this development as well as means to *enargia*. Cf. the first 'energy' in T. Blount's *Glossographia*.

[3] *Sermons*, ed. John Brown (Cambridge, 1909), pp. 116, 60, 53, respectively. Other

His basic style is hardly less curt in its members, if less elliptical, than that of Andrewes; but it is less discontinuous in effect because less asyndetic. Its natural form is the aphoristic, and it makes points with less expense in words and schemes than Lyly's aphoristic vein, but not with less than Bacon's.[1] Adams's longer flights are usually marked by an accumulation of parallelisms or multiplication of parts ordered by emphasis, the common method of elaborating the pointed style for oratorical use.

His later Character style may be illustrated from 'The Soul's Sickness', which embraces a series of moral sketches in the witty vein of Overbury: 'His words are precise, his deeds concise; he prays so long in the church, that he may with less suspicion prey on the church.'[2] But again he is more like Hall:

He was no talkative fellow: that to every short question returns answer able to fill a volume; with as many parentheses in one sentence as would serve Lipsius all his life. I have read of two sorts of ill answers. Come to one of them, and ask where his master is: he replies, He is not within; and goes his way, not a word further. Demand so much of another: he answers, My master is gone to the Exchange, to talk with a merchant of Turkey, about the return of a ship which went out in April, laden with, &c.; a voluble, tedious, headless, endless discourse. This son is one of the former; he doth not trouble his father with many words: he is short with him, as if he wanted breath, or were loath to draw out the thread of his speech too long: *Nolo*, 'I will not go.'[3]

If there is no certain progress in Adams, generally his style moves between Lyly on the one hand and Overbury on the other. In the history of the new style he is a significant transitional figure, whose prevailing mode is best described as a mixture of Andrewes and Hall.

examples are: 'The unicorn's horn, that in a wise man's hand is helpful, is in the beast's head hurtful. If a man be a beast in his affections, in his manners; the more skilful, the more wilful. . . . The greatest scholar without his two eyes, of discretion and honesty, is like blind Samson; apt to no good, able to much mischief.' 'Related things are long in getting, quick in forgetting; therefore God commanded his law should be written' (pp. 67, 110). 'The Fatal Banquet' alone is sufficient to illustrate the variety of paromoion or Senecan word-play in Adams.

[1] Cf. Adams (ibid., p. 60): 'It is observable that Solomon's proverbial says are so many select aphorisms, containing, for the most part, a pair of cross and thwart sentences, handled rather by collation than relation, whose conjunction is disjunctive.' This is perhaps the best contemporary definition of the curt Senecan style.

[2] Ibid., p. 227.

[3] Ibid., pp. 197–8: 'The Two Sons.' For Cornwallis these two might have been a Senecan and a Ciceronian.

The stylistic aims once expressed by Donne are typically Senecan —when he tells his audience that he will open the meaning of the text 'with such succinctness and brevity as may consist with clearness, and perspicuity, in such manner, and method, as may best enlighten your understandings, and least encumber your memories'.[1] In 1710 Steele remembers Donne in connexion with such aims. Having remarked that Boccalini sentences a laconic writer, for using three words where two would have served, to read all the works of Guicciardini, Steele quotes—apparently from memory—Donne's comment on the prolixity of Guicciardini as opposed to the brevity of Moses.[2] It should be added that Donne includes Livy in his charge against Guicciardini, and thus brings prolixity into a context appropriate to a Senecan indictment.

In sermons Donne, like Andrewes, uses the schemes in disjointed sentences, terse of member; but employs far less paromoion than Andrewes. Often by joining his terse members by a repeated connective like *that*, or by proportioning his parallelisms, pulling them out, he achieves a more flowing, less clipped, movement than Andrewes. Both use schemes not only for rhythm or memorable phrasing, but to bring out points as well.[3] A single sermon will illustrate the pattern of Donne's rather more schematic and less pointed oratory:

One of the most convenient Hieroglyphicks of God, is a Circle; and a Circle is endlesse; whom God loves, hee loves to the end: and not onely to their own end, to their death, but to his end, and his end is, that he might love them still. His hailestones, and his thunderbolts, and his showres of bloud (emblemes and instruments of his Judgements) fall downe in a direct line, and affect and strike some one person, or place: His Sun, and Moone, and Starres (Emblemes and Instruments of his Blessings) move circularly, and communicate themselves to all.[4]

---

[1] *Works*, ed. Alford (1839), vi. 146.

[2] *Tatler*, no. 264; cf. Donne, ed. Alford, iv. 491.

[3] To illustrate pointed oratory Croll (*PMLA*, xxxix. 290 n.) quotes this sentence from Muret's imitation of Pliny's Panegyric: 'O felicissimam Catharinam, regis matrem, quae, cum tot annos admirabile prudentia parique sollicitudine regnum filio, filium regno conservasset, tum demum secure regnantem filium adspexit.' Antimetabole, for which Playfere was famous, is illustrated in 'regnum filio, filium regno'—an easy way to point and transverse paromoion. Here of course it plays into polyptoton, a Tacitean way to point. Cf. Croll's example of medieval polyptoton quoted earlier.

[4] *Donne's Sermons: Selected Passages*, ed. L. P. Smith (Oxford, 1919), p. 134. Yet here Donne is hardly less pointed than in the essay prose of his *Devotions*.

There is more 'point' in this, centring in the play on 'end', than in the much more famous passage on the divine seasons.

This illustrious passage is full of cunning rhetoric; Hoskins's figures of repetition, for example, contribute much to its art; figures of parallelism establish its pattern and rhythm.

> God made Sun and Moon to distinguish seasons, and day, and night, and we cannot have the fruits of the earth but in their seasons: But God hath made no decree to distinguish the seasons of his mercies; In paradise, the fruits were ripe, the first minute, and in heaven it is alwaies Autumne, his mercies are ever in their maturity. We ask *panem quotidianum*, our daily bread, and God never sayes you should have come yesterday, he never sayes you must againe to morrow, but *to day if you will heare his voice*, to day he will heare you. If some King of the earth have so large an extent of Dominion, in North, and South, as that he hath Winter and Summer together in his Dominions, so large an extent East and West, as that he hath day and night together in his Dominions, much more hath God mercy and judgement together: He brought light out of darknesse, not out of a lesser light; he can bring thy Summer out of Winter, though thou have no Spring; though in the wayes of fortune, or understanding, or conscience, thou have been benighted till now, wintred and frozen, clouded and eclypsed, damped and benummed, smothered and stupified till now, now God comes to thee, not as in the dawning of the day, not as in the bud of the spring, but as the Sun at noon to illustrate all shadowes, as the sheaves in harvest, to fill all penuries, all occasions invite his mercies, and all times are his seasons.[1]

Instead of the basic metaphor or emblem of the former example, this passage employs a basic antithesis, which is worked out in terms of lesser antitheses. While the temporal order is committed to transitions between its opposites, day and night, summer and winter, the spiritual order is not. In working out this antithesis the rhetoric never fails to exploit both pairs of opposites; after the initial statement, the dual reference remains constant. In the smaller pair, of course, the transition between night and day is the 'lesser light', to which the 'dawning of the day' refers. The temporal order which is contravened becomes insistent in the rhetoric of contravention: not yesterday or tomorrow, but today, today; though 'be-

---

[1] *Donne's Sermons: Selected Passages*, ed. L. P. Smith (Oxford, 1919), pp. 139-40. Note the subtle inversions of established orders which point the sense and vary the rhythm. The pairs toward the end that qualify the states of fortune, understanding, and conscience are examples of Hoskins's 'shorter *compar*', or caesural measure.

nighted till now' and 'wintred' till now, now comes broad day and ripe summer. The points of antithesis are there, and reinforced by parallelism and repetition; but the rhythmic balance is so insistent that the final impression is less pointed than schematic. The effect is Isocratic with less articulation, though both polysyndeton and gradation contribute to continuity.[1] Donne has moved farther than Andrewes from the curt style; here he moves between the schematic and the modulated loose period.

Though Donne's admirers, by contemporary testimony, fancied that 'Golden Chrysostom was alive again', the Puritans were of another mind:

> They humm'd against him; And with face most sowre
> Call'd him a strong lin'd man, a Macaroon,
> And no way fit to speake to clouted shoone,
> As fine words (truly) as you would desire,
> But (verily) but a bad edifier.[2]

Though subject to confusion, a Macaroon with his fine words was by intention one thing, and a strong-lined man another; in Donne's fourth *Satyre* a strong-lined man portrays a Macaroon. The 'hard words' of strong-lines were supported by the Senecan cult, which might be epitomized in its 'abruptae sententiae et suspiciosae'. St. Ambrose, as 'charactered and censured by Erasmus', appears in Wilkins's *Ecclesiastes* as a strong-lined man: 'Ambrosius habet argutiae, & sententias affectatas, saepe etiam subobscuras.'[3] Thus a transmitter of the Senecan heresy, according to Savile, and the sanctifier of *sententiae*, according to Hoskins, illustrated the tendency toward obscurity which had appeared brilliantly in Tacitus. Senecan 'point' reached its limit in the 'darkness' of Persius and Tacitus, and through the fathers supported the obscurity of 'metaphysical' conceit in the sermon. For Andrewes and Donne, as for Balzac, point often consisted in a bold comparison, a giddy hyperbole, an un-

---

[1] Cf. Fénelon's *Dialogues concerning Eloquence*, Dial. II, where he criticizes scheme and point, and the influence of Isocrates on French preaching; especially, 1760 ed., pp. 111 ff.

[2] 'In memory of Doctor Donne: By Mr. R. B.', Donne, *Poems*, ed. Grierson (1933), p. 356. Pocock, the great Orientalist, was not a strong-lined man: 'His care not to amuse his hearers, with things which they could not understand, gave some of them occasion to entertain very contemptible thoughts of his learning, and to speak of him accordingly ... *Our parson is one Mr. Pocock, a plain, honest man; but ... no Latiner*' (Twell's *Life of Dr. Edward Pocock*).   [3] *Ecclesiastes* (London, 1675), p. 108.

expected opposition of terms, or a play on words.[1] And the ways to point, including brevity, were the ways to strong lines.

If the more witty prose forms were inclined to point, Senecan preaching wavered between the two extremes of brevity, leaning to the pointed in Andrewes and to the plain in Hall. It is perhaps in oratory, where brevity is least expected, that we can observe the most striking contrast between them, culminating in the criticism of the pointed Andrewes by the plain South. This contrast is observable even in the books relating to oratory, of which two will be examined. Though heretofore the similarity of Stoic and Senecan style has been emphasized, the difference may now be used to distinguish the plain and the pointed brevity. The extent to which Seneca has appeared to exceed the Stoic requirements of style provides us with the margin by which the pointed brevity outdoes the plain. It is largely a matter of the presence or absence of what I have called schematic point, of the Gorgian tricks that Seneca retained for antithesis.

The character which Fuller gives Bishop Hall, on the authority of Sir Henry Wotton, presents a contrast to Bacon's view of Senecan style: 'He was commonly called our English Seneca, for the pureness, plainness, and fulness of his style.'[2] But Milton, as we know, saw only agonizing brevity in that style, though he recognized its wit, while Doddridge found it too prodigal with antitheses and witty turns. Hall claimed to be a pioneer in two forms that were exploited by the Senecan style, the character and the epistle. His dedication of the *Epistles* to Prince Henry, as we have seen, sounds a familiar Senecan note: 'Thus, we do but talk with our friends by our pen, and express ourselves no whit less easily; somewhat more digestedly.'[3] While this epistle emphasizes the informal, conversational manner of discourse, another epistle which I have quoted emphasizes brevity: 'for both the powers of good advice are the stronger, when they are thus united; and brevity makes counsel more portable for memory, and readier for use'.[4] His view of brevity

---

[1] Cf. G. Guillaumie, *Guez de Balzac et la prose française*, p. 451.

[2] *Worthies of England*, ed. J. Nichols (1811), i. 566: 'Not unhappy at *Controversies*, more happy at *Comments*, very good in his *Characters*, better in his *Sermons*, best of all in his *Meditations*.'

[3] 'Epistle Dedicatory', *Epistles, Meditations and Vows* (London, 1614).

[4] Ibid., p. 593: Decad. 6, Ep. 10.

is no less Senecan, or Baconian. If such affirmations suggest that Hall's early style was committed to Lipsian ideals, a sermon preached in 1624 does not alter the impression:

We have an old saying, that Cases that rarely happen are neglected of Law-givers: The newes of a few Enemies is entertained with scorne; Many are dreadful, and call upon our best thoughts, for their preventation, or resistance. The World is apt to make an ill use of multitude: On the one side arguing the better part by the greater: on the other arguing mischief tolerable because it is abetted by many. The former of these is the Paralogisme of fond Romanists; The other of time-serving Politicians. There cannot be a worse, nor more dangerous Sophistry then in both these.[1]

For this disjunctive style Milton denounced Hall as a 'tormentor of semicolons'. But of the schemes Hall makes use only of those of structure, to set off resemblances or oppositions of thought.

If Hall's sermons in general are less terse than his works in the essay style, his later sermons are less terse, less spasmodic, more continuous in style than his early sermons. Milton's appraisal is truer of the earlier Hall, and Fuller's of the later Hall. But even in the later Hall a basic terseness emerges from time to time, reminding us that he, like Lipsius, sought to harmonize brevity and continuity. His earlier style has not been renounced but modified, though rather slightly, in such a passage as this:

Time is the common measure of all things, the Universal metwand of the Almighty, *Eccles.* 3. 1. There is a time for all things saith wise *Solomon*, and but a time; for the motions of time are quick and irrevocable, ye cannot think of it but with wings; It is but a short word, a monosyllable; yet, whiles we are speaking of it, it is gone. As for the Time of our sojourning; *Moses* reckons it by years, *Job* by moneths, and those of vanity; old *Jacob*, and *David* by dayes; the Apostle shuts it up closer; and cals the very age of the World, *hora novissima*, the last hour: all imply a quicknesse of passage. It is a true observation of *Seneca*, *Velocitas temporis* (saith he) the quick speed of time is best discerned when we look at it past, and gone, and this I can confirm to you by experience. It hath pleased the providence of my God so to contrive it, that this day, this very morning fourscore years ago I was born into the World: a great time since, ye are ready to say; and so indeed it seems to you that look at it

---

[1] 'A Sermon Preacht at Hampton-Court', *The Remaining Works* (London, 1660), p. 11. Note the sophism of the Baconian 'colour' that Hoskins called 'division'.

forward, but to me that look at it as past, it seems so short that it is gone like a tale that is told, or a dream by night, and looks but like yesterday.[1]

In another passage there is no modification at all:

Time is that whereof many of us are wont to be too prodigall; we take care how to be rid of it; and (if we cannot otherwise) we cast it away, and this we call Pass-time: wherein we do dangerously mistake our selves; and must know that time is, as the first, so one of the two most precious things that are: Insomuch as there are but two things which we are charged to redeem, Time and Truth.[2]

Yet it does add initial connexion to the style of our first selection. But the preceding passage is less discontinuous in effect than this, and emphasizes the direction in which his style was modified, even to modest eloquence. Though Hall was 'elegant and polite', if too witty, for Doddridge, he was pure, plain, and full for his own age, if we except Milton. He was not inadequate to the requirements laid down in Wilkins's *Ecclesiastes*, which best defines his Senecan qualities; but he was none the less Stoic in his affiliations.

Long before the Restoration, witty preaching began to provoke criticism. On 6 October 1629 John Rous records in his diary that upon asking the news, he was told of a sermon preached at Whitehall by Dr. Lushington, Oxfordiens: 'I asked the drift of it; he told me "wit". I asked what was remarkable; he said, first the beginning. "What news? Every man asks what news? Every man's religion is known by his news; the Puritan talks of Bethleham Gabor, &c.".'[3] Rous concludes his report with evident disapproval. Before the death of George Herbert the 'wit' and 'division' of Andrewes, which have analogues in Seneca, had begun to arouse criticism. For his 'country parson' Herbert prescribes another style and method, more appropriate to the 'clouted shoone':

The parson's method in handling of a text, consists of two parts: first, a plain and evident declaration of the meaning of the text; and secondly, some choice observations drawn out of the whole text, as it lies entire, and unbroken in the Scripture itself. This he thinks natural, and sweet, and grave. Whereas the other way of crumbling a text into small parts, as, the person speaking, or spoken to, the subject, and object, and the like, hath neither in it sweetness, nor gravity, nor variety, since the

---

[1] 'A Sermon Preacht at Higham', *Remaining Works*, p. 205.
[2] Ibid., pp. 206–7, misnumbered 226–7.
[3] *Diary*, ed. Mary Anne Everett Green (Camden Society), p. 44.

words apart are not Scripture, but a Dictionary, and may be considered alike in all the Scripture.[1]

Thus Herbert anticipates the method of Tillotson and condemns that of Andrewes, in which Donne was a lesser offender. Herbert began his criticism of witty preaching in these significant words:

> By these and other means the parson procures attention; but the character of his sermon is holiness; he is not witty, or learned, or eloquent, but holy. A character, that *Hermogenes* never dreamed of, and therefore he could give no precept thereof.[2]

It might have been retorted upon Herbert that his Character of the country parson reveals the profit to be derived from Senecan brevity. Of course Senecan wit was not 'metaphysical' wit, or patristic wit, but Seneca had provided the urgent classical model of a witty prose style.

The criticism of Andrewes's practice of division even reached the stage of parody. Such a parody is called 'A Sermon on Malt' in *A Book of Seventeenth-Century Prose*,[3] where it is attributed to Suckling; it is called 'A Preachment on Malt' in *Humour, Wit, & Satire of the Seventeenth Century*,[4] which provides a much better text; and it is called 'The Ex-ale-tation of Ale' in *Baconiana*, where Thomas Tenison remarks on the injuries of the press to eminent writers:

> The Press hath been injurious in this kind, to the Memory of Bishop *Andrews*, to whom it owed a deep and solemn Reverence. It hath sent forth a Pamphlet upon an Idle Subject, under the venerable Name of that great Man, who (like the Grass in hot Countries, of which they are wont to say that it groweth Hay) was born Grave and Sober: And still, further to aggravate the Injury, it hath given to that Idle Subject, the idler Title of the *Ex-ale-tation of Ale*.[5]

This title, with its punning play on the 'division' of a word, suggests

---

[1] *Works* (London, 1836), i. 17–18. *The Priest to the Temple* was first printed in 1652. Herbert is supposed to have acted as Latin scribe to Bacon.

[2] Ibid., pp. 15–16. While the 'pyrotechnics' of the witty preacher were used to procure attention, they were not adapted, as Herbert knew perhaps too well, to country people, 'which are thick, and heavy, and hard to raise to a point of zeal'. Such people, however, found Pocock no 'Latiner'.

[3] Ed. R. P. T. Coffin and A. M. Witherspoon, New York, 1929.

[4] Ed. John Ashton (New York, 1884), p. 411. Ashton reprints it from *Coffee House Jests Refined and Enlarged* (London, 1686.)

[5] 'A Discourse by Way of Introduction', *Baconiana* (London, 1679), p. 76. Impropriety of subject is the apparent injury to a grave man, not given to such idleness.

the nature of the parody which Tenison's age left to the memory of Andrewes. And the parody itself makes abundantly clear how Andrewes's division contributed to his broken, abrupt, and yet frequently balanced style.

The true stylistic doctrine of Tenison's age first found its place in the manuals in John Wilkins's *Ecclesiastes*, published in 1646. Of Wilkins himself Edmund Gosse has remarked: 'But his style deserves great praise. His sentences are short, pointed, and exact. He has little or nothing of the redundant languor of his contemporaries; and justice has never yet been done to him as a pioneer in English prose.'[1] This was not the view of Dryden. So described, this 'pioneer' would probably have been called a Senecan or Laconic in his own time. In *Ecclesiastes*, under the head 'Concerning Expression', Wilkins considers the style of preaching. 'The *Phrase*', he begins, 'should be plain, full, wholesome, affectionate.' In the paragraphs devoted to the first two requirements of this 'phrase', R. F. Jones has discovered the spirit of Baconian experimental philosophy.[2] But Wilkins's discussion, even without his references, might remind others of Senecan doctrine. In short, it is doubtful whether Wilkins was moved by the scientific spirit when he laid down the requirements of sermon style; if so, it must have added to the fears of opponents of the Royal Society. While the practice of Seneca advanced the pointed style, his doctrine encouraged the plain style; and if Wilkins's programme is Senecan, it points to the style of Hall and South rather than that of Andrewes and Donne, though both may be called Senecan.

In developing the first requirement, upon which Jones lays most emphasis, Wilkins declares that expression

must be plain and natural, not being darkned with the affectation of *Scholastical* harshness, or *Rhetorical* flourishes. Obscurity in the Discourse, is an Argument of Ignorance in the mind. The greatest learning is to be seen in the greatest plainness. The more clearly we understand any thing our selves, the more easily can we expound it to others. When the notion it self is good, the best way to set it off, is in the most obvious plain expression. . . . And it will not become the Majesty of a Divine Ambassage,

---

[1] *A History of Eighteenth Century Literature* (New York, 1927), p. 76. Here is another candidate for honours in the simplification of prose; but the change is not to be explained by a change from languid redundance to pointed shortness.

[2] 'Science and English Prose Style, 1650–1675', *PMLA*, xlv (1930), 979.

to be garnished out with flaunting affected Eloquence. How unsuitable is it to the expectation of a hungry Soul, who comes unto this Ordinance with a desire of spiritual comfort and instruction, and there to hear only a starched speech, full of puerile worded Rhetorick? How properly may such a deceived hearer take up that of Seneca, *Quid mihi lusoria ista proponis? Non est jocandi locus, ad miseros vocatus es, opem te laturum naufragis, captis, aegris, intentae securi subjectum praestantibus caput, quo diverteris? quid agis?* 'Tis a sign of low thoughts and designs, when a man's chief study is about the polishing of his phrase and words. *Cujus-cunque orationem vides politam & solicitam, scito animum in pusillis occupatum.*[1]

Now we might conclude, with Bacon in mind, that this passage begins its attack against the Scholastic and the Ciceronian style; or, without Bacon and more immediately, against 'metaphysical' obscurity and the Andrewes style of preaching. On the relation of mind and speech Hoskins has similar doctrine, which is reported in Jonson's *Discoveries* under the heading 'De Optimo Scriptore'. But, except for a short Biblical section which I omit,[2] this paragraph depends upon the authority of Seneca, which is indicated by marginal references to *Epistles* 6, 49, and 21.

The first reference, set opposite the 'hungry Soul' passage, follows this marginal quotation, 'Non quaerit aeger medicum eloquentem, sed sanantem', from *Epistle* 75. 'The sick man seeketh not out an eloquent Physitian, but such a one as knoweth how to cure well'; that, in Lodge's words, is an expression of one of Seneca's favourite ideas: philosophy affects not words, but things, although it may use eloquence if 'it rather express the matter than itself'. The other references apply to the passages from Seneca in the text.[3] The first

---

[1] *Ecclesiastes* (London, 1675), pp. 199–200. No change in stylistic doctrine is found in this edition. In 1668 David Lloyd (*Memoires*, p. 511) describes the style of Dr. Brown, Dean of Hereford, in the phrases of this paragraph. The *Directory for Public Worship* (1644) had been more particular on the 'Preaching of the Word': 'Abstaining also from an unprofitable use of unknown tongues, strange phrases, and cadencies of sounds and words; sparingly citing sentences of ecclesiastical or other human writers, ancient or modern, be they never so elegant'; cf. W. F. Mitchell, *English Pulpit Oratory*, p. 105. Again 'cadencies' are not related to rhythm but to Savile's 'rhyming harmony'; this is the common confusion that Nashe turned against Harvey.

[2] Composed of some Pauline passages on Paul's manner of preaching, especially its lack of pretension to learning and rhetoric. The requirements for 'Divine Ambassage' set out by St. Paul are amplified from Seneca and thus connected with Stoic theory. But do not forget, for example, Heylin's espousal of plain brevity.

[3] *Ep.* 75 is one of the important letters on style. For the passage from *Ep.* 21 (115) Burton gives the reference 'Epist. lib. i. 21'; Wilkins gives no book divisions.

passage comes from *Epistle* 48, in which Seneca objects to the logical quibbles that Stoic philosophy offers humanity instead of counsel. And so the objection, in Lodge's words:

Why proposest thou vnto mee these toyes? There is no place of iesting; the miserable craue thy assistance. Thou hast promised that thou wilt helpe such as are ship-wrackt, captiue, poore, such as subiect their heads to axe and blocke: whither art thou diuerted? what doest thou?[1]

The second Latin passage, for which the reference is *Epistle* 21, and of which Wilkins gives his own translation in the preceding sentence, is from the first part of *Epistle* 115. This argues the same doctrine of style that is found in *Epistle* 75, and was a favourite passage with the Anti-Ciceronians. It is the doctrine, even to the passage, by which Burton justifies his own style in 'Democritus to the Reader'. And this quotation, if completed—'in scriptis nil solidum'—as Burton completed it, provides an antithesis found in the '*solid* business' of Wilkins's next paragraph.

The qualities of style appropriate to a moral physician or philosopher are also appropriate to the preacher, since instruction is for both a serious business; and all that Wilkins says in this first paragraph has its justification in Seneca. We may argue that Wilkins anticipates the revolt against obscurity and extravagance which is expressed by Samuel Butler:

All Authors of all Sorts of Bookes about Queen Elizabeths time, usd to excuse themselves in their Epistles and Dedications and Praefaces for writing plainly, and not using Scholastical Tearms and Rhetoricall Phrases, which are since found to be the Fopperys, and impertinent Follys of all writers. So certain it is, that some men may do better by being below, as well as others by being above all Phantastique and Ridiculous Impertinencys.[2]

We may associate 'scholastical harshness' and 'rhetorical flourishes' with the school of Andrewes; we may observe that these phrases describe the faults of style which are castigated by Sprat; but the fact remains that objection to the former is justified by *Epistle* 48, and to the latter by *Epistles* 75 and 115.

---

[1] This letter criticizes Stoic dialectics and was used by Bacon. Lodge leaves out the 'sick' who relate this passage to Wilkins's 'Physitian'. Seneca concludes, in the words of Lodge, that 'open and simple things become honestie and goodnesse' (*aperta decent et simplicia bonitatem*).

[2] *Characters and Passages from Note-Books*, ed. A. R. Waller (Cambridge, 1908), p. 412.

Of these *Epistles* the main rhetorical burden is that the philosophic or essay style should be plain and natural.[1] It is in *Epistle* 75 that Seneca takes his extreme position: 'If it were possible ⟨that a man⟩ might understand that which I think, I had rather express it by signs, than by words.' And *Epistle* 115 gives a well-known instance of his fundamental doctrine that speech reflects the mind—a doctrine which justifies most of Wilkins's requirements of style for the preacher. Hence 'obscurity in the discourse, is an argument of ignorance in the mind', or indulgence in logical subtleties and verbal flourishes is 'a sign of low thoughts and designs' in the preacher. It is important to observe that Wilkins is recommending the essay rather than the oratorical style.

The requirement that the phrase be 'full' finds no specific support in the *Epistles* to which Wilkins refers, although it might suggest Seneca's discussion of the proper philosophic style in Fabianus, who forms the subject of *Epistle* 100. Burton, who had to acount for an extemporaneous fullness, relies upon this *Epistle* in his own defence. However, 'full' is not used in the sense that we usually have in mind; it does not mean 'copious':

It must be *full*, without empty and needless Tautologies, which are to be avoided in every *solid* business, much more in *sacred*. Our expressions should be so close, that they may not be obscure; and so plain, that they may not seem vain and tedious. To deliver things in a crude confused manner, without digesting of them by a previous meditation, will nauseate the hearers, and is as improper for the edification of the mind, as raw meat is for the nourishment of the body.[2]

And in this sense also 'full' could find support in Seneca on Fabianus. Even if 'full' means 'solid', Jones's suggestion that ' "solid business" is equivalent to scientific matters' appears far-fetched. It may be admitted that Seneca's physician was engaged in a 'solid business', in which tautology was out of place and confusion dangerous; but

[1] La Mothe le Vayer, in *L'Éloquence françoise*, excuses Seneca's philosophical eloquence for not observing all the rules of oratorical eloquence; he also expounds the doctrine that style is the man on the basis of *Epp*. 114 and 115, which relate style to moral character (cf. *Œuvres*, Dresden, 1756, II. i. 233, 285–6).

[2] *Ecclesiastes* (1675), p. 200. Cf. Hobbes on Thucydides when he quotes Cicero's *De Oratore* 'for the pithiness and strength of his style': 'For he is so full of matter, that the number of his sentences doth almost reach to the number of his words; and in his words he is so apt and so close, that it is hard to say whether his words do more illustrate his sentences, or his sentences his words' (*English Works*, ed. Molesworth, vol. viii, p. xxiii). Here 'sentences' mean 'thoughts'.

after the medical analogy in *Epistle* 75, Seneca makes his own business clear: 'Are you concerned about *words*? Rejoice this instant
if you can cope with *things*.'

In its context 'full' seems to require that there be no 'words without sense'; it involves the concern that Bacon attributed to the
schoolmen 'to avoid circuit of speech'. The 'phrase' must be significant, for empty tautology is a loss of fullness; therefore expressions
should be close or precise, so as not to be obscure; plain or clear,
so as not to be either vain or tedious.[1] Perhaps this significant speech
will ensure the Royal Society of 'so many things almost in an equal
number of words'; certainly the consequence is to combine brevity
and perspicuity. But this intention is as thoroughly Senecan as the
references in Wilkins's text.[2] The latter part of this paragraph is
not only a warning that significant and ordered speech requires
study, but a blow at the preaching which prided itself on delivering
things 'without digesting of them by a previous meditation'. Whitlock was more forthright: 'With ruder Ignorance, and blind zeal,
what is above the level of extempore Non-sense, is Popery.'[3] Thus
far Wilkins has described a style that is to be plain, natural, close,
yet clear; he is concerned with significant speech.

The third requirement—that the phrase be wholesome—which
is obviously opposed to Nonconformist preaching, and the fourth—
that it be affectionate—which founds persuasion upon emotional
sincerity, have less relevance to the doctrine of plainness and no
explicit reference to Seneca, but rather to Biblical sources.[4] Much
of their argument, however, could find justification in the Epistles
of Seneca cited by Wilkins.

Among 'Authors proper for a Divine' Wilkins includes Seneca,

---

[1] Glanvill later observes (*An Essay concerning Preaching*, 1678, p. 63) that 'some
Sermons lose their efficacy and force by being too full, and close'. Quintilian (IV. ii.
40–7) has some relevant doctrine on the relation of brevity to superfluity.

[2] Many years later Richard Ward, who employs the schematic method of *Ecclesiastes*,
sounds like a disciple of Wilkins or Burton when he asks the reader 'to expect sound
and soul-saving matter from me, but strong lines, neat phrases, polite and eloquent
Expressions, sweet and mellifluous Words from others. I naturally affect Matter more
than Words, and sound Sentences than set Speeches: My study is to express *Multa
paucis*, much matter in few Words; and my care is, in whatsoever I write, to keep such
a measure, that it may neither be so brief, that it cannot well be understood, nor so
tedious as to breed dislike' (*Two Theological Treatises*, 1673). Like Burton, this Senecan
declaration—in a late allusion—disclaims 'strong lines'.

[3] *Zootomia* (1654), p. 251.

[4] For the latter requirement Quintilian (VI. ii. 25–9) had provided relevant doctrine.

with this comment, 'Seneca in traducendis vitiis salsus & elegans, ac vehemens etiam'. Among the Church Fathers we find those stigmatized by Savile, but here 'charactered and censured by Erasmus':

Cyprianus apertus, vehemens, serius nec infeliciter fluens.

Ambrosius habet argutias, & sententias affectatas, saepe etiam subobscuras. . . .

Augustinus in genere extemporali faelix est & argutus, sed dulcior est quam gravior. . . .

Bernardus, festivus, jucundus, nec segnis in movendis affectibus.[1]

It should be observed that wit rather than rhyming harmony is marked in these characters, as in that of Seneca; but it cannot be concluded that they qualify in the requirements laid down by Wilkins.

Wilkins's discussion of the 'phrase' may remind us, both in style and sense, less of Bacon than of Jonson in *Timber*, particularly the section 'De stylo epistolari', which was drawn from Hoskins. The Senecan scheme which Jonson sets forth anticipates much that is found in Wilkins, especially his demands on plainness, brevity, and perspicuity. Although his emphasis on plainness could anticipate either Robert South or the Royal Society, it was also concerned—as in Jonson—with order. One thing, however, would have placed Wilkins as a Senecan in the seventeenth century, and that is his leaning toward brevity. Like Jonson, he is afraid that some stroke of wit or art may 'darken' language, and yet he finds expression threatened more by tautology than by closeness. It can hardly be doubted that Wilkins is an advocate of plain brevity, or that his doctrine of style derives more from Seneca than from science, which, being a subject matter, could at best provide only a standard of propriety.

For the subsequent doctrine of brevity in oratory, let us inspect a rhetoric published thirteen years later. Obadiah Walker's *Instruc-*

---

[1] *Ecclesiastes* (1675), pp. 105, 108–9. Under the 'Authors proper for a Divine' Wilkins includes these writers among 'such as concern the study of Antiquity'. His 'Heathen Moralists' give chief place to the Stoics; and to these he adds, among others, Bacon's *Essays* and Lipsius's *Manuductio ad Stoicam Philosophiam*. Of Plutarch he remarks, 'De moribus nemo felicius scripsit quam Plutarchus'. But on their use see p. 24, 1669 ed. Wilkins is indebted to Erasmus's *Ecclesiastae*. David Lloyd (*Memoires*, pp. 521–2) mentions preachers who 'preached Seneca and St. Bernard so much, till they attained a sententiousness as happy as theirs'.

tions concerning the Art of Oratory points its rhetorical teaching toward oratory, but, unlike Wilkins, distinguishes between the style directed to an auditor and the style directed to a reader. Walker is especially relevant because his Latin examples, for the most part, have been 'taken out of *Plinius Secundus* his *Panegyrick* and *Epistles*',[1] and because his English authorities are mainly Hooker, Bacon, and Andrewes. Now Bacon put Pliny among the 'aculeate' writers, and Croll turns to his *Panegyric* for an example of the oratorical use of that style. Therefore the reader, if he remembers Croll's insistence on asymmetry, may be surprised to learn that Walker's rhetoric is concerned with correspondence in the period.

The section 'Concerning Periods' begins with this statement:

Every *Period* is constituted of two members at least, except it be a sentence: but to speak always sententiously, is not Oratorlike; since they, being single Propositions, are not *Reasoning*; and many of them together, if without connexions, but implicite argumentation at most.[2]

The requirements of the period, in his view, are based on the requirements of the enthymeme, and 'sentences' without connexion are destructive of both. It is, moreover, one of the chief rules of oratory that exact correspondency, as far as the matter will permit, be observed between members. The transposition of words to the beginnings and ends for emphasis not only facilitates correspondence but introduces another attribute of the period:

Therefore 'tis usual, to *commence* with *things*, rather than *persons*: with the *Accusative*, rather than the *Nominative*; which also may have more reference to what next precedes: again, to *conclude* with that, without which the sense is not perfect (to keep the Auditor in an attentive suspense, till all is said:) and upon which the rest chiefly depend. . . .[3]

---

[1] Hence both oratorical and epistolary models are drawn upon. White Kennet in justifying his adaptation of the 'Panegyric' to *An Address of Thanks to a Good Prince* (London, 1686) refers to Walker's *Instructions* (Oxford, 1682) in these words: 'one of our best Instructours for Oratory illustrates and exemplifies most of his ornamental Tropes by instances drawn from this single Tract' (p. vii). Imitation and adaptation of this 'Panegyric' were common in the seventeenth century.

[2] *Some Instructions concerning the Art of Oratory* (London, 1659), p. 37.

[3] Ibid., p. 42. The latter 'is commonly a Verb, a Participle, or Adjective; words muchwhat of the same *power*: and all of much more than the rest, being words expressing some action or passion about the rest'. And conjunctions must be of such a character that 'as they serve for chains to link the several clauses of a period together; so likewise for signs, to suspend the Auditors attention, till that which corresponds to them, is inferred' (p. 20). They must be illative, not copulative. Let the reader test Milton by this doctrine.

In English this is the counterpart of Farnaby's statement of the suspended character of the period in relation to sense, which became the accepted definition in the eighteenth century.

Transposition also promotes 'sweeter Cadence and Rhythme', and 'cadence' here involves paromoion, especially like-endings. Examples of the powers of transposition in a modern, undeclined language are 'borrowed out of Hooker, one in our Language very eloquent'.[1] They illustrate the more artificial structure of Hooker, but as examples of correspondence involving paromoion they fall far short of Walker's Latin examples,[2] which could be more nearly matched in *Euphues*.

On the rhythm of the period Walker is somewhat more comprehensive than Farnaby. While he is concerned with the effect of correspondence upon rhythm, he treats the proper rhythm of the period under 'Pronunciation'. In the cadence of the period the chief orators, though negligent of all the rest, have observed certain measures in four or five of the last syllables. He then discusses the requirements of this cadence in terms of these measures.[3] Otherwise, periodic style requires only that the clauses be 'of a like and proportionable extension'. Their length is ascertained by analogy with the longest and shortest verse 'usual in any Language':

And by these metrical members of Poetry (which were onely first used, because found more to please; the Orators aim, as well as the Poets) all our prose also is tacitely modelled: though it must alwayes avoid the appearance thereof, lest it should seem to be more affected, less natural, less masculine, by so much trimming; as also to be strict therein would be too troublesome.[4]

This states explicitly the principle on which the period introduced

---

[1] Ibid., pp. 46 ff.

[2] Ibid., pp. 44–6. Although Rainolds was Hooker's tutor, he did not infect him with schematic excess.

[3] Ibid., pp. 121 ff. 'A due and tunable clause therefore of a Period after the last Pause that is made before it (i.e. the Comma or other Point that precedes &c.) ought to be ordinarily at least of four syllables; because the voice begins its variation some Notes before the syllable that concludes: (For who can conclude handsomely that knowes not of it, before he is enter'd into the last word or syllable?) And these syllables are better all *long*, than all *short*; those having more stability and weight; better *long* and *short* interchangeably, than all *long*; the *short* being far more smooth and sweet, and the voice also requiring by courses some syllables, wherein to spare (as in the *short*) and some again, wherein to extend it self (as in the *long*.)' Long and short are determined by emphasis.

[4] Ibid., pp. 124–5. This 'tacit modelling' makes the changes in verse relevant to the changes in prose.

rhythm into the formal support of prose. Of this proportioning, for instance, Ralegh's famous apostrophe is a shining example:

> O eloquent, just and mightie Death! whom none could advise, thou hast perswaded; what none hath dared, thou hast done; and whom all the world hath flattered, thou only hast cast out of the world and despised. Thou hast drawne together all the farre stretched greatnesse, all the pride, crueltie, and ambition of man, and covered it all over with two narrow words, *Hic iacet.*[1]

In the rhythmic design of these sentences the syllabic proportioning of members is surprisingly equal, and the antithesis which accompanies the rhythmic balance induces a balance of stresses. The play of antithesis, however, in which Lyly provided instruction, is heightened by no more than a touch of the letter or syllable. It will be observed how the final and climactic member of each sentence lengthens out. Once again we have encountered the doctrine by which the period is given rhythmic limitation.

If Walker finds that separate *sententiae*, being implicit argument at best, are not properly oratorical, he does not find that *synoeciosis* and *contentio* are similarly deficient. These are treated as 'Dissimiles and Contraries', and are distinguished by the way in which the contraries are expressed: '*Dissimilitudes*; or Comparisons with, and illustrations by *Contraries—Contraria juxta se posita magis elucescunt*. This conducing much also to the suspension, and gravity; parity and equal balancing of a sentence.'[2] Antithesis contributes not only to correspondency but also to suspension in the period; it has the same relation to the figures of symmetry as in Hoskins. Walker distinguishes, but does not name, three varieties of dissimilitude. If the contraries are expressed by 'disjunction' the result is antithesis; if by 'conversion' the result is antimetabole. But synoeciosis (or oxymoron) is obtained when contraries are 'denominated' one of another: 'Which because commonly not done without strength of fancy in the Orator, is the more remarked and admired by the Auditor, much taken to see opposites agree, and contradictions true.'[3] His final example of this figure gives us the 'boyisms' or

---

[1] In the broader scheme of the conclusion it may be observed that 'all the pride, crueltie, and ambition of man' becomes in effect a member amplifying 'the farre stretched greatnesse', only to be telescoped again in 'covered *it*'.

[2] *Some Instructions*, p. 63; sect. vi on 'Ornaments of Speech'.

[3] *Ibid.*, p. 65; cf. p. 67 on the use of 'Conversion' or antimetabole. Hoskins made a

turns which Dryden found in Ovid and might have found in himself:

> (*Myrrha* enamour'd on her Father.)
> Now, in that mine, not mine: *Proximity*
> *Dis-joyns us: nearer*, were we not *so nigh*.[1]

Although writing half a century after Hoskins, Walker certainly does not suggest that the days of antithetic wit and rhetorical point are over.[2]

In Section VII Walker treats of style, and it should be remembered that his rhetoric is based on examples from the 'pointed' Pliny. After the usual advice 'to be perpetually varied', he particularizes:

> You are not every where to use either flourishing *Metaphors*, as some of our Moderns: or grave sentences, as *Seneca*: or acute, and exactly-according periods, as *Tacitus*: or sweet and consenting cadencies, as *Isocrates*: but, interchangeably, something of them all; now one, now another.[3]

Here Walker selects the main characteristic of significant models for his 'young student', for whom he, like Hoskins, collected his book. In further directions for style Walker distinguishes between the requirements of spoken and written composition:

> For *speaking*, 'tis necessary, that you observe a fuller and opener style; a stricter for the *pen*. For the same man, when an Auditor, is not so curious and vigilant, as when a Reader. Repetitions here, and doubled sentences, and enlargements by Synonymal words &c. before the shutting up of the period, are but necessary. . . . There what can be more tedious? All the force also and smartness, and sting of the speech being lost by languishing explications, dilatations and paraphrases.[4]

similar comment on this figure. Its surprise is the pole on which seventeenth-century wit turns, whose 'intimation' works by metonym as well as antonym. Its intellectual basis is suggested by a eulogist of John Hall's *Paradoxes* (1653):

> Errour and truth *each other doth* comprise,
> *And men* demonstrate Contradictories;
> *What th'*Authour *saies as* Paradox, *may be*
> *A sacred* truth *vail'd in a* prophecy.

[1] Ibid., p. 65. Here paradox turns on paronomasia in good pointed fashion.

[2] In 1657 Michael Radau, in his *Orator Extemporaneus*, had treated these 'points' or *acumina* as requirements of the age, which was devoted to striking expression. And in 1671 John Newton, in *An Introduction to the Art of Rhetorick*, repeated Radau on the sharpness of wit that derives from agreeing discord or discordant concord in the relation of disparate or ambivalent ideas. Thus the 'aculeate' style criticized by Bacon was taught in the rhetorics.

[3] *Some Instructions* (1659), pp. 87–8.

[4] Ibid., p. 95. Thus Montaigne found Cicero tedious.

'Extemporal Eloquence especially must use a long and compassing style' rather than 'acute sentences, and concise Periods: and generally must rather imitate Tully than Tacitus'.[1] The 'concise period' is defined by the other reference to Tacitus as of the antithetic sort, which depends upon correspondence.[2] But Tacitus is his chief example of elliptical omission for the sake of economy, and the short sentences of Andrewes serve to illustrate the powers of transition and gradation.[3]

Walker advises his student to addict himself rather to that style to which his natural abilities incline him, whether it be long or short—the main divisions of style for Walker and his century. Of style, he observes, 'there is no one sort but hath its proper graces and defects':

A *short* period loseth so much of smoothness, as a *long* and round one of acuteness: One is more harsh, and the other blunt. One suits with reason; the other with the passions, better: and the Rhetorick of the one is more sweet, of the other more powerful. If the one seem more learned, the other seems more natural and unaffected; and if this hath an elegancy, the other hath a simplicity that pleaseth one. One entertains naturally some sorts of figures, which the other cuts off; as the *short* is adverse to *Metaphor* &c. the *long* to exact *correspondence*, and libration of its parts.[4]

Thus Walker sums up the short and long, or Senecan and Ciceronian, styles from his point in time; for this kind of summary Bacon had set the chief example. And it is to be noted that he regards the Gorgian symmetries as naturally adapted to the short period and pointed style.

The extremes of both styles meet in a common difficulty:

Either very long, or very short, periods are subject to obscurity: one not opening and spreading the matter enough; the other over-burdening the Auditors memory. Yet who so will not lose the acuteness and elegancy

---

[1] *Some Instructions* (1659), p. 96.

[2] W. C. Summers, on the contrary, states the general view, 'that he avoids symmetry and parallelism of construction' (*The Silver Age of Latin Literature*, p. 189). The frequent use of pointed balance does not characterize Tacitus as it does Seneca. Cf. Walker in *Of Education* (1673), pp. 165–6.

[3] *Some Instructions* (1659), pp. 77, 89, 76, 21–2. '*Gradation*: Which, from the less considerable, orderly ascends to what is more. A Rule to be observed in the whole Oration; in every period; in every clause; and in every *Articulus*.' These are the means by which Andrewes achieves some connexion and continuity in his short sentences.

[4] Ibid., p. 97. In the propriety of figures to styles the divergence from Croll should be noted. The last sentence might be applied to *Euphues* and *Arcadia*.

in the one, or suffer the dismembring in the other, must in some things hazard the imperspicuity of his stile.[1]

Since perspicuity is threatened from both sides, complete perspicuity in the short style may entail some loss of 'acuteness and elegancy', and in the long some sacrifice of periodicity. To attain perspicuity 'in a Laconic style you must use a multiplication of the like expressions; and the substance of what is said briefly, must be said more than once'; in a long style 'one of those longer periods must be answered with a heap of these smaller, and the magnitude of the one equalled with the multitude of the other'.[2] This advice about a Laconic style, though directed toward oratory, may help to explain not only the practice of the Senecan stylists but also the criticism that was levelled against them.

Both in his theory and in his practice Walker's allegiance to pointed brevity is apparent; even in oratory he seems to prefer the style prepared for the eye, which is not Ciceronian. His advice to practise ellipsis, of which Tacitus is the great exemplar, may exaggerate but it does not pervert his attitude;[3] 'such a conciseness, not only avoiding a kind of Tautology, but savouring of a great deal more acuteness, force, and clearness of conceit', especially in things written to be read. But most revealing, perhaps, are his suggestions for overcoming the defects of brevity when used in oratory, for one should follow his bent.

Walker's attention to paromoion may have been influenced by the character of his chief models,[4] but critics of sermon style like Eachard and Glanvill show that preaching still 'jingled' in their day. And rhetoric, as Dryden might have observed, also extended the benefit of clergy to decayed or decaying fashions.[5] Of course, even

---

[1] Ibid., p. 98.

[2] Ibid., p. 107. Walker quotes the sentence from Quintilian (IV. ii. 41) that Hoskins renders in his discussion of brevity: 'there is a briefness of parts sometimes that make the whole long'. Walker (p. 98) urged 'a sufficient perspicuity' as essential to communication.

[3] Ibid., pp. 35–6.

[4] Yet he wrote for a young student and recognized (p. 50) the difficulties of like-endings in English. His book went into a second edition in 1682.

[5] Cf. Dryden's *Defence of the Epilogue* (1672): 'This was then the mode of wit, the vice of the age, and not Ben Johnson's; for you see, a little before him, that admirable wit, Sir Philip Sidney, perpetually playing with his words. In his time, I believe, it ascended first into the pulpit, where (if you will give me leave to clench too) it yet finds the benefit of its clergy; for they are commonly the first corrupters of eloquence, and the last reformed from vicious oratory' (*Essays*, ed. Ker, i. 173).

among the clergy revolt against this fashion had appeared before Eachard. In the essay style required by Wilkins like-sounds properly found no place, but their relation to oratory was traditional. Walker's *Instructions* centres our attention upon elements of rhetoric that came into crucial conflict during the course of this century. The reaction against rhyming harmony not only sharpens the criticism of Senecan style, but defines the fortunes of scheme and point in pulpit oratory, the course of which may be said to turn on Robert South.

It is possible to discern the passage from Euphuism to pointed Senecan prose by considering what happened to agnomination—the central feature of Euphuism—when the figures of parallelism became less elaborate and less obtrusive in Senecan writing. If we may differentiate parallel terms, which did not enjoy equal spans of life, we may consider agnomination as chiefly echoes of the sound of words (jingles) and paronomasia as chiefly plays upon the sense of words (quibbles), and then we may conclude that the latter term and meaning tends to displace the former. The 'rhyme' of Euphuistic prose came to be employed less in its schematic function than in its witty function, more as the likeness which points a difference of sense than as the likeness which gives pattern to sense. It is another instance of the shift to a less verbal, more intellectual wit, which can no longer be defined merely as the 'allusion of words'.

In this passage from sound-play to word-play, imitation of the Church Fathers prolonged a more mixed effect in the Andrewes school of preaching. Pointed wit of the Senecan variety, however, was rejected by Dryden early in his career: "Tis not the jerk or sting of an epigram, nor the seeming contradiction of a poor antithesis . . . nor the jingle of a more poor paronomasia; neither is it so much the morality of a grave sentence.'[1] Now, indeed, the antithetic rhetoric of Hoskins—joined with the paronomasia that he assigned to Euphuism—is no longer the most proper for amplification, at least in fortifying the heroic poem. According to Dryden, quibbles were still popular in the court of Charles II, although criticism was setting against them;[2] but jingles of the Euphuistic kind were then to be found only in preaching.

[1] 'Account of *Annus Mirabilis*', 1667. Here rejected as 'the proper wit of an Heroic or Historical Poem'.

[2] Cf. *A Discourse concerning Satire* (1693): 'But it may be puns were then in fashion,

Perhaps no one was more opposed to rhyme than Milton, for whom a proper Latin style meant Cicero. Elsewhere I have pointed out his opposition to the Senecan fashion.[1] In his earliest tract, 1641, he has this to say about style:

He that cannot understand the sober, plain, and unaffected style of the scriptures, will be ten times more puzzled with the knotty Africanisms, the pampered metaphors, the intricate and involved sentences of the fathers, besides the fantastic and declamatory flashes, the cross-jingling periods which cannot but disturb, and come thwart a settled devotion, worse than the din of bells and rattles.[2]

Here Milton ascribes to the Church Fathers the traits which the Restoration frowned upon, and to the Scriptures the qualities which it praised. But it is the 'cross-jingling periods' that concern us. They are illustrated both in Croll's examples from medieval Latin and in Euphuism, but are found in Seneca and some of the fathers with less complication in the cross-jingle. In criticizing the style of the *Eikon Basilike*, Milton alludes to the quibbles of a court sermon, which were encouraged by the 'cymbal' fathers:

That his head was divided from his body, because his heart was divided from the King: two heads cut off in one family for affronting the head of the Common-wealth; the eldest son being infected with the sin of his Father, against the Father of his Countrie. These petty glosses and conceits on the high and secret judgements of God, besides the boldness of unwarrantable commenting, are so weake and shallow, and so like the quibbl's of a Court Sermon, that we may safely reck'm either fetcht from such a pattern, or that the hand of some houshold preist foisted them in; least the World should forget how much he was a Disciple of those Cymbal Doctors.[3]

These quibbles had a proper source in 'those Cymbal Doctors' who tinkled in imitation of the fathers.

Donne, no doubt, would have been a cymbal doctor for Milton, and may therefore be heard on the cross-jingling fathers:

Pax non promissa, sed missa (says St. Bernard, in his musical and as they were wit in the sermons of the last age, and in the court of King Charles the Second' (*Essays*, ed. Ker, ii. 95).

[1] See Chap. VII.

[2] *The Student's Milton*, ed. F. A. Patterson (New York, 1934), p. 453. Cf. Robert Boyle's *Considerations touching the Style of the Scriptures* (1663) on the faults of Biblical style and the relation of Seneca and Cicero to his defence, especially in method and rhetoric (see third and eighth objections).

[3] *The Columbia Milton*, v. 146-7. Milton too became a disciple when, forgetting his own criticism, he introduced quibbles into his Latin *Defences*.

harmonious cadences,) not promissd, but already sent; *non dilata, sed data*, not treated, but concluded; *non prophetata, sed praesentata*, not prophesied, but actually established.[1]

And he comments more generally on the style of the fathers:

> The Holy Ghost is figurative; and the fathers are wanton in their spiritual elegancies, such as that of St. Augustine, (if that book be his) *Hiems horrens, Æstas torrens*, and *Virent prata, vernant sata*, and such other harmonious, and melodious, and mellifluous cadences of these waters of life.[2]

It need hardly be remarked that scriptural style for Donne would not have entitled the Holy Ghost to membership in the Royal Society. If Donne was appreciative of the paromoion of the fathers, he could also plead their example for his occasional indulgence:

> It is a blessed termination, *Mission*; it determines and ends many words in our language; as *permission, commission*, and *remission*, and others, which may afford good instruction, that as the Holy Ghost, did for his, so we may be content to stay God's leisure, for all those *missions*. A consideration which I presume St. Bernard, who evermore embraced all occasions of exalting devotion from the melodious fall of words, would not have let pass; nor St. Augustine, for all his holy and reverend gravity, would have thought *Nimis juvenile*, Too light a consideration to have insisted upon. And therefore I may have leave, to stay your meditations a little, upon this termination, these missions.[3]

These examples of patristic rhyming harmony ought to recall rather sharply not only the examples by which Jackson defended Rainolds but also the general character of Seneca's prose. Needless to say, the motives for jingles and quibbles which Donne ascribes to the fathers were also sufficient for him and his contemporaries. Very far from Donne is Milton's general condemnation of rhyme as a thing of 'no true musical delight; which consists . . . not in the jingling sound of like endings, a fault avoided by the learned Ancients both in Poetry and all good Oratory'.[4]

But when Milton thus extended his antipathy to 'jingling', it had again become a fault to be avoided in all good oratory. It could no

---

[1] *Eighty Sermons*, Ser. 1; *Works*, ed. Alford, i. 11. These illustrate the simpler sound-patterns of the fathers and of Seneca.

[2] Ibid., Ser. 73; *Works*, iii. 324–5. Note the connexion of cadence and paromoion.

[3] Ibid., Ser. 28; *Works*, i. 524. The 'melodious fall of words' is *similiter cadens*, for which all occasions were not embraced by Donne.

[4] Prefatory note on 'The Verse', *Paradise Lost*, 1668.

longer even be regarded as 'wit'. In the 'Preface to Gondibert' Davenant had described 'that which is not, yet is accompted, Wit'. Young men, he said, 'proceed to the admiration of what are commonly called Conceits, things that sound like the knacks or toys of ordinary Epigrammatists'; but 'old men, that have forgot their first Childhood and are returning to their second, think it lies in *agnominations*, and in a kind of an alike tinkling of words'.[1] Thus the taste of old men belonged definitely to the past, but the taste of young men inclined to the vogue of the epigrammatic, which included Senecan prose.[2] Hobbes, who resented the aspersion on old men, found in such word-play—of which epigram was by no means devoid—an instance of the value of judgement in works of the fancy:

Again, in profest remissenesse of mind, and familiar company, a man may play with the sounds, and aequivocall significations of words; and that many times with encounters of extraordinary Fancy: but in a Sermon, or in publique, or before persons unknown, or whom we ought to reverence, there is no Gingling of words that will not be accounted folly: and the difference is onely in the want of Discretion.[3]

Though the fancy may be extraordinary—a significant admission—judgement determines the propriety of such play, and it is not appropriate to the sermon.

Robert South would have agreed, in fact did; but his wit was less submissive. In the verses on punsters quoted by Oldmixon, immediately after the lines on Andrewes, are these:

> But cou'd you hear grave *South*, without a Grin,
> Cry, *Death the Wages, who can live by Sin?*
> Yet I've wish'd often of a *Levi's* Son,
> Rather than be so dull, that he wou'd *Pun*.[4]

[1] *Critical Essays of the Seventeenth Century*, ed. J. E. Spingarn, ii. 21–2. Davenant was one of the first to engage in the re-definition of wit.

[2] Richard Flecknoe adds his testimony in an epigram 'Of Epigrams in General':
> Poets can't write, nor Orators declame,
> But all their wit is chiefly Epigram:
and in an epigram 'Of the difficulty of making them now-a-days' he says that 'in former times'
> A little gingle on the words wou'd do't.

[3] *Leviathan*, Everyman ed., p. 34. This is followed by the famous statement making judgement the *sine qua non* of wit; but of wit as an intellectual virtue, not of wit as fancy. Thus, regardless of the quality of the fancy, 'if the defect of Discretion be apparent . . . the whole discourse will be taken for a signe of want of wit'.

[4] *The Arts of Logick and Rhetorick* (London, 1728), p. 20. Glanvill was not quite so averse to dullness.

With all the acclaim of plainness, more than one critic of sermon style would have been uneasy if confronted by this dilemma. South met it with characteristic decision. At the same time that he cultivates the Senecan qualities which pass into Restoration style, he succumbs to some of the wit that he condemns in Andrewes or disparages by association with Seneca.

South was not only Senecan in style, but his ideals of style were definitely Senecan, in the better sense of brevity and plainness rather than 'point'. No one can overlook his clearly Senecan requirements for style in *A Discourse against Long and Extempore Prayers*, nor explain them merely by the sectarian motive. Still inclining to epigram, if not to point, his rather Baconian view finds expression in one short paragraph, which translates his argument into other fields:

In fine, brevity and succinctness of speech is that, which, in philosophy or speculation, we call *maxim*, and first principle; in the counsels and resolves of practical wisdom, and the deep mysteries of religion, *oracle*; and lastly, in matters of wit, and the finenesses of imagination, *epigram*. All of them, severally and in their kinds, the greatest and noblest things that the mind of man can shew the force and dexterity of its faculties in.[1]

Here we are reminded of the value which Bacon attached to aphorism as a form of expression in philosophy, practical wisdom, and matters of wit. This taste makes South seem more old-fashioned, more Senecan, than his famous rivals in the pulpit; and his vigour of analogy, which was rather Hobbesian, along with his antithesis, contributes to this impression. On the occasion of his attack on the florid style of Jeremy Taylor, in a sermon at Christ Church, Oxford, in 1668, he made a more direct plea for plainness in sermon style, declaring that preaching should be 'plain, natural, and familiar'.[2] But—and it was a frequent addition—never dull. In this declaration,

---

[1] *Sermons* (Oxford, 1842), i. 338. South, like Donne, praises the style of Genesis for its brevity; unlike Donne, he refers to Longinus in this connexion. John Hall's preface to his contemporary translation gives a vivid description of the Laconic style.

[2] See ibid. iii. 317 ff. The ability of speech conferred upon the apostles included 'great clearness and perspicuity, an unaffected plainness and simplicity, and a suitable and becoming zeal or fervour'. Preaching 'was to be easy, obvious, and familiar; with nothing in it strained or far-fetched: no affected scheme, or airy fancies, above the reach or relish of an ordinary apprehension'. South, like Wilkins, opposes St. Paul to the rhetoric represented by Taylor. The reader who came to replace the 'understander' of earlier prefaces (Donne, Jonson) is defined by 'an ordinary apprehension', which more and more represents the main audience.

and in his practice as a whole, South remains stoutly Senecan in the plainer fashion of Bishop Hall.

In *The Scribe Instructed*, preached in 1660, South had given 'a just and severe reproof' to two extremes in pulpit oratory. Preachers of the Andrewes school 'disparage and detract from the grandeur of the gospel, by a puerile and indecent levity'; preachers of the Puritan school, by a 'mean, heavy, careless, and insipid way of handling things sacred'. It may be added that in subsequent criticism of sermon style these remain the extremes to be avoided.[1] The former style is attacked on these grounds:

All vain, luxuriant allegories, rhyming cadencies of similary words, are such pitiful embellishments of speech, as serve for nothing but to embase divinity. . . . What Quintilian most discreetly says of Seneca's handling philosophy, that he did *rerum pondera minutissimis sententiis frangere*, break, and, as it were, emasculate the weight of his subject by little affected sentences, the same may with much more reason, be applied to the practice of those, who detract from the excellency of things sacred by a comical lightness of expression: as when their prayers shall be set out in such dress, as if they did not supplicate, but compliment Almighty God; and their sermons so garnished with quibbles and trifles, as if they played with truth and immortality; and neither believed these things themselves, nor were willing that others should.[2]

But, since the 'insipid way' must also be avoided, it is not so much wit as the kind of wit that South finds at fault.

For he continues, 'as this can by no means be accounted divinity, so neither can it pass for wit':

Such are wholly mistaken in the nature of wit: for true wit is a severe and manly thing. Wit in divinity is nothing else, but sacred truths suitably expressed. It is not shreds of Latin or Greek, nor a *Deus dixit*, and a *Deus*

---

[1] Abraham Wright's *Five Sermons in Five several Styles* (1656)—his imitations of the several ways of Andrewes, Hall, Maine and Cartwright, Presbyterian, and Independent—gives a fair conspectus of sermon styles at this time. His purpose was to show the difference between university and city preaching as they related to education; his imitations fall into a similar division, and so divide South's extremes. Compared to 'the plain easie way of Doctrine and Use', Donne was 'strong-lined'. On Wright's *Five Sermons* Mitchell's *Pulpit Oratory* should be corrected by Anthony Wood or Wright's own preface; Thomas Birch (*Life of Tillotson*, 1752, p. 20) knew that these sermons were all imitations by Wright. See Evelyn's letter to William Wotton, 12 Sept. 1703, on Sir William Petty's ability to imitate the various pulpit styles.

[2] *Sermons* (1842), ii. 359. Thus Seneca's *sententiae* failed not as 'maxim' but as 'point'. Yet South had already declared (p. 345), no doubt with the Puritan school in mind, 'that piety engages no man to be dull'. In this respect Glanvill followed South rather than Wilkins.

benedixit, nor those little quirks, or divisions into the ὅτι, the διότι, and the καθότι, or the *egress*, *regress*, and *progress*, and other such stuff (much like the style of a lease), that can properly be called wit. For that is not wit which consists not with wisdom.[1]

As he specifies learned quotations, word-play, and echoing divisions, the allusion to Andrewes becomes unmistakable. Thus taking part in the re-definition of wit, South is purging the pointed sermon style of its levity—in the sense in which Quintilian found it an enemy to *gravitas*. Again we meet a criticism of paromoion, 'rhyming cadencies of similary words', and—as if to verify Savile—discover that a criticism of Seneca applies with even more reason to that 'lightness of expression' for which Donne found an excuse in the fathers. Both jingles and quibbles belong to this levity, and both are condemned by a preacher who thinks that 'no man's dulness is or can be his duty, and much less his perfection'.[2]

That sort of wit, agrees Eachard ten years later, contributes much to the discredit of the clergy; but it is acquired at the university, where a 'Latin-Wit' is 'highly admired in some Academic Exercises'.[3] Youthful indulgence in this 'Academic Wit' disposes one to punning, trifling, and jingling; to quibbling with 'the lucky ambiguity of some word or sentence' and to 'wreathing here and there an old Latin Saying into a dismal Jingle'.[4] After attacking this wit, Eachard elaborates the deficiencies of sermon style, and remarks:

[1] *Sermons* (1842), ii. 359. Cf. Quintilian, IV. v. 25. Thus South helped to define wit as it is sponsored by Glanvill nearly twenty years later.

[2] William Lupton, in a letter quoted in Robert Nelson's *Life of Dr. George Bull* (London, 1713, p. 490), remarks that Bull 'abhorred Affectation of Wit, Trains of fulsome Metaphors, and nice Words wrought into tuneful, pointed Sentences, without any substantial Meaning at the Bottom of them'. But Lupton thought that 'True Wit' deserved 'the utmost Praise, in Sermons as well as in other Discourses'.

[3] *The Grounds & Occasions of the Contempt of the Clergy* (London, 1670), p. 33. This academic wit accounts for the defects of sermon style: hard words, high notions, learned quotations, extravagant metaphor, ridiculous similitude, all the excesses of the 'metaphor-mongers' as well as of the jinglers and quibblers. It may be recalled that this 'Latin-Wit' had even affected the 'Academic Exercises' of Milton.

[4] In commenting on the schemes of words, of which there are both good and bad, James Arderne alludes to Eachard's criticism and explains why this wit was 'academic': 'That which I account bad is the use of schemes relating to words of the same sound: this hath been sufficiently exposed by a late Author; so that nothing is left for me to do, but to refer you thither, and to plead in behalf of the Authors without defending their practice, that they herein erred with *Cicero*, who at the same time imitated the best *Attick* wits, and it was so common a mistake, that you find it taught and enjoyn'd by most Rhetoricians; so that all that with modesty can be said against the usage is, that the general suffrage of our times, (which gives laws to stile) hath decried and voted

For when the *Gallants* of the World do observe, how the *Ministers* themselves do jingle, quibble, and play the fool with their *Texts*, no wonder if they, who are so inclinable to *Atheism*, do not only deride and despise the *Priests*, but droll upon the Bible. . . .[1]

It should be added that the Puritan school as well as the Andrewes school of preaching comes in for castigation at the hands of Eachard.

When N. N. employs a translation of Rapin's well-known work on eloquence to instruct those who were still smarting under the lash of Eachard, to whom he refers, he makes a few significant remarks of his own. Mostly he stresses the tumidity of the 'metaphor-mongers' that Eachard had observed in current style. In 'The Epistle to the Reader', no doubt partly as means to end, he registers his admiration for Bacon:

I have often blushed with indignation at the reading of some of our Late Writers; so much are also their stiles vitiated and depraved: and to see so few Imitators of that vigorous and majestick stile of our illustrious *Bacon*, which was the legitimate off-spring of his fine pregnant and powerful Imagination.[2]

Deprecating the pompous and figurative extravagance of this vitiated style, he nevertheless protests his own regard not only for Bacon but for 'Elocution':

I am as much in love with elegant words and noble expressions, which may adorn our Language, as any are: But yet, with *Quintilian*, I would have them serve to unfold a sence yet more considerable. *Curam ergo verborum, rerum volo esse solicitudinem*; A too great care of words and their disposition is equally blameable, with a too great neglect.[3]

Bacon apparently satisfied such demands—as Fabianus did for Seneca. Cowley might have made this doctrine effective, for in a postscript to his translation N. N. adds to the lament of Sprat:

The death of the most excellent Mr. *Cowley* is very much to be

it down' (*Directions concerning the Matter and Stile of Sermons*, 1671, pp. 85-7). It is worth remarking that here the oral schemes are separated from the structural schemes and voted down by the general suffrage of the times, 'which gives laws to style'; authority now cannot prevail against 'general suffrage'.

[1] Ibid., pp. 130-1. Rainolds, Andrewes, Seneca, and the Church Fathers are all brought to mind by his examples (p. 67) of division combined with jingle: '*Accusatio Vera: Comminatio Severa*. A Charge full of verity; a Discharge full of severity. . . . There is in the words *duplex miraculum; Miraculum in modo*, and *miraculum in nodo*.'

[2] *Reflections upon the Eloquence of these Times*, London, 1672. This is not to be confused with the translation printed at Oxford in the same year. The consequences of Eachard's attack were considerable, and that attack was certainly not prompted by any sponsorship of the Royal Society.   [3] Ibid., 'Epistle'.

lamented, which with that of his Life, gave an unhappy period to the design he had conceived to give us the pattern of several Stiles fitted for several Subjects: His example might have put some bounds to that Poetick rage, from whose invasion our holy places have not escaped: Certainly none knew better than he, how modestly to confine that Wanton: And in this it may be truly affirmed, he hath left very few successors. The Stiles of our most witty men, seem the dictates of the same spirit which inspires them in their raptures.[1]

Thus Cowley might have defended even the holy places from invasion by 'Poetic rage'; now Rapin must serve.

Glanvill and Burnet also found such a threat to sermon style; and Burnet, as we have seen, was original enough to associate it with the heroic play. But they were both subsequent in time. In his instructions for sermon style, in 1678, Glanvill remembered Cowley: 'Rather than all be Wit, let none be there.' For Glanvill, however, this allusion stated an extreme: 'I do not by this reprehend all Wit whatsoever in Preaching, nor any thing that is truly such.' He then defined wit:

For true Wit is a perfection in our faculties, chiefly in the understanding, and imagination; Wit in the understanding is a sagacity to find out the nature, relations, and consequences of things; Wit in the imagination, is a quickness in the phancy to give things proper Images; now the more of these is in Sermons, the more of judgment and spirit, and life: and without Wit of these kinds Preaching is dull, and unedifying. The Preacher should indeavour to speak sharp, and quick thoughts, and to set them out in lively colours; this is proper, grave, and manly wit, but the other, that which consists in inversions of sentences, and playing with words, and the like, is vile and contemptible fooling.[2]

Glanvill might have been amplifying South out of Dryden. But 'sharp and quick thoughts' would not exclude *sententiae*, and his products of fancy would limit rather than banish the 'metaphormongers'. Even when the Senecan style passed, the problem of wit remained. Its definition was a central concern, in which many parti-

---

[1] *Reflections upon the Eloquence of these Times* (London, 1672), pp. 157–8. This aspect of Cowley's reputation is commonly obscured by the 'metaphysical' aspect. For N. N. the distinction between poetry and prose has been ignored.

[2] *An Essay concerning Preaching* (London, 1678), pp. 63, 71–2. This is his version of the definition formulated by Hobbes, Dryden, and others. It may be compared with the discussion of wit in Dryden's 'Preface to Annus Mirabilis' (1667), which had since been developed in a significant way. See also Glanvill's *Essays* (1676), Essay VII, pp. 41–6; and Robert Boyle's *Occasional Reflections* (Oxford), pp. 34, 36–8, 43.

cipated—even Sprat, but apart from the programme of the Royal Society. Here Glanvill speaks as one committed to the plain style, though not as defined by Sprat.

But by the time Glanvill writes his *Essay concerning Preaching* he has to relate a somewhat worn tale, and can do little more than repeat his predecessors. 'There is', he says, 'a bastard kind of eloquence that is crept into the Pulpit, which consists in affectations of wit and finery, flourishes, and cadencies.' Even now 'cadencies' must be included. But, after Eachard, this recognition is belated; for even the 'florid strain' later decried by Burnet was passing, if not worn out, by this time. What had lately crept in was the plain style of Tillotson, then the foremost exemplar of 'the Plain Way of it'. Tillotson's style was most nearly prescribed, at least in its earlier form, by Wilkins's *Ecclesiastes*; but perhaps Glanvill found him dull, for the rogue seldom hazards a metaphor. In fact, Tillotson's style was almost a calculated antithesis to that which Dryden defended, though not for prose, in his *Apology for Heroic Poetry and Poetic Licence*.

Tillotson's labour with Wilkins on the *Real Character*, says Birch in his *Life*, 'led him to consider exactly the truth of language and style';[1] but his first printed sermon, *The Morning Exercise at Cripplegate* published in 1661, Birch characterizes 'as a discourse full of good sense, though inferior to his later performances in elegance of style, and exactness of composition'.[2] Henry Felton, whom Birch quotes, had found Tillotson's diction 'not in the naked terms of the things he speaks of, but rather metaphorical', though easily so. The Cripplegate sermon, which Birch reprints, illustrates the character of style given Tillotson in the *Memorials* of John Beardmore, which Birch also prints; and it elucidates Burnet's famous description of his style, which Birch copies. This character centres in the observation: 'His more grave discourses were very weighty; he spoke apophthegms.'[3] But of this sermon it might be said, as Birch

[1] Tillotson's preface to his 1682 volume of Wilkins's sermons observes 'the suitable manner of handling them, in a stile of so much clearness, and closeness, and strength, as was fitted (as he himself was wont to wish) to the capacity of the weakest, and the conviction of the strongest' (*Ecclesiastical Biography*, ed. C. Wordsworth, iv. 692). This is the preacher of *Ecclesiastes*.

[2] *Life of Tillotson* (London, 1752), p. 17. Modern readers would be inclined to view this as indeed damning with faint praise.

[3] *Life*, pp. 415, 424-5.

says of Hall, that it reveals 'no ill copier of Seneca's sententious manner'.

It is no less devoted to the short sentence than Andrewes, but without the trimmings; it is, however, logical rather than rhetorical, and avoids metaphor, except for the most commonplace sort. Its most florid moment comes in the effort 'to move' found in his peroration:

> God doth many times by his providence order things so, that in this life mens unrighteousness returns upon their own heads, and their violent dealings upon their own pates. There is a divine *Nemesis*, which brings our iniquities upon ourselves. No man hath any vice or humour alone, but it may be match'd in the world, either in its own kind, or in another. If a man be cruel and insolent, *a* Bajazet *shall meet with a* Tamerlane: if a man delight to jeer and abuse others, *no man hath so good a wit, but another hath as good a memory*; he will remember it to revenge it. He, that makes a trade of deceiving and cozening others, doth but teach others to cozen him; and there are but few masters in any kind, but are out-done by some of their scholars. But however we may escape the hands of men, how shall we escape our own consciences, either trouble of conscience in this life, or the worm of conscience in the next? How shall we escape the hands of the living God? How shall we escape the damnation of hell?[1]

Although this passage reveals his shortness of member—indeed that 'he spoke apophthegms'—it is less curt and more fluent than the staple of the sermon. But the affinity of this style to the plain Senecan style of Hall is just as evident as its conformity to the principles of Wilkins's *Ecclesiastes*. When Tillotson became less curt and more elegant, the change was not easy to explain by any work on the *Real Character*. For he came to be appreciated for qualities other than those prescribed by the Royal Society or those required by his antithesis to Andrewes. No doubt he reached his apotheosis when he joined Shakespeare and Milton to illustrate *Longinus on the Sublime* in William Smith's eighteenth-century translation.

Much of what was now considered false wit may be summed up in the jingle of words, to which in one form or another various critics have directed our attention. As late as 1678 Glanvill had thought it necessary to criticize jingling cadences. Through the eyes

---

[1] Birch, *Life of Tillotson*, pp. 487–8.

of Thomas Baker, writing at the end of the century, we can see the jingling style fall into perspective. Although Baker wrote in the knowledge that 'Oratory may be thought to be now at its full height' he was sceptical of the verdict of the future. The virtue of his account does not lie in novelty:

A Reformation in Religion brought with it an advancement in Learning, and as Elegancy begun then to be restor'd to the Latine Tongue, so in Queen *Elizabeth's* Reign, the Writers of that age, seem to have affected a *Ciceronian* style in English, both in the length of their periods, and often by throwing the verb to the end of the Sentence: The succeeding Reign degenerated rather than improv'd, when the generality run into an affected way of writing and nothing would please, without a fantastick Dress and jingle of Words. And tho in the following Reign, this way of writing was much laid aside, yet even then they larded their Discourses so thick with Sentences of Greek and Latin, that as things now are, it would be a hard matter to excuse them from Pedantry. What sort of Oratory obtain'd in the late times of Confusion, is well known, especially in the Pulpit: As if the observation of our Neighbours had been calculated for them, little Similitudes and odd Examples, and a worse sort of Cant, was the Eloquence of these times, which notwithstanding charm'd the People to that degree, that it hurry'd them besides themselves, and almost out of their Wits.[1]

If style is regarded more on the level of diction than of composition, Euphuism can merge with Senecan style more completely than it did for Bacon, leaving only 'a fantastic Dress and jingle of Words' to follow the Ciceronian style.[2] Neither Euphuism nor Senecan style can evade that description—however intended—since they shared at least the 'jingle of words', though hardly the Jacobean reign. Both scheme and point are involved in the jingle of words; and 'a fantastic dress' would cover the excesses of both styles. But they also shared the antithetic rhetoric, even when Senecan style renounced the jingle; the criticism against that rhetoric, however, took

---

[1] *Reflections upon Learning* (London, 1700), p. 48. Baker remarks of Linacre (p. 38) that when '*Cicero* was study'd almost to the neglect of our Bibles, yet one of our Great Critics in the Latine Tongue, could never be reconcil'd to a *Ciceronian* Stile'. But Arderne (*Directions*, pp. 69–70) attributes the improvement in pulpit oratory to the 'late times of Confusion', which sharpened both styles and swords.

[2] Baker, in deflating rhetoric, observes (p. 42): 'There are few that read Seneca, that do not imagine, he writes with great force and strength, his thoughts are lofty, almost every line in him is a Sentence, and every Sentence does seem a Reason'; yet Malebranche finds 'that there is little more in him at the bottom, than a Pomp of Words'.

much longer to gather force.[1] This it did in Neo-Classical times, when antithesis was generally damned and generally practised—for it was the age of Pope.

[1] In 1671, for example, Arderne observes (*Directions*, pp. 83–4): 'There is likewise in great reputation that which we call *Antithesis*, or the opposition of things very different: this gives comeliness, as shadowing colours do to pictures, if it be used with discretion, and in measure: The like too may be said of all sorts of distributions, where the parts are set answerably one over against another.' He is speaking of the figures of parallelism, of which the oral ones have now been cried down.

9. *Reform and the Royal Society*

The stylistic programme of the Royal Society, which has been thought crucial to the reform of prose style in the Restoration, repeats in effect Bacon's revolt against Ciceronian *copia*, and associates itself with Senecan requirements. Cicero had not ceased to be the great model of eloquence. In the *History of the Royal Society* there are two sharply contrasted attitudes toward eloquence, of which no one is more aware than Sprat. These attitudes may represent his dual role as a member both of the Royal Society and of its committee for improving the English tongue. But in a larger way they represent two different ambitions of his time, literary and scientific, relative to different ends of writing.

These ends are old and have old associations; for style they may still be distinguished as philosophic and rhetorical. One of the eulogists of Glanvill's *Vanity of Dogmatizing* credits him with resolving the conflict:

> You have remov'd the old *Antipathy*
> 'Tween *Rhetorick*, and *Philosophy*.

His modern praise insists that, influenced by the Royal Society, he developed by restoring the antipathy. To the Royal Society, then, our question is not the general question which they repeatedly answered—'What have the Royal Society done?' but the particular question, what they did for style.

The reform of style was not a novelty when Sprat and Wilkins made their pronouncements for the Royal Society. Various critics, some who became members of the Society and some who did not, had already spoken. But the early group which led to the Society contained few critics of style, none worthy of mention save Wilkins or Boyle; Evelyn joined the group later. While the Society stated its own requirements, it reflected rather than initiated a stylistic reform; even its own requirements for philosophic style resembled not only those of Bacon but also those of the despised Aristotelians. This reform of style cannot be regarded as exclusive with the Royal Society, nor as divorced from the Anti-Ciceronian movement.

Both Erasmus and Bacon had been confronted by the conflict between scholastic and Ciceronian style—varieties of the philosophic and the rhetorical—and to Bacon the former was plainly less of a hindrance to the advancement of learning. If the Royal Society, as represented by Sprat, rejected the scholastic style, it did not reject a philosophical style, for it was most vehement against the rhetoric which had been associated with Ciceronianism. The Anti-Ciceronian style, on the other hand, rejected not only the rhetoric of the Ciceronian, but the logic of the scholastic, which became its most reprehensible feature. As it was the Anti-Ciceronian style that Bacon advanced, so it is the Anti-Ciceronian style from which the Royal Society programme derived.[1] But the reform of style which preceded the Royal Society must first engage our attention.

Of Wilkins's 'ambiguity of words by reason of Metaphor and Phraseology' many were aware long before the publication in 1668 of *An Essay towards a Real Character and a Philosophical Language*, but they did not therefore become candidates for the Royal Society.[2] In 1645 Alexander Ross made a premature bid for membership: 'Expect not here from me Rhetorical flourishes: I study matter, not words: *Good wine needs no bush.*'[3] If the proverb was a handicap, he could answer that it was used against Sir Thomas Browne. Though Ross admits that the author of *Religio Medici* 'tells us, that many things in it are not to be called unto the rigid test of reason, being delivered Rhetorically', yet he suspects 'that Religion, which is trimmed up with too many Tropical pigments, and Rhetorical dresses'.[4] Objecting to Browne's definition of nature, he asserts

---

[1] For a different view see R. F. Jones, 'Science and English Prose Style in the Third Quarter of the Seventeenth Century', *PMLA*, xlv (1930), 977–1009; 'The Attack on Pulpit Eloquence in the Restoration', *Journal of English and Germanic Philology*, xxx (1931), 188–217; 'Science and Language in England of the Mid-Seventeenth Century', ibid. xxxi (1932), 315–31.

[2] Cf. John Wilkins, *An Essay* (London, 1668), p. 17. For evidence of this awareness see 'The Restoration Revolt against Enthusiasm', *Studies in Philology*, xxx (1933), 571–603.

[3] *Medicus Medicatus*, 'Epistle Dedicatorie'. Wilkins's *Ecclesiastes* was published a year later. Ross lived to attack Hobbes; he survives in *Hudibras* (i. ii): 'There was an ancient sage philosopher | That had read Alexander Ross over.'

[4] Ibid. 'Tropical' of course refers to tropes.

that the end of a good definition 'is to bring us to the knowledge of the things defined: therefore Aristotle in his *Topics* will have us to avoid Metaphors, which cast a mist upon the thing defined; every Metaphor being more obscure than proper words'.[1]

Ten years later Meric Casaubon is still making the same reference to Aristotle: 'But this very reason that makes them so pleasing in ordinary language, hath brought Metaphors out of credit with Philosophers, that seek not the pleasures of the senses, but the naked truth of things. Aristotle, in his *Topics* condemneth them.'[2] Need one add that Aristotle was not eligible for membership in the Society, which at this date was only an informal group? The year before, when Wilkins had written to urge an answer to Webster's *Academiarum Examen*, he had nominated Ross: 'I should think that Mr Alex: Ross might in some respects be very fit to enter the lists with this Champion. But I know not how far he may at present be engaged in the Confutation of some better Book.'[3] In what respects Ross might be less fit does not appear; but his orthodoxy, including his Aristotelianism, was unchallenged, and Webster was a Baconian of sorts.

Again in 1645 Ross attacked a rhetorician who was subsequently not unwelcome in the Royal Society; his object was Kenelm Digby's *Discourses*:

If you lay the fault of this upon your *Rhetoricall* expressions, I must answer you, that *Rhetorick* in such a subject may well be spared: use your *Rhetorick* when you will work upon the *affections*, but not when you will *informe* the *understanding*; for in this regard you do but cloud, not cleere the intellect.[4]

Ross hammers his lesson: 'naked truth cares not for such dressings' and 'Philosophical arguments sort not well with Rhetorical flourishes,

[1] Ibid., pp. 20–1. Cf. Sprat, *History* (1702, p. 111): 'Who can behold, without Indignation, how many mists and uncertainties, these specious *Tropes* and *Figures* have brought on our Knowledg?'

[2] *A Treatise of Enthusiasme* (1655), p. 181. Cf. Samuel Parker, *A Free and Impartial Censure of the Platonick Philosophie* (1666, pp. 73 ff.), for an attack on metaphorical language in philosophy by a member of the Royal Society. But even Parker, although Anti-Aristotelian, cites Aristotle among the critics of Plato's metaphorical style.

[3] *Vindiciae Academiarum* (Oxford, 1654), p. 6. This is chiefly by Seth Ward. Both authors sign by the last letter of each name, Wilkins being N. S. and Ward, H. D. Wilkins may have been speaking from experience, for Ross had attacked him in *The New Planet no Planet* (1646).

[4] *The Philosophicall Touch-stone* (1645), p. 92. This is the end of rhetoric commonly held in the Restoration.

and Tullian pigments'.[1] Ciceronian rhetoric is not appropriate to philosophy; a rigid Aristotelian did not have to be taught that.

But Sir Thomas Browne, as Ross indicates, had some perception of these rhetorical principles, and some awareness of how solid knowledge could be eaten out by words. In the first book of his *Vulgar Errors* he is, of course, echoing the doctrine of Bacon, even as the work itself constitutes one of Bacon's 'kalendars'; none the less it is Browne who observes, for example, 'that strict and definitive expressions are always required in philosophy';[2] who discusses verbal deception, especially the danger of 'converting metaphors into proprieties' or confusing metaphors with proper words.[3] When he speaks of the Egyptians as 'using an alphabet of things, and not of words', he is thinking—if he has anyone in mind—of Bacon and not of Wilkins.[4] He even shows some knowledge of the reasons for Sprat's advice to wits and writers; brought up on mythology, they acquire perverted notions of elegance:

For, were a pregnant wit educated in ignorance hereof, receiving only impressions from realities, upon such solid foundations, it must surely raise more substantial superstructions, and fall upon very many excellent strains, which have been justled off by their intrusions.[5]

Yet it is not for Browne to anticipate the proper basis of wit in nature and truth that Sprat was to announce and Addison to sanction. He cannot, however, be convicted of being wholly ignorant of some of the principles that animated the Royal Society; he had even considered, in his own way and after Bacon, similar problems of language and learning. Nor was he quite excluded from that group, if we remember Dr. Walter Charleton, who exemplified, without rebuke from that august assembly, a style which had been 'carminated' by Sir Thomas Browne.

Among the earlier expressions of Wilkins's views of style is that found in his *Discourse concerning the Gift of Prayer* (1653). This popular work contains a doctrine of expression not unlike that of his *Ecclesiastes*, but more likely to produce the familiar style of the

---

[1] *The Philosophicall Touch-stone* (1645), pp. 93, 117.
[2] *Vulgar Errors*, bk. I, chap. ix. In the preceding chapter he is concerned with the *ipse dixit* of fabulous histories, including the natural.
[3] Ibid., chap. iv.   [4] Ibid., chap. ix.
[5] Ibid.; cf. Sprat, *History*, part III, sect. 35. Sprat also charged rhetorical excesses upon education.

Restoration. 'There are', he says, 'two extremes to be avoided in our Expression, namely, Negligence, Affectation.' These extremes— often charged to the sermon styles of this time—he defines as follows:

Negligence, when men vent their thoughts in a rude, improper, unseemly phrase; as if they had no awe upon their spirits, and did not care how they spoke.

Affectation, either of too much neatness and elegance, or else of a mystical kind of phrase, not to be found either in Scripture, or any sober Writer, (though much in fashion amongst some men in these times) which, it may be, sounds well to vulgar ears; but being reduced into plain English, will appear to be wholly *empty*, and to signifie nothing, or else to be *full* of vain repetitions.[1]

The affectation of 'a mystical kind of phrase' played a large part, as Wilkins constantly testifies, in bringing about the reform of style. This stylistic doctrine, like that of *Ecclesiastes*, has connexions with that of the Royal Society, but even more obvious differences, chiefly in its concern for elegance. If this was coerced by a particular religious style, that other favourite pair of extremes, empty and full, provide significant and characteristic restraints. But the more literary extremes, apart from their relation to a special subject matter, offer a better means of defining the familiar style of the Restoration than is offered by the extremes set forth in Sprat's *History*. They come closer to defining Sprat's style as described by Glanvill, whose own doctrine of style resembles that of the earlier Wilkins. But while they would define the elegance of the plain style in Wilkins or Tillotson, they would not explain why Tillotson enjoyed a reputation for style that Wilkins did not.[2]

Wilkins was concerned with the universal character at least as early as 1654, when he and Seth Ward criticized John Webster's

[1] *Discourse* (London, 1678), p. 48. These are also South's extremes. The final remarks are echoed in Wilkins's *Essay* and represent the doctrine of significant speech.

[2] Certainly Tillotson resented the one that Wood gave Wilkins in *Historia et Antiquitates Universitatis Oxoniensis*, for he objected: 'The latter part of it consists of flat and ill-favoured commendations; as, that he was *philosophiae et mathematicae addictissimus*, a great well-willer to philosophy and the mathematics; the exact character of an empirick and an almanack maker, when these two excellencies happen to be in conjunction: and then, that to the study of divinity he added, *eloquentiam in concionando non contemnendam*, an eloquence in preaching not to be despised: which though it be but a very cold and slender commendation both of his divinity and his eloquence, yet I must own something of kindness in it, because there is in good earnest a sort of eloquence in preaching that is to be despised' (*Ecclesiastical Biography*, ed. C. Wordsworth, v. 693).

universal character and language of nature in their *Vindiciae Academiarum*.[1] Although he had already suggested a universal character, it was to Seth Ward that Wilkins owed his first 'distinct apprehension of the proper course' in such an undertaking.[2] Wilkins is sharp on Webster's 'Torrent of affected insignificant tautologies'; but Ward is more particular about his universal character.[3] He argues that a sign language like that of mathematics would bring 'no other benefit besides a communication without language'; this reduces Sprat's 'mathematical plainness' to pure metaphor. The only language that might claim to be a natural language would be not only one which was 'utterable' but 'where every word were a definition and contained the nature of the thing'. He remarks that such a design has been undertaken by 'one in this University', but only 'as far as the tradition of real learning, by which I understand the Mathematics, and Natural Philosophy, and the grounds of Physic'.[4] This limitation of *real* should not be forgotten in the relation of the real character to real learning; the real character was a philosophical or scientific language. The subject of literature, as Hobbes said, 'is the manners of men, not natural causes'. But Ward apparently was not ready to push the universal character as far as the Baconian Webster, to whose phrase Wilkins chiefly objected.

The middle of the century is marked by an outbreak of English rhetorics, of which we should take notice, not merely because Sprat involved the study of rhetoric in the corruption of style. 1651 produces *A Compendium of the Art of Logick and Rhetorick*, which contains Hobbes's *Briefe* of Aristotle and Dudley Fenner's Ramist *Rhetorike*.[5] 1652 produces John Hall's aptly named version of Lon-

[1] See the preliminary letter by Wilkins, p. 5; and the response by Ward, pp. 18–22, esp. p. 22. Webster's book was *Academiarum Examen, or the Examination of Academies*, London, 1654.

[2] See 'The Epistle to the Reader', *An Essay towards a Real Character and a Philosophical Language*, London, 1668.

[3] Here Ward gives a public account of the ideas that are basic to Wilkins's *Essay* (cf. 'Epistle to the Reader'). Wilkins tells us that Ward mentions his own 'considerable preparations' toward the achievement of this design.

[4] In 1657 when Walter Charleton gives an account of the advancement of science in England, he observes that 'in the Colledge of Physicians in London . . . you may behold *Solomons House* in reality'. After celebrating its achievements, he notices the advances in learning at Oxford, particularly in astronomy, 'Optiques', and the 'Universal Character and Language'. For the latter he reports the 'most ingenious discourse' in *Vindiciae Academiarum* (cf. *The Immortality of the Human Soul*, London, 1657, pp. 33–48).

[5] Identified by my student, Miss Mary C. Dodd, to whom I am indebted for other

ginus, *The Height of Eloquence*, which Blount knew. 1654 produces Thomas Blount's *Academie of Eloquence*, which draws upon Bacon and Hoskins. 1657 produces John Smith's *Mysterie of Rhetorique Unvail'd*, which uses Fenner, Hoskins, and Farnaby; also Alexander Richardson's *Logicians School-Master*, teaching 'Talaeus his Rhetorick', which Fenner had abridged. 1659 produces Obadiah Walker's *Instructions concerning the Art of Oratory*, which employs English models and relies chiefly on Quintilian; also John Prideaux's *Sacred Eloquence, or the Art of Rhetorick*. Of these Smith and Prideaux, like Fenner, related rhetoric to the Scriptures. For the most part they were rhetorics of 'elocution' and dealt with the figures. The popular rhetorics, Blount and Smith, were also the only ones that retailed the rhetoric of Hoskins. Especially in Blount and Smith this decade might claim to have produced the rhetoric of the Restoration. Indeed, as it was a unique decade for English rhetoric so it was a critical decade for English style.

Glanvill, like Browne, offered this excuse for part of his preface to *The Vanity of Dogmatizing*: 'That some grains must be allowed to a rhetorical display, which will not bear the rigour of a critical severity.'[1] When the *Vanity* of 1661 was presented to the Royal Society in 1665 as *Scepsis Scientifica*, his 'display' was called 'a dress, that possibly is not so suitable to the graver Geniuses, who have outgrown all gaieties of style and youthful relishes'.[2] Is this what the Royal Society had done about style? Glanvill attributed his own rhetoric to youth.[3] His growing distaste for that style he attributed to his 'humour', but not to the influence of the Royal Society. In his 'Address to the Royal Society', prefixed to *Scepsis Scientifica*, he missed an opportunity when he wrote:

For I must confess that *way* of *writing* to be less agreeable to my

details about rhetorics. The *Compendium*, minus the Ramist logic of Robert Fage, is still found in the Molesworth edition of Hobbes. Hoyt H. Hudson has identified Hoskins in Blount and Smith. And Farnaby's *Index Rhetoricus* was not forgotten in the rhetorics of this decade. The second edition of Thomas Horne's *Rhetorices Compendium, Latino-Anglice* (1648), which contains 'A Short Epitome of Rhetorick' in English, also appeared in 1651.

[1] In the *Vanity* he says that Aristotle 'transgres't his own *Topicks*' in definition; in the preface to *Plus Ultra* he admits the value of Aristotle's *Rhetoric*.

[2] Here Glanvill cites the principle of the literary men: 'And there is nothing in words and styles but suitableness, that makes them acceptable and effective.'

[3] The *Vanity* had been written by a wit against the wits, and therefore in a brisker style than that of the 'Address', which is quite formal.

present relish and *Genius*; which is more gratified with *manly sense*, flowing in a *natural* and *unaffected Eloquence*, then in the *musick* and curiosity of *fine metaphors* and *dancing periods*.[1]

After he became a member of the Society he could only continue to develop his new taste and genius, which carried him away from Sir Thomas Browne, with no thanks to the Society.

But apart from the line of thought in the *Scepsis*, Glanvill had more to offer the Society than his style. His 'Address' was the first defence against the wits, who are explicitly mentioned, and he thus anticipated a concern of Evelyn, Cowley, and Sprat.[2] His *Vanity of Dogmatizing* does not fail to get honorable mention from Sprat, and under its first title—a circumstance that seems to neglect both its style and the 'Address', which contains several topics elaborated by Sprat.[3] At best the statement that Glanvill's style was altered by the influence of the Royal Society is only an inference from Sprat's *History* to Glanvill's change. Even the wits, advertised as enemies by the Society itself, disciplined their style with the Restoration; Cowley's career was not unique. And South, Butler, Hobbes, Eachard—all wits rather than advocates of the Royal Society—all criticized the style represented by the early Glanvill. In the Society itself the presence of the florid Charleton, Wilkins's pupil and Dryden's sponsor, is enough to confuse the issue, or at least to suggest that the Society failed to discipline its own members.

The circumstances attending the *History of the Royal Society* are important to its evaluation. Of concern to its stylistic programme is the provision in the Statutes of 1663:

In all Reports of Experiments to be brought into the Society, the

---

[1] There is no real evidence in the 'Address' that Glanvill was either adapting himself to or aware of a Royal Society programme for style. His 'address' is to their *gravitas*. 'The Authors Apology for his Style' merely explains why he did not reply to Thomas White in Latin, 'the universal Language'.

[2] But Thomas Baker (*Reflections upon Learning*, p. 84) suggests that Glanvill's *Scepsis* was doubtful advertising for the Royal Society: 'Nothing has done them more injury, than the vanity of some few Men, who have been so *Planet-struck* as to dream of the possibility of a Voyage to the Moon, and to talk of making wings to fly thither, as they would of buying a pair of Boots to take a journey.' Baker also mentions Wilkins directly (pp. 17–18): 'an extraordinary Person, but very projecting', whose projection of a *Real Character and Philosophical Language* may be ranked with such 'wings'. These 'planet-struck' men made the Society vulnerable to the wits.

[3] This choice may be explained by the fact that the second title was more provocative of the prejudices Sprat was trying to allay.

matter of fact shall be barely stated, without any prefaces, apologies, or rhetorical flourishes. . . . And if any Fellow shall think fit to suggest any conjectures, concerning the causes of the phaenomena in such Experiments, the same shall be done apart.[1]

Not only must the matter of fact be 'barely stated'; it must be separated from conjecture. In reports 'to be brought into the Society' both words and thoughts in excess of the facts are to be avoided. These requirements concern the 'reports of experiments'; that they have a wider application is not suggested.

Several actions of the Society are related to the contents of the *History*. On 7 December 1664 the 'committee for improving the English language' was voted. At the same meeting Glanvill's *Scepsis Scientifica* was presented, 'the dedication of which was read'. In this dedication Oldenburg and others were gratified to find the design of the Society 'so well understood at last by some'.[2] On 24 November 1664 Oldenburg, in a letter to Boyle, had expressed dissatisfaction with the manuscript of the *History*, remarking that 'he knew not whether there was enough said in it of particulars'.[3] On 21 December 1664 a committee, which included Wilkins, was appointed 'to consider of the particulars to be inserted in the relation of the Society's institution'. This was followed on 16 May 1665 by 'a committee for reviewing Mr. Sprat's relation concerning the institution and design of the Royal Society'. Only Wilkins was a member of both committees. Meanwhile, on 18 January 1665 'it was ordered, that Dr. Wilkins meet the first time (at least) with the committee for improving the English tongue; and that particularly he intimate to them the way of proceeding in that committee, according to the sense of the council, viz. chiefly to improve the philosophy of the language'.

This committee originally had been suggested because 'there were several persons of the Society, whose genius was very proper and inclined to improve the English tongue, and particularly for philosophical purposes'. Wilkins had not been appointed to the com-

---

[1] Cf. C. R. Weld, *A History of the Royal Society* (London, 1848), ii. 527. If both brevity and plainness are suggested here, Sprat is more emphatic on brevity.

[2] Cf. Thomas Birch, *History of the Royal Society* (London, 1756), i. 500, note *i*. No doubt Sorbière's misunderstanding (cf. *Relation*, 1664) aggravated the situation.

[3] Ibid. ii. 197, note *d*. After it was printed he (ibid.) was still dissatisfied with the 'notice of the performances' and looked to Glanvill for satisfaction.

mittee; hence this order serves to emphasize improvement 'for philosophical purposes', though it says 'the philosophy of the language'. If this was the proper end of the committee—and it is an end appropriate to the requirements of the Society—not all of the genius on this committee, as we shall see, was inclined the way of the council; nor does the council make their 'sense' the exclusive concern of the committee. This confusion of interests is represented in Sprat's *History*, which speaks both of improving the tongue for philosophy and of polishing it for literature. Considering the ubiquitous Wilkins, the *History* is more remarkable for its inclusions than for its omissions. Glanvill's *Plus Ultra* (1668), which is also an apology for the Society, is more strictly scientific, and has nothing to say about the stylistic programme.

Shortly before the publication of the *History*, on 12 March 1667, Evelyn wrote to Cowley asking for the ode which Sprat had already requested to introduce his 'eulogies on the Royal Society'. Although Evelyn declares that he need not instruct Cowley how to answer or confound those who have asked 'What have the Royal Society done?' his letter is full of suggestions:

Or if their insolence press, you are capable to show how they have laid solid foundations to perfect all noble arts, and reform all imperfect sciences. It requires an history to recite only the arts, the inventions, and phenomena already absolved, improved, or opened.

Citing the limitations with which the Royal Society is obliged to struggle, in spite of all its advantages, he remarks, 'and yet we are sometimes the subject of satire and the songs of the drunkards'. Perhaps that is one more reason why he was so anxious to secure a spirit like Cowley to raise up benefactors of the Royal Society, for he is 'even amazed at the wretchedness of this age that acknowledges it no more'. It appears that Evelyn was of one mind with Sprat in appreciating the necessity of showing the wits and writers where their advantage lay. In Cowley's reply to Evelyn, 13 May 1667, he acknowledges the value of Evelyn's suggestions:

I could not comprehend in it many of those excellent hints which you were pleased to give me, nor descend to the praises of particular persons, because those things afford too much matter for one copy of verses, and enough for a poem, or the History itself; some part of which I have seen, and think you will be very well satisfied with it. I took the boldness to show him your letter, and he says he has not omitted any of those heads, though he wants the eloquence in expression.[1]

Though Cowley did descend to praise Sprat, it should not be forgotten that Sprat envied the elegance of Pellisson's *Historie de l'Académie françoise*.

In the *History of the Royal Society* Sprat tells us that the Society has been most solicitous about its manner of discourse, 'which, unless they had been very watchful to keep in due temper, the whole spirit and vigour of their Design had been soon eaten out by the luxury and redundance of speech':

The ill effects of this superfluity of talking have already overwhelm'd most other *Arts* and *Professions*, insomuch that when I consider the means of *happy living* and the causes of their corruption, I can hardly forbear recanting what I said before, and concluding that *eloquence* ought to be banish'd out of all *civil Societies*, as a thing fatal to Peace and good Manners.[2]

To this opinion he should wholly incline, if he did not find that eloquence is available to good and bad alike, and that by renouncing it virtue would only expose itself to malice. 'This', he concludes, 'is the chief reason that should now keep up the Ornaments of speaking in any request.' But the 'easy vanity of fine speaking'—which suggests a current definition of rhetoric—snatches many rewards that are due to more profitable and difficult arts: 'And, in few words, I dare say that, of all the Studies of men, nothing may be sooner obtained than this vicious abundance of Phrase, this trick of Metaphors, this volubility of Tongue, which makes so great a noise in the World.' This rhetoric or 'beautiful deceit' is now preferred by Englishmen to 'undeceiving expressions', and largely because they have laboured so long after it in the years of their education that ever after they think kinder of it than it deserves. Of course Bacon had found rhetoric a hindrance to the advancement of learning.

'It will suffice my present purpose', says Sprat, 'to point out what has been done by the Royal Society towards the correcting of its

[1] Evelyn remarks on Sprat's pulpit style (*Diary*, 23 Nov. 1679): 'His talent was, a great memory, never making use of notes, a readiness of expression in a most pure and plain style of words, full of matter, easily delivered.'

[2] Part II, sect. 20. What he said before concerned an academy, which will be considered in the next chapter. The Puritan interregnum is never far from Sprat's mind.

excesses in Natural Philosophy, to which it is, of all others, a most profest enemy.' The Royal Society has put into execution 'the only Remedy that can be found for this extravagance'—a new version of the Baconian remedy—

and that has been a constant Resolution to reject all amplifications, digressions, and swellings of style; to return back to the primitive purity and shortness, when men deliver'd so many *things* almost in an equal number of *words*. They have exacted from all their members a close, naked, natural way of speaking, positive expressions, clear senses, a native easiness, bringing all things as near the Mathematical plainness as they can, and preferring the language of Artizans, Countrymen, and Merchants, before that of Wits and Scholars.[1]

And there is one thing 'which will render this established custom of the Society well nigh everlasting, and that is the general constitution of the minds of the English'. It is assured by these characteristics: 'that they have commonly an unaffected sincerity, that they love to deliver their minds with a sound simplicity, that . . . they are not extremely prone to speak, that they are more concerned what others will think of the strength than of the fineness of what they say'.

One begins to wonder why the Royal Society was so afraid of being 'eaten out by the luxury and redundance of speech', how the English could have become so debauched by the general mischief of eloquence, or why any reform was necessary. It is to be remembered that Sprat speaks of this reform of style as directed primarily toward the requirements of natural philosophy.[2] But when he devotes a short section at the end of his book to the consideration of possible benefits from experiments to wits and writers, his chief standard of value for wit is whether the comparisons derive from things apparent to the senses. Here his standard for style may reflect that requirement: 'so many *things* almost in an equal number of *words*'—not

[1] Part II, sect. 20. As Aristotle said (*Rhetoric*, III. i. 6), nobody uses style in teaching geometry. This standard of diction will not exclude terms of art, which Dryden tried in *Annus Mirabilis*. Thomas Baker (*Reflections upon Learning*, p. 15) observes that 'matters of Science', being abstruse, are not easy to express in proper terms that cannot be misunderstood: 'Such particularly are Terms of Art, that must needs be obscure as being too comprehensive, and taking in more notions than one under the same Word: Which tho' of good use, as being designed to make knowledge more compendious, yet have frequently turn'd the other way, by requiring large Comments.' But Dryden's object was to be more particular.

[2] Sprat really amplifies the Statute in Baconian terms, for he develops the vanities which Bacon found hindrances to science, especially the vanity of words.

'things and notions', as Wilkins puts it. For Sprat's antipathy to the abstractions of the schoolmen colours his definition, preferring the language of those who deal in things before the language of those who deal in notions. Viewed in the light of his discussion of wit, this would be only another aspect of the doctrine of plainness as perspicuity.

But when Sprat spoke of 'so many things almost in an equal number of words', some of his readers may have been reminded of a passage in Cicero's *De Oratore* which Hobbes had used in praising the pithiness of Thucydides. Hobbes had said, with the turn of antimetabole:

For he is so full of matter, that the number of his sentences [thoughts] doth almost reach to the number of his words; and in his words he is so apt and close, that it is hard to say whether his words do more illustrate his sentences, or his sentences his words.[1]

Seneca (*Ep.* 114) had found in Sallust more thoughts than words, or still greater brevity. Thus Sprat's remark would associate the Royal Society programme with Senecan brevity rather than Ciceronian copiousness; the degree of brevity may be located on Jonson's scale of succinct styles. It was a brevity like that for which Wilkins had argued in his *Ecclesiastes*, and it was hardly a novelty then. It certainly was not the prerogative of natural philosophy, though Bacon had pointed to their ancient association.

In the first part of his *History* Sprat takes pains to show that almost from the beginning philosophy had been corrupted by the arts of speech. Eloquence, however, was not a positive fault with the schoolmen:

I will not insist long on the Barbarousness of their Stile; though that too must justly be censur'd: For all the *ancient Philosophers*, though they labour'd not to be full and adorn'd in their Speech, yet they always strove to be easie, natural, and unaffected. *Plato* was allow'd by all to be the chief Master of *Speaking*, as well as of *Thinking*. And even *Aristotle* himself, whom alone these Men ador'd, however he has been since us'd by his *Commentators*, was so careful about his Words, that he was esteem'd one of the purest, and most polite Writers of his Time. But the want of good Language, not being the *Schoolmen's* worst defect, I shall pass it over, and

---

[1] *English Works*, ed. Molesworth, vol. viii, p. xxiii; cf. *De Oratore*, II. xiii. 56. Cicero's words are 'ut verborum prope numerum sententiarum numero consequatur'.

rather stop a while, to examine the *Matter* it self, and *Order* in which they proceeded.[1]

Did the ancient philosophers, then, write in a manner acceptable to the Royal Society? Certainly Plato did not for Samuel Parker, another Fellow. But if the schoolmen fell short of Aristotle in politeness, their worst fault was their method of disputation. Their 'notional war' could never do any great good towards the enlargement of knowledge, 'because it relied on general Terms, which had not much Foundation in Nature, and also because they took no other Course, but that of Disputing'.[2] So to their lesser defects of style we add a reliance on general terms that have not much relation to things.

The significance of Sprat's insistence upon the corrupting influence of the arts of speech in philosophy—also a problem for Bacon—appears when Sprat discusses 'A Model of their whole Design' in relation to language: 'And to accomplish this, they have endeavoured, to separate the Knowledge of Nature, from the Colours of Rhetoric, the Devices of Fancy, or the delightful Deceit of Fables.'[3] The necessity of such a procedure is supported by Sprat's discussion of romantic histories of nature as opposed to true histories.[4] If Sir Thomas Browne were kept out of the Royal Society for any of these reasons, it was not because he was ignorant of these principles. Of course the extreme step contemplated by the Royal Society in this direction is to be found in Wilkins's *Real Character and Philosophical Language*. The essential purpose of this scheme was to get words back to a univocal relation to things by means of a system of marks which would define those things. It looked to an artificial language that would avoid, and help to correct in natural languages, all equivocation, ambiguity, or redundance. Sprat celebrates this

[1] Part I, sect. 9. On the schoolmen Sprat echoes Bacon, but not in this concern for elegance. Bacon explained their efforts to avoid 'circuit of speech'; Sprat seems to have forgotten his thesis.

[2] In an epistle 'To the Learned Tho. Albius', included in *Scepsis Scientifica* (1665), Glanvill says that his aim 'was the Advance of Science by discrediting empty and talkative notionality'.

[3] Part II, sect. 5.

[4] Part II, sect. 13. See Bacon's third vanity of learning on the necessity of separating fact and opinion—as required by the Royal Society statute—and the consequence of failure to do so, natural history 'being fraught with much fabulous matter' (*Advancement*, Everyman ed., pp. 28–9).

work, although it was not yet published, as one designed 'to teach a Communion of Speech amongst all Philosophers'.[1]

Among 'modern experimenters', says Sprat, in a section which has its bearing on style,

I shall only mention one great Man, who had the true Imagination of the whole Extent of this Enterprise, as it is now set on foot; and that is, the Lord *Bacon*; in whose Books there are every where scattered the best Arguments, that can be produc'd for the Defence of experimental Philosophy, and the best Directions, that are needful to promote it: All which he has already adorn'd with so much Art; that if my Desires could have prevail'd with some excellent Friends of mine, who engag'd me to this Work, there should have been no other Preface to the *History* of the *Royal Society*, but some of his Writings.[2]

The *History* certainly makes one realize the truth of this insistence on the relation of Bacon to the Society; for instance, their 'way of registering' and their 'Histories' both have antecedents in the *Advancement of Learning*.[3] But the interesting point is that Sprat finds no impropriety between Bacon's writings 'adorned with so much Art' and the requirements of the history of the Society.[4] What that art was Sprat proceeds to describe:

He was a Man of strong, clear, and powerful Imaginations; his Genius was searching and inimitable; and of this I need give no other Proof, than his style it self; which as, for the most part, it describes Men's Minds, as well as Pictures do their Bodies, so it did his above all Men living. The Course of it vigorous, and majestical; the Wit bold, and familiar; the Comparisons fetch'd out of the Way, and yet the more easie: In all expressing a Soul, equally skill'd in Men, and Nature.

Although his wit is bold, Bacon's limitation, which Sprat also defines,

[1] Part II, sect. 37.

[2] Part I, sect. 16. Nevertheless Sprat has plundered Bacon sufficiently. His friends are the two secretaries, Wilkins and Oldenburg, whose duty it is 'to publish whatever shall be agreed upon by the Society', and from whom, adds Sprat, 'I have not usurp'd this first imployment of that kind; for it is onely my hand that goes, the substance and direction came from one of them' (Part II, sect. 15). Be that as it may, Wilkins by his actions must share the responsibility; but Oldenburg was not satisfied. One obvious inference from this is that Sprat is not representing his own opinion so much as that of Wilkins.

[3] On the former see *History*, Part II, sect. 20. 2. Sect. 21 marks the break in writing occasioned by the plague and fire.

[4] Cf. his 'Advertisement to the Reader': 'The Style perhaps in which it is written, is larger and more contentious than becomes that Purity and Shortness which are the chief Beauties of historical Writings.' Of course it has a rhetorical purpose, for it is a defence.

is not one of style; rather it is that which must always belong to individual effort in the large field of science, the co-operative nature of which Sprat, like Bacon, is never tired of repeating. Yet Sprat could still argue from the doctrine of propriety that supported the cult of expressiveness, which Seneca had developed and Jonson asserted under 'oratio imago animi', holding that 'Language most shows a man: speak that I may see thee'.[1]

But, we may ask, could Sprat tolerate the metaphorical character of Bacon's style? The answer is that he used it as a bribe in his attempt to placate the wits. His theme is the benefit of experiments to wit, and so to wits and writers:

The use of Experiments to this Purpose is evident, by the wonderful Advantage that my Lord *Bacon* receiv'd from them. This excellent Writer was abundantly recompenc'd for his noble Labours in that *Philosophy*, by a vast Treasure of admirable *Imaginations* which it afforded him, wherewith to express and adorn his Thoughts about other Matters. But I will not confine this *Observation* to one single *Author*, though he was one of the first and most artificial Managers of this way of Wit. I will venture to declare in general of the *English Tongue*, that as it contains a greater Stock of *natural* and *mechanical Discoveries*, so it is also more enrich'd with beautiful *Conceptions*, and inimitable *Similitudes*, gather'd from the *Arts* of Men's Hands and the *Works of Nature*, than ever any other *Language* could produce.[2]

Here, indeed, Sprat was exceeding the programme of the Society, or at least of Wilkins. If this were merely propaganda—to persuade the wits, as Evelyn quoted Bacon, against despising to 'converse with mean Experiments'—he was placing himself in the awkward position of having to explain why figurative expression must be banished if the language were so indebted to natural philosophy. To be consistent, Sprat would have to reply that the exclusion applied only to the language of philosophy, and that seems to be his general position, although it is sometimes obscured in the *History*.

The third part, which asserts 'the Advantage and Innocence of this Work', deals with the most delicate issues raised by the Society. In education the only alteration which Sprat will acknowledge is that to be made in natural philosophy; but we observe the con-

---

[1] See Seneca, *Epp.* 40, 75, 114, 115; Jonson, *Timber*, 'Oratio imago animi'.
[2] Part III, sect. 35. Was this a consequence of 'preferring the language of Artizans, Countrymen, and Merchants, before that of Wits and Scholars'?

temptuous dismissal of metaphysics, 'that Cloudy Knowledge' of which its lovers 'are wont to boast, that it is an excellent instrument to refine, and make subtil the minds of men'; and the judgement that in logic or the 'Art of Discourse . . . mankind has been already rather too curious, than negligent'. What of grammar and rhetoric?

First then I will make no scruple to acquit *Experimental Philosophy*, from having any ill effects, on the usual *Arts*, whereby we are taught the Purity, and Elegance of *Languages*. Whatever discoveries shall appear to us afresh, out of the hidden things of *Nature*, the same words, and the same waies of Expression will remain. Or if perhaps by this means, any change shall be made herein; it can be only for the better; by supplying mens Tongues, with very many *new things*, to be nam'd, and adorn'd, and describ'd in their discourse.[1]

Thus any change means addition rather than subtraction, or the profit which Bacon derived from experiments. And the 'new things' are allowed not only to be named but 'adorned' in discourse. This benefit is made clearer in the section addressed to wits and writers. It we recall that in Sprat's outburst against eloquence what made it so 'utterly desperate in its Cure' was that we 'labour so long after it in the Years of our Education', we must again suspect Sprat or else believe that he intended to limit plain speech to natural philosophers. The weight of evidence in the *History* points toward that conclusion.

Mention of the benefit of experiments to wits and writers—'which perhaps it will scarce become me', says Sprat, 'to name amidst so many Matters of greater Weight'—has this excuse:

But this I am provok'd to mention by the Consideration of the present *Genius* of the *English Nation*; wherein the Study of *Wit*, and Humour of *Writing* prevails so much, that there are very few Conditions, or Degrees, or Ages of Men who are free from its Infection.[2]

Are we to conclude that the English genius is suffering from another 'Astrological humour'? Or should we look further into this excuse?

And now I hope what I have here said will prevail something with the *Wits* and *Railleurs* of this *Age*, to reconcile their Opinions and Discourses

[1] Part III, sect. 2. Robert Hooke's manuscript note (Weld, *History of the Royal Society*, i. 146) likewise limits the object of the Society: 'To improve the knowledge of naturall things, and all useful Arts, Manufactures, Mechanick practises, Engynes and Inventions by Experiments—(not meddling with Divinity, Metaphysics, Moralls, Politics, Grammar, Rhetorick, or Logick).'

[2] Part III, sect. 35.

to these *Studies*: for now they may behold that their Interest is united with that of the *Royal Society*; and that if they shall decry the promoting of *Experiments*, they will deprive themselves of the most fertil Subject of *Fancy*: and indeed it has been with respect to these terrible Men, that I have made this long Digression. I acknowledge that we ought to have a great Dread of their Power: I confess I believe that the *new Philosophy* need not (as *Caesar*) fear the pale or the melancholy, as much as the humorous and the merry: For they perhaps by making it ridiculous because it is *new*, and because they themselves are unwilling to take pains about it, may do it more Injury than all the Arguments of our severe and frowning and dogmatical *Adversaries*.

This may be disingenuous; but the latter half of it, being addressed to his colleagues rather than his opponents, becomes a kind of personal tribute to the literary power which the Royal Society feared, but, Sprat suggests, not enough. One would like to know what he thought when the humorous Shadwell took pains to show the failure of the Virtuoso to understand that wit and wisdom are related to 'the manners of men, not natural causes'.[1] Against the wits, then, Sprat plays his trump card, self-interest; he has, however, another trump:

> But to gain their good Will, I must acquaint them, that the Family of the *Railleurs* is deriv'd from the same Original with the *Philosophers*. The Founder of *Philosophy* is confess'd by all to be *Socrates*; and he also was the famous Author of all *Irony*.

This is rather disingenuous, for Sprat wants 'philosophy' here to mean natural philosophy, but his first mention of Socrates is connected with the contamination of the 'Knowledge of Nature' by that of 'Discourse' and 'human Actions'.

The alteration in wit follows the change in education that is to be effected by natural philosophy. The best wit, says Sprat, requires 'that it be founded on such Images which are generally known, and are able to bring a strong and a sensible Impression on the Mind'. This definition illuminates his description of Bacon's wit, which was both strong and sensible. When Sprat dismisses the 'Wit of the Fables and Religions of the ancient World' he adds another criterion: 'especially seeing they have this peculiar Imperfection,

---

[1] Cf. Hobbes (*Answer to Davenant*): 'But the subject of a Poem is the manners of men, not natural causes; manners presented, not dictated; and manners feigned, as the name of Poesy imports, not found in men.'

that they were only Fictions at first; Whereas Truth is never so well expressed or amplified, as by those Ornaments which are true and real in themselves'. With these criteria in mind, we are ready to observe that the subjects of education which he treated somewhat contemptuously receive a similar treatment as the matter of wit:

The *Sciences* of Mens Brains are none of the best Materials for this kind of *Wit*. Very few have happily succeeded in *Logical, Metaphysical, Grammatical*, nay even scarce in *Mathematical Comparisons*; and the reason is, because they are most of them conversant about Things remov'd from the Senses, and so cannot surprize the *fancy* with very obvious, or quick, or sensible Delights.[1]

Thus of the more approved subjects grammar is rejected, but mathematics more reluctantly. With respect to logic we may recall Sprat's remark—as he recalled Bacon's—that the 'promoters of Experiments' condemn men 'for being wholly employed about the productions of their own minds, and neglecting all the works of Nature, that are without them'. The rejection of the schoolmen in philosophy is reflected in this rejection of the scholastic wit of the earlier part of the century; it might be summed up as the rejection of 'metaphysics', for scholastic notions had come to be nothing but 'general terms' or bad metaphors.

The great improvement in education was to be in natural philosophy, and so it is in wit. 'It is apparent, that the Defect of the Ancients in natural Knowledge did also straiten their Fancies'; the few things which they knew and applied have been almost worn out. But this poverty will be relieved by 'Experiments':

The Comparisons which these may afford will be intelligible to all, because they proceed from Things that enter into all Mens Senses. These will make the most vigorous Impressions on Mens *Fancies*, because they do even touch their *Eyes*, and are nearest to their *Nature*. Of these the Variety will be infinite, for the Particulars are so from whence they may be deduc'd: These may be always new and unsullied, seeing there is such a vast Number of *Natural* and *Mechanical Things*, not yet fully known or improv'd, and by Consequence not yet sufficiently apply'd.

Common intelligibility was not a scholastic virtue; as Thomas Baker said, 'Nicety is the great fault of the Schools, her Doctors have been

[1] The proper sources are 'the Arts of Men's Hands and the Works of Nature'. Cf. Robert Boyle's view of wit in *Occasional Reflections* (Oxford, 1848), pp. 34, 36-8, 43.

styled Profound, Subtle, Irrefragable; Titles which they have most valued themselves upon, and seem not much to have affected the Reputation of being Familiar and Easy.'[1] And we may recall that according to Sprat the worst defect of the schoolmen was their reliance 'on general Terms, which had not much Foundation in Nature'. The products of wit derived from the new philosophy will have both the intelligibility and the 'particulars' which derive from a report of the senses.

That wit or eloquence was to be banished out of all writing is certainly not the conclusion of Sprat. It can hardly be argued that by wits and writers he does not mean prose writers, since Bacon is his only example of a writer and 'he was one of the first and most Artificial Managers of this way of Wit'. The course for the future apparently was not away from Bacon. It will be remembered that after his tirade against eloquence in general Sprat concluded: 'It will suffice my present Purpose, to point out, what has been done by the Royal Society, towards the correcting of its Excesses in natural Philosophy; to which it is, of all others, a most profest Enemy.' This is a limited statement both of the opposition between philosophy and rhetoric and of his office as the spokesman of the Society. To make good that last clause is the chief function of the first part of the *History*. To the question whether this programme extended to other writing, Sprat's criticism of literature must supply the answer, for it is he who suggests the question.

On the basis of available evidence the stylistic programme set forth by the *History of the Royal Society* seems to be indebted chiefly to the doctrine of Wilkins and the tumid exposition of Sprat.[2] The Statutes of the Society define a method of reporting the results of investigation more than a style for such reports. The Society sought to prevent, after the teaching of Bacon, the confusion of fact and conjecture rather than of words and things; but to Wilkins, no doubt, they came to the same thing. If the Horatian motto, *Nullius in Verba*, speaks for the Society, the minutes of the Society suggest

---

[1] *Reflections upon Learning* (1700), p. 220.

[2] Note the appeal to the Society for support which Wilkins makes in his 'Epistle Dedicatory' to *An Essay*. Here he argues that if 'the polishing of their language' is worthy of the 'united labour and studies' of Academies, 'certainly then, the Design here proposed, ought not to be thought unworthy of such assistance; it being as much to be preferred before that, as things are better than words, as *real knowledge* is beyond *Elegancy of speech*'. Sprat's contrast of Academy and Society may be compared.

that Wilkins was most concerned about the improvement of the language for philosophical purposes. He is the agent of the special instructions to that end which were given to the committee of which Sprat was a member; his official relation to the *History*, though limited to supervision of the particulars to be included and to final review, may have been as considerable as Sprat indicates. Moreover, Wilkins's interest in a philosophical language, as we have seen, goes back clearly at least to 1654, though he began to work on it much later.[1]

Wilkins's *Essay towards a Real Character and a Philosophical Language*, published a year later than Sprat's *History*,[2] contains the same stylistic doctrine as the *History*; and this doctrine ultimately returns to his *Ecclesiastes*, where it is associated with Seneca, not with science. But here the doctrine is negative; it concerns the removal of 'defects and imperfections' that hinder communication in extant languages.[3] This proposal includes 'a Real universal Character, that should not signify words, but things and notions';[4] and a 'Philosophical Language' by which this Character can be translated into letters and sounds and made utterable.[5] As an artificial medium, this philosophical language could have no direct effect on English prose style; its indirect effect at best would be to make the diction more exact. For this proposal Wilkins, like Sprat, finds contemporary motivation in 'the late times, wherein this grand imposture of Phrases hath almost eaten out solid knowledge in all professions'.[6] For Wilkins 'words' as opposed to 'things and notions'

[1] That is, the 'interest' indebted to Seth Ward, which finally materialized in the *Essay*. Cf. the 'Epistle to the Reader': 'It was some considerable time after this, before I had any thought of attempting any thing in this kind.' Yet 'this Work was first undertaken, during that vacancy and leasure which I formerly enjoyed in an Academicall station'. Probably he began work on it just before the Restoration.

[2] But it too was delayed, for the printing had been nearly finished when it was burnt in the Great Fire (1666).

[3] Cf. *Essay*, part I, esp. chaps. iv and v.

[4] *Essay* (1668), p. 13. The sentence continues, 'and consequently might be legible by any Nation in their own Tongue; which is the principal design of this Treatise'. By means of a Dictionary the words of any language, in all their various senses, could be defined as things or notions by reference to the Philosophical Tables. Such a dictionary for English has been provided in this work by Dr. William Lloyd.

[5] See part IV for the Real Character, or the signs by which things are defined by their genus, difference, and species; and also for the Philosophical Language, by which these signs are translated into letters and sounds, or made utterable. Remember Ward's criticism of Webster.

[6] Ibid., p. 18. The context of 'solid' is not limited to science in the narrow sense, and

have much the same significance that 'general terms' have to Sprat: they have too little 'Foundation in Nature'. If in Butler's words, they are not 'nominals' rather than 'reals', they are not close enough to things; they are names, not definitions.[1] 'General terms' are most removed from 'things', but they provide the 'Philosophical Tables' by which words are defined as less general things and notions.[2] Thus the two terms, words and things, give significance to that other set of terms often in Wilkins's mind when discussing style, empty and full.

When Wilkins published the *Real Character* he realized, we may be sure, his idea of the office of the committee for improving the English tongue. In fact, outside of the *History*, the only discernible result of the special intention of improving the language for philosophical purposes was the subsequent publication of Wilkins's *Real Character*. His prefatory epistles show that if he was not sure of the Society, he was sure of the necessity of the 'real character' to the advancement of learning.[3] But many of the benefits which he claims for his design were already being realized, and the criticism of reform, including his own, had been growing for more than two decades. Indeed, Hobbes had behind him two decades of labour at 'unmasking many wild errors, that shelter themselves under the disguise of affected phrases' and turn out to be 'inconsistencies and

this defect of the late times is not new in Wilkins. Here he contemplates the application of this language to religion as well as to natural knowledge. Incidentally, here we find not only the 'trick of metaphors' but Sprat's very metaphor.

[1] Hudibras, it may be remembered, was

> Profound in all the Nominal
> And Real ways, beyond them all:
> And, with as delicate a hand,
> Could twist as tough a rope of sand.

[2] Cf. *Essay* (1668), p. 24: 'Tho *particulars* are first in the order of *Being*, yet *Generals* are first in the order of *Knowing*, because by these, such things and notions as are less general, are to be distinguished and defined. Now the proper end and design of *Metaphysic* should be to enumerate and explain those more general terms, which by reason of their Universality and Comprehensiveness, are either *above* all those Heads of things stiled Predicaments, or else *common to several of them*.'

[3] He presented it to the Society as 'those Papers . . . which by severall Orders of the Society have been required of me'. But he also urged it upon their attention, unless he was really addressing the public through the Society. Thomas Baker, however, remained sceptical: 'For this Language being design'd not to express words but things, we must first be agreed about the nature of things, before we can fix Marks and Characters to represent them, and I very much despair of such an agreement' (*Reflections upon Learning*, p. 17). Already, he continues, the order upon which Wilkins built is passing, 'Accidents' are giving way to 'Modes', thus tumbling his house of cards.

contradictions'.[1] But it may be doubted whether Wilkins would have joined Hobbes in finding the scholastic 'incorporeal substance', even if 'this way examined', to be 'either nonsense, or very flat and jejune'. Yet Hobbes, without benefit of the Royal Society, was just as deadly an enemy of the metaphor in philosophy.[2] Nor was he the sole voice of protest against such 'ambiguity of words'.

Wilkins reminds us in several ways that he stands behind Sprat's expression of the stylistic programme of the Royal Society:

And though the varieties of Phrases in Language may seem to contribute to the elegance and ornament of Speech; yet, like other affected ornaments, they prejudice the native simplicity of it, and contribute to the disguising of it with false appearances.[3]

Yet Sprat never brought himself to state such an unqualified position with respect to the literary use of language; and Bacon, who previously had remarked this 'disguising of it with false appearances', never set forth so simple a doctrine. Wilkins again recalls Sprat when he adds to the disability of such phrases the fact that they are things of fashion: 'witness the present Age, especially the late times, wherein this grand imposture of Phrases hath almost eaten out solid knowledge in all professions; such men generally being of most esteem who are skilled in these Canting forms of speech, though in nothing else'.[4] The verbal similarity to Sprat has been remarked, but in this longer quotation we get the addition of the present age

[1] See 'The Epistle Dedicatory' to An Essay. Hobbes could have pointed to passages in his De Cive, Human Nature, Answer to Davenant, and Leviathan for early criticism of this sort.

[2] Cf. Wilkins, An Essay (1668), pp. 17–18; Hobbes, Leviathan, part I, chaps. iv and v. In these chapters Sprat's 'general terms' and 'trick of metaphors' are sufficiently ventilated as dangers to science or knowledge. Chap. v treats 'the use of Metaphors, Tropes, and other Rhetoricall figures, in stead of words proper'. Hobbes also insisted on definition, reference to things, absence of contradiction, and the dangers of eloquence.

[3] An Essay (1668), p. 18. To the objection that some of the 'Enquiries' in the Essay are trivial, Wilkins replies in the 'Epistle to the Reader': 'Such Persons may know, that the discovery of the true nature and Cause of any the most minute thing, doth promote real Knowledge, and therefore cannot be unfit for any Mans endeavours, who is willing to contribute to the advancement of Learning.' This scientific creed was to the Wits, however, to whom it was no doubt addressed, as flagrant a violation of values as Milton discovered when Satan 'on the Tree of Life . . . Sat like a Cormorant' (PL, iv. 194 ff.).

[4] Ibid. This reference becomes a little tiresome from one whose 'Canting forms' found other expression. Of course Wilkins did not have in mind the prose of Howell, Suckling, or Cowley; but we cannot therefore forget that such prose was written in 'Canting' times. H. C. Wyld (A History of Modern Colloquial English, p. 153) observes that in Suckling 'we find, almost for the first time, the accents of that age which has given to succeeding generations the models of clarity, elegance, and urbanity'.

and its esteem for the forms of speech, both of concern to Sprat. The threat to learning against which Bacon spoke now wears a new fashion; it is no longer Ciceronianism, but the canting speech of the Commonwealth. At least that is one of the most obvious charges made by Wilkins and Sprat, and it is supported by various attacks upon the jargon of 'enthusiasm'.[1] It is hard to resist the conclusion that the expansion in the *History* of the method of reporting prescribed in the Statutes derives more from Wilkins than from Sprat and gives a peculiar bias to that account. In doctrine the likeness of the *History* to Sprat's other work identifies Sprat, but the difference identifies Wilkins.

John Evelyn, in a work for the Royal Society, makes an explicit subscription to the stylistic programme of that group, and thus provides us with some actual testimony to its operation. It is found in the conclusion to his preface to *Pomona* (1664):

It now remains, that I should make some *Apology* for my self, to extenuate the tumultuary *Method* of the ensuing *Periods*. Indeed it was not intended for a queint or elaborate piece of *Art*; nor is it the design of the *Royal Society* to accumulate *Repetitions* when they can be avoided; and therefore in an *Argument* so much beaten as is that of dressing the *Seminary*, *Planting*, and modes of *Graffing*, it has been with Industry avoided; such rude, and imperfect *Draughts* being far better in their esteem (and according to my Lord *Bacon's*) than such as are adorn'd with more *Pomp*, and ostentous *Circumstances*, for a pretence to *Perfection*.[2]

[1] To the significance of 'canting' other members of the Royal Society have testified. For instance, Evelyn writes of the Presbyterians in 'A Character of England': 'In divers places they read not the Scriptures at all; but up into the pulpit, where they make an insipid, tedious, and immethodical prayer, in phrases and a tone so affected and mysterious, that they give it the name of canting, a term by which they do usually express the gibberish of beggars and vagabonds; after which, there follows the sermon (which, for the most part, they read out of a book) consisting (like their prayers) of speculative and abstracted notions and things, which, nor the people nor themselves well understand: but these they extend to an extraordinary length and Pharisaical repetitions. . . .' And Boyle brings 'canting' into science, for in his preface to *The Sceptical Chymist* he declares that he will not answer replies to his arguments 'if any impertinent person . . . shall write against them in a canting way, I mean shall express himselfe in ambiguous or obscure termes, or argue from experiments, not intelligibly enough delivered'. Such criticism of the canting of the 'enthusiasts' is very common, for it was one of the main objects of reform.

[2] Prefixed to the Discourses that follow *Pomona* is an 'Animadversion' concerned with the running 'Title of Aphorisms', which was extended by a printer's error. It should not, says Evelyn, be taken as a sign of dogmatism, which is contrary to the spirit of the Royal Society; rather, the general form of the Discourses does not 'pretend to fine and elaborate Methods'. But the style of Bacon's *Essays* has often been taken as a sign of dogmatism.

Evelyn concludes that the time may come when a history of agriculture can be written; he has followed the method of the Royal Society by providing 'materials'. This method is explained by what Sprat says of their 'way of Registering' and its stylistic aspect by their 'manner of Discourse'.[1] The whole matter is summed up by Bacon's discussion of the proper method of delivery for science; in style this method leads to 'writing in aphorisms' rather than to 'writing in Method'.[2]

As writing in aphorisms promotes a 'tumultuary Method', Shaftesbury, who associated such a method with Seneca, might have called Evelyn's method Senecan. For both Bacon and the Society the facts were to be 'barely stated', and hence the lack of elaboration mentioned by Evelyn. It is clear that for Evelyn a 'piece of Art' and a discourse for the Royal Society are two different things, and that he feels some need of apologizing for such a discourse when it is presented to the public in this form. Evelyn's 'Repetitions', it need hardly be said, are Sprat's 'superfluity' and 'redundance of Speech'; they were equally to be avoided by Bacon's 'aphorisms'.

Evelyn's public vindication of the Royal Society is to be found in his preface to *Sylva*, which was printed with *Pomona* and by order of the Society.[3] In its first form the preface is more of a eulogy; in its later form more of a vindication, amplifying his letter to Cowley. His original attitude may be suggested by one remark: 'I will not exasperate the Adorers of our ancient and late Naturalists, by repeating of what our Verulam has justly pronounced concerning their Rhapsodies.'[4] But he must have exasperated them not a little when he later described the Royal Society as earnestly trying to sort out 'any thing of sincere and useful among this Pedantic Rubbish' couched in '*alti-sonant* Phrases'.

[1] *History*, part II, sect. 20. This section is divided into their 'manner of Discourse' and their 'way of Registring'. The latter avoids the fourth error of learning stated in the *Advancement of Learning* (bk. 1) by adopting the Baconian 'kalendar'. The avoidance of this 'over early and peremptory reduction of knowledge into arts and methods' entails its delivery in 'aphorisms and observations'.

[2] See *De Augmentis*, VI. ii, and the corresponding place in the *Advancement*; or Chap. VI of the present work. Recall Burton's quotation of Lipsius on the method of Seneca and the Stoics.

[3] First published in 1664, it was enlarged in 1670 and 1679. The preface was likewise enlarged.

[4] In the first edition (1664) Evelyn stops with this affront, and speaks of his indebtedness to them. This is all that I quote from the first edition. Though he praises the Royal Society, his vindication is of subsequent date.

That Evelyn was not above being somewhat high-sounding himself, even while defending the Royal Society, may be shown by the following passage from this preface:

Witness you *Great Alexander*, and you the *Ptolemees, Caesars, Charlemain, Francis* the First; the *Cosimo's, Frederic's, Alphonsus's*, and the rest of *Learned Princes*: Since when all the *Pomp* and Noise is ended; They are those *little things* in *black*, (whom now in scorn they term *Philosophers* and *Fopps*) to whom they must be oblig'd, for making their *Names* outlast the *Pryamids* whose *Founders* are as unknown as the Heads of *Nile*; because they either deserv'd no *Memory* for their *Vertues*, or had none to transmit them, or their *Actions* to *Posterity*.[1]

Sir Thomas Browne, though damned by his 'alti-sonant Phrases', might have spoken thus, and better, for the Royal Society.[2] But Evelyn illustrates the 'alti-sonant' lift that comes with the employment of periodic structure and its sustained rhythm. He concludes his vindication by quoting Bacon on a pertinent theme: 'Some Men (like Lucian in Religion) seek by their Wit, to traduce and expose useful things; because to arrive at them, they converse with mean Experiments.' Sprat also found it expedient to remind the wits of Bacon; but this passage, like many in Sprat, reminds us that no small element in the antipathy to the Royal Society was the humanist tradition, which assumed comic form in Shadwell's *Virtuoso*. It is clear, however, that for Evelyn a report to the Society restricted one to bare statement, but a defence of the Society permitted another character of style, not without pomp and circumstance. His testimony is valuable because he was indifferent neither to style nor to the Society, but produced some of the first works that were published by order of the Society.

---

[1] And of 'this Illustrious Assembly' he writes: 'But they have aimed at *greater things*, and *greater things* produc'd, namely, by *Emancipating*, and freeing themselves from the *Tyranny* of *Opinion, delusory* and fallacious shews, to receive nothing upon *Trust*, but bring it to the *Lydian Touch*, make it pass the *Fire*, the *Anvil* and the *File*, till it come forth perfectly *repurged*, and of consistence.' One thing which they rejected, according to Sprat, was 'this trick of metaphors'.

[2] Cf. Browne (*Religio Medici*, Everyman ed., pp. 70-1): 'It is not meer Zeal to Learning, or Devotion to the Muses, that wiser Princes patron the Arts, and carry an indulgent aspect unto Scholars; but a desire to have their names eternized by the memory of their writings, and a fear of the revengeful Pen of succeeding ages; for these are the men, that, when they have played their parts, and had their *exits*, must step out and give the moral of their Scenes, and deliver unto Posterity an Inventory of their Virtues and Vices.'

10. *Polishing the English Tongue*

Some of the defenders of the Royal Society were likewise advocates of an academy. Before the appearance of Sprat's *History*, the Royal Society had made abortive efforts in the direction of establishing an arbiter of language and style in a domain wider than that of natural philosophy. On 7 December 1664 a committee including Sir John Berkenhead, Dryden, Evelyn, Sprat, Waller, and others, with Sir Peter Wyche as chairman, had been appointed 'for improving the English tongue'; later it was given instructions by Wilkins. Earlier in the year Dryden had included a plea for an academy in the dedicatory epistle of his *Rival Ladies*, which was not only his first criticism but criticism directed toward language and style. For him, as for other literary members of the committee, it was the natural interest. Our only knowledge of the deliberations of this committee, besides the hints in Sprat's *History*, is contained in the letter of 'indigested thoughts' which Evelyn sent to Sir Peter Wyche, on 20 June 1665, as his contribution. But the writings of some members of this committee may tell us what ideas they would have brought to its purpose, and how they were disposed toward style; thus we may ascertain both the nature of their design and its relation to antecedent styles.

We learn of a few meetings of this committee in a letter from Evelyn to Samuel Pepys on 12 August 1689. Here he remarks 'how obliging a thing it were . . . if, as there is a Society for the Improvement of Natural Knowledge, and which was fit should be first, since things were before words, so there was an Academy for that of Art and Improvement of speaking and writing well'.[1] As the consequence

---

[1] *Critical Essays of the Seventeenth Century*, ed. J. E. Spingarn, ii. 327. In 1660 the *New Atlantis Continued* by R. H. suggested an academy, perhaps prompted by the translation of Pellisson's *History of the French Academy* (1657). Edmund Freeman, who called attention to this proposal (*Modern Language Review*, xix. 291–300), makes Sprat disclaim his academy rather than his 'first general Head' as 'what was before very well known, and what passes about in common discourse'.

of such an academy, whose place is not taken by the Royal Society, Evelyn declares,

We should not then haue so many crude and fulsome rhapsodies impos'd vpon the English world for genuine witt, language, & the stage, as well as on the auditors and spectators, which would be purg'd from things intollerable. It would inflame, inspire, & kindle another genius and tone of writing, with nervous, natural strength & beauty, genuine and of our owne growth, without allways borrowing & filching from our neighbours.

In 1689 this seemed to Evelyn the possible effect of an academy. That the Royal Society as constituted ought to have an effect upon literary style does not occur to him, for he continues to Mr. Pepys:

And indeede such was once design'd since the restauration of Charles the Second (1665), and in order to it three or fowre meetings were begun at Gray's Inn, by Mr. Cowley, Dr. Sprat, Mr. Waller, the D. of Buckingham, Matt. Clifford, Mr. Dryden, & some other promoters of it. But by the death of the incomparable Mr. Cowley, distance & inconvenience of the place, the contagion, & other circumstances intervening, it crumbled away & came to nothing.[1]

As 'an inferior labourer' Evelyn offers Pepys what material he had gathered towards 'that intended pyramid'.

It is significant that Evelyn speaks of 'the plan I drew and was laying before them for that design, which was, I said, the polishing of the English tongue'.[2] Such a plan he had included in his letter to Sir Peter Wyche; and since it was the same as that mentioned to Pepys, it ought to give us a fairly accurate notion of the kind of ideas that were considered by the committee for the achievement of their design. It may throw some light on Dryden's occasional remarks on language and style, or suggest the appropriate background for the attacks on his style by Martin (Matt.) Clifford and the Duke of Buckingham; and perhaps it will serve to give perspective to the programme for style announced in the *History of the Royal Society*.

First, however, we need to consider Sprat's own proposal of an

---

[1] *Critical Essays*, ii. 329. The promoters seem to have included some unofficial members; the original committee did not include Cowley, Buckingham, or Clifford.

[2] Wilkins, on the other hand, was ordered to 'intimate to them the way of proceeding in that committee, according to the sense of the council, viz. chiefly to improve the philosophy of the language'.

academy in the *History*, for it also supplies perspective. When he proposes the erecting of an English Academy, he observes that the English character and the English habits of life are discouragements to his proposal.[1] 'I know indeed that the English Genius is not so airy and discoursive as that of some of our neighbors, but that we generally love to have Reason set out in plain, undeceiving expressions, as much as they to have it delivered with colour and beauty.'[2] However, the need is great:

But besides, if we observe well the *English Language*, we shall find that it seems at this time more than others to require some such aid to bring it to its last perfection. The Truth is, it has been hitherto a little too carelessly handled, and, I think, has had less labor spent about its polishing then it deserves.[3]

In the late Civil Wars 'it received many fantastical terms, which were introduced by our Religious Sects, and many outlandish phrases, which several Writers and Translators in that great hurry brought in and made free as they pleased, and with all it was enlarged by many sound and necessary Forms and Idioms which it before wanted'.

If an academy were to act as arbiter of the language, he concludes that 'our Speech would quickly arrive at as much plenty as it is capable to receive, and at the greatest smoothness which its derivation from the rough German will allow it'. Improvement as well as corruption has taken place in Sprat's view, and it need hardly be added that *copia* or 'plenty' was not Wilkins's idea of further improvement. But this new academy is not to be 'confined only to the weighing Words and Letters'; it is to be 'a fixt and Impartial Court of Eloquence, according to whose Censure all Books or Authors should either stand or fall'. This is remote indeed from the purpose

[1] Part I, sect. 20. In the same section of part II he sets down the counter-proposal for Royal Society style.

[2] Cf. Dryden (Ker ed., i. 176) on the effect of the example of the court and king after the Restoration: 'The desire of imitating so great a pattern first awakened the dull and heavy spirits of the English from their natural reservedness; loosened them from their stiff forms of conversation, and made them easy and pliant to each other in discourse.' Even if you deny the cause, this change was for Dryden a cardinal fact in the development of style; it is not to be ignored in the *Essay of Dramatic Poesy*. By all accounts Dryden was such an Englishman as he describes.

[3] Sprat, like Evelyn, speaks of 'polishing'; he anticipates one of Dryden's most persistent themes. The whole passage in Sprat suggests the literary context for Wilkins's 'negligence—affectation' as criteria for style.

for which Wilkins was associated with the committee on improving the English tongue. Thus spoke the writer who sought to emulate Pellisson's *History of the French Academy*, though he said, 'it is only my hand that goes'.[1]

Evelyn prefaces his plan, which is much more detailed, with some remarks on language:

> I conceive the reason both of additions to, and the corruption of, the English language, as of most other tongues, has proceeded from the same causes; namely, from victories, plantations, frontieres, staples of com'erce, pedantry of schooles, affectation of travellers, translations, fancy and style of Court, vernility & mincing of citizens, pulpits, political remonstrances, theatres, shopps, &c.
>
> The parts affected with it we find to be the accent, analogy, direct interpretation, tropes, phrases, and the like.[2]

This is a much more complete inventory of the possible sources of growth or corruption than that given by Sprat, and wholly devoid of the bias of the *History* in its programme for style. To Evelyn a preference for 'the language of Artizans, Countrymen, and Merchants, before that of Wits and Scholars' apparently made little sense. Evelyn sets forth his plan under twelve heads. The first three propose a grammar, an orthography, and 'new periods and accents' for reading aloud; the next seven heads concern a lexicon, made up of various collections.[3] Perhaps reflecting the desire for urbanity, Evelyn finds English deficient in courtly expressions and words that will translate various French and Italian idioms. With regard to exotic words he makes an interesting comment:

> There are some elegant words introduc'd by physitians chiefly and philosophers, worthy to be retained; others, it may be, fitter to be abrogated; since there ought to be a law as well as a liberty in this parti-

---

[1] Not that he minimized his 'hand'. The whole composition of the *History* suggests that the 'particulars' and 'performances', upon which Oldenburg insisted, were for Sprat little more than matter intractable to elegance. While apologizing for his digression on an academy, he ventures to 'affirm that the *Royal Society* is so far from being like to put a stop to such a business, that I know many of its Members, who are as able as any others, to assist in the bringing it into practice'.

[2] *Critical Essays*, ed. Spingarn, ii. 310.

[3] The following collections: 'pure English words', those 'derivative from others', and 'symbolical'; 'technical words, especially those of the more generous employments'; better interpretations of weights, measures, &c.; 'exotic words'; 'dialects, idioms, and proverbs'; 'quaint and courtly expressions'; and necessary additions from 'old layd-aside words and expressions' or other languages.

cular. And in this choyce there would be some reguard had to the well sounding and more harmonious words, and such as are numerous and apt to fall gracefully into their cadences and periods, and so recommend themselves at the very first sight, as it were; others, which (like false stones) will never shine, in whatever light they be placed, but embase the rest.[1]

Thus Evelyn insists that even in terms of art some regard be paid to the qualities which adapt words to eloquence. Earlier writers, such as Sir Thomas Browne, had used their Latinisms with an ear to 'such as are numerous and apt to fall gracefully into their cadences and periods'. Evelyn adds that there is a vocabulary peculiar to universities, 'as may be observed in Cleveland's Poems for Cambridge'.

So far Evelyn has been concerned with what Sprat calls 'the weighing Words and Letters'; his last two heads relate to style.

Something might likewise be well translated out of the best orators & poets, Greek and Latin, and even out of the moderne languages, that so some judgement might be made concerning the elegancy of the style, and so a laudable & unaffected imitation of the best reco'mended to writers.

Finaly, there must be a stock of reputation gain'd by some public writings and compositions of the Members of this Assembly, and so others may not thinke it dishonor to come under the test, or accept them for judges and approbators; and if the designe were ariv'd thus far, I conceive a very small matter would dispatch the art of rhetoric, which the French propos'd as one of the first things they reco'mended to their late academitians.[2]

Obviously the Society's 'manner of discourse' had no such aspirations, though its *History* may not have convinced the wits that it lacked pretensions. Dryden's labours in translation were not unconcerned with the ends suggested here. Evelyn is inclined to minimize rhetoric and to preach by example rather than precept. And Sprat's

---

[1] Cf. Sprat's requirements for the language of science.

[2] This plan as sent to Pepys in the letter of 4 Oct. 1689 (cf. *Letters and the Second Diary of Samuel Pepys*, ed. R. G. Howarth, pp. 205 ff.) shows some revision in details. For example, 'translations' have been omitted from the sources of growth and corruption in language, and the section on translation (11) has been enlarged: 'Nor should there be wanting *copia* of epithets, and variety of expressing the *same thing, several ways*, such as the *Dicerie Poetiche* of *Tomaso Caraffa*, for the help of poets, preachers, orators, &c.' This revision seems to put translation wholly on the credit side, and it implements the *copia* which Sprat implied in his 'plenty'. The *Dicerie Poetiche* appeared in 1655.

History subsequently gained 'a stock of reputation', but not for the 'Members of this Assembly'.

In Sprat's discussion of an academy and its labours there are points that suggest his presence with Evelyn on the committee for polishing the English tongue; for instance, 'some emendations in the Accent and Grammar', the stress on 'smoothness', the notion that translation is a source both of corruption and growth, or the remark 'that we only want a few more standing Examples, and a little more familiarity with the Ancients, to excel all the Moderns'. Of course the last remark goes beyond the English genius which discouraged Sprat. The 'standing Example' which Sprat, prompted by Cicero and the spirit of prophecy, set for his 'Impartial Court of Eloquence' was a history of the Civil Wars. He had already defended the eloquence of the man who wrote it, and much of it had been written when he spoke.

The eloquence of Clarendon is illustrated by the *History of the Rebellion*, but it is a prose suspended between the old and the new. In its opening it is reminiscent of the old, for its periodic structure reflects the tone and sentiment of the preface to *Laws of Ecclesiastical Polity*:

That posterity may not be deceived, by the prosperous wickedness of these times, into an opinion, that less than a general combination, and universal apostasy in the whole nation from their religion and allegiance, could, in so short a time, have produced such a total and prodigious alteration and confusion over the whole kingdom; and so the memory of those few, who, out of duty and conscience, have opposed and resisted that torrent, which hath overwhelmed them, may lose the recompense due to their virtue; and, having undergone the injuries and reproaches of this, may not find a vindication in a better age; it will not be unuseful, at least to the curiosity if not the conscience of men, to present to the world a full and clear narration of the grounds, circumstances, and artifices of this rebellion. . . .[1]

Confronted by this oratorical prose, which nevertheless tends to loosen and sprawl, we may remember that along with his plan Evelyn sent to Sir Peter Wyche 'that attempt upon Cicero which you enjoined me'. But this attempt, although it bears witness to the wider interests of the committee, does not promise the new, more

---

[1] In its informing tone and sentiment this defence of a 'lost cause' derives its similarity to Hooker from the same philosophic basis; its structure from the oratorical pattern.

conversational, prose. If such specimens could represent their 'standing Examples', they brought no conflict to the ideas of an academy held by Sprat and Evelyn. If Sprat contradicted those ideas in expressing the aims of the Royal Society, he was aware of the contradiction and did not assert that the Society should govern literature.

Sprat is concerned with literature in a controversial work which he published two years before the *History*, indeed for which he interrupted the *History*. It was provoked by Sorbière's *Voyage to England*, and appeared as a letter written to Dr. Wren. Sprat's *Observations on Sorbière* was both a national defence and an institutional defence, for the Royal Society felt that it had been deceived and insulted.[1] When Sorbière allows Clarendon to be eloquent but 'utterly ignorant of the Belles Lettres', Sprat replies:

Whence did he fetch this Idea of Eloquence? Let him produce his Notes out of *Aristotle*, *Tully*, *Quintilian*, *Seneca*, or any of the Rhetoricians of Antiquity, and then let him tell me whether they do not all with one Voice consent that an Orator must of necessity be acquainted with all Sorts of useful Knowledge?[2]

If one is reminded of the charge against More in the *Ciceronianus* of Erasmus, it is clear that this Fellow not only knows the teachers of eloquence, but is ready to use them to save the polite learning of an eloquent Fellow.

Sprat's defence of Hobbes, however, is invidious, for Sorbière makes much of Hobbes at the expense of Wallis:

But however, to comfort Mr. *Hobbs* for this affront, I dare assure him, that as for *Monsieur de Sorbiere's* Part he understands not his Philosophy. Of this I will give an unanswerable Testimony, and that is *the Resemblance that he makes of him to the Lord* Verulam, between whome there is no more likeness than there was between St. *George* and the Waggoner. . . . I scarce know Two Men in the World that have more different Colours of Speech than these Two Great Wits: The Lord *Bacon* short, allusive, and abounding with Metaphors, Mr. *Hobbs* round, close, sparing of Similitudes, but ever extraordinary decent in them. The one's Way of Reasoning proceeds on Particulars, and pleasant Images, only suggesting new Ways of experimenting, without any Pretence to the Mathematicks.

---

[1] Evelyn contributed to this work in a letter to Sprat on 31 Oct. 1664, even suggesting that he write in Latin.

[2] *A Voyage to England, with Observations* (London, 1709), pp. 154-5.

The other's bold, resolv'd, settled upon general Conclusions, and in them, if we will believe his Friend, *Dogmatical*.[1]

Bacon's way of reasoning conforms to that of the Royal Society, for it 'proceeds on particulars' rather than on generals; but his style, 'abounding with Metaphors', seems less proper than that of Hobbes, 'sparing of Similitudes'. Where Bacon is short and allusive, Hobbes is full and definitive; Bacon's thinking is 'suggestive', Hobbes's 'settled'. The contrast reminds one of Bacon's opposition of 'aphorisms' and 'methods'. That there is a propriety of style and thought in each is clearly implied by Sprat; the problem of distinguishing between them arises from Sorbière's failure to understand Hobbes's philosophy. We might conclude that the terse Senecan style had a propriety to the Royal Society way of thinking which was more important than the fault of 'abounding with metaphors'. Yet Sprat repeats Bacon when opposing the new philosophy to the old: 'That does neither practise nor cherish this humour of Disputing, which breaks the force of Things by the subtilty of Words; as Seneca was said to do by his Style.'[2] This is not, however, the words-things opposition; but, as in Bacon, the opposition that distinguished the schoolmen, and that now obtains between Bacon and Hobbes.

'Concerning the English Eloquence', observes Sprat, 'he bravely declares, that all their Sermons in the Pulpit, and Pleadings at the Bar, consist of nothing but mean Pedantry.' And Sprat responds:

> But to shew him that we can better judge of *Monsieur de Sorbiere's* Eloquence, I must tell him, that the *Muses* and *Parnassus* are almost whipt out of our very Schools: That there are many Hundreds of Lawyers and Preachers in *England*, who have long known how to contemn such Delicacies of his Stile.[3]

By 'such Delicacies of his Style' Sprat refers to a manner which he regards as more romantic than that of the French romances. Though he writes to one member of the Royal Society in Wren and has the assistance of another in Evelyn, Sprat, nevertheless, neglects to mention the efforts of the Royal Society towards such a reform of

---

[1] *Voyage*, pp. 163–4. The resemblance to Bacon was to be found in the Royal Society. But Hobbes, though dogmatic, was not given to 'this trick of metaphors'.

[2] Cf. *History*, part III, sect. 6: 'The *Art* of *Experiments* . . . consists not in *Topicks* of reas'ning, but of working.'

[3] *Voyage*, pp. 169–70. On Sprat's defence of English drama see 'The Occasion of the Essay of Dramatic Poesy', *Modern Philology*, xliv (1946), 1–9.

style. But no doubt national pride could explain the lapse, even though Sorbière had failed to understand the true character of the Society. Declaring that northern men 'may justly come into Competition with the best of these Southern Wits', this member of the Royal Society adds:

And, to speak particularly of *England*, there might be a whole Volume composed in comparing the Chastity, the Newness, the Vigor of many of our *English* Fancies, with the corrupt and the swelling Metaphors wherewith some of our Neighbours, who most admire themselves, do still adorn their Books.[1]

If national pride has removed 'swelling metaphors' from English style momentarily, it is at least apparent that Sprat knows what he means by 'this trick of metaphors', and that he anticipates the consequences of the Society in the way of wit. Sprat asserts 'that in the first Restoration of Learning the English began to write well as soon as any, the Italians only excepted; and that if we may guess by what we see of the Italians at this Day, the English have continued to write well longer than they'. The 'first Restoration of Learning'— that is a stroke of wit; but it helps to locate the corruption of English style where Sprat locates it in the *History*, during the Puritan interregnum.

Sprat celebrates English writers from 'that Time down to this', and he does not forget philosophers:

We have had many Philosophers of a strong, vigorous and forcible Judgment, of happy and laborious Hands, of a sincere, a modest, a solid and unaffected Expression; such who have not thought it enough to set up for Philosophers, only to have got a large Stock of Fine Words, and to have insinuated into the Acquaintance of some of the Great Philosophers of the Age.[2]

If Sprat's tense here is a little expansive, it is surely unnecessary, for the Royal Society alone, it might be presumed, would have served to point the personal rebuke to Sorbière. But these philosophers are certainly moulded in the image of the Royal Society.

---

[1] *Voyage*, pp. 171–2. This achievement relates to what Sprat calls 'the Lighter Studies of Ornament and Humanity'. The extent to which Sprat reflects the doctrines of French reform that were reported in Pellisson's *History of the French Academy*, with which he was acquainted, remains a question.

[2] Ibid., p. 173. Sorbière's 'Acquaintance' included Hobbes.

The work of the philosophers is crowned by the *Eikon Basilike*, upon which Sprat rests the case of English eloquence:

> And above all, we have one small Book which we dare oppose to all the Treasures of the *Eastern* and *Western* Languages; it is that which was written by our late King and Martyr; whose Majestical Stile and Divine Conceptions have not only mov'd all his Readers to admire his Eloquence, but inclin'd some of the worst of his Enemies to relent their Cruelty towards him.[1]

It is not likely that Sprat would rest his defence merely on a compliment to Charles the Second. That the *Eikon Basilike* was regarded as a masterpiece of style is not a strange opinion to readers in this period, but it may appear strange in the mouth of Sprat.[2]

An illustration of its style may not be out of place—the opening of the final section, 'Meditations upon Death', a common seventeenth-century theme:

> As I have leisure enough, so I have cause more than enough, to meditate upon; and prepare for my Death: for I know, there are but few steps between the Prisons & Graves of Princes.
>
> It is Gods indulgence, which giveth me the space; but mans crueltie, that giveth me the sad Occasions for these thoughts.
>
> For, besides the common burthen of mortality, which lies upon me, as a Man; I now bear the heavie load of other mens ambitions, fears, jealousies, and cruell passions, whose envie or enmitie against me makes their own lifes seem deadly to them, while I enjoy any part of mine.[3]

This passage may be contrasted to Clarendon. Seventeenth-century sentences of the loose variety had to learn not to sprawl. Everybody, including the author of the *Eikon*, wrote much better short sentences. The critical step in disciplining the loose style, aside from violations of formal unity, was to strengthen its connexions. For

---

[1] *Voyage*, pp. 173-4. In this work, however, Milton (cf. *Eikonoklastes*) found the quibbling style of the 'Cymbal Doctors'.

[2] William Ramsay in *The Gentlemans Companion: or a Character of True Nobility and Gentility* gives a list of great books which in 1672 would contribute to his purpose: 'I shall here contract his Study into these few Books following; in which he may indeed reade all that is requisite, and of Substance' (p. 127). The list, which runs to two pages, includes the *Eikon Basilike* and such English prose writers as Hooker, Andrewes, Bacon, Boyle, Digby, Browne, Charleton, Glanvill, Ralegh, Howell, Burton, and Selden. The new science gets a prominent place, but there is no Sprat. Yet Cleveland, Cowley, Butler, and Dryden are included among the later writers.

[3] Notice the tendency to iambic movement, the use of balance and antithesis, the measured phrases which overlay the blank verse suggestion, the imposition of rhetorical stress.

unity and coherence sentences involving several thoughts are more efficiently organized by periodic structure. But periodic structure in English had to learn not to pile up its subordinations. In firmness of structure the Clarendon period does not approach this passage.

But—to return to Sprat—for the same spokesman to praise English eloquence for qualities which he was to announce two years later as either the desiderata or the objects of a general reform in style would, to say the least, be still more astonishing than his praise of the *Eikon Basilike*. No such discord would appear in the advocacy of an academy to bring the language to its last perfection. Yet corruption could be imputed to Nonconformist prose, scholasticism could be blamed for reducing natural philosophy to words, and a stylistic reform in that field could be announced without nullifying the effect of either book or seriously abating English patriotism. For his exuberance in that announcement, however, Sprat ought to have felt some embarrassment.

In his *Account of the Life and Writings of Mr. Abraham Cowley* Sprat had the assistance of Martin Clifford, to whom it is addressed. It appeared a year after the *History*, and more closely concerned the work of the committee for improving the English tongue. Sprat declares that he takes the 'liberty of censure' because he does not 'pretend to a professed Panegyric'.

As in Bacon, so in Cowley Sprat finds 'that in all the several shapes of his Style, there is still very much of the likeness and impression of the same mind'. Of Cowley's words Sprat remarks 'that he had no manner of affectation in them: he took them as he found them made to his hands; he neither went before nor came after the use of the Age. He forsook the Conversation, but never the Language, of the City and Court'.[1] Not even in his village retreat, then, did this former member of the Royal Society prefer the language of countrymen before that of wits. Yet 'he was not wonderfully curious in the choice and elegance of all his words'—as the earlier wits had been.

'He excelled', says Sprat, 'both in Prose and Verse':

He never runs his Reader nor his Argument out of Breath. He perfectly practises the hardest secret of good Writing, to know when he has

---

[1] *Critical Essays*, ed. Spingarn. ii. 129. The curt Senecan or character style, it could be argued, has had its effect on Sprat's own expression.

done enough. He always leaves off in such a manner that it appears it was in his power to have said much more. In the particular expressions there is still much to be Applauded, but more in the disposition and order of the whole. From thence there springs a new comliness, besides the feature of each part.[1]

If this principle of economy or restraint sounds like the injunction to avoid 'swellings of style' and to practise 'shortness', it was an old literary principle, having had a famous application to Ovid; and Dryden had already drawn Sprat's first sentence from the theory of Davenant and the practice of Waller. But the principle of order is a classical principle without counterpart in the programme of the Royal Society. Then Sprat praises Cowley's observance of 'the rules of Decence' or propriety—a principle of which Sprat is sufficiently aware.

Sprat resembles Savile (as reported by Bacon) in his attitude toward poetry. The Pindaric way of writing is to be preferred because of 'its near affinity with Prose'.

But now this loose and unconfin'd measure has all the Grace and Harmony of the most Confin'd. And withal it is so large and free, that the practice of it will only exalt, not corrupt our Prose, which is certainly the most useful kind of Writing of all others, for it is the style of all business and conversation.[2]

The Royal Society programme was not intended to exalt prose, but this exaltation was criticized in other quarters. Sprat does recall, though not mention, the *History* on the subject of wit, when he defends the *Davideis* against the charge of debasing Divinity to make it a subject of fancy. He musters the same arguments and gives the same example of the 'durable impression' of such wit: 'Of this we have a powerful instance amongst the Ancients. For their Wit has lasted much longer than the Practise of any of their Religions.'[3]

Sprat finds Cowley 'very happy in the way of Horace's Speeches' or Epistles—'the very Original of true Raillery': 'I know some Men disapprove it, because the Verse seems to be loose, and near to the plainness of common Discourse.' But such verse reflects 'natural easiness and unaffected Grace'; and this 'familiar way of verse',

---

[1] *Critical Essays*, ed. Spingarn, ii. 130.

[2] Ibid., p. 132. Cowley found antithesis rather than affinity between the proper styles of the two.

[3] Ibid., p. 134.

says Sprat, 'puts me in mind of one kind of Prose wherein Mr. Cowley was excellent, and that is his Letters to his private Friends'.[1] Such letters, however, are not for publication:

The truth is, the Letters that pass between particular Friends, if they are written as they ought to be, can scarce ever be fit to see the light. They should not consist of fulsom Complements, or tedious Politicks, or elaborate Elegancies, or general Fancies. But they should have a Native clearness and shortness, a Domestical plaines, and a peculiar kind of Familiarity, which can only affect the humour of those to whom they were intended.[2]

It may be observed that the letters which are not 'fit to see the light' are described in terms that recall the stylistic programme of the Royal Society, while their opposites suggest the style that it rejected. Yet such a style for letters had been set forth in Jonson's *Timber*, to which it descends from Seneca by way of Lipsius and Hoskins. Perhaps Sprat really thought 'the style of all business and conversation' none the worse for a touch of the Pindaric; at least, that a more rhetorical manner was necessary for public address. In familiar letters, he explains, 'the Souls of Men should appear undressed, and in that negligent habit' they are not fit 'to go abroad into the Streets'. If this prudishness does not extend to style, Sprat seems to feel that the familiar way even in prose requires some apology.

It is appropriate that Sprat should pass from Cowley's letters to his essays—'the last Pieces that we have from his hands'—for he gives them a similar character:

These he intended as a real Character of his own thoughts upon the point of his Retirement. And accordingly you may observe that in the Prose of them there is little Curiosity of Ornament, but they are written in a lower and humbler style than the rest, and as an unfeigned Image of his Soul should be drawn without Flattery. I do not speak this to their disadvantage. For the true perfection of Wit is to be plyable to all occasions, to walk or flye, according to the Nature of every subject. And there is no doubt as much Art to have only plain Conceptions on some Arguments as there is in others to have extraordinary Flights.[3]

Though they were 'upon some of the gravest subjects', would the Royal Society reformer of style feel any need of saying, 'I do not

---

[1] Ibid., p. 137. The English, says Sprat, are now superior to all in this way.
[2] Ibid. Here propriety seems to leave Sprat in a quandary.
[3] Ibid., p. 138.

speak this to their disadvantage'? It sounds less odd in the mouth of one who refused to publish Cowley's letters partly on account of their style. But Sprat is defending the familiar style against a more rhetorical taste or even a charge of impropriety. To assert that 'the true perfection of Wit is to be pliable to all occasions' is to counter the levelling tendency imputed to the programme of the Royal Society. But the ground of propriety here is revealing: though subject is mentioned, it is not subject; 'a real Character' of the mind should be 'unfeigned'. Cowley's style, which is here less elevated than his 'grave' subjects, exhibits one of the favourite doctrines of Seneca, that speech is the image of the mind: 'Oratio vultus animi est.'[1] This is the chief form of propriety for the Anti-Ciceronian cult of expressiveness. Although Sprat applied it to Bacon and Hobbes, it naturally found no place in the programme of the Royal Society. Because of the nature of his mind Cowley's prime excellence emerges in his use of the familiar plain style.

While in retirement Cowley 'entered with great advantage', says Sprat, 'on the studies of Nature': 'He betook himself to its Contemplation, as well furnished with sound Judgment and diligent Observation and good Method to discover its Mysteries, as with Abilities to set it forth in all its Ornaments.'[2] To set Nature forth 'in all its Ornaments' was not the function of a Fellow, but the privilege of a Wit. And this quondam Fellow had another contribution to make, one of special interest to the committee on improving the English tongue:

Besides this, we had perswaded him to look back into his former Studies and to publish a Discourse concerning Style. In this he had design'd to give an account of the proper sorts of writing that were fit for all manner of Arguments, to compare the perfections and imperfections of the Authors of Antiquity with those of this present Age, and to deduce all down to the particular use of the English Genius and Language.[3]

Apparently the initiative for this project came from Sprat and Clifford. Cowley, like Sprat, recognized that there were 'proper

---

[1] Cf. *Ep.* 115. La Mothe le Vayer quotes and adapts it; Gibert reports it from him: 'il suffit quelquefois d'entendre parler un homme pour le connoître' (Baillet's *Jugemens des Savans*, Amsterdam, 1725, viii. 279). Consider the Senecan precept (*Ep.* 75): 'quod sentimus loquamur, quod loquimur sentiamus; concordet sermo cum vita.'

[2] *Critical Essays*, ed. Spingarn, ii. 142.

[3] Ibid. Besides 'this labour about Natural Science'.

sorts of writing' for different subjects, and believed that the ancients and moderns could be compared to the profit of the English genius and language. Sprat vouches for Cowley's fitness for the subject, which concerned the Academy, 'it being most proper for him to be the Judge who had been the best Practiser'. But Cowley did not live to accomplish the task, and Sprat almost despairs 'ever to see it well accomplished', unless Clifford should undertake it. Clifford did go so far as to write some notes on Dryden.

For literature, then, the discourse on style remained to be written. Since Sprat helped to persuade Cowley to undertake it, he could not have thought that the *History of the Royal Society* supplied the needs of literature with respect to style. It is possible to say that, up to a certain point, the stylistic programme of the *History* corresponded to his personal taste in style, even in literature. Beyond that point his taste is better defined by the familiar or conversational essay style, the requirements of which associate it with the Senecan mode. The dislike for 'this trick of Metaphors', apart from the criticism of philosophical prose, belonged as much to a reaction against the 'metaphysical' in poetry and prose as to the attitude of the Royal Society. This reaction was already vigorous before the Society was instituted; its voice may be heard in the eulogies to Cartwright's *Poems* in 1651. The reform of prose as it related to the Royal Society concerned the philosophic style, which, though opposed to rhetoric, had behind it a Stoic tradition in which Seneca the philosopher was not without authority. This tradition was already effective in the teaching of Bacon.

Although Cowley failed to give us his projected discourse on style, he did not leave us quite ignorant of his opinions. Here and there, in poems or notes to poems, he has given us hints of his views on style. It is important to remember that Cowley was a late 'metaphysical' poet, and yet the first master of Dryden; that he was interested in organizing the Royal Society, contributing a plan, and yet dedicated by Sprat and Clifford to write on literary style.[1] Among

[1] In *A Proposition for the Advancement of Experimental Philosophy* Cowley offers a scheme of education which resembles Milton's in several respects. But while it, too, emphasizes natural philosophy, it does not forget that professed enemy, rhetoric. For rhetoric the students are to have Cicero, Quintilian, Aristotle, and perhaps Hermogenes and Longinus. 'They should likewise use to declaim in Latin and English, as the Romans did in Greek and Latin.' Then Cowley had not had the advantage of reading any part of the *History of the Royal Society*, in which this *Proposition* is given serious consideration.

the seeming contradictions which appear to characterize Cowley, perhaps none is more revealing than that he should have espoused 'metaphysics' as a poet and opposed metaphysics as a philosopher. It is with the opposition to metaphysics that his opinions on style become most significant, for that opposition is to him, even more than to Sprat, a matter of language.

Sprat has told us, like many others in that time, with something like damnable iteration, that the schoolmen reduced philosophy to words. But Cowley first celebrates the restoration of philosophy in connexion with Hobbes. In the Pindaric ode 'To Mr. Hobs' Cowley traces the course of Aristotle's 'universal Intellectual reign' until it perished in the schoolmen:

> Then nought but *Words* it grew,
> And those all *Barb'arous* too.

Philosophy was discovered anew by Hobbes, that 'great Columbus', and restored to eloquent words:

> I little thought before . . .
> That all the *Wardrobe* of rich *Eloquence*,
> Could have afforded half enuff,
> Of *bright*, of *new*, and *lasting* stuff,
> To cloath the mighty *Limbs* of thy *Gigantique* Sence.

And this sense is a philosophy so 'solid' that, like Nature, it detests 'emptiness'. Of course, this restoration of philosophy has nothing to do with the Royal Society, or with a renunciation of eloquence; but it does involve the cultivation of new fields after the exhaustion of the old. It is also a renovation of language such as Carew celebrated in Donne, for language is expanded by new meaning. On the schoolmen Cowley expresses himself with more particularity in his notes to 'Life and Fame':

The Distinctions of the *Schoolmen* may be likened to *Cobwebs* (I mean many of them, for some are better *woven*) either because of the too much fineness of the work which makes it slight, and able to catch only little Creatures; or because they take not the materials from *Nature*, but spin it out of *Themselves*.

In the poem such distinctions seem insufficiently 'nice' to Cowley's wit, but in science their chief disqualification was the last named, as Bacon and Sprat insist. And for Sprat, remember, the correction of this altered the sources of wit.

In the ode 'To the Royal Society', where philosophy is limited to natural philosophy, Cowley returns to the theme that philosophy has been perverted by words:

> That his own business he might quite forget,
> They' amus'd him with the sports of wanton Wit,
> With the Desserts of Poetry they fed him,
> In stead of solid meats t' encrease his force;
> In stead of vigorous exercise they led him
> Into the pleasant Labyrinths of ever-fresh Discourse:
> In stead of carrying him to see
> The Riches which doe hoorded for him lie
> In Natures endless Treasurie,
> They chose his Eye to entertain
> (His curious but not covetous Eye)
> With painted Scenes, and Pageants of the Brain.

The first lines suggest how the Metaphysical poets, like the guardians of scholasticism, perverted philosophy to their own ends, and by such means as he enumerates in 'The Muse'.[1] Here Cowley brings to his theme the new disqualification that 'they take not the materials from Nature, but spin it out of Themselves'. Bacon, however, 'broke that Scar-crow Deitie', authority, and liberated philosophy:

> From Words, which are but Pictures of the Thought,
> (Though we our Thoughts from them perversly drew)
> To things, the Minds right Object, he it brought:
> Like foolish Birds to painted Grapes we flew;
> He sought and gather'd for our use the True.

Thus Bacon freed the mind from the bondage of words by turning it to things; Cowley cannot mention eloquence in Bacon, for in the advancement of learning it was a delusion. If Cowley did not think eloquence irrelevant to Bacon, he saved his praise for a more important use:

> And ne're did Fortune better yet
> Th' Historian to the Story fit:
> As you from all Old Errors free
> And purge the Body of Philosophy;
> So from all Modern Folies He
> Has vindicated Eloquence and Wit.

For Cowley the peculiar fitness of the historian to the story is that

---

[1] '*Figures, Conceits, Raptures,* and *Sentences,* In a well-worded *Dress.*'

just as the Royal Society has purged philosophy from 'all Old Errors' so Sprat has 'vindicated Eloquence and Wit' from 'all Modern Follies'. It was a labour of the Academy.

The follies are a good deal more recent than the errors, and the rest of the stanza describes Sprat's style.

> His candid Stile like a clean Stream does slide,
>   And his bright Fancy all the way
>   Does like the Sun-shine in it play;
> It does like *Thames*, the best of Rivers, glide,
> Where the God does not rudely overturn,
>   But gently pour the Crystal Urn,
> And with judicious hand does the whole Current Guide.
> T' has all the Beauties Nature can impart,
> And all the comely Dress without the paint of Art.

Sprat, after all, has no touch of the Pindaric and no 'painted Grapes'. Cowley describes his style as lucid, smooth, disciplined; neither plain nor without art: 'bright Fancy' still plays in it, drawing upon the 'beauties' of nature rather than the 'paint' of art. In short, his style is judicious; it avoids modern follies; it vindicates eloquence and wit, is not devoid of them. There is nothing here to suggest the plain style of the scientists; Sprat is not much plainer in his 'comely Dress' than Hobbes in his wardrobe 'of bright, of new, and lasting stuff'. As Denham, far from the Pindaric fury, yearned to flow like the Thames, so Sprat has the achievement thrust upon him. But Samuel Butler, one of the wits feared by the Royal Society, set down this 'Contradiction' in his *Note-Books*: 'The Historian of Gresham Colledge, Indevors to Cry down Oratory and Declamation, while He uses nothing else.'[1] The difference is worth noting, for here is one who found contradiction in Sprat.

Although we cannot be sure that Cowley was aware of the 'vindication' of wit at the end of Sprat's *History*, we can be reasonably certain of what he regarded as 'modern follies'. His ode 'Of Wit' gave him authority in such matters. One of the commonplaces of Restoration criticism was his counsel against excessive ornament:

> Rather than *all things Wit*, let *none* be there.[2]

[1] *Characters and Passages from Note-Books*, ed. A. R. Waller (Cambridge, 1908), p. 424.
[2] Another commonplace was
> Much less can that have any place
> At which a *Virgin* hides her Face.

In the fifth stanza of this ode he stresses the judgement which he has given to Sprat. Then he enumerates types of false wit, such as gilding 'that shows more Cost, than Art', clenches 'when two like words make up one noise', and the following:

> 'Tis not such *Lines* as almost crack the *Stage*
> When *Bajazet* begins to rage.
> Nor a tall *Meta'phor* in the *Bombast way*,
> Nor the dry chips of short lung'd *Seneca*.
> Nor upon all things to obtrude,
> And force some odd *Similitude*.

There was no gilding in Sprat, and his bright Fancy avoided the other excesses. The 'dry chips of short lung'd Seneca' not only admits prose to these excesses, but frowns upon the sententious wit of Seneca, which was word-play at its worst and antithesis at its best. Many of the sins of expression were covered by such strong 'Lines', by the hyperbole or catachresis of a 'tall Metaphor', or by the artifice of an 'odd Similitude'.

Cowley again deals with false wit in 'An Answer to a Copy of Verses sent me to Jersey'. In Jersey rhyme comes hard, and tropes and figures are unknown; yet something can be said for the honour of the place:

> That by Gods extraordinary *Grace*
> (Which shows the people 'have *Judgment*, if not *Wit*)
> The land is *undefil'd* with *Clinches* yet.
> Which in my poor opinion, I confess,
> Is a most sing'ular blessing, and no less
> Then *Irelands* wanting *Spiders*. And so far
> From th' *Actual Sin* of *Bombast* too they are,
> (That other *Crying Sin* o' th' *English Muse*)
> That even *Satan* himself can accuse
> None here (no not so much as the *Divines*)
> For th' *Motus primo primi* to *Strong Lines*.

By including the first line I have preserved Cowley's own play upon the ambiguity of 'judgement', which introduces his basic metaphor. Cowley sets up no antagonism between wit and tropes and figures, but between wit and excesses in them; he does single out clenches and strong lines as the most offensive, the latter being associated with bombast. All of these modern follies, except the 'sentences' of Seneca, can be verified in Butler's character of 'A Small Poet'. The reaction against such 'metaphysical' faults began long before anyone knew about the programme of the Royal Society. If in practice Cowley often echoed the past, in theory, and indeed in practice, he set the pattern for the future.

In his survey of wit at the close of the *History*, Sprat must have had Cowley in mind when he wrote about the wit available in the Bible and in mythology. As his comments on *Davideis* in the *Account* of Cowley reflect his appendix on wit, so his appendix on wit reflects Cowley's own comments on the *Davideis*.[1] Cowley and Sprat also seem to have been of one mind about metaphysics. Sprat expresses his contempt for metaphysics in his *History*,[2] and that contempt affects his evaluation of the wit derived from it. Cowley, in his essay 'Of Agriculture', enumerates the arts and sciences with a similar qualification: 'Metaphysick, Physick, Morality, Mathematics, Logick, Rhetorick, &c. which are all, I grant, good and usefull faculties, (except onely Metaphysick which I do not know whether it be any thing or no).'[3] But then he had found it words and presumably 'conversant about things removed from the Senses'. Cowley is certain that good poetry and obscurity are not compatible; significantly his comment relates to Persius, 'who, you use to say, you do not know whether he be a good Poet or no, because you cannot understand him, and whom therefore (I say) I know to be not a good Poet'.[4] The cult of obscurity, to which strong lines were related, obviously was not sanctioned by Cowley.

For Cowley poetry and prose each had its own propriety. In the notes for his ode 'To Mr. Hobs' Cowley comments on his imitation of Claudian in the sixth stanza: 'Tacitus has the like expression . . . which is too Poetical for the Prose even of a Romance, much more of an Historian.'[5] In note 89 to Book II of his *Davideis*, commenting on an objection raised by Seneca the Elder, he declares that an expression may be poetically, though not literally, true; but 'I confess indeed in a Declamation I like not those kind of Flowers so well'. Both of these comments show that Cowley frowned upon poetic excesses in prose, and allowed greater licence to poetry.

[1] In his preface to the *Poems* of 1656 Cowley argues for Biblical as opposed to mythological wit.   [2] Cf. part III, sect. 2.
[3] *Essays, Plays, and Sundry Verses*, ed. A. R. Waller (Cambridge, 1906), p. 404.
[4] Ibid., p. 454: 'The danger of Procrastination.'
[5] Cowley adds, 'See likewise *Seneca*, Epist. 79'. In this Epistle Seneca criticizes Lucilius for wanting to gratify his taste for fine writing in a description of Mount Aetna.

This distinction might have made R. F. Jones hesitate to declare, while trying to account for the style of the *Essays*, which Sprat referred to propriety, that 'the best expression of his changed attitude appears in "The Garden" '.[1] This change, we are told, is to be attributed to the influence of the Royal Society; and the new attitude appears in this quotation: 'You may wonder, Sir, (for this seems a little too extravagant and Pindarical for Prose) what I mean by all this Preface.'[2] Although this statement agrees with Cowley's belief that prose has its own propriety—a belief which he had made known as early as 1656—we may ask what 'Pindarical' had meant to him in 1656, or ten years before he addressed 'The Garden' to Evelyn.

Cowley makes himself quite clear on this point in his notes to the *Pindarique Odes*. His first note on 'The 34. Chapter of the Prophet Isaiah' is especially interesting:

> The manner of the Prophets writing, especially of *Isaiah*, seems to me very like that of *Pindar*; they pass from one thing to another with almost *Invisible connexions*, and are full of words and expressions of the highest and boldest flights of *Poetry*, as may be seen in this Chapter, where there are as extraordinary Figures as can be found in any *Poet* whatsoever; and the connexion is so difficult, that I am forced to adde a little, and leave out a great deal to make it seem *Sense* to us, who are not used to that elevated way of expression . . . for the old fashion of writing, was like *Disputing* in *Enthymemes*, where half is left out to be supplyed by the Hearer: ours is like *Syllogisms*, where all that is meant is exprest.[3]

For emphasis we may add a remark from the first note to 'The Resurrection': 'This Ode is truly Pindarical, falling from one thing to another, after his Enthusiastical manner.' Here 'Pindarical' is associated with the style of 'enthusiasm', which so many critics condemned. Now if you will look at the writing which precedes Cowley's remark about being too 'Pindarical for Prose', you will not find any occasion to believe that 'Pindarical' has changed its meaning to that of 'unscientific'. Of course, his apology is in the vein of whimsical exaggeration, but since the Pindaric ode was for Cowley the most licensed form of poetry, any suggestion of it in prose was open to criticism.

[1] See *PMLA*, xlv (1930), 999.
[2] See *Essays*, ed. A. R. Waller, p. 421.
[3] If he was then less intolerant of 'difficulty', he still had to 'make it seem Sense'.

The striking characteristics which Cowley ascribes to the Pindaric manner, namely, the ellipsis or lack of connexions and the boldness of figure, were not unlike certain aspects of the Senecan fashion of writing, particularly in the Character. Hence it is interesting that Cowley should characterize the modern fashion of writing, though in relation to verse, as explicit, requiring that both syntax and meaning be fully exhibited. Of course, Cowley was making his contrast over a much wider space of time; but even in his century, in which older fashions were revived, some change of this kind took place in style.[1] Yet Cowley seems to have admired brevity, which was fundamental to the curt Senecan style; at least, he hints at such a taste when he remarks in 'The Garden': 'Or as Virgil has said, Shorter and Better for me.' Again, Cowley observes in his notes to 'Destinie' that Thucydides says something 'with admirable shortness and weight'; and then adds, 'Which Sallust imitating, renders yet shorter; and beats him, as Seneca says, at his own weapon'. This comment reveals some admiration of brevity, but more knowledge of the models of Anti-Ciceronian rhetoric.

If we may conclude that we are not quite ignorant of Cowley's ideas of style, we may declare that there is little or nothing to support the alleged influence of the Royal Society. His view did not change after its institution. Most of Cowley's remarks derive their force from a doctrine of propriety and their point from the abuses of the time. Like Dryden later, he is much concerned with the definition of wit and, conversely, with the practices that make re-definition imperative. Here Bacon's shift—as it seemed to them—in the mental theatre of operation was significant to Cowley as well as to Sprat.

We know that Dryden had the highest regard for the prose of

[1] Cf. Greneway's translation of Tacitus with that of Dryden. Greneway completed Savile's translation, and Dryden translated a part that falls into Greneway's portion. The most obvious feature of Dryden's translation is that it is filled out, the ellipses have been filled up; the logical relationships have been more exactly expressed; a more natural order has resulted, though some of his sentences are periodic; his vocabulary is more abstract; in short, the expression is more complete in Dryden, and he is less like Tacitus. In Greneway, although a lesser writer, the very hiatuses produce an imaginative effect, which frequently intensifies the sinister implication of Tacitus; the result, as in Tacitus, is greater density and greater weight. Greneway's translation gives the effect of a mind working in private, while Dryden gives the impression of a mind attentive to a public; Greneway is more suggestive and more poetic, even in vocabulary. In Greneway the syntax is more Pindaric than prosaic; in Dryden the prose virtues have been developed to a much higher degree.

Etherege, that he once spoke of 'the other harmony of prose', and, on Congreve's authority, that his own prose was indebted to Tillotson. If by mentioning harmony Dryden became a prophet of a still later watchword in prose, by his own concern with propriety he was chiefly responsible for the stylistic doctrine which Hughes formulated in 1698. We may rightly believe that his views on prose style are less evident today than they must have been to Hughes. But need we conclude that his written word, except as example, is actually mute on prose style? Matthew Arnold, of course, would have said that all of Dryden's remarks on style are relevant since he is a classic of our prose; and except for the reason, there is much to be said for this conclusion.

Before it can be said, however, we should recall that Dryden was a member of the Royal Society from November 1662 to July 1666, when he was dropped for not paying his dues. Moreover, on 30 March 1664, he was assigned to the uncongenial committee for 'collecting all the phenomena of nature hitherto observed, and all experiments made and recorded'—perhaps a consequence of his poem 'To Dr. Charleton on his learned and useful Works'; and the same year, on 7 December, he became a member of the committee 'for improving the English language'.[1] Of his work on these committees all we know is that Evelyn mentions his name in connexion with three or four meetings held by the latter committee. But for ten years after his admission Dryden's work reveals a special awareness of the Royal Society; after 1672 allusions to things for which the Society stood are harder to find, though not absent. Until the 'Defence of the Epilogue' and later, scarcely a preface comes from Dryden without some allusion to the principles or projects of the Royal Society, the *Essay of Dramatic Poesy* being richest in these allusions. In general the Society supplied Dryden with analogies for literary arguments, analogies which were pointed against dogmatism, or the tyranny of the past, and toward improvement in literature.

As an instance of the way in which Dryden used the support of the Royal Society, we may cite the preface which proved most

---

[1] See Birch, *History of the Royal Society*, i. 407, 499–500. The former committee seems to have had for its object Bacon's 'kalendar of works' (cf. *Advancement*, Everyman ed., pp. 101–2).

offensive to his contemporaries, his 'Defence of the Epilogue'. Here Dryden uses the attitude of the Royal Society to justify his own work toward the aim of the committee on language: 'For we live in an age so sceptical, that as it determines little, so it takes nothing from antiquity on trust; and I profess to have no other ambition in this *Essay*, than that poetry may not go backward, when all other arts and sciences are advancing.'[1] To make good such an attitude in literature Dryden makes clever use of Horace to prove 'that antiquity alone is no plea for the excellency of a poem; but that, one age learning from another, the last (if we can suppose an equality of wit in writers) has the advantage of knowing more and better than the former'. Having committed himself to a false analogy between science and literature, Dryden could have cited the *Advancement of Learning*, though not on poetry. 'It is therefore my part', says Dryden, 'to make it clear, that the language, wit, and conversation of our age, are improved and refined above the last; and then it will not be difficult to infer, that our plays have received some part of those advantages.' Thus Dryden employed the attitude of the Royal Society to justify his most definite effort to assist a project which had been attempted by the Society itself. And at this very time he was himself the victim of a burlesque written by other members of that same committee on language, for we may recall that not only Buckingham but also Sprat and Clifford have been associated with *The Rehearsal*. The antagonism which met the 'Defence of the Epilogue' may be some indication of how the wits and writers might have greeted the intrusion of the Royal Society into their province.

Although the connexion between prose and verse is clear enough in this preface, we may properly ask how Dryden distinguished between them in point of style. In answering this question we shall determine the extent to which his remarks on the style of verse are applicable to the style of prose. First, was there any distinction in vocabulary? None, except that new words were less permissible in prose. Dryden's early work bears witness to this view; and in 1666 he writes to Sir Robert Howard about some innovations in diction, 'which, as I offer not to introduce into English prose, so I hope they

---

[1] *Essays*, ed. W. P. Ker, i. 163. Evelyn's 1670 preface to *Sylva* strikes this note, 'to receive nothing upon Trust'.

are neither improper, nor altogether unelegant in verse'.[1] In the days of Sir Thomas Browne prose had been more indulgent in this respect. Was there any distinction between prose and verse in composition or the order of words? Of course Dryden considered blank verse as *prose mesurée*, and we may recall that he twice criticized blank verse for placing words 'unnaturally, that is, contrary to the common way of speaking'.[2] He laid down as a general rule for verse that 'for the most part, the words be placed as they are in the negligence of prose'.[3] Obviously the order of words in the common way of speaking was to be the standard of naturalness in both prose and verse.

Finally, was there any distinction between prose and poetry in the use of tropes and figures? It is no doubt commonplace to define poetic licence as the liberty 'of speaking things in verse, which are beyond the severity of prose'; but it is important to know whether the severity of prose excluded the ornaments of style. These are Dryden's words on such ornaments: 'for if this licence be included in a single word, it admits of tropes; if in a sentence or proposition, of figures; both which are of a much larger extent, and more forcibly to be used in verse than prose.'[4] Tropes and figures, therefore, are not to be excluded from prose, but their range and force are to be restricted. Similes in prose are to be used by way of illustration; they are not the same as argument: 'I am almost fearful of illustrating anything by similitude, lest he should confute it for an argument.'[5] Metaphorical expression is improper in definition, as Dryden suggests by turning to direct expression with an apologetic 'or without metaphor';[6] here he recognizes current criticism. In conclusion we may say that what Dryden did not allow in verse he would not allow in prose; or, conversely, that prose is the norm from which he defines the licence of verse.

It is impossible to determine the effect which membership on the committee for improving the English language had upon Dryden's activities in that direction. It is possible to say that those activities were more particular and precise down to about 1680; but Dryden is never unconcerned about the improvement of the language. Just as Sprat, another member of this committee, spoke of

---

[1] *Essays*, ed. Ker, i. 17.
[2] Ibid., p. 95.
[3] Ibid., p. 98.
[4] Ibid., p. 189.
[5] Ibid., p. 129. Spoken in irony of course.
[6] Ibid., p. 14.

an academy, of language, style, and wit, in his *History of the Royal Society*, so Dryden has much to say on these subjects in the period specified. In 1679 he is again enthusiastic about the projection of an academy;[1] still later he corrects the language of *An Essay of Dramatic Poesy*. Perhaps a survey of his views on these subjects will set him in his proper relation to Sprat, especially if the survey is made primarily before 1672, the year of Rapin's work on eloquence and two years after Eachard's renewal of the attack on style.

In 1664 Dryden mentioned an academy while regretting the lack of any certain standard of English:

> I have endeavoured to write English, as near as I could distinguish it from the tongue of pedants, and that of affected travellers. Only I am sorry, that (speaking so noble a language as we do) we have not a more certain measure of it, as they have in France, where they have an Academy erected for that purpose, and endowed with large privileges by the present king. I wish we might at length leave to borrow words from other nations, which is now a wantonness in us, not a necessity. . . .[2]

If Dryden was also opposed to the language of 'scholars', he did not prefer to draw from countrymen rather than wits; but he remained, on the whole, a defender of 'received words'. The endeavour to separate English from affectation may remind us of Evelyn's plan, but Dryden is obviously much more hostile to further borrowing. Thus in his first critical preface Dryden rather unusually declares a purpose of endeavouring 'to write English'.

In 1666 Dryden is interested in terms of art or 'particulars' in poetry: 'the terms of art in every tongue bearing more of the idiom of it than any other words'.[3] The desire to write English in an idiomatic way perhaps explains some of the attraction of terms of art, but it is not the explanation given by Dryden: 'And certainly, as those who, in a logical dispute, keep in general terms, would hide a fallacy; so those, who do it in any poetical description, would veil their ignorance.' Here Dryden joins Sprat in the revolt against 'general terms', which in poetry may offer the reader a 'fatal tissue' instead of a handkerchief, though not for the same reason. But Dryden was to discover reasons for preferring general terms. According to Evelyn's plan, terms of art were to be compiled by the

---

[1] See the 'Dedication of Troilus and Cressida'.
[2] *Essays*, ed. Ker, i. 5. [3] *Ibid.*, p. 13.

committee. Certainly the revolt against the schoolmen was accompanied by a rejection of their terms of art, not only by the Royal Society but also by the poets; yet, despite a preference for a common language, the Royal Society was obliged to use terms of art. Not to use such 'proper' terms could oblige one to metaphor.

Dryden's remarks testify to the sense of idiom upon which, having no academy, he relied for a 'measure' of English.[1] In the same essay, speaking of his borrowings from Virgil, he remarks that his 'expressions also are as near as the idioms of the two languages would admit of in translation'.[2] A sense of English idiom was sharpened for Dryden by the same means that had brought a keener sense of idiom to writers in the course of the seventeenth century, that is, translation and imitation of Latin authors. The assimilation of English to Latin forms had produced the learned style of which Flecknoe spoke, which disturbed Dryden even in Ben Jonson.

On the state of the language Dryden, like Sprat, has much to say. In 1668, speaking of Beaumont and Fletcher, he remarked: 'I am apt to believe the English language in them arrived to its highest perfection: what words have since been taken in, are rather superfluous than necessary.'[3] Again we have Dryden the defender of received words, in relation to which this 'perfection' is defined. In the 'Defence of the Epilogue' in 1672, however, Dryden undertakes to show how the language has improved:

That an alteration is lately made in ours, or since the writers of the last age (in which I comprehend Shakespeare, Fletcher, and Johnson), is manifest. Any man who reads those excellent poets, and compares their language with what is now written, will see it almost in every line; but that this is an improvement of the language, or an alteration for the better, will not so easily be granted. For many are of a contrary opinion, that the English tongue was then in the height of its perfection; that from Johnson's time to ours it has been in a continual declination. . . .[4]

Now this view brings Dryden into some divergence of opinion with Sprat, who, in offering his proposal of an English academy, had held

---

[1] In the 'Dedication of Troilus and Cressida' he confesses: 'For I am often put to a stand in considering whether what I write be the idiom of the tongue, or false grammar, and nonsense couched beneath that specious name of *Anglicism*; and have no other way to clear my doubts but by translating my English into Latin, and thereby trying what sense the words will bear in a more stable language.'

[2] *Essays*, ed. Ker, i. 17.

[3] Ibid., p. 81. Ibid., p. 164.

that the late Civil Wars were mainly an interruption in the improvement of the language, and 'that it seems at this time, more than others, to require some such Aid, to bring it to its last Perfection'.[1] The chief difference between their views, and it is an important one, is that for Dryden there has been improvement rather than interruption, and the improvement is now established, thanks to writers like Suckling and Waller or to the example of the Court. Dryden believes that 'improprieties are less frequent, and less gross' in his day than in the last age; he illustrates various defects in the judicious Jonson.[2] Thus Dryden deals with the labour of rejection, which is one part of the refinement of a language.

The principles which ought to govern the choice of words should now be clear; the best measure, as Horace said, is 'custom and common use'.[3] Likewise in 1668 Dryden tells us 'that wit is best conveyed to us in the most easy language'; and by this standard he can praise Donne for his 'common language' while he condemns Cleveland for 'his new way of Elocution', which is 'to express a thing hard and unnaturally'.[4] Dryden calls it catachresis; Evelyn, 'university language'. In this passage Dryden sets up an ultimate audience of the 'meanest apprehensions', or the audience that Burnet considered in his *Discourse of the Pastoral Care*. Having a wider range, these principles of diction also cover the requirements of the Royal Society. Although Dryden mentions science, it is never in support of any qualifications of style. Now the point is simply that if wit is to be independent of words, 'abstruse words' are no longer proper, even for deep thoughts. The revolt against such words is perfectly obvious in literature as early as 1651, when it appears in the numerous eulogies to Cartwright's *Poems* and in Hobbes's 'Epistle to Davenant'.

The order of words is unnatural even in rhymed verse when the words are placed 'as no man would in ordinary speaking':

but when 'tis so judiciously ordered, that the first word in the verse seems to beget the second, and that the next, till that becomes the last word in

---

[1] *History*, part I, sect. 20.

[2] Among such defects he enumerates perplexed sense, false grammar, '*synchysis*, or ill-placing of words' (of which Cicero often complains in oratory), the terminal preposition, redundance, ill syntax, misuse of words, and Latinisms.

[3] *Essays*, ed. Ker, i. 51.

[4] Ibid., p. 52. In the poem 'To Dr. Charleton' Dryden reduces scholastic philosophy to 'hard words'.

the line, which, in the negligence of prose, would be so; it must then be granted, rhyme has all the advantages of prose, besides its own.[1]

In its context this 'begetting' involves the choice of words as well as the order. It is interesting that in specifying the advantages of prose, as he saw them in 1666, Dryden should have described a negligent prose evolving in the same organic manner as the 'loose period' or the style Burton defended out of Seneca. At this time Dryden also detected a blank-verse movement in prose, 'into which the English tongue so naturally slides, that, in writing prose, it is hardly to be avoided'.[2] Dryden's next words reinforce his principle of order, which he may have learned at school:

And therefore, I admire some men should perpetually stumble in a way so easy, and inverting the order of their words, constantly close their lines with verbs, which though commended sometimes in writing Latin, yet we were whipt at Westminster if we used it twice together.[3]

But it would be strange if Dr. Busby, amidst all the rules of rhetoric, were teaching prose in this crucial period to follow the order which men use in ordinary speaking.

Perhaps it will help to consolidate our notions of Dryden's view of style if we look at his criticism of the styles of two men, one of his own time and one of the last age. First of Jonson:

If there was any fault in his language, 'twas that he weaved it too closely and laboriously, in his serious plays: perhaps too, he did a little too much Romanize our tongue, leaving the words which he translated almost as much Latin as he found them: wherein, though he learnedly followed the idiom of their language, he did not enough comply with the idiom of ours.[4]

Dryden later changed 'serious plays' to read 'comedies especially', and for the latest editors of Jonson his verse and prose deserve the same character of style. Dryden's criticism, which finds Jonson's

[1] Ibid., p. 7.
[2] We may recall his phrase, 'the other harmony of prose'. Evelyn in his *Diary* for 24 Feb. 1665, notes that 'Dr. Fell, Canon of Christ Church, preached before the King . . . a very formal discourse, and in blank verse, according to his manner; however, he is a good man'.
[3] *Essays*, ed. Ker, i. 6. Terminal prepositions were more puzzling to Dryden.
[4] Ibid., p. 82. In 1672, in the 'Defence of the Epilogue', he criticizes in Jonson 'the preposition in the end of the sentence; a common fault with him, and which I have but lately observed in my own writings' (ibid., p. 168). When he corrected this fault in his *Essay* (1684, cf. ibid., p. xxvii), he was less true to idiom than to the requirements of the period. Obadiah Walker in *Instructions for Oratory* (1659, pp. 27-8) supplied appropriate doctrine.

language neither loose nor natural enough, but deficient in the negligence of prose, is actually directed at a curt Senecan style, which he later criticized in the person of Seneca. His characterization of Howard's prose style is, of course, not without malice; but it points at real faults which he does not hesitate to particularize:

> I cannot but give this testimony of his style, that it is extreme poetical, even in oratory; his thoughts elevated sometimes above common apprehensions; his notions politic and grave, and tending to the instruction of Princes, and reformation of States; that they are abundantly interlaced with variety of fancies, tropes, and figures, which the critics have enviously branded with the name of obscurity and false grammar.[1]

No doubt this has its fling at Howard's verse, but Dryden is replying to his preface to *The Duke of Lerma*, and suggesting that even his prose is poetical, or given to improprieties that prose should avoid.

Since Dryden obviously adopts a conversational standard for style, it is intelligible that he should make so much of the improvement in conversation, 'the last and greatest advantage of our writing'.[2] The Court gave this conversational standard, after the example of the king had loosened the courtiers 'from their stiff forms of conversation, and made them easy and pliant to each other in discourse'. If we take this remark as no more than a flattering fiction, we cannot deny its veracity as the description of something that happened in prose, something that distinguishes the *Essay of Dramatic Poesy* from earlier critical writing. Although Burton also adopted a conversational norm, it was his own, not that of a social group. A conversational norm had appeared in the drama and modified blank verse, which in turn modified the lyric verse of Donne; but 'stiff forms of conversation' had still prevailed in the drama, and Dryden found that only Beaumont and Fletcher partially escaped from them. It is such a view that explains the stress that Dryden lays on 'easiness' in writing, which became a byword in 'easy Suckling'.

But it is through his long consideration of wit that Dryden reached his restrictive canon of style, and chiefly affected later theory and practice. His concern with the problem may first be

---

[1] *Essays*, ed. Ker, i. 119. It suggests the faults of Cleveland. For Dryden's dislike of florid prose see 'A Parallel of Poetry and Painting'; of florid verse, see Ker, i. 203.
[2] Ibid., p. 175.

noticed in his criticism of the wit of the former age, both in its ancient models and in its own writers. In his first attempt to define wit in 1666, like Cowley he declared what wit was not:

'Tis not the jerk or sting of an epigram, nor the seeming contradiction of a poor antithesis (the delight of an ill-judging audience in a play of rhyme), nor the jingle of a more poor paronomasia; neither is it so much the morality of a grave sentence, affected by Lucan, but more sparingly used by Virgil. . . .[1]

Dryden, like Cowley, was in fact rebuking current conceptions of wit. Lucan, of course, was a favourite of the seventeenth century, and to condemn his wit was also to condemn the wit of Seneca, who employed all of these devices in prose. In 1672 Dryden still refers to Lucan as one who 'crowded sentences together, was too full of points, and too often offered at somewhat which had more of the sting of an epigram, than of the dignity and state of an heroic poem'.[2] Here he is again criticizing Senecan traits. From the first Dryden is clearly opposed to the wit which characterized the Anti-Ciceronian models of the seventeenth century.

In the same fashion he condemns Shakespeare's wit: 'his comic wit degenerating into clenches, his serious swelling into bombast'.[3] Both of these aspects of wit, which remind us of the range of meaning embraced by the word, had been condemned by Cowley before him. Jonson is likewise condemned for his clenches, and Sir Philip Sidney for 'perpetually playing with his words', to which Hoskins found his style not 'much beholding'.

In his time, I believe, it ascended first into the pulpit, where (if you will give me leave to clench too) it yet finds the benefit of its clergy; for they are commonly the first corrupters of eloquence, and the last reformed from vicious oratory. . . .[4]

This was said in 1672, after the publication of Eachard's *Grounds*

[1] Ibid., pp. 14–15. And implied in Howard. For Butler on wit see 'The Rhetorical Pattern of Neo-Classical Wit', *Modern Philology*, xxxiii. 73 ff.

[2] *Essays*, ed. Ker, i. 152. Later, in the 'Preface to Oedipus', he remarks that 'Seneca, on the other side, as if there were no such thing as Nature to be minded in a play, is always running after pompous expressions, pointed sentences, and philosophical notions, more proper for the study than the stage'. Thus Seneca also 'affects the metaphysics . . . where nature only should reign' (ibid., ii. 19).

[3] Ibid. i. 80.

[4] Ibid., pp. 173–4. Twenty-one years later, speaking of Horace, he completes the indictment: 'But it may be puns were then in fashion, as they were wit in the sermons of the last age, and in the court of King Charles the Second' (ibid. ii. 95).

and Occasions of the Contempt of the Clergy. Then Dryden's general verdict on wit was something like this:

> Yet, as Mr. Cowley (who had a greater portion of it than any man I know) tells us in his *Character of Wit*, rather than all wit, let there be none. I think there is no folly so great in any poet of our age, as the super-fluity and waste of wit was in some of our predecessors. . . .[1]

On the subject of wit there is no doubt that Cowley was a greater authority than Sprat, and a Cowley who antedated the Royal Society; even Glanvill remembered his lessons when he wrote on sermon style. In general Dryden is in agreement with Cowley on what rightly is not wit in his day, but which was in the last age.

The kind of wit that Dryden wanted, especially in comedy, could be detected among the writers of the last age only in Beaumont and Fletcher. This was the one ground for preferring them to either Shakespeare or Jonson: 'they understood and imitated the con-versation of gentlemen much better'.[2] And imitation of the conversa-tion of gentlemen was the right imitation of nature in matters of style. Later, in 1672, Dryden concludes that the wit of his age is much more courtly; it does not suffer from the 'allay of pedantry'; in the wit of his predecessors 'there was ever somewhat that was ill-bred and clownish'.[3] Urbanity is the word that comes nearest to the desideratum in comic wit; in serious wit, not to be 'pestered with figurative expressions'.

In the same essay, however, Dryden first clearly stated a distinc-tion between two senses of 'wit' that led him, five years later, to give up wit in the narrow sense for the larger wit of his famous definition. Dryden admits that even propriety in poetic imitation 'is wit in a larger signification' than 'wit in the stricter sense, that is, sharp-ness of conceit'.[4] But wit in the larger sense—which he accepts with some reluctance, partly no doubt because it was urged by Shadwell—had been in his mind when he wrote the 'Preface to Annus Mirabilis'. It was the natural consequence of his various speculations, and he soon developed it into the governing principle of style. More than any single thing, this shift marks Dryden's orientation toward the classical order; it makes propriety more im-

---

[1] *Essays*, ed. Ker, i. 139–40. Yet one could be too provident, like Jonson.
[2] Ibid., p. 81.
[3] Ibid., p. 174.
[4] Ibid., pp. 172–3.

portant than expressiveness; it is the culmination of his ideas about style.[1]

In 1677, then, at the close of his 'Apology for Heroic Poetry', and as a consequence of his position in that essay, he first stated his celebrated definition of Wit: 'that it is a propriety of thoughts and words; or, in other terms, thoughts and words elegantly adapted to the subject'. When Addison objected that this 'is not so properly a Definition of Wit, as of good Writing in general', he was right enough; Dryden intended it to be a definition of 'wit written'.[2] But standards for language remained to be established; for these Dryden still looked toward an academy. Again, in the 'Dedication of Troilus and Cressida', he observed:

Propriety must first be stated, ere any measures of elegance can be taken. Neither is one Vaugelas sufficient for such a work; it was the employment of the whole Academy for many years; for the perfect knowledge of a tongue was never attained by any single person. The Court, the college, and the town, must be joined in it.[3]

Thus propriety led toward a doctrine of correctness, which remained to be announced. Meanwhile, Dryden found his standard in the Court or the conversation of gentlemen.

Finally, we may glance at Evelyn in a literary capacity which provides an appropriate contrast to his scientific capacity. In 1688

---

[1] In the 'Dedication of the Spanish Friar' (1681) Dryden applies the doctrine of propriety to his own work and early taste. Now 'nothing is truly sublime that is not just and proper'. He condemns as abominable fustian 'thoughts and words ill-sorted, and without the least relation to each other', and figures not 'suited to the occasion, the subject, and the persons'. Now 'the propriety of thoughts and words . . . are the hidden beauties of a play'. It is an aspect of the *Essay of Dramatic Poesy* that was then only touched on, but had since been fully developed.

[2] Addison, in his papers on wit, is already separating wit from imagination, or the serious and the facetious fancy which are included in 'wit' for Dryden, who did not deny the heroic poet the element of surprise.

[3] Knowledge of the languages that have contributed to English is also required, and 'a conversation with those authors of our own, who have written with the fewest faults in prose and verse'. In the 'Preface to Sylvae' in 1685 he asserts: 'There are many who understand Greek and Latin, and yet are ignorant of their mother-tongue. The proprieties and delicacies of the English are known to few; 'tis impossible even for a good wit to understand and practise them, without the help of a liberal education, long reading, and digesting of those few good authors we have amongst us, the knowledge of men and manners, the freedom of habitudes and conversation with the best company of both sexes; and, in short, without wearing off the rust which he contracted while he was laying in a stock of learning' (*Essays*, ed. Ker, i. 253). At this point John Hughes began *Of Style*.

or thereabouts Evelyn, in the role of improver of the English tongue, wrote to Lord Spencer:

> Having now tempted and sufficiently provoked your Lordship in Plautus, Cicero, Pliny, Seneca, Lipsius, &c. (for your Lordship is master of all styles) I give it over. On my word, your Lordship has tamed the shrew, and it is more than time for me to leave off the pedant, and write henceforth in my mother tongue.

Evelyn is concerned with letters; but, although he is no partisan, all but one of the writers mentioned are Anti-Ciceronian models. Of course it was precisely in his Epistles that Seneca became the model of Lipsius and a force in modern prose. Evelyn not only has put his Lordship through his paces in such Latin; he has set models in his own letters. Evelyn, moreover, wonders at the dearth of familiar epistles that have 'adorned the part of elegancy' among the English:

> Sir Francis Bacon, Dr. Donne, and I hardly remember any else who have published any thing of considerable, and they but gleanings; or cabal men, who have put many things in a heap, without much choice or fruits, especially as to the culture of the style or language, the genius of the nation being almost another thing than it was at that time.[1]

James Howell, adds Evelyn, has published his *Ho-Elianae*, which is now preserved for its matter, 'but which, were the language enlightened with that sort of exercise and conversation, I should not question its being equal to any of the most celebrated abroad'. Howell's view of 'the part of elegancy' may be recalled. Presumably his Lordship has the culture of style that Howell lacks; for, concludes Evelyn, if you were to condescend, 'you who are so perfect a master in the learned tongues, how would you embellish your native language!' Thus spoke an ardent supporter of the Royal Society about a style which was plain enough, surely, to escape the worst strictures of the Society, but not elegant enough for a potential Academician.

Eventually Evelyn found himself apologizing for the style of one of the most illustrious members of the Royal Society. In a letter to William Wotton, 30 March 1696, Evelyn contributes memoranda

---

[1] By withholding Cowley's letters Sprat may have contributed to this dearth. For the genius of the nation, which in Bacon and Donne had been Senecan, apparently was now more capable of the proper 'elegance'.

for a life of Boyle, and makes this interesting comment on his style:

I have said nothing of his style, which those who are better judges think he was not so happy in, as in his experiments. I do not call it affected, but doubtless not answerable to the rest of his great and shining parts; and yet, to do him right, it was much improved in his 'Theodora' and later writings.[1]

Evidently the style of one member of the Royal Society might be called affected by some judges, but to another member of the Society his style is not answerable to his other abilities, though definitely a matter of concern. Obviously the meaning of 'answerable' here has no reference to the stylistic programme of the Royal Society. But if affectation touched the great Boyle, much could be forgiven the 'spruce' Glanvill, and even more the florid Charleton, who sponsored the master of the new prose in Dryden.

[1] In an early work, *Considerations touching the Style of the Scriptures* (1661), Boyle declared 'To the Reader': 'And (to dispatch) I might add, That Oratours may not unjustly bear with some Rudenesses in the Style of a Person that Professes not Rhetorick, and Writes of a Subject that needs Few of her Ornaments, and Rejects Many, as Indecencies misbecoming its Majesty: and that Severer Divines may safely Pardon some Smoothness in a Discourse Written Chiefly for Gentlemen, who would scarce be fond of Truth in every Dress, by a Gentleman who fear'd it might misbecome a Person of his Youth and Quality Studiously to Decline a fashionable Style.' Although his sentiments are a little broad, Boyle must have felt easier in the Royal Society.

11. *Pert Style in Neo-Classic Times*

As the fourth quarter of the century opened, Dryden was preparing to take his final step in defining wit as a literary product. When he took that step in his 'Apology for Heroic Poetry and Poetic Licence', he thought Rapin 'alone sufficient, were all other critics lost, to teach anew the rules of writing'. Propriety was a central doctrine for Rapin, and in the way of prose he had recently figured in the argument over the eloquence appropriate to the pulpit. Some years before, Sprat had represented the Royal Society as preferring, though on the grounds of proximity to 'things', the language of the artisan before that of the scholar. By the close of the century the controversy about style was settled in favour neither of the scholar nor of the artisan, but of the gentleman.

While both Dryden and Glanvill believed that learning is necessary to the writer, John Hughes in 1698 is more concerned that his learning be polite. The philosopher is now to be saved from the 'Rust of the Academy' by 'Polite Learning', which gives the mind a 'free Air and genteel Motion'. 'In a Word', says Hughes, 'it adds the Gentleman to the Scholar';[1] and this was the addition that in contemporary eyes gave Boyle the advantage over Bentley. Soon Henry Felton found even Dryden too much the scholar.[2] In Hughes the plainness of Glanvill gives way to propriety as the quality of prime importance, for which 'People of Fashion' provide a standard.

The style which discovers a mean between brevity and prolixity—or extremes of Seneca and Cicero—was suggested in Blount, established in Glanvill, and maintained in Hughes. It developed, in so far as it derived from classical models, out of the loose unexpected period of Seneca rather than out of the formal expected period of Cicero. To Henry Felton early in the eighteenth century a just style

[1] 'Of Style', *Critical Essays of the Eighteenth Century*, ed. W. H. Durham (New Haven, 1915), p. 79.
[2] *A Dissertation on Reading the Classics and Forming a Just Style* (London, 1715), pp. 64–5.

was threatened by obscurity from two directions: either by labouring to be concise, or by running into a 'Prodigality of Words'.[1] Of course Jonson had been aware of this, but he had nevertheless emphasized brevity. Studying to be concise produced 'close contracted Periods', which were now outlawed; on the other hand, there could be no return to the copious periods that Bacon had condemned in the Ciceronians.

I

If English style had worked itself out of such contrary affectations, it had not made itself any easier to describe. The relaxed or loose Senecan style, which adopted a conversational norm, prevailed after the Restoration; but the more taut, epigrammatic form did not disappear. The conflict between epigram and speech which appears in Dryden's dramatic verse is not absent from the prose of Halifax; but the curt rhetoric belongs, for the most part, and except for epigrammatic forms, to the past. Of course the periodic form did not vanish, but it acquired a more native and disciplined character. The analysis of a loose Senecan style, as of the plain style in general, presents the problem that wit presented to Cowley; it is easier to define by negatives. None the less the problem of making discriminations beyond those which define its 'loose' character becomes critical in this time, and hence some review of the elements of the problem is necessary.

The qualities found in a prose writer, so far as style is concerned, must be definable in the elements of prose, or words and their arrangement, though not unqualified by thought. We tend to speak of qualities without reference to their rhetorical causes, where the older rhetoricians would have defined an effect of elevation in terms of hyperbole and the like, or irony in terms of its figure, or catachresis as the particular manner of Cleveland. If the style seems rhythmical, we describe it by epithet, without referring the rhythm to a principle of balance or movement. If we involve the general characters of style—plain, grand, and florid—we ignore their propriety to end, or neglect this limitation of their rhetoric. No doubt we are motivated by the feeling that rhetoric provides terms in

---

[1] Cf. *A Dissertation*, pp. 92–3, for a condemnation of the close, contracted style of sententious writers.

337

which to define the means to general effects rather than terms in which to explain the nature of particular effects. When Dryden moved from the position 'that those things which delight all ages must have been an imitation of Nature', he declared, 'Therefore is Rhetoric made an art; therefore the names of so many tropes and figures were invented; because it was observed they had such and such effect upon the audience'.[1] Therefore Dryden could, without apology to Cleveland, include catachreses and hyperboles among the acceptable means of art; for in practice the imitation of nature became something more than its means. But the effects of art were not independent of their means.

In so common a medium as prose, style, as Aristotle saw, can only be defined by its difference, its foreign air. Prose acquires this air most obviously by departures from the customary or the expected. Such matters as the relations between language and thought and end, so far as style is concerned, come down to the choice of words and their arrangement. The writer's choice of words and use of tropes will help to define his qualities and distinction. The arrangement of those words into figures of language, extending to the periodic figure, and including the figures of rhythm, will supplement this definition of effect or distinction. It is in the plain and loose style that definition becomes most difficult, because there rhetoric is most restricted, formal principles most limited, the foreign air itself a contradiction. However, even here, if there is style, there must be elements of distinction; otherwise the critic finds what the *Bourgeois Gentilhomme* discovered he had been speaking all his life. In the plain style, if words should represent things, is arrangement determined by perspicuity and the end of instruction? Presumably things ordered by these requirements will give the proper order of thought in this style, and hence of representative words. On the other hand, words chosen for more than their representative value will require an ordering which exhibits or develops

[1] See his 'Apology for Heroic Poetry and Poetic Licence'. But Dryden does not assume that to identify these tropes and figures is to exhaust the causes of these effects. The matter in which these figures are embodied, for one thing, will always qualify their effect. Without reference to thought we can speak of formal principles only in relation to words, and hence of their arrangement; without reference to style the formal principles of thought become matters of logic; and, as Demetrius remarked, the form of an enthymeme is not the form of a period. But any particular style is indefinable in these terms alone. Of course this study is concerned with general patterns of style.

those other values; formal values will require a formal frame. Periodology exploits such formal values, for pleasure is an end of such words and arrangements. But except for some of the effects of parallelism, such formal values are denied to the plain style.

In diction Aristotle assumes that the uncommon is more pleasing than the common, though less clear. Here the plain style may find distinction if it is willing to compromise with mere representation and therefore with clarity and plainness. But its very nature compels it to modesty. The standard of diction which was most commonly accepted in this century specified the oldest of the new and the newest of the old. While both requirements guarded the interest of perspicuity, they represented a compromise between the common and the distinctive, or between perspicuity and ornament. In arrangement also the plain style, while accepting the conversational order as the standard, could make a similar compromise in the interest of emphasis or distinction; and what was not required by perspicuity might contribute both to pleasure and to effectiveness. When the range of possibilities is limited, or the formal principles are negative rather than positive, the discriminations must be the nicer. As individual speech may vary from current speech, so this style, which approaches that speech most closely, may reflect such variations. The way in which one speaks or puts thought together, and represents it by style, will reveal patterns or variations in patterns that are definable, if not in terms of rhetoric, at least as arrangements contributing to a certain effect.

It may be said that the order in which words and phrases enter the mind of the reader is crucial to certain effects, but also dependent on custom. Let us take a modern example—a sentence of A. E. Housman in his preface to *Lucan*. After saying that 'Horace was as sensitive to iteration as any modern', he writes this sentence: 'Virgil was less sentitive, Ovid much less; Lucan was almost insensible, but not, like the scholars I speak of, quite.' Consider the effect of placing the scholars in the disjunction (hyperbaton) of 'not' and 'quite'. Could any other location be quite so damaging? Here the scholars are left quite insensible rather than almost, or still lower than Lucan. Now this climax depends upon an unusual separation, which puts the sting of the sentence in its very tail, and by means of a relatively insignificant word. Of course parallelism and opposition play their parts in building up the effect, in which a series of discriminations suddenly becomes an order of sarcasm. And consider the difference in effect if Housman had used the more formal, 'like the scholars of whom I speak'; it would have diminished the emphasis of that devastating adverb. The colloquial idiom covers the artificial disjunction, so that it becomes less obtrusive. In diction there is only one unusual word, and that is 'insensible' instead of 'insensitive', apparently introduced to vary expression; but it is a malicious choice, and gives the final twist to 'quite', in a connexion for which the reader is made to wait. Of course the short members increase the force of the final word in each, and march the whole sentence off in the manner of the curt style, so that we are left with something more than merely a loose sentence.

Nevertheless, these principles serve to describe the novel as well as forceful way that Housman has taken to distinguish the sensitivity of Lucan from the sensitivity both of his rivals and of his commentators. Dryden's treatment of Lucan may remind us that where he found Lucan insensitive Housman later found him insensible. The novelty of comparing Lucan's sensitivity with that of his commentators is manifested by the slight alteration in expected words and arrangement which makes Housman's expression distinctive. It shows how a cutting mind manipulates the common medium in an uncommon way to achieve cutting expression. To such economy of means the plain style is limited, and the air of distinction is correspondingly hard to achieve, and to describe. The problem is to speak the language such as men do use, not quite as they speak it, but not so differently as to be mannered.

This was the problem of the Restoration. The third quarter of the century performed the labour of rejection that, as Dryden saw, was necessary to establish such a speech. Dryden knew and quoted Sir John Berkenhead, who expressed what they were all trying to learn when he wrote that Cartwright

> Knew the right mark of things, saw how to choose,
> (For the great Wit's great work is to *Refuse*).[1]

And Berkenhead, who afforded more in precept than in example, knew and quoted Cowley's ode 'Of Wit', which he turned into

[1] See Dryden's 'Defence of an Essay' and Berkenhead's elegy in Cartwright's *Poems* (1651).

epigram. The last quarter of the century was the first to achieve this common speech in the realm of style, or to achieve it so effectively as to make the discrimination of styles correspondingly difficult. By that time writers had been disciplined in the propriety of certain kinds of words and arrangements to certain kinds of writing. They sought a mean between the extremes of the curt Senecan and the copious Ciceronian styles; they found that mean in a loose but not sprawling style, which was closest to the conversational ideal of Seneca. Individualism in style had been checked by the formulation of general standards to which the individual was obliged to submit and by which he was disciplined if he rebelled. No one knew this better than Dryden, who helped to formulate the standards by which his style was criticized.[1] Then a corporate criticism supported generally accepted requirements of style, which produced a common speech.

The tendency both in poetry and in prose during the seventeenth century was towards the conversational norm, towards a dramatic immediacy in communication. The difference between early and late seventeenth-century prose may be put in this way: the earlier prose suggests an extension of the soliloquy in Elizabethan drama, and is in this sense a private communication from mind to mind; but the later prose, like dialogue, feels and manifests the pressure of the social scene. Sir Thomas Browne, for instance, indulging the privacy of his thought, can call upon resources of the poet and create his medium in a way that requires one to learn his language; while Cowley, only a little later, is more concerned with the public quality of his thought because he is more conscious of speaking a common language. Again, the earlier prose seldom has the sense that it may be answered, except in another declamation; hence it lacks that precise sense of mind accommodating itself to mind which we may call the social sense; it is, in a way, too private. There is some truth in the paradox that seventeenth-century verse developed prose virtues before seventeenth-century prose did. This was largely because of the conversational or dramatic immediacy which the verse affected; witness Donne, whose verse is often more conversational

---

[1] Two notorious catachreses became the subject of much ridicule: In *Astræa Redux*, 'An horrid Stillness first invades the ear'; in *The State of Innocence and Fall of Man*, the angels 'all dissolved in hallelujahs lie'. Cf. *Essays*, ed. Ker, i. 188. Dryden, as critic, often developed ideas that were first stated by others.

than his prose. But in time a new corporate sense moulded prose as well as verse to a common style. And it cannot be insisted too much that the discipline exercised upon verse, then as in other periods, was of great consequence for prose.[1]

The progress in conversational style may be illustrated in Dryden, who is at first reminiscent of Cowley, but later admits less ceremony in his style. Dryden opened the *Essay of Dramatic Poesy* with this sentence:

> It was that memorable day, in the first summer of the late war, when our navy engaged the Dutch; a day wherein the two most mighty and best appointed fleets which any age had ever seen, disputed the command of the greater half of the globe, the commerce of nations, and the riches of the universe.[2]

He opened the 'Preface to the Fables' with this sentence:

> 'Tis with a Poet, as with a man who designs to build, and is very exact, as he supposes, in casting up the cost beforehand; but, generally speaking, he is mistaken in his account, and reckons short of the expense he first intended.

The oratorical idiom predominates as much in the first sentence as the conversational does in the second; the difference appears not only in the diction and turn of phrase but also in the sweep and modulation of members. This appears nowhere more clearly than in the way the phrasing of the second follows the various movement of the mind; it commits itself less obviously to any continuous development. In all respects, from diction to rhythm, the first is as formal as the second is informal. Yet the first is not all ceremony, nor the second all negligence. In the second, however, he has managed to seem more natural without being mean; he achieves distinction with less deviation from ordinary language. If these two opening sentences exaggerate the progress of Dryden in conversa-

---

[1] Atterbury, though speaking of the poets before Waller, preaches a lesson that prose also had to learn: 'Besides, their verses ran all into one another; and hung together, throughout a whole copy, like the hooked atoms that compose a body in Descartes. There was no distinction of parts, no regular stops, nothing for the ear to rest upon; but, as soon as the copy began, down it went, like a larum, incessantly, and the reader was sure to be out of breath before he got to the end of it' (preface to Waller's *Poems*, 1690). Dryden had made this point long before. In the structure of prose Lyly erred chiefly in making the stops too regular.

[2] This sentence recalls the opening of Cowley's *Discourse concerning the Government of Cromwell*.

tional prose, they do not falsify his real advance in adapting the conversational idiom of his time to the dignity of various occasions.

In Dryden's time the divisions of discourse with respect to style were new neither in kind nor in intention. Essentially they were the same as those of Bacon. The Restoration simply made up its mind more decisively and more generally about the propriety of certain kinds of words to certain kinds of ends or things, and then proceeded to discipline the recalcitrant. One statement is Hobbes's:

> Now eloquence is twofold. The one is an elegant and clear expression of the conceptions of the mind; and riseth partly from the contemplation of the things themselves, partly from an understanding of words taken in their own proper and definite signification. The other is a commotion of the passions of the mind, such as are *hope, fear, anger, pity*; and derives from a metaphorical use of words fitted to the passions. That forms a speech from true principles; this from opinions already received, what nature soever they are of. The art of that is logic, of this rhetoric; the end of that is truth, of this victory. Each hath its use; that in deliberations, this in exhortations; for that is never disjoined from *wisdom*, but this almost ever.[1]

This statement of the old division of discourse, which now calls both eloquence, divides it more sharply between reason and passion, and makes style a more important means of distinction. Or, to put it another way, the conventional ends of eloquence are separated and referred to particular kinds; the end of one is to prove or instruct, of the other to move. It is still the old philosophic and rhetorical opposition; but the eloquence of the former now suggests the Stoic in its logic and the Attic in its elegance.[2] Another statement is Dryden's:

> The Expressions of a Poem designed purely for Instruction ought to be Plain and Natural, and yet Majestic: for here the Poet is presumed to be a kind of Law-giver, and those three qualities which I have nam'd are proper to the Legislative style. The Florid, Elevated, and Figurative way

---

[1] *Philosophical Rudiments concerning Government and Society* (*De Cive* in English); *English Works*, ed. Molesworth, ii. 161–2. Cf. Bacon's distinction between logic and rhetoric, cited in Chap. VI.

[2] Cicero encouraged this division of eloquence in several ways: by dividing oratory into accurate argument and emotional appeal (*Brutus*, 89), and making the latter more effective; by distinguishing between the intellectual appeal of the plain style and the emotional appeal of the grand style (*Orator*, 20); and by relating the three functions of oratory to the three styles, with the conclusion that the grand style of persuasion 'summed up the entire virtue of the orator' (*Orator*, 69).

is for the Passions; for Love and Hatred, Fear and Anger, are begotten in the Soul by shewing their Objects out of their true proportion; either greater than the Life, or less; but Instruction is to be given by shewing them what they naturally are. A Man is to be cheated into Passion, but to be reason'd into Truth.[1]

Thus a similar division serves to distinguish styles with respect to the ends of poetry, for the division is essentially rhetorical and borrows two ancient characters of style, the plain and the elevated.

Style when it addresses itself either to the understanding or to the passions must alter itself accordingly. No one was more concerned than Hobbes with language as it relates to reason, and no one more concerned than Dryden with language as it relates to the passions. Sir George Mackenzie, however, considered the two kinds of discourse as they relate to the bar. In arguing 'What Eloquence is fit for the Bar', he states the common position that

where Passions are to be excited, as they are by the Pulpit and Theatre, or where Statesmen endeavour to reclaim a mutinous Multitude; there, Eloquence is not only allowable, but necessary (Eloquence being the true Key of the Passions); yet since no Passions are allowed in judging, and the Object of that excellent Science being Truth, and not Humour, Eloquence should not be allow'd in Discourses there.[2]

To this he responds by defining an eloquence which resembles Dryden's legislative style:

To which my Answer is, That Eloquence does not only consist in Tropes, Figures, and such extrinsic Ornaments, whereby our Fancy is more gratified than our Judgment, and our Discourse is rather painted than strengthned; but when I mean that an Advocate should be eloquent, I design thereby, that he should know how to enliven his Discourse with Expressions suitable to the Subject he treats; That he should choose Terms that are significant, and which seem full of the Thing which they are to express, and so lodge his Reasons handsomly. . . .[3]

Such significant expression is also like Hobbes's elegant logical

[1] Preface to *Religio Laici.* Cf. Thomas Baker (*Reflections upon Learning*, p. 41): 'The truth of it is, our common Eloquence is usually a cheat upon the Understanding, it deceives us with appearances, instead of things, and makes us think we see reason, whilst it is tickling our sense: Its strongest proofs, do often consist in an artificial turn of words, and beautiful expressions, which if unravel'd, its strength is gone and the reason is destroyed.'

[2] *Works* (Edinburgh, 1716), i. 12.

[3] Ibid. When 'he is to debate upon probable Themes . . . he may use a more florid and elegant Stile'.

discourse. The whole passage serves to emphasize the kinds of expression thought proper to different ends, and the relation of these styles to rhetoric. The figurative way is the speech of the passions and appropriate where they are to be aroused, but the legislative style is not without its proper elegance in counsel or instruction.

With these kinds of discourse we may connect Dryden's distinction between Plutarch and Seneca. It may be recalled that the arguments of Plutarch, 'drawn from reason, work themselves into your understanding, and make a deep and lasting impression'; but those of Seneca, 'drawn from wit, flash immediately on your imagination, but leave no durable effect'. These consequences of appealing primarily to judgement or to fancy have their causes in the style and discourse of each. And, Baker would add, rhetoric has its effect on the people:

An apposite Similitude is argument with them, and a quaint saying will go farther than a substantial Reason, for being guided by Imagination, they are most affected with sensible resemblances, and not having capacity to penetrate into things, that which is easiest and lies uppermost perswades them most: So that unless we could make them wise, they will be easie and credulous, and will be lead by appearances instead of Truth.[1]

Received opinion found the office of figures in moving the affections, not in appealing to reason. Though Dryden was prompted to his comparison by the fact that Montaigne had unduly honoured Seneca by ranking him with Plutarch, the times presented him with a more immediate reason for disparaging the style of Seneca.

In 1678 L'Estrange had published *Seneca's Morals*, which at once became very popular and lived to be crowned with praise for its 'bright Expression and surprizing Turn'.[2] From another point of view L'Estrange added pertness to the style of Seneca. In the preface 'To the Reader' L'Estrange urges as one reason for his abstract of Seneca that 'his Excellency consists rather in a Rhapsody of Divine, and Extraordinary Hints, and Notions, than in any Regulated Method of Discourse'. This manner, which Dryden had in mind, had often been described as a fault, and L'Estrange reminds

---

[1] *Reflections upon Learning* (1700), p. 42. This is essentially Bacon's view.
[2] Preface to the *Critical Works of Rapin* (London, 1706): 'which we are charm'd with in Sir *Roger L'Estrange's Seneca*, and Mr. *Collier's Antoninus*'.

his contemporaries that among the ancients Seneca had three professed enemies:

Caligula; who call'd his Writings, *Sand without Lime*; alluding to the
starts of his Phancy, and the Incoherence of his Sentences . . . Fabius;
who taxes him for being too bold with the Eloquence of former times,
and failing in that point himself; and likewise for being too Queint and
Finical in his Expressions . . . Agellius, who falls upon him for his Style,
and a kind of Tinkling in his Sentences. . . .[1]

But L'Estrange also quotes the Church Fathers in his favour,
Lactantius especially. In the work itself the Third Part, or the
Epistles, presents in the first four epistles an abstract of Seneca's
rhetorical doctrine, dressed in the new pert diction. Here Seneca
the philosopher appears very prominently as an advocate of the
plain but not careless style.

As an example of L'Estrange's less pert expression, let me quote
a favourite requirement of Seneca's:

It is the Excellency of Speaking, and Writing, to do it Close; and in
Words accommodate to the Intention; and I would yet have somewhat
more to be signify'd, than is Deliver'd: It being also a Mark of Strength
and Solidity of Judgment. . . . As to forc'd *Metaphors*, and wild *Hyperboles*, I would leave them to the *Poets*. And I am utterly against Fooling
with Tinckling Conceipts, and Sounds.[2]

L'Estrange makes Seneca's taste for smart brevity more than
obvious, but not his 'Tinkling Conceits and Sounds'. The style of
the *Morals* offers a new imitation of the Senecan manner, and
L'Estrange, who belonged to Cowley's generation, can be regarded
as the renewer of an older fashion. What was merely old had no
vogue. As late as 1683 Evelyn heard an old man preach 'much after
Bishop Andrews's method, full of logical divisions, in short and
broken periods, and Latin sentences, now quite out of fashion in
the pulpit'.[3] And Evelyn praises the new fashion of the pulpit,
'which is grown into a far more profitable way, of plain and practical
discourses'.

---

[1] 'Of Seneca's Writings' —appendix to his preface, extracted out of Lipsius.
[2] *Seneca's Morals* (London, 1685), pp. 246–7. This is Seneca simplified. Here is
another favourite doctrine (p. 244): 'Speech is the *Index* of the Mind; When you see
a Man Dress, and set his Cloths in Print, you shall be sure to find his Words so too, and
nothing in them that is Firm and Weighty; It does not become a *Man* to be *Delicate*.'
[3] See *Diary*, 15 July 1683.

Of this new way there was a fashion of plain brevity, more like the logical eloquence of Hobbes, which may be called the Latitudinarian style. It was more austere than the style described by Glanvill, and was expounded by Burnet after the example of Tillotson. In 1692 Burnet rang the changes on the defects of sermon style which had been repeated so often. 'Pert Wit and luscious Eloquence', he declared, 'have lost their relish.'[1] His prescription for the pastoral function was, as we shall see, the style of Tillotson. For those with a gift for eloquence—and only those should employ it—the best modern guide was 'Rapin's little Book of Eloquence'.[2]

As to the *Stile*, Sermons ought to be very plain; the Figures must be easy, not mean, but noble, and brought in upon design to make the Matter better understood. The Words in a Sermon must be simple, and in common use; not savouring of the Schools, nor above the understanding of the People. All long *Periods*, such as carry two or three different Thoughts in them, must be avoided; for few Hearers can follow or apprehend these: Niceties of *Stile* are lost before a common Auditory.[3]

No strain was to be put upon the audience, and hence plain brevity still enjoyed the benefit of clergy. In method 'the impertinent Way of dividing Texts is laid aside' and 'Sermons are reduced to the plain opening the Meaning of the Text, in a few short Illustrations of its Coherence with what goes before and after, and of the Parts of which it is composed'.[4] The Latitudinarian sermon did not remind one of Seneca either in subtlety or lack of coherence.[5]

The description of Tillotson's style found in the Funeral Sermon by Bishop Burnet is handed on by Birch, who also adopts the explanation that his labour on the *Real Character* accounts for his style.

Together with the pomp of words he cut off likewise all superfluities and needless enlargements. He said what was just necessary to give clear

---

[1] *A Discourse of the Pastoral Care* (London, 1692), p. 108; chap. ix, 'Concerning Preaching'.

[2] Ibid., p. 112.

[3] Ibid., p. 111. Cf. Feltham's *Resolves*, First Century, xx, 'Of Preaching'.

[4] *Discourse*, p. 108. George Herbert's *Priest to the Temple* had anticipated this reformation. On 4 Apr. 1679, Evelyn records in his *Diary*: 'The Bishop of Gloucester preached in a manner very like Bishop Andrews, full of divisions, and scholastical, and that with much quickness.' Burnet warns that 'too close a Thread of Reason, too great an Abstraction of Thought, too sublime and too metaphysical a Strain, are suitable to very few Auditories, if to any at all'. You were not thus to 'flat the Auditory'.

[5] But when Burnet (p. 117) urges the preacher to make a collection of moral thoughts, he advises that 'Seneca will be of great use to him'.

ideas of things, and no more. He laid aside all long and affected periods. His sentences were short and clear; and the whole thread was of a piece, plain and distinct. No affectations of learning, no torturing of texts, no superficial strains, no false thoughts nor bold flights. All was solid and yet lively, and grave as well as elegant.[1]

Such a style of rather Senecan brevity had already been prescribed for the pulpit by South, who set the pattern for Restoration criticism of sermon style.[2] But this is the preacher of the *Pastoral Care*, and Burnet explains his origin in the *History of his own Time*.

There we are told that the Latitudinarians were formed under Whichcote, Cudworth, Wilkins, More, and Worthington; and that Tillotson, Stillingfleet, Patrick, and Lloyd were the most eminent Latitudinarians.[3] Burnet credits this set of men with the reformation of preaching by means of the method and style which he describes in the *Pastoral Care* and the funeral sermon for Tillotson. Lloyd's description of Wilkins's preaching will illustrate this style:

As for his Preaching, it was sometimes famous near this place; tho' he sought rather the Profit, than the Praise of his Hearers. He spoke solid Truth, with as little Shew of Art as was possible. He express'd all Things in their true and natural Colours; with that Aptness and Plainness of Speech, that grave natural Way of Elocution, that shewed he had no Design upon his Hearers. . . . He applied himself rather to their Understanding than Affections.[4]

[1] Thomas Birch, *Life of Tillotson* (London, 1752), pp. 21-2. If the *Real Character* (1668) explains the style of Tillotson, his connexion with it (which Wilkins fails to mention) began before the Restoration. His first printed sermon appeared in 1661, or before the institution of the Royal Society, of which he did not become a member until 1672, the year of Wilkins's death.

[2] If Wilkins anticipated him in some respects, South formulated the complete doctrine, even if he did not impose it.

[3] *History of his own Time* (London, 1840), i. 127-9. Burnet next deals with the Royal Society, but says nothing about its effect on style. Here Wilkins forms a link with the Latitudinarians, but Burnet makes nothing of that link. In 1662, however, Simon Patrick's *Brief Account of the new Sect of Latitude-Men, together with some Reflections upon the New Philosophy* purports to answer a letter which associated the Latitudinarians with the new philosophy. But the relation between philosophy and religion was a controversial question which set the Cambridge Platonists against the separation urged by Bacon, and later confronted the apologists for the Royal Society. Cf. Glanvill's *Essays* (1676), Essay VII, 'Anti-fanatical Religion and Free Philosophy', or *Plus Ultra* (1668).

[4] *A Funeral Sermon*, 12 Dec. 1672; printed with Wilkins's *Principles and Duties of Natural Religion*. This is the Latitudinarian style of plain brevity, at times relieved and pointed by antithesis, or supported by parallelism. James Greenwood's *English Grammar* (cf. preface) remembers to quote Wilkins on the ambiguity of words and to praise Lloyd's *Dictionary*—which was appended to the *Real Character*—as 'the best English Dictionary that was ever published'.

But of these writers Lloyd is most worthy of Jonson's words: 'Pure and neat language I love, yet plain and customary.' The style which the Latitudinarians reformed Burnet describes much as in his preface to *Utopia*: 'The common style of sermons was either very flat and low, or swelled up with rhetoric to a false pitch of a wrong sublime.'[1] These were common extremes, for they are the extremes of faulty poetic style described in the opening of Dryden's *Essay of Dramatic Poesy*; they suggest that the proper style was to be defined between the extremes of flatness and extravagance. By the time Burnet announced his views there was little novelty left in them; but they served to prolong the fashion of plain brevity, which he exemplified with a Senecan cast of his own.

The curt Senecan style did, moreover, acquire some new prestige from French example, which provoked imitation, and will concern us in due course. Walsh in writing to Dryden, probably about 1691, raises the old opposition in French terms. He is speaking of Balzac, famous for his letters:

By the way do you think Boileau has so extremely well succeeded in his Imitation of him. I confess I allways thought it a chef d'Oevre, till looking upon it again after the receipt of your letter; it does not appear to mee so well as formerly, & I will tell you my reason, that you may inform mee better if I am in the Wrong. Balzac you know was the first that brought the French Prose to any thing of Excellence. No Modern in any language has imitated the beauty of Ciceros Numbers like him, & there is nothing more full, more musical, round, more majestical or more harmonious than his Numbers (his connexion very fine). Hee writes in that Sublime Stile that Longin talks so much of, & this has sometimes carryd him too far, into too bold Metaphor & too strong Hyperboles. Now pray how does Boileau imitate this. His periods are short, rough, & unmusical, no connexion at all between em, more like Seneca or Lipsius than Cicero or Balzac; but to make amends hee has given you three times more Hyperboles than ever Balzac made use of in the same compass.[2]

[1] *History* (1840), i. 131. Edward Fowler in *The Principles and Practices of certain Moderate Divines* (London, 1670, p. 104) says that the Latitudinarians 'affect not Bumbastic words, trifling Strains of Wit, foolish Quibbling, and making pretty sport with Letters and Syllables in their Preaching; but despise those doings as pedantick and unmanly. But on the contrary, they use a Style that is very *grave*, and no less significant.' They avoided, in short, the stylistic occasions for the contempt of the clergy which were described by Eachard in the same year. On the relation of Fowler's defence to South's attack see Birch, *Life of Tillotson* (1752), pp. 351–2.

[2] *The Letters of John Dryden*, ed. C. E. Ward, pp. 46–7. Walsh recognizes the tumour

Here Balzac is regarded as completely Ciceronian, and Boileau's imitation as Senecan, for appropriate reasons. The reasons offer a good summary of the opposing styles, and particularly noteworthy is the emphasis on connexion.[1] This exchange between Dryden and Walsh not only confirms Dryden's interest in prose style and Walsh's sensitiveness to basic differences, but also points the Senecan and Ciceronian opposition within the epistolary form.

There is a letter on the same subject by Mrs. Evelyn which anticipates the elegance that was in request in Walsh's day. It also illuminates the progress of epistolary style. She writes to Mr. Bohun, 21 May 1668, objecting that she must not thank him for entitling her to the great name of Balzac because she does 'not admire his style'. To support her opinion, she adds:

There is a lucky hit in reputation, which some obtain by the defect in their judges, rather than from the greatness of their merit: the contrary may be instanced in Doctor Donne, who, had he not been really a learned man, a libertine in wit and a courtier, might have been allowed to write well; but I confess in my opinion, with these qualifications he falls short in his letters of the praises some give him.

Voiture seems to excel both in quickness of fancy, easiness of expression, and in a facile way of insinuating that he was not ignorant of letters, an advantage the Court air gives persons who converse with the world as books.[2]

These are the qualities that now superannuate Balzac and Donne, motivate Dryden, and bring Voiture closer to the requirements of Hughes. Dr. Bohun, in his 'Character of Mrs. Evelyn', described

and abuse of metaphor that Croll calls Asianism for us but a consequence of Atticism for Balzac's time. On Balzac's Ciceronian cult of form see G. Guillaumie, *Guez de Balzac et la prose française*, esp. the chap. on *L'Harmonie*. Guillaumie finds (p. 471) *le style coupé* also in Balzac, above all in his later works, and imitated from Seneca and Tacitus. He observes (p. 470) 'that it is false to pretend that the *style coupé* is a creation of the end of the seventeenth century' and 'that it is substituted little by little for the periodic style'. Both are found in the earlier part of the century, and in the same writer, as in England.

[1] The change in French style Guillaumie explains (p. 470) as follows: 'Above all, writers have tended to a more exact symmetry. Moreover, symmetry in juxtaposed or coordinated members is more satisfying, and more easy to obtain than that which unites the subordinate with the subordinated.' Hence the periodic style was preferred in the earlier time, which prized the difficulty conquered. In France the *style coupé* was not praised until the last part of the century, when Richesource declared that 'le style coupé et succinct ou laconique est fort mignon, il est dégagé, rien ne l'embarrasse'. Incidentally, asymmetry does not distinguish the *style coupé* for Guillaumie.

[2] See her letters and the 'Character' by Bohun in the *Diary and Correspondence of John Evelyn*, ed. William Bray (London, 1854), vol. iv.

her style as 'equal and chaste', confined to 'the purity of the English tongue', without any 'perplexed sentence':

The expressions are clear and unaffected, the sentences frequent and grave, the remarks judicious, the periods flowing and long, after the Ciceronian way; yet though they launch out so far, they are strict to the rules of grammar, and ever come home at last without any obscurity or incoherence attending them.

In 1695, then, Mrs. Evelyn's periods seemed to Dr. Bohun, despite 'sentences frequent and grave', to be 'after the Ciceronian way', which for Walsh was that of Balzac.[1] Yet they escaped the suggested pitfalls of Ciceronian imitation. Indeed, it may be added, they give less evidence of the 'perplexed sentence' than those of her Royal Society husband. But Mrs. Evelyn did not achieve the ease which she admired and might have found in 'easy Suckling', whose secret, as Dryden knew, was that he found both his syntax and his diction in the conversation of gentlemen.

It remained for an early member of the Royal Society to relate the letter to the familiar style in a manner reminiscent of Sprat, but without his scruples. It was by way of apology for Thomas Barlow's *Genuine Remains* that Sir Peter Pett remarked in 1693,

. . . the first draught of the thoughts of an Author, and such as at once finished up, are to pass from him in a Letter, strike the Eye more with the appearance of the likeness of his Soul and genius, than do the following productions of his Mind, in which Art is exerting it self with variety of labour, and with its colours and shadowings doth often rather hide than illustrate nature.[2]

No doubt Dryden's indifference to revision helped to preserve

---

[1] In 1718 when the tropes and figures are brought up to date in Anthony Blackwall's *Introduction to the Classics*, two figures especially are connected with the period: '*Suspension* begins and carries on a Period or Discourse in such a Manner as pleases the Reader all along; and keeps him in expectation of some considerable thing in the Conclusion' (p. 190). But nothing is worse than 'to usher in an arrant Trifle with the Formality of Preface and solemn Preparation'. Again, '*Amplification* is when every chief Expression in a Period adds Strength and Advantage to what went before; and so the Sense all along heightens, till the Period be vigorously and agreeably clos'd' (p. 208). These figures point to the same end, though the effect in one is beauty, in the other force; they were also part of the 'Ciceronian way'.

[2] 'Epistle to the Reader', *Genuine Remains* (London, 1693). William Walsh is more specific: 'The Stile of Letters ought to be free, easy and natural; as near approaching to familiar Conversation as possible' (Preface to *Letters and Poems Amorous and Gallant*, 1692). His next sentence makes the requirement polite: 'The two best Qualities in Conversation are good Humour and good Breeding; those Letters are therefore certainly the best that shew the most of those two Qualities.'

the familiar, conversational tone and loose structure of his prose. Of course this familiar manner, based on nature, was a Senecan ideal, which had also been illustrated in letters. Barlow himself commends the brevity of William Ames: 'when he 's out, you lose not much; and when he 's right, you have it in a little time.'[1] And this, as Montaigne and Cornwallis would testify, was not a Ciceronian consideration. The point is not that Barlow is a Senecan, but that such qualities, if not imitated from Seneca, had been defended by his authority. Pett goes farther and relates the informal manner of letters to learning: 'Nor are any Learned Works more grateful to Critical Readers than such as are Comprised in the way of Epistles.' This is remote indeed from the formality which required the oratorical style to lend dignity to learning. Dryden, it should be remembered, found his legislative style, and Sprat the familiar style of Cowley, in the Epistles of Horace.

What Dryden called the legislative style, and Burnet considered Latitudinarian, Dennis called the didactic style. For Dennis brevity still had its appropriate place in relation to the end of discourse. In *The Impartial Critic* of 1693 he objects to the 'Pleasantry' of Rymer's style, for the critic 'should keep to the Didactic Style'; and this he defines as 'a Style that is fit for Instruction, and must be necessarily upon that account pure, perspicuous, succinct, unaffected, and grave'.[2] For Dennis the didactic style differs from other styles in its demands upon succinctness and gravity. It is to be inferred that Rymer's style is defective chiefly because it lacks gravity; for true gravity, which derives from wisdom and virtue, gives an air of authority that makes a deeper impression.[3] Thus a style having a Stoic end becomes Stoic in its requirements, and should find its proper place in that tradition, which was essentially that of plain brevity. But Rymer's style, though it might claim to be succinct, had no more gravity than L'Estrange's *Seneca*, but rather what was called a pert air. These are the important ways in which brevity or its opposite appeared in the consideration of style near the turn of the century.

---

[1] *Genuine Remains*, p. 47. Though Pett edited his *Remains*, Barlow had written letters to Sir J. B. (John Berkenhead?) against the new philosophy of the Royal Society (ibid., pp. 151–9).

[2] *Critical Essays of the Seventeenth Century*, ed. J. E. Spingarn, iii. 157.

[3] Ibid., p. 158.

II

The curt Senecan style did not pass into memory with the age of Dryden; it was still a small but lively voice at the opening of the eighteenth century; it had, in fact, yet to receive its most extensive criticism. To Shaftesbury this conclusion would certainly be under-statement, for the prevailing style in his view was found in the *Epistles* of Seneca:

> He falls into the random way of miscellaneous writing, says everywhere great and noble things, in and out of the way, accidentally as words lead him (for with these he plays perpetually), with infinite wit, but with little or no coherence, without a shape or body to his work, without a real beginning, a middle, or an end.[1]

But Seneca's *gravitas*, paronomasia, and wit concern Shaftesbury less than his cult of *sententiae* or violation of 'order and method'. He remarks that whole pages or letters may be divided or combined at pleasure; 'every period, every sentence almost, is independent, and may be taken asunder, transposed, postponed, anticipated, or set in any new order, as you fancy'. This possibility had been demonstrated in L'Estrange's *Abstract*.

After this analysis of Seneca, he turns to his own time:

> This is the manner of writing so much admired and imitated in our age, that we have scarce the idea of any other model. We know little, indeed, of the difference between one model or character of writing and another. All runs to the same tune, and beats exactly one and the same measure. Nothing, one would think, could be more tedious than this uniform pace. The common amble or *canterbury* is not, I am persuaded, more tiresome to a good rider than this see-saw of essay writers is to an able reader.[2]

Thus Shaftesbury characterized the style which had corresponded

[1] *Characteristics*, ed. J. M. Robertson (London, 1900), ii. 170; Misc. 1, chap. iii. Of Seneca the dramatist Thomas Rymer (*Tragedies of the Last Age*, 1692, p. 97) had said: 'He crumbles every *thought* into all the little *points* that ever he can strain it to; and all these *points* (for, or against him, it matters not) must one way or other be apply'd.'

[2] Ibid., p. 171. For Shaftesbury this antithetic 'see-saw' is the 'witty' style of the modern letter, essay, or miscellany. The figures employed by Attic prose, says Croll, 'are not the "schemes", or figures of sound, which characterize oratory, but the figures of wit, the rhetorical means, that is, of conveying thought persuasively' (*Studies in Philology*, xviii. 116). These are chiefly antithesis, point, and metaphor. In particular, metaphor 'is as much the characteristic possession of the essay style as the musical phrase is of the oratorical'. This aspect is studied by D. S. Mead in *The Literary Comparison in Jacobean Prose*, Princeton, 1926.

to the Jacobean taste for mingled wit and gravity, but which now threatened to compete with the heroic couplet. 'If your Poets are still Mr. Bays's', asked Shaftesbury, 'and your Prose-Authors Sir Rogers, without offering at a better Manner; must it follow that the Manner itself is good, or the Wit genuine?'[1] Senecan style remained for some time—as late as Blair—one of the extremes between which eighteenth-century theory charted its course; but in practice it was no longer the alternative to the Ciceronian.

The general names for these extremes Blair borrowed from the French, who had borrowed them from Cicero. Gibert provides them in his summary of La Mothe le Vayer's *Considérations sur l'éloquence françoise de ce temps*, published in 1638: 'L'opposé du style périodique est le style coupé.'[2] It is proper, as Blair also remarks, to mix the two styles—an art which Cicero explains in his *Orator* (221). The cut style mentioned by Cicero was described by La Mothe le Vayer in this fashion: 'it resembles the speech of asthmatics . . . or in short the manner in which magpies advance: they go only by bounds. It is true that points, verbal allusions, and sentences acquire in this style both pomp and wonderful brilliance'. While La Mothe le Vayer observed that Caligula imputed the 'asthmatic' style to Seneca, he himself imputed it to Malvezzi, the discourser upon Tacitus, who imitated the 'magpie' movement or Lipsian character of style. This is the background for the terms to which Blair gives a place in English rhetoric.[3]

When John Hughes wrote his essay 'Of Style' in 1698, the reign of the plain style was over, and the reign of the correct, just, or accurate style had begun.[4] Certainly as early as 1672 the doctrine

---

[1] *Characteristics*, Misc. v, chap. ii. Shaftesbury provided rhetoricians like Blair with their prime example of a periodic oratorical style; he was Ciceronian.

[2] Cf. Baillet's *Jugemens des savans* (Amsterdam, 1725), viii. 278.

[3] In 1716 Myles Davies (*Athenae Britannicae*, 'Preface', p. 72) names three styles, Asiatic, Ciceronian, and Laconic, which had been Asiatic, Rhodian, and Attic for Erasmus. The Asiatic is 'lofty and spaciously flowing'; the Ciceronian is 'Majestick Eloquence'; the Laconic is 'Elegancy it self, with a Sententious Pungency and an Awful Cogency'. His exemplars, especially for the first two styles, are often more curious than informing. Baxter and Bunyan, being copious, are Asiatic; Clarendon is Ciceronian; but Seneca, Epictetus, and Lipsius are Laconic.

[4] Glanvill's definition of the former may be recalled: 'Plainness is a Character of great latitude, and stands in opposition, First, to *hard words*; Secondly, to *deep* and *mysterious notions*; Thirdly, to *affected Rhetorications*; and Fourthly, to *Phantastical Phrases*.' Since this is chiefly on the level of diction, his comment on borrowed words should be added: 'which when they are once brought into common use, they may be spoken

of correctness had been preached in Dryden's 'Defence of the Epilogue', and only five years later the standard of correctness in style had been enunciated by Dryden as 'a propriety of thoughts and words; or, in other terms, thoughts and words elegantly adapted to the subject'.[1] In his final allusion to this definition of wit—obviously a much larger term than Addison's captious criticism implies[2]—Dryden adds this qualification: 'which I imagined I had first found out, but since am pleasingly convinced that Aristotle has made the same definition in other terms'.[3] Now Aristotle's definition of 'thought' in the *Poetics* as 'the ability to say what is possible and appropriate' covers but part of Dryden's definition, and not the part of style; but his requirement that diction be both clear and uncommon not only indicates the way to dignity or distinction of style but makes propriety its fundamental literary principle.[4] All expression beyond adequate communication comes within the province of style, which is ruled by propriety.[5]

John Hughes developed Dryden's definition of wit, whether by design or not, into a theory of style which laid greatest stress on

without blame of affectation; yea, there is sometimes vanity and affectation in avoiding them.' He illustrates this vanity by the Saxonisms which Nathaniel Fairfax substituted for Latinisms in *A Treatise of the Bulk and Selvedge of the World*. Fairfax, in his preface 'To the Reader', shows that he for one took Sprat's *History* seriously on the subject of diction. He also contributed to the pert colloquial diction which became so popular.

[1] In 1685 (*Albion and Albanius*) he is more specific: 'Propriety of thought is that fancy which arises naturally from the subject, or which the poet adapts to it. Propriety of words is the clothing of those thoughts with such expressions as are naturally proper to them; and from these, if they are judiciously performed, the delight of poetry results.'

[2] By quoting Dryden as saying 'a Propriety of Words and Thoughts adapted to the Subject', Addison (*Spectator*, 62) telescopes 'elegantly' right out of the definition, and as elegance goes out Euclid comes in.

[3] See *The Life of Lucian*, probably written in 1696, but not published until 1711. The allusion to Aristotle has been identified as *Poetics*, vi. 22: 'Third comes "thought". This means the ability to say what is possible and appropriate.' But words are also involved, and of words the *Poetics* (xxii. 1) says: 'The merit of diction is to be clear and not commonplace.' While the common ensures clarity, the unusual gives dignity or distinction. T. S. Eliot in 'Little Gidding' calls these two elements 'the common word' and 'the formal word'.

[4] As a way to avoid the commonplace, all tropes are analogous for Anthony Blackwall (*An Introduction to the Classics*, p. 171): 'that in all of them a Man uses a foreign or strange Word instead of a proper one; and therefore says one thing and means something different'.

[5] See also the related discussion in the *Rhetoric* (III. ii), where clarity and distinction are required, and the uncommon again gives distinction but is subject to propriety—because, as Dryden says, it must seem 'natural'. In the *Rhetoric* 'thought' belongs to proof.

propriety. When he summarized the qualities of a good style as propriety, perspicuity, elegance, and cadence, he added: 'And each of these, except the last, has some relation to the Thoughts, as well as to the Words.'[1] Therefore, each quality, except the last, is considered in this twofold relation. Since most of his attention is given to propriety, the other qualities may be summarized briefly. For perspicuity, of course, your thoughts must be clear in order that your words may, and your expression must be adequate. Elegance of thought is wit, and to the elegance of words belong all the figures of rhetoric, though it is best learned by example. Cadence 'consists in a Disposing of the Words in such Order, and with such Variation of Periods, as may strike the Ear with a sort of musical Delight'.[2] It should be added that style is primarily a matter of words, and that elegance actually becomes a propriety of the polite world: 'Elegance consists very much in a genteel Ease and Freedom of Expression.' Here it is not amiss to recall, by way of giving content to this phrase, the vogue of 'easy Suckling'. Elegance becomes the highest attribute of words, though justness remains their basic requirement.

The propriety of thoughts is twofold: the first requires that the thoughts be proper in themselves, or sense rather than nonsense; the second that they be proper to the occasion. 'Propriety of Words, the first Qualification of a good Style, is when the Words do justly and exactly represent, or signify, the Thoughts which they stand for.'[3] This is the very foundation of the correct, just, or accurate style; but the standard for this propriety is to be found neither in Hobbes nor in the Royal Society, but rather in 'general Acceptation', which is established by 'the most correct Writers' and 'the Conversation of People of Fashion'. In prose the most correct writers are Temple, Sprat, and Tillotson. In this list the presence of Sprat is no more surprising than the absence of Dryden, but

---

[1] *Critical Essays of the Eighteenth Century*, ed. W. H. Durham, p. 80.

[2] Ibid., pp. 82–3. Shaftesbury also was interested in harmony, in prose as well as verse; he notes some improvement in periods: 'They have of late, 'tis true, reform'd in some measure the gouty Joints and Darning-work of *Whereunto's*, *Whereby's*, *Thereof's*, *Therewith's*, and the rest of this kind; by which, complicated Periods are so curiously strung, or hook'd on, one to another, after the long-spun manner of the *Bar* or *Pulpit*' (Misc. v, chap. i). This was not only to improve in composition and harmony, but also to shorten perplexed periods.

[3] *Critical Essays*, ed. Durham, p. 80.

neither circumstance is to be explained by any principle deriving from the Royal Society.

It is more to the point to recall the education which Philip Doddridge received in Jennings's academy at Kibworth. In a letter to the Rev. Mr. Saunders, dated 16 November 1725, he describes the exercises set in that academy: 'Bacon's Essays were often used on this occasion and our exercises were a kind of comment upon some remarkable sentences in them. We were often set to translate Tillotson into Sprat's style, and *vice versa*.'[1] Since Sprat and Tillotson have been called representatives of the Royal Society style, it will be interesting to see how a man so trained describes their styles:

Tillotson. There is such an easiness in his style, and beautiful simplicity of expression, as seems easy to be imitated, yet nothing more difficult....

Sprat. His language is always beautiful, but many of his sentences are very weak.—The *Ciceronian* style is too much laboured.—Tully is translated for many sentences together in some of his sermons, though not mentioned.[2]

Tillotson could be a Royal Society stylist, Sprat hardly; they are sufficiently diverse to provide an exercise in translation. To a man schooled in imitation, even of English writers, the official spokesman of the Society preferred laboured Ciceronianism to 'native easiness', at least in sermons.[3] This suggests his appropriateness as a contrast to Tillotson in an academic exercise.

Having described the four qualifications of style, Hughes considers two kinds of 'Manner', which are only other aspects of propriety. The first is the individual manner of the writer; it is language as the image of a mind. The second is 'the different Manner to be used by the same Writer, according to the Subject he treats of'.[4]

[1] *Works* (Leeds, 1804), v. 561. For themes Bacon's 'sentences' thus replaced the adages of Erasmus.

[2] Ibid., pp. 435–6. For comparison here is Doddridge on Wilkins (p. 435): 'His method is very exact, but too scholastic.—His style is almost as easy and pure as Tillotson's.' His method is not Tillotson's.

[3] Richard Bentley, in justifying one of his expressions, argues that 'particularly it's adopted by our English *Cicero*, the Right Reverend the Bishop of *Rochester*, in his History of the *Royal Society*; where Philosophy and Eloquence have renew'd as strict an Acquaintance, as they had in *Cicero's Philosophica* Seventeen Hundred Years ago' (*Dissertation upon Phalaris*, 1699, p. xcvi). Bentley, who was more expert in language than Wilkins, knew that Sprat's *History* contained the expression 'first inventor', but he had missed, or else ignored, the programme which separated philosophy and eloquence.

[4] *Critical Essays*, ed. Durham, p. 85.

While philosophy, for instance, requires a plain style, 'Morality and Divinity are capable of all the Ornaments of Wit and Fancy'.[1] To show that each author has his own manner, Hughes gives short characters of Temple, L'Estrange, and Sprat.

Temple is distinguished by harmony and wit; he is the orator. L'Estrange's talent is humour; he is a master of idiomatic expression, in whom the Englishman speaks. But how does the author of the *History of the Royal Society* strike Hughes?

The elegant Dr. *Sprat* is, in my Judgment, one of the most genteel and exact Writers we have. His Style is grave and manly, infinitely preferable to Sir *Roger's*, and having all that is beautiful in Sir *William Temple*, only (if 'tis possible) with more Correctness and Decency. There appears in him all the Sweetness and Fluency, handsom Turns and apt Expressions, that can be desir'd. He has united the most charming Elegance to the strictest Propriety, and is witty without the least Shadow of Affectation. The soft Cadence of his Periods, methinks, resembles the Current of a pleasant Stream; It makes but little Noise, yet affects you with a calm Delight, which, if it were heard louder, wou'd be lost.[2]

Whether or not Sprat ever illustrated the programme of style described in his *History*, he qualified easily for the laurel in Hughes's programme. But his plainness appears, if at all, only in the epithets 'grave and manly', which describe the style appropriate to philosophy. Apparently, for Hughes too, Dryden failed to add the gentleman to the scholar.

Only one writer mentioned by Hughes is celebrated for simplicity, one of the two qualities which constituted plainness for the *Royal Society*, and that writer is 'the Incomparable Tillotson, who always writes the best Sense, and in the best Manner':

That which particularly recommends him is an Easiness and beautiful Simplicity in all his Expressions, which every one that reads him is apt to think may be imitated without much Difficulty, and yet nothing perhaps is so hard in the Experiment.[3]

---

[1] Thus propriety to the subject limits the style of Sprat's *History*, but would justify his 'Ciceronian' style in sermons.

[2] Ibid., p. 84. Waller is mentioned because 'he has scarce any Equal' for 'Propriety both of Thoughts and Words'. The figures of repetition were called 'Turns' in Neo-Classical times; but care had to be taken not to 'affect a trifling Sound and Chime of insignificant Words'. See Anthony Blackwall, *An Introduction to the Classics*, p. 201; and observe Dryden's interest in them, located by the Ker index under 'Turns of words and thoughts'.

[3] See Durham, pp. 84–5. The agreement with Doddridge is striking.

'Easiness' not only qualifies Tillotson in 'elegance' but associates him with 'easy Suckling'. For Hughes his simplicity could hardly derive from the language of artisans, countrymen, and merchants. Only Tillotson among the prose writers seems to deserve mention for propriety of thoughts, for Sprat's propriety is chiefly of words.

The weight which Hughes attaches to perspicuity may be suggested by the fact that he praises no writer explicitly for that quality, though it may be involved in 'simplicity'. It was, of course, the other component of plainness for the Royal Society. Since perspicuity in some measure is essential to communication, it becomes significant in programmes of style chiefly by reason of its relation to other qualities.[1] And so it is in Hughes's programme: 'Here an Extreme is to be shunned, lest, while you aim to make your Meaning fully understood, you become Verbose. So that the Art lies in expressing your Thoughts clearly in as few Words as possible.'[2] Just as 'purity', although not mentioned among the qualifications, is associated with propriety of words, so brevity, likewise unmentioned, is associated with perspicuity.[3] Verbosity is set up as the more undesirable extreme, and the art lies in getting as much brevity as is consistent with clarity. For Shenstone this was the very essence of Pope's art; for Wilkins it had belonged to the proper sermon style. For Hughes's own practice this is a very significant fact because it associates him with a theory of style by which he had been judged before his own view was published.

While Hughes suggests the curt Senecan style in his concern for brevity, by associating it with cadence he was seeking qualities that formerly would have been regarded as antithetic. But that his inclination was not unrelated to Senecan style may be attested by a contemporary criticism of his practice. In *A Dissertation concerning the Perfection of the English Language* Leonard Welsted, digressing to the state of prose in 1724, remarks that prose has been improved more than poetry, particularly 'in this Circumstance of Politeness';

---

[1] Aristotle remarked (*Rhetoric*, III. ii. 2) that without perspicuity a speech 'will not perform its proper function'. But he himself was not a waster of words.

[2] *Critical Essays*, ed. Durham, p. 82.

[3] Purity also finds its standard in 'modern Use'. For Aristotle (*Rhetoric*, III. v) purity, which is the foundation of style, depends upon rules of composition that contribute to exactness or perspicuity; it is correct and precise usage.

but, though now 'little inferior to the French for Neatness and Perspicuity of Style', it is still short of perfection.

A late very popular Author, has, I own, carried the Essay-Turn of Writing to a great Height, and left behind him fine Models of a terse and chast Diction; his Defect, if he has any, seems to be, that he lies too much in *courte* Sentences, that do not run cleverly into one another, and are not so connected as to depend naturally enough together; the Chain is sometimes wanting, and the full Stop, or Close of the Period, returns too frequently upon us; which is the Vice also of the *French* Writers. . . [1]

This late author has been identified as Addison, but Addison was not addicted to '*courte* Sentences'. Welsted puts us on the right track when he adds: 'The English Author, I am speaking of, as he followed, or seemed to follow very closely in the Traces of Fontenelle, and to have much studied his Manner, so did he succeed extremely well in it.' Of late essayists in 1724 none fits this description so well as the translator of Fontenelle, John Hughes. If he had studied the manner of Fontenelle, he had simply followed his theory of style, believing that 'good Examples are the best Instruction'. Thus Hughes is not only described as a curt Senecan stylist, but one after the French model provided by Fontenelle; moreover, he has had imitators.

It is interesting that a programme of style which so well describes the prose of the first part of the eighteenth century should still reflect the curt Senecan tradition, and should even produce a variety of that style in the practice of its author. If, as Welsted suggests, Hughes achieved elegance in this variety of Senecan style, the basic character of that style remained antipathetic to cadence or harmony, which supersedes propriety in later stylistic theory. It is apparent that even after Shaftesbury's complaint Senecan style was still a force to be reckoned with. Swift detected its characteristic movement in Burnet's *History of His Own Time*, which, though antecedent, had only recently been published. Quoting from Burnet a passage of short, disconnected sentences in the Character style, Swift comments: 'Pretty jumping periods'.[2] To his readers that phrase would still have meant Seneca or Lipsius. And William Stevenson, in translating Fénelon's *Dialogues concerning Eloquence*,

---

[1] *Critical Essays*, ed. Durham, p. 385. Prose, it seems, reflected the discipline of the couplet.

[2] 'Remarks on Burnet's History of His Own Times', *Works*, ed. Scott, xii. 193.

gives his testimony both to the French *style coupé* and to its charm
for him. In apology for his translation of the dialogues, he remarks:
'their style is extremely concise; sometimes obscure'; and later adds:

> Some critics will think I have too often neglected such connecting
> particles as for, but, seeing, &c. there is a peculiar beauty in this omission:
> and I should have left out many more, if I had closely followed our
> author's example, or my own judgment. but too much must not be
> attempted at once.[1]

These are marks of the curt Senecan style; they are imitated by the
translator in his 'Advertisement'.[2]

But these are not the writers who provoked the main Anti-
Senecan criticism. And this criticism was not concerned solely, or
even chiefly, with their brevity, but rather with their wit and colloquialism. Hughes describes the manner of one of these writers, even
though he does not illustrate the doctrine of correctness. L'Estrange,
says Hughes, is a master of idiom and proverbial expression, though
not without affectation in their use; 'yet, generally speaking, his
Style is pleasant, smooth and natural; and that Gaiety and seeming
Negligence, which is peculiar to him, entertains you with a familiar
sort of Delight, like that of witty and facetious Company'. This is
not the elegance which 'consists very much in a genteel Ease and
Freedom of Expression'; it is colloquial ease minus the gentility.

This colloquial ease, which was much sought after, ran the gamut
in diction from slang to preciosity; and it was not new in Senecan
style. About it, and particularly on its vulgar side, centred the
criticism against the new Senecans, chiefly Collier and L'Estrange.
The authors of *Peri Bathous* devote a special category to it as 'The
Pert Style', which 'does in as peculiar a manner become the low
in wit, as a pert air does the low in stature':

> But the beauty and energy of it is never so conspicuous, as when it is
> employed in *Modernizing* and *Adapting* to the *Taste of the Times* the
> works of the *Antients*. This we rightly phrase *Doing* them into English,

---

[1] See 'The Translator's Advertisement'; first published, London, 1722. 'Tho' I
admire conciseness', says Stevenson, 'I prefer perspicuity, when I cannot be both
short and clear.' Another translator from the French remarks in his Dedication: 'Had
he not been so very studiously *concise*, and so elegantly *Sententious*, I should conceive
less Reason to apprehend the Success of my Attempt' (Edward Combe's *Art of being
Easy*, London, 1724; translated from the French of Des Landes).

[2] For Gibert's criticism of Fénelon's views see *Jugemens des savans* (Amsterdam,
1725), viii. 379-87.

and *Making* them English; two expressions of great Propriety, the one denoting our *Neglect* of the *Manner how*, the other the *Force* and *Compulsion* with which it is brought about.[1]

Here the allusions include the Senecan bias of L'Estrange and Collier: 'Tully is as short and smart as Seneca or Mr. Asgill, Marcus Aurelius is excellent at Snipsnap.' It may be recalled that Blair found Pope given to the French manner of being 'short and smart'; but the manner made the difference.

Where this attack, made in 1727–8, seems to find more of a target in L'Estrange, the simultaneous attack made by Oldmixon is directed against Collier. This attack is found in *An Essay on Criticism*, and incidentally in his paraphrase of Bouhours, *The Arts of Logick and Rhetorick*, both published in 1728.[2] In the *Essay* he begins with the pertness of Collier's style, 'which was mistaken for Vivacity', and proceeds to a detailed indictment. Collier's faults include cacophony, affected metaphor and colloquialism, frequent use of proverbs, and especially the 'huddling of Metaphors'. It is a 'Declamatory Style', straining for point and often repetitive in effect; its spasmodic or Senecan character is suggested by an indecent simile: 'The Stream is the same still, but . . . it comes by Spirts.'[3] In the *Arts* he indicts Collier of 'Phebus's Figure' or glittering nonsense, which defines his kind of obscurity. And he epitomizes Collier's faults in one sentence: 'Collier's Style is extremely vicious, by his affecting to heap Metaphors one upon another, and to think and speak out of the common Road.'[4] In effect the sum of this criticism is to derive Collier's style from the schools of declamation.

When Coleridge took up the theme of low diction in Restoration style, it was by annotations on a copy of Collier's translation of Marcus Aurelius, which had been ridiculed in *Peri Bathous*. Coleridge found that although 'colloquial barbarisms' made Collier's style less disgusting to him than 'Johnsonian magniloquence or the

---

[1] Pope, *Works* (London, 1751), vi. 205: 'The Art of Sinking in Poetry.' The comment illustrates the colloquial impropriety.

[2] In the latter work Oldmixon shows himself aware of the *Art of Sinking*, from which, despite his attack on Pope and Swift, he may have borrowed, though his criticism is much more comprehensive. In the 'Introduction' to the *Arts* he calls the *Essay* 'a Sketch of Father *Bouhours's* Manner of Criticism'; of the *Arts* he says, Sir Samuel Garth 'put me upon this Work'. Others for whom Bouhours was a voice of authority include Addison and Constable.

[3] *An Essay on Criticism* (London, 1728), pp. 49–52.

[4] *The Arts of Logick and Rhetorick* (London, 1728), pp. 368, 397–8.

balanced metre of Junius', their cultivation resulted in a loss of precision and an acquisition of the mean and ludicrous in conversational prose. Thus he comments on the 'Picture of Cebes', included in this volume:

This is worth reading as a Masterpiece of *Black-guard Slang*, which passed for easy writing from the Restoration of Charles & of the Royalist Party to the accession of Queen Anne. I cannot remember any one, but Cowley, that was not more or less infected with it. Even Dryden, masterly as his Prose Style is, not free from it.[1]

When Coleridge adds, 'I believe, Sir Roger L'Estrange was the Introducer of this Thames-Waterman's Language', he is selecting L'Estrange for an honour which Hughes put somewhat differently, though not in contradiction. As one reason why some idioms 'degrade the Diction and render it mean and ludicrous', Coleridge offers 'the indefiniteness of the phrase, which marks a vulgar mind'.

But the age thus impugned also knew that the pursuit of easy writing could fall into low or vulgar diction, and even a second-rate critic like Oldmixon condemned Collier on such grounds. This verdict has simply been handed down to our time. If Oldmixon is too late for Coleridge's period, most of the culprits mentioned by Pope and Swift write before the age of Anne. Although the Royal Society might claim to have encouraged the language of artisans, countrymen, and merchants, certainly Dryden could not. Dryden would have set up an academy; meanwhile he laboured at turning brick into marble. The language sponsored by the Royal Society was no more acceptable to the wits than to the scholars, and the day now belonged even more to the wits than to the scholars. Witnesses of the Bentley–Boyle controversy, in fact, would probably have held that the scholars were much less responsible in such matters. What passed for easy writing, however, was not written solely by the masters of 'blackguard slang'.

Colloquial locutions alone do not make conversational prose; nor does studied brevity convey the impression of its easy, if not careless, syntax. In this kind of prose Addison provides a useful contrast to Collier; and Addison's effects have never been better described than by Dr. Johnson—as a model for the middle style—'always

[1] See B. Ifor Evans, 'Coleridge on Slang', *T.L.S.* Correspondence, 29 May 1937, p. 412.

equable, and always easy, without glowing words, or pointed sentences'. Phoebus's figure and Collier's way do not lead to this style:

It was apparently his principal endeavour to avoid all harshness and severity of diction; he is therefore sometimes verbose in his transitions and connexions, and sometimes descends too much to the language of conversation; yet if his language had been less idiomatical, it might have lost somewhat of its genuine Anglicism. . . . His sentences have neither studied amplitude, nor affected brevity: his periods, though not diligently rounded, are voluble and easy.[1]

What Addison avoided Collier achieved. If L'Estrange had the Anglicism, he lacked the correctness; if Collier was idiomatic, he was also glowing and pointed. Both lacked the easy transitions and connexions which distinguish conversation but not affected brevity; neither was 'familiar but not coarse, and elegant but not ostentatious'. Hughes's doctrine would dictate the same conclusion, and it is no accident that he was welcome to the pages of the *Spectator*.

A very popular work written in 1709 supports Hughes's doctrine and examples of style, and that is Henry Felton's *Dissertation on Reading the Classics and Forming a Just Style*, which later supplied Dr. Warton with an example of the 'Finical Style' described in the *Art of Sinking*. Felton's examples of the chief models of English style tally with Hughes's down to their individual qualities; and his doctrine is summarized in propriety, which supplies the rules for forming a just style: matter suited to the subject, thoughts suited to the matter, words suited to the thoughts. Moreover, although both brevity and prolixity threaten perspicuity, Felton is inclined to favour brevity as exemplified by Thucydides and Sallust. He appraises L'Estrange as a translator in terms of propriety, but does not object that he makes Cicero 'as short and smart as Seneca':

Sir *Roger L'Estrange*, who was a perfect Master of the familiar, the facetious and jocular Style, fell into his proper Province, when he pitched upon *Erasmus* and *Æsop*. *Tully's* Offices were suitable enough for their Plainness and Familiarity to his Genius; but he could never rise to the Solemnity and Dignity of his Orations.[2]

Compared with the *Art of Sinking*, the *Dissertation* excuses L'Estrange for his Cicero, but also damns his Josephus for its

---

[1] Conclusion to Johnson's *Life of Addison*. Hughes warned against verbosity; Johnson retreated too far from the language of conversation.

[2] *Dissertation*, 5th ed. (London, 1753), p. 129. Felton, if finical, is not above pertness.

'Levities and low Expressions'. Neither for Felton nor for Hughes does L'Estrange represent the 'genteel Way of writing' that belongs to elegance, indeed to 'Quality'. But they are both more sympathetic to brevity, if not 'affected brevity', than to 'studied amplitude'.

The most extensive attack on Senecan style, particularly as represented by Collier, was apparently written for the most part about 1713, though not published until 1731. It was John Constable's *Reflections upon Accuracy of Style*, containing, he avows, 'the Chief Rules to be observed for obtaining an Accurate Style'.[1] Constable's *Reflections* 'were really occasioned by conversation' with an extreme admirer of Callicrates or Collier, and this circumstance suggested their dialogue form. Eudoxus, Constable's mouthpiece, succeeds in converting two admirers of the 'short and smart style' by exploring the grounds of style in general. Of course the 'new style' of Collier turns out to be an old style which has marked Seneca, Lipsius, and Feltham: 'Feltham, Sir, as old as he is, writes in almost as new a Style as Callicrates.'[2]

This book is remarkable chiefly for its thorough recapitulation, at this late date, of the arguments for and against Senecan style. The main Lipsian arguments for Senecan style are advanced, and the main Anti-Senecan arguments from Quintilian down are marshalled against them. As Constable completes the indictment made by Shaftesbury and accumulates the occasional criticism of Collier, he sets forth the doctrine of the just style and points toward the newer stress on harmony. In this shift Dryden returns to favour, for he had suffered from the criteria of justness and gentility. After Constable rhetoric directs its attention much more largely to harmony, producing a number of works on that subject alone; the new emphasis may be observed in Blair or Johnson.[3]

Constable makes it abundantly clear that Callicrates stands for Collier; indeed, Collier's style is the only individual style mentioned

---

[1] Printed, London, 1731; with a new title-page in 1734 and 1738. Cf. preface, p. xi, for date of composition.

[2] *Reflections upon Accuracy of Style* (London, 1734), p. 69. Feltham was still being published in the reign of Queen Anne.

[3] See, for example, Edward Manwaring, *Of Harmony and Numbers in Prose and Poetry*, London, 1744; James Geddes, *Essay on the Composition and Manner of Writing of the Ancients*, Glasgow, 1748; John Mason, *Essay on the Power and Harmony of Prosaic Numbers*, London, 1749, 1761. Cf. W. Vaughan Reynolds, 'Johnson's Opinions on Prose Style', *Review of English Studies*, ix (1933), 433–46.

in the topics enumerated on the title-page of 1734. Collier's 'flashing' style is in general characterized in these terms:

Those concise Sentences, those short Cuts, those continual Metaphors, and that which I call the *Tic-Tac*, of an *Antithesis*, strikes indeed at first, but will seldom bear the test of a reflection. . . . You know how much you admired at first *Lipsius's* hopping style: yet, as I told you then, you soon changed your opinion, and with a great deal of reason. . . . Now, methinks, the *English* of *Callicrates* is something like *Lipsius's Latin*.[1]

One consequence of such a style is lack of variety:

I find by daily experience the like effect from those Styles in prose, which are *homogeneal*, by their perpetual ending in a short cut of an anti-thesis, or something like it. It is as bad as perpetually to make rhymes, clinches, or blank verse. . . . Thus in some people's prose, my ear rings with the following sound, before my eye has reached the word, and I laugh if I meet the fall I expected, and wonder if I do not; and either way, think more of the sound than of the meaning.[2]

If this explains the basis of expectation in the antithetic period, such styles enter into his discussion of harmony because of 'the oddnesses of their abrupt, and yet expected and foreseen cadences'.[3] The intention of this style is the same as that of the schools of declamation—to secure applause; and Constable deals with it in terms reminiscent of Quintilian's influential chapter on *sententiae*:

Thus a perpetual *Laconism* strikes at first, but upon reflection you will find it extremely weak. The imagination cannot always keep up to that constraint. 'Tis above the capacity of man to be always extraordinarily witty, and whoever aims at it in every sentence, must of necessity fall into affectation, false conceits, flat and impertinent ideas.[4]

The consequence of this intention is that 'they give their every period something like the air and turn, but not the solidity of an Apothegm'.

---

[1] *Reflections* (1734), pp. 8–9.

[2] Ibid., p. 91.

[3] Ibid., pp. 89 ff. and 96. The abrupt style of Sallust, Seneca, and the like, does not seem to end, but fall; its antithetic completions are prone to ellipsis, hence to abrupt rather than smooth endings.

[4] Ibid., p. 21. Cf. Quintilian, *Institutes*, VIII. v. Bacon noted the same disappointment in Senecan style. Relative to harmony, Quintilian (VIII. v. 27) had observed that by the 'pursuit of fine thoughts . . . language is rendered too unconnected, and being composed not of members, but of bits (*non membris, sed frustis collata*), has no proper construction; for these round and polished portions refuse to unite with each other'. Cf. Quintilian, IV. v. 25 and IX. iv. 19.

'Even of the very best of them one may say,' remarks Cleander, 'as I have been told Callicrates in another work says of Seneca: *he moves by start and sally. He flashes a hint in your face and disappears. This looks like an apparition of philosophy.*'[1] This is the pointed style for which Aristotle also provided the doctrine of *sententiae*—if not of sententious style—and which leads to 'writing in surprizing, disjointed Phrases'. From intention to consequence such a style must be damned:

> Nay, oftentimes it is a sharpness of wit that depraves the Style. *Chrysippus*, says *Seneca*, *was a great man, and of an acute wit. But the edge of it was so fine, that every thing turned it: and he might be said in truth rather to prick the subject that he handled, than to pierce it through.* This is often the character of *Seneca* himself, and commonly that of sententious Authors.[2]

This is followed by another itemizing of the various elements of this style, where 'all is sharp points and oppositions'. And the criticism runs from 'the obscurity which generally attends the pretended sententious way of writing' to the paradox of the 'long-short-lung'd Seneca', whose brevity is actually prolix.[3] The 'new-coined words', especially Latinisms, are another abuse of this style, which Feltham also illustrates.[4]

Finally, Eudoxus sums up the requirements of an accurate style as perspicuity, 'genuine and proper words', metaphor in moderation, cadence neither grating nor monotonous, and periods neither too long nor too short. Certainly, those authors 'who seem afraid of making a period reach beyond a line' cannot be called eloquent. 'In a word', says Eudoxus, 'the Style of those books which are often entitled *Characters*, I never admired in those very books, and much less when used in other matters.'[5] Again, style should neither run, jump, nor creep, but maintain 'a moderate equal tenour'. To his *Reflections* Constable adds a summary of Quintilian's doctrine—so long basic to the criticism of Senecan style, and hence relevant to Collier.

Since for Constable this style is essentially the Character style applied to other matters, an eighteenth-century description of that

---

[1] *Reflections*, p. 129. It is from the work used by Coleridge.

[2] Ibid., pp. 130–1. The reference is to L'Estrange's Abstract of *Seneca's Morals* (*Ep.* 2), where Seneca's stylistic doctrine was available in the new 'pert style'.

[3] Ibid., pp. 127, 133.   [4] Ibid., pp. 84 ff.   [5] Ibid., pp. 184–6.

style will not be out of place. To a translation of Theophrastus, Henry Gally prefixed 'A Critical Essay on *Characteristic-Writings*' in which he defines their style from Libanius out of Casaubon:

'When you describe Manners you must use a plain, concise, florid, easy Style, free from all artificial Turns and Figures.' Every Thing must be even, smooth, easy and unaffected; without any of those Points and Turns, which convey to the Mind nothing but a low and false Wit, in which our Moderns so much abound, and in which they seem to place their greatest Beauties.[1]

While Gally agrees with Constable on the false wit to which the moderns have turned such a style, he emphasizes the need of brevity for the Character:

In *Characteristic-Writings* both the Way of Thinking and the Style must be Laconic: Much must be contain'd in a little Compass. Brevity of Diction adds new Life to a good Thought: And since every perfect Stroke ought to be a distinct Representation of a particular Feature, Matters shou'd be so order'd, that every perfect Sentence may contain a perfect Thought, and every perfect Thought may represent one Feature.[2]

But this was also the way to make every thought in the declamation of the Roman schools, as well as every thought in the aphoristic essay, as telling as possible; and neither Seneca nor Bacon, nor the other pointed stylists, failed to observe its possibilities. Yet, if they wrote epigrams, they did not have to make them jingle or play upon words; but the temptation was there, given the Gorgian resources, and many of them succumbed. Few, if any, can be found innocent of the wit that turns, as Addison noticed, upon the opposition of ideas—a wit still so attractive that the eighteenth century threatened to classify it altogether as false wit. If Seneca still furnished Blair with an example of the excessive use of antithesis, Pope was his modern example of the *style coupé*; but Shaftesbury was damned, with faint praise at least, for his rather stilted Ciceronianism.

During the course of the Senecan fashion, which continued after it ceased to rule, we have seen successive standards or principles of prose style come and go. Brevity long maintained its appeal, if not its primacy, in the hierarchy of stylistic virtues; at worst, it was

---

[1] *The Moral Characters of Theophrastus* (London, 1725), p. 42. The proper style is one of plain and easy brevity, not the pointed brevity of the moderns.

[2] Ibid., p. 43. Hence a thought acquires 'the force of emphatic condensation', as Demetrius had pointed out.

a less undesirable extreme than prolixity. Though prose style is not reducible to a single pattern in any period, yet, if we posit the Theophrastian virtues of style as the general desiderata, we may observe a shifting emphasis in our century and beyond. First, however, we must recall that the Stoics added brevity to these virtues—namely, clearness, correctness, ornateness, appropriateness—and restricted the ornament in practice to what Hoskins calls life or wit. Then out of the Stoics came Seneca; out of Seneca, Lipsius; and out of Lipsius, Hoskins. This Neo-Stoic pattern dropped correctness—which as a restricted definition of purity of language was a Ciceronian virtue—and replaced ornateness, except for wit, by plainness; but wit or energy had long been the one relief allowed the plain style, Attic or Stoic. Now it was plainness that succeeded brevity in seventeenth-century esteem, but its relation to wit varied as between Wilkins and Glanvill. Meanwhile, Senecan brevity did not oust Ciceronian *copia*. In composition Blount asserted the 'mediocrity' which replaced brevity and prolixity in the period, and the cadence which became important later. Although Hughes insisted on cadence, he made propriety the first requirement of style, which was founded upon accuracy or correctness. Thence the just style held sway until cadence or harmony, after Ciceronian example, became the great desideratum. By this time we have returned to the cult of form which, with the fetish of Ciceronian correctness, preoccupied the Ciceronians of the Renaissance and inspired the Anti-Ciceronian movement. Thus, as both an attack on the latest form of Senecanism and a defence of the newest form of Ciceronianism, Constable's *Reflections* brings our study of the cult of expressiveness to a fitting conclusion.

The curt Senecan style naturalized a pattern which English prose assumes from time to time, commonly with the impulse to brevity or epigram or smart expression. Long after Blair defined the *style coupé*, a glittering exemplar of that style arose in Macaulay. He serves to condense a long story, for he not only has provided a parallel to Hegesias, but has shown how the nineteenth century could be 'excellent at Snipsnap'. In the *Essay on Milton* a modern Bishop Hall, though as little to Milton's taste, defends the Puritans with the same 'snapping adages'. If Macaulay presents the modern form of this style, John Lyly began to fashion it, leaving it to be

handed on in a greatly improved form in his last plays. His achievement for English prose was perhaps greater, though less complete,
than Dryden's. Both simplified the sentence structure of their time,
and this meant chiefly reducing the number and subdependence of
clauses, or rejecting Latin relatives and inversions. Dryden left the
conversational style perfected in its 'diligent kind of negligence',
but Lyly first taught English prose to manœuvre with precision.
And the smart step of that manœuvre, modified by later development, is still visible in Macaulay. Even in our day a popular magazine has fostered the asyndetic smartness of Senecan style.

Index of Authors

The defining subjects of this history are found in the table of contents, the terms of art in Chapter II. The index 'n.' limits the page reference to footnotes.

PRINTED IN
GREAT BRITAIN
AT THE
UNIVERSITY PRESS
OXFORD
BY
CHARLES BATEY
PRINTER
TO THE
UNIVERSITY